HISTORY OF BRAZIL, 1500–2000

HISTORY OF BRAZIL, 1500–2000

Politics, economy, society, diplomacy

JOSEPH SMITH

WITH

FRANCISCO VINHOSA

An imprint of **Pearson Education**

London · New York · Toronto · Sydney · Tokyo · Singapore · Hong Kong · Cape Town
New Delhi · Madrid · Paris · Amsterdam · Munich · Milan · Stockholm

Pearson Education Limited

Head Office:
Edinburgh Gate
Harlow CM20 2JE
Tel: +44 (0)1279 623623
Fax: +44 (0)1279 431059

London Office:
128 Long Acre
London WC2E 9AN
Tel: +44 (0)20 7447 2000
Fax: +44 (0)20 7240 5771
Website: www. history-minds.com

First published in Great Britain in 2002

© Pearson Education Limited 2002

The right of Joseph Smith and Francisco Vinhosa to be identified
as Authors of this Work has been asserted by them in accordance
with the Copyright, Designs and Patents Act 1988.

ISBN 0 582 25771 9

British Library Cataloguing in Publication Data
A CIP catalogue record for this book can be obtained from the British Library

Library of Congress Cataloging in Publication Data
A CIP catalog record for this book can be obtained from the Library of Congress

10   9   8   7   6   5   4   3   2   1

Typeset in 11/13.5pt Columbus by Graphicraft Limited, Hong Kong
Printed and bound in Malaysia

The Publishers' policy is to use paper manufactured from sustainable forests.

CONTENTS

CONTENTS

PREFACE

I was attracted to the idea of writing a book covering the history of Brazil because I have long been fascinated by that country and its people. As a teacher of Latin American history I have also wanted to write a general work of synthesis that would be useful and informative for students taking survey courses in Brazilian history. When I started on the project there was a lack of up-to-date textbooks in English, but this has been rectified in the past few years by the publication of a number of excellent scholarly works. Students now have an enviable luxury of choice.

My own studies have been aided by travel grants from the British Academy that enabled me to make research visits to Brazil. I am also very grateful to the Arts and Humanities Research Board for a Research Leave grant that gave me a period of release from teaching and administrative duties and was a crucial factor in helping me to complete this particular book.

I am indebted to my co-author, Francisco Vinhosa, for his friendship and hospitality. Francisco prepared material in Portuguese that I translated and edited to form the basis of the chapters on the colonial and imperial periods. I hope that the final text lives up to his expectations. My greatest personal acknowledgement is, as always, to Rachael for her encouragement and support.

Exeter, August 2001

MAPS

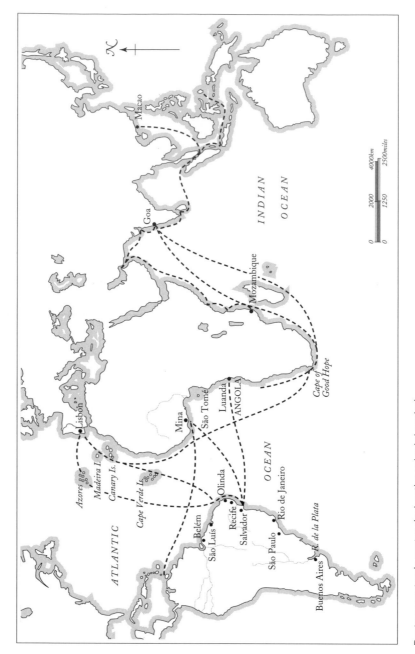

Portuguese trade routes during the colonial period

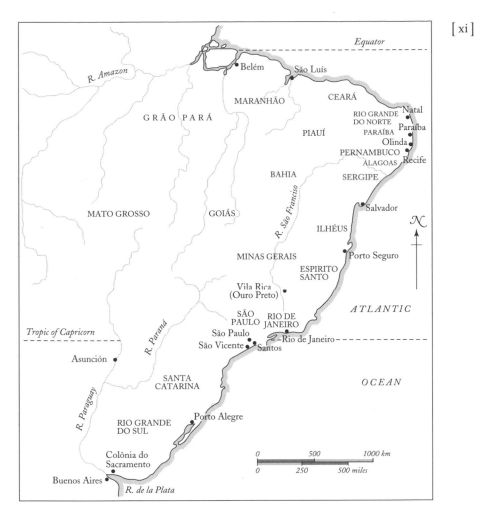

Colonial Brazil

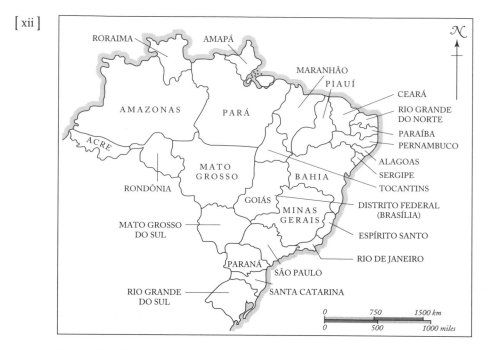

Modern Brazil

CHAPTER 1

COLONIAL BRAZIL

Politics and diplomacy

Discovery

Although it had been traversed and occupied by indigenous peoples for centuries, the large area of the Americas that would become the nation known to people all over the world as Brazil was not formally discovered and claimed by Europeans until 1500.[1] The encounter occurred when a Portuguese fleet en route to India sighted an unknown land to the west on April 22, 1500. On coming ashore two days later the leader of the expedition, Pedro Álvares Cabral, declared the territory to be the possession of the king of Portugal. The land therefore became part of the Portuguese overseas empire, and its history for the next three centuries would be greatly influenced and shaped by Portuguese political, economic and cultural values and requirements.

The discovery appeared accidental, but to the Portuguese it was one more sign of their nation's divine mission to expand overseas. For over a century since 1385 the relatively tiny kingdom of Portugal under the ruling House of Avis had been actively involved in organizing voyages of discovery and exploration. Interest in the wider world reflected the country's geographical position bordering the Atlantic Ocean. The resulting sea-going tradition of the people of the coast was reinforced by contemporary improvements in cartography and navigational techniques and especially the development of the caravel, a sailing ship that combined stability on the high seas with the capacity to carry large cargoes of merchandise. In addition, the Portuguese monarchy, of which Prince Henrique 'the Navigator' was a prominent member, gave enthusiastic backing to merchants in their schemes to circumvent the traditional land passage across Europe and Asia and discover a new

[2]   route by sea to the precious metals and spices of the Orient. But economic factors were not the only reason for overseas expansion. Religion also played an important part. Like their Spanish[2] Christian neighbors, the Portuguese had fought a successful *Reconquista* (War of Reconquest) to reclaim their portion of the Iberian peninsula from the Muslims who had invaded during the eighth century. The spirit of the *Reconquista* endured in the desire to serve God by spreading the Catholic faith overseas and was illustrated in the emblem of the Cross that appeared on the sails of Portuguese vessels.

The first stage of Portuguese overseas expansion was directed to North Africa, where the fortress of Ceuta was seized from the Muslims in 1415. Although a desire for further territorial conquests existed, the policy that evolved was eminently practical in emphasizing trade rather than permanent colonial settlement or civilizing mission. Various strategic points along the coast of West Africa were captured and used as *feitorias* (fortified trading posts) for the exchange of goods with local Africans. The most valuable items traded were gold, sugar and slaves. To facilitate and protect the new trade, a network of important naval bases in the Atlantic Ocean was established during the fifteenth century in Madeira, the Azores and the Cape Verde Islands. The route to the Indian Ocean was opened in 1488 when Bartolomeu Dias succeeded in safely sailing past the Cape of Terrors, which was renamed the Cape of Good Hope.

Portuguese overseas expansion was copied by its larger and more powerful neighbor, the Kingdom of Castile, which sponsored the celebrated expedition organized by Christopher Columbus that discovered the Indies in 1492. The success of Columbus raised the question of ownership of the previously unknown territories and those still to be discovered in what Europeans would refer to as the 'New World.' In 1493 Pope Alexander VI sought to resolve the issue by drawing a line running from the north to the south about 100 leagues (1,700 miles) west of the Cape Verde Islands. In return for an undertaking from the monarchs of Spain and Portugal to spread Christianity, the pope stated that the lands to the west of the line belonged to Spain while those to the east were the exclusive possession of Portugal. King João II of Portugal, however, did not agree with the division, alleging that the pope had been too sympathetic to Spain. In June 1494 Portugal and Spain signed the Treaty of Tordesillas that was more acceptable to Portugal because it moved the pope's line to 370 leagues west of the Cape Verdes. No other European rulers were consulted in the arrangement. In effect, the two kingdoms were unilaterally dividing the New World between themselves.

Shortly after the conclusion of the Treaty of Tordesillas, Portuguese ambitions were greatly elevated by reports that Vasco da Gama had followed the route of Bartolomeu Dias around Africa and had reached India in 1498. A new and larger expedition was prepared to repeat his achievement. The fleet of thirteen ships contained 1,200 persons and was commanded by a prominent aristocrat, Pedro Álvares Cabral. Though a desire to promote the Catholic faith was evident, the emphasis of the expedition was placed on securing trade and treasure. Most of all, King Manoel I (king from 1495 to 1521) wanted Cabral to arrange an alliance with the Sultan of Calcutta that would establish profitable commercial relations. The fleet left the Tagus on March 9, 1500, followed the regular route to the Canaries and the Cape Verde Islands, but then chose to take a more westerly route than normal. Whether the change of course was deliberate or accidental is not known. On April 21 the fleet caught sight of land and made a brief landing before proceeding on the next day to what is today the state of Bahia, where they anchored in a sheltered harbor that was appropriately named Porto Seguro ('Safe Port'). April 22 later became recognized as the official date of discovery. Between that day and May 2, a reconnaissance was made along the coastline. The newly discovered territory was claimed for Portugal and called the 'Island of the Holy Cross.'

Conquest and commerce

The stop in Brazil was treated as a temporary diversion and Cabral quickly resumed his voyage to India. A single ship, however, was sent back to Lisbon to report the discovery of what was initially believed to be an island of indeterminate size. A letter dated May 1, 1500 and prepared by Pero Vaz de Caminha, a scribe who was a member of Cabral's fleet, informed the king that 'the country is so well-favored that if it were rightly cultivated it would yield everything.'[3] The popular image of Brazil as a land of infinite natural resources and great economic potential was tempered, however, by the major disappointment that no evidence had been found of the presence of any gold or silver. The lack of precious metals, jewels or spices was confirmed by a second and smaller fleet of three ships that was dispatched from Portugal in 1501 and surveyed a long stretch of the Brazilian coastline. The fleet brought back samples of a local dyewood, however, that was considered valuable in Europe and had previously only been available in limited quantities from the Orient. The dye produced from the bark was known in Latin as 'brasile' so that the newly-discovered land was referred to as 'the land of brasil' and the dyewood as brazilwood (*pau-brasil*). In Europe, 'Brazil' soon became the accepted name for the new country in preference to Cabral's 'Island of the Holy Cross.'[4]

[4]   While the Portuguese Crown quickly declared its possession of the new territory under the terms of the Treaty of Tordesillas, it showed no desire to incur any expenses to set up a colonial administration or to emulate Spain and embark on a great civilizing mission in the New World. Despite the general attitude of indifference, however, Brazil was not completely neglected. Even though there was no easily accessible gold and silver, the Portuguese monarchy recognized that respectable profits could be made from trade. As had been the practice in West Africa, most of the expenses arising from the fitting out of ships and conducting trade were incurred by private individuals. This was achieved by the grant of royal leases to set up *feitorias* to trade with the local people. In return, merchants agreed to pay a fixed share of their profits to the Crown and maintain the trading station as an outpost of the Portuguese empire. In 1502 a monopoly of the trade in brazilwood was given to the New Christian merchant, Fernão de Noronha, who undertook in return to organize the defense of the coast and to send out further exploratory missions. *Feitorias* were established along the coast, but Portuguese merchants had little incentive to go further inland. In marked contrast to Spanish America, there was no sign of the proximity of either precious metals or substantial native populations or advanced civilizations. Moreover, physical movement beyond the coastline was seriously impeded by the proximity of dense forest and jungle, high mountain ranges and swift-flowing rivers. In addition, there was the threat of hostile Indians, wild animals, poisonous insects and snakes. The *feitorias* in Brazil proved therefore to be precarious footholds and did not initially have much significance. By comparison 'golden Goa' in India was the center of the empire and was considered a much more attractive financial proposition by Portuguese merchants and adventurers.

The desultory attitude of the Portuguese Crown towards Brazil was disturbed by encroachment from French competitors who were also attracted by the availability and economic potential of the brazilwood trade. A French ship reportedly reached the Brazilian coast in 1504. While the French rarely chose to establish *feitorias* on shore, their ships engaged in direct trade with the Indians. Not only did this pose a challenge to the Portuguese claim to monopolize the brazilwood trade, but it also increased supplies to Europe and thereby reduced prices and profits. The Portuguese king denounced the French traders as pirates and sent ships to patrol Brazilian waters. Conscious that the king of France did not recognize the Portuguese and Spanish claims laid down in the Treaty of Tordesillas, King João III (king from 1521 to 1557) decided to pre-empt possible interference from other nations by asserting his own control over Brazil. To achieve this, however, required the provision of a permanent Portuguese military and civilian presence in the new territory.

The captaincy system

In December 1530 Martim Afonso de Sousa set sail for Brazil in command of an expedition consisting of five ships and more than 400 men. Martim Afonso was under royal instructions to establish fortified settlements that would provide bases for naval action to prevent the French interlopers from trading with the Indians. The forts would also assist the search for gold and precious metals, a prospect that was enhanced by the news of the treasure discovered in Mexico by the Spanish conquistador, Hernán Cortés. In January 1532, after completing a survey of the coast, Martim Afonso chose São Vicente near present-day Santos as the site of his preferred headquarters and main fortified point. São Vicente was, therefore, the first permanent Portuguese colony in Brazil. In 1554 Jesuits traveled further inland and founded a smaller settlement in a village that was named after the River Piratininga. This village would ultimately grow into the city of São Paulo. Martim Afonso acted as a virtual viceroy in establishing the machinery of royal government in Brazil. In doing so, he affirmed his king's sovereignty over the country and ensured the continuation of Portuguese control.

In 1534, in order to colonize and develop the interior, João III divided the area between the coast and the supposed line of the Treaty of Tordesillas into land grants known as captaincies (*capitanias*). By 1536 fifteen separate captaincies of varying size had been created extending from Maranhão in the North to Santa Ana in the South. They were distributed among twelve donataries (*donatários*), most of which were wealthy Portuguese aristocrats. An arrangement resembling a feudal compact was made between the king and each donatary in which the latter and his heirs received the royal gift of land (*carta de doação*) and in return pledged not only to pay taxes to the king but also to settle and develop the land and to provide for its defense against the Indians and foreign invaders. Like the leases for the trade in brazilwood, the donataries and their heirs assumed the full costs of establishing the captaincies. The donatary, however, exercised powers of civil and criminal jurisdiction and was also allowed to sub-divide his captaincy into smaller and separate lots of uncultivated land known as *sesmarias*. Initially there was so much available land that some individual *sesmarias* were huge. The largest varied in size from 40 to 100 square miles and established a precedent for creating vast estates that would be a prominent feature of the future distribution of land-holding in Brazil.

It was soon evident that the captaincy system was too ambitious and impractical. Not enough Portuguese aristocrats, merchants or peasants were willing to emigrate to a country as vast and undeveloped as Brazil. By

[6] contrast, Africa and India still remained more attractive and less dangerous destinations. Indeed, five captaincies were never actually colonized because the donatary did not choose to make the journey to Brazil. Of the donataries who took up their captaincies, four were killed by Indians who frequently attacked and often destroyed the fledgling settlements. Only the captaincies of São Vicente and Pernambuco were initially successful. Although he did not personally assume control of the captaincy of São Vicente, Martim Afonso delegated his powers to efficient administrators. They effectively contained the Indian threat and established profitable sugar plantations. The captaincy of Pernambuco in the Northeast also prospered under its donatary, Duarte Coelho, who was unusual in stressing the importance of cooperating with the local Indians. This ensured reliable supplies of brazilwood and food and enabled him to exploit the fertile local soil which proved ideal for the successful cultivation of tobacco and especially sugar.

The success of São Vicente and Pernambuco was exceptional. The other captaincies were in a state of chaos. 'If Your Highness does not shortly aid these captaincies,' a brother of one donatary pleaded to King João III in 1548, 'You will lose the land.'[5] In fact, a decision to evacuate remained a distinct possibility so long as Brazil appeared as a remote and forbidding wilderness. However, the success of the sugar industry in São Vicente and Pernambuco demonstrated a potential to produce regular income and good profits. The dream of finding '*el dorado*' also still lingered. Recent reports of the Spanish discovery of the great silver mines of Potosí in 1545 rekindled the hope that precious metals might still be found in Brazil.

Royal government

King João III recognized that timely royal intervention was necessary to prevent the collapse of the captaincy system and the possible loss of his American empire to foreign rivals. In 1548 he announced the appointment of Tomé de Sousa as resident governor-general of the colony. The captaincy of Bahia was also reclaimed as royal land. Sousa arrived in Brazil in March 1549 with a powerful fleet of six ships and more than 1,000 soldiers. In accordance with his instructions, he subsequently founded a powerful fortress at Salvador (da Bahia) overlooking the Bay of All Saints. Although some individual captaincies survived into the eighteenth century, the founding of Salvador as the capital of the colony and seat of the new central government marked the direct and visible assertion of royal authority for the first time in Brazil and, consequently, signified the abandonment of the captaincy system as the Crown's preferred model of colonial government. In fact, the donataries were required to give up their exclusive powers in relation to the collection of taxes, administration of justice and defense of territory.

The sending of military reinforcements proved sensible because Sousa and his successors, most notably Mem de Sá who was governor-general from 1558 to 1572, had to combat French attempts to seize possession of Brazilian territory. The most serious threat emerged in 1555 when a French fleet commanded by Admiral Nicolas Durand de Villegaignon entered Guanabara Bay and in alliance with the Tamoios Indians, founded a small community known as 'French Antarctica' on Sergipe Island. The ostensible aim was to establish a refuge for French Huguenots. Similar French attempts were made in South Carolina and in St. Augustine, Florida. The Portuguese response to Villegaignon's Brazilian venture was uncompromising. After a series of attacks by Portuguese forces from 1565 onwards, the French were eventually expelled in 1567. The excellent harbor and strategic location of Guanabara Bay led the Portuguese to establish a new town which was called (São Sebastião do) Rio de Janeiro. Though French threats would persist, especially in the North where Daniel de la Touche, Sieur de la Ravardière, founded the short-lived settlement of St. Louis (São Luís) in 1612, they were never militarily powerful enough to undermine Portuguese control of Brazil.

Military operations directed against the French resulted in the establishment of new fortified Portuguese settlements along the Brazilian coastline extending from São Vicente up to the Amazon Valley. In the process, there was frequent conflict with local Indians resulting in their subjugation and expulsion. Efforts were made, however, to convert the Indians to Christianity. In fact, six Jesuits had arrived with Tomé de Sousa's fleet in 1549. Led by Father Manoel da Nóbrega, they played an important role in promoting the policy of pacifying and acculturating the Indians. The authority and influence of the Church was considerably enhanced by the creation of the diocese of Bahia in 1551. By the second half of the sixteenth century Portuguese attitudes towards Brazil had markedly changed. Although the vast interior still remained virtually unexplored and unknown to Europeans, Brazil was no longer merely a collection of *feitorias* but a colony containing several permanent fortified settlements, a central government and diocese located in the capital city of Salvador, and the beginnings of a flourishing sugar industry.

In 1580 Portugal fell under Spanish rule when King Philip II of Spain (king from 1556 to 1598) claimed the vacant Portuguese throne as Philip I of Portugal. The Iberian Union or Dual Monarchy lasted until 1640. During

[8]   this period Portugal was neither annexed by Spain nor governed by Spanish officials. In fact, Portugal was allowed relative political autonomy. Although the Portuguese legal code was changed by the passage of the Philippine Ordinances (*Ordenações filipinas*) in 1603, legislation specifically concerning the colonies continued to be passed in Lisbon. In practice, the Portuguese empire remained a separate unit and distinct from its Spanish counterpart. In 1604 the Council for India and Overseas Conquests (*Conselho da India e Conquistas Ultramarinas*) was created with responsibility for administering the whole of the Portuguese empire including Brazil. During the period of union the colony did experience two visitations from the Inquisition, the first of which took place in Bahia and Pernambuco from 1591 to 1595 and the second in Bahia in 1618. But enforcement of legislation and regulations was not so strict in Brazil as in the Spanish-American colonies. Acknowledgement of Brazil's growing importance was evident in the delegation of important judicial powers to the High Court of Appeals (*Tribunal da Relação*) that was set up in Bahia in 1609. Indeed, the colony was considered so large to administer that it was split into two sections in 1621, a recognition of the existence of 'two Brazils.' Most of the territory that had been settled during the sixteenth century was retained by the *Estado do Brasil* (State of Brazil) with its capital at Salvador. To the north and west, the captaincies of Grão-Pará, Maranhão and Ceará were formed into the new State of Maranhão with its capital at São Luís. Both states would have their own separate governments and governors-general. The governor-general at São Luís reported directly to Lisbon, a reflection of the fact that, in terms of sailing time and communications, Portugal was actually closer to Maranhão than Salvador.

Despite the attempted centralization of colonial government in Salvador and São Luís, a decentralized system remained firmly in place for most of the colonial period because geographical distance and the difficulties of communications meant that the capacity of the governor-general to interfere in local affairs was very limited. Moreover, colonial Brazil provided a marked contrast to Spanish America in failing to develop major cities and administrative centres such as Mexico City and Lima from which royal power and authority radiated. In fact, mainly for economic reasons and security the population of Brazil preferred to congregate in municipalities (*municípios*) composed of small towns and villages, many of which were located close to large sugar plantations. The municipalities were, therefore, the focus of local government. The powerful local landowners and planters known as '*homens bons*' ('leading citizens') served as councillors (*vereadores*) in the senate or town council (*senado da câmara*) which was the equivalent of the Spanish-American *cabildo*. The exact composition of councils varied, but they were usually presided over by a resident magistrate (*juiz ordinário*) who also acted as a permanent law officer. Under the Philippine Ordinances the town council possessed wide political, fiscal, judicial and police powers and its jurisdiction usually extended far beyond the municipality to cover the surrounding countryside. Intended as an instrument of royal authority, the council generally collaborated with the Crown but could take an independent stance if specific local interests were perceived to be threatened. For example, councils were usually resistant to attempts by royal officials to prevent the forced labor of Indians and the organization of expeditions to hunt for slaves. Intervention by the Crown took the form of the dispatch of *ouvidores* (superior circuit judges) from the High Court of Appeals in Salvador on annual visits to supervise the work of the councils. After 1696 the Crown sought to exercise greater control by appointing resident external or district magistrates (*juízes de fóra*) to replace the *juiz ordinário*. These appointments, however, were confined to the cities and the principal towns. Although remote rural councils continued by default to enjoy a wide latitude of political maneuver, their status and importance were gradually eroded during the eighteenth century by political and economic developments that gave more power to the governor of the captaincy.[6]

War with the Dutch

The principal threat to Portuguese control of Brazil that originated from the Iberian Union was the Dutch invasion of the Northeast. Since the beginning of the sixteenth century Dutch ships and merchants had been active participants in Portugal's trade with Brazil, providing ships, credit and markets. This relationship was undermined by Holland's[7] declaration of independence from Spain in 1581. In retaliation, Spain sought to prohibit Portuguese merchants from conducting trade with the Dutch. When a period of truce between Holland and Spain ended in 1621, the Dutch resolved to launch military expeditions against Brazil, which they regarded as a legitimate target because it was ruled by the king of Spain. While French attacks during the previous century had been confined to remote and unsettled points on the coast, the Dutch sought to seize control of the wealthy sugar plantations and thereby directly threatened the center of the colony's wealth. The result was the most serious and sustained effort to strip Portugal of its Brazilian possession during the colonial period. A large Dutch fleet attacked and invaded Bahia in 1623. The Dutch eventually withdrew in 1624, but returned with another powerful military expedition that invaded Pernambuco in 1630. On this occasion, Recife was captured and held for more than two decades. Under Dutch control, Recife was transformed from a small village to a

[10] flourishing port. In the first years of occupation the local plantation owners resisted the invasion. An agreement was later reached between the plantation owners and Johan Maurits of Nassau–Siegen, Count Maurice of Nassau, who represented the Dutch West India Company as governor of 'New Holland' from 1637 to 1644. During his period of rule the Dutch colony was extended from Pernambuco to the mouth of the River Amazon.

The conflict with the Dutch illustrated the vulnerability of Brazil's long coastline to external attack. It also highlighted the strategic significance that Brazil had acquired in the European struggle for international power during the seventeenth century. Not only did the Dutch seize the most economically profitable region of the colony, they also attacked Portuguese ships and *feitorias* in West Africa and Angola. As a result, they took temporary control of the flourishing transatlantic slave trade originating from the Mina Coast. Indeed, the Dutch possession of Pernambuco and their military successes in the Atlantic Ocean disrupted Portuguese and Spanish access by sea to the Orient and also threatened Spain's control over its South American empire.

Violent conflict recurred after the departure of Count Maurice in 1644. A series of naval battles took place and a fierce struggle known as the Pernambucan Insurrection was fought on land, which eventually succeeded in expelling the Dutch in 1654. The victory represented a success for the fighting abilities of local Pernambucan volunteers. But there was also a high price to be paid in terms of cane fields destroyed, machinery burned, and production lost. Peace was formally concluded in 1661. In fact, Brazil was never threatened again with a serious foreign invasion.

During the struggle against the Dutch, Portugal had separated itself from Spain in 1640 and the unpopular Iberian Union was brought to an end. Dom João IV (king from 1640 to 1656) of the House of Braganza was acclaimed as the new king of Portugal. The growing importance attached to Brazil was acknowledged by the fact that the colony became a principality and the title of 'Prince of Brazil' was accorded to the heir to the throne. Though distance and poor communications still militated against effective administration of Brazil from Lisbon, an attempt to reform the structure of colonial government was made in 1642 with the creation of an Overseas Council (*Conselho Ultramarino*).

Territorial expansion

The Iberian Union facilitated the territorial exploration and settlement of Brazil because it removed the boundary restrictions dividing the continent

that had been set by the Treaty of Tordesillas in 1494. But the main motive [11]
for European exploration into the interior was still the search for precious
metals. Added to this was a desire to capture Indians to work as slaves in
the rapidly expanding sugar plantations. The most celebrated expeditions
(*entradas*) were those organized by the *bandeirantes* of São Paulo. The
bandeirantes were a combination of Indians and Europeans, many of whom
were a mixture of white and Indian origin and known as *mamelucos*. They
gained their name from the distinctive *bandeiras* (flags or banners) that they
carried to identify themselves. Travelling enormous distances on foot for
weeks, months and even years, the *bandeirantes* acquired a formidable and
heroic reputation. A Jesuit priest remarked: 'They go without God, without
food, naked as the savages, and subject to all the persecutions and miseries
in the world. Men venture for 200 or 300 leagues into the sertão, serving
the devil with such amazing martyrdom, in order to trade or steal slaves.'[8]
Expeditions varied greatly in size and duration. One expedition in 1628
included 69 whites, 900 *mamelucos* and 2,000 Indians. The *bandeirantes*
were ruthless pioneers whose forays assisted the spread of Portuguese rule
and authority and thereby stimulated further settlement and commercial
development of the interior.

Exploration and settlement were also influenced by a concern to prevent
other European nations from encroaching upon Portuguese territory, especially along the northern coastline. Fortified points were founded at Filipéia
(present-day João Pessoa) in 1585, Natal in 1599, and Fortaleza in 1611.
São Luís was captured from the French in 1614 and became the first capital
of the State of Maranhão which was created in 1621. An important military
base was established at Belém in 1616 to control the mouth of the River
Amazon. An expedition organized by Pedro Teixeira left Belém in 1637 and
spent two years navigating the vast river. Although Portugal duly claimed
sovereignty over the whole Amazon Valley, Portuguese settlement was
restricted for much of the seventeenth century to the cities of São Luís and
Belém. Beyond the coastal cities, royal authority was represented by the
establishment of military outposts and the missionary activities of the Religious Orders. Franciscans, Jesuits and Carmelites established *aldeias* (villages)
in which communities of local Indians were brought together for purposes
of conversion to Christianity and acculturation.

In the Northeast, the bulk of the European population was located close
to the sugar plantations along the coasts of Bahia and Pernambuco. The growing requirement for food and for animals to provide transportation for the
sugar industry stimulated the development of cattle ranching. During the

[12] seventeenth century cattle herds gradually spread beyond the coast and into the surrounding grasslands of the interior or 'backlands', known as the *sertão* (or *sertões*), and more specifically in Bahia as the *sertões de dentro*, and in Pernambuco as the *sertões de fora*. Further expansion into the interior was discouraged by the lack of roads and trails, the extremely dry climate and the hostility of the Indians. It was not until the discovery of gold in Minas Gerais at the end of the seventeenth century that there would be a large and sustained movement of people from the coast to the *sertão*.

In the south of the colony, the city of Rio de Janeiro took advantage of its excellent natural harbor facilities to develop as a major port. São Paulo also emerged as an important base for commercial exchange and the starting point for the *bandeirantes* to organize their expeditions into the interior. Few Europeans ventured further south. The exceptions were Jesuit missions set up to protect and acculturate the Indians and a few fortified points such as Laguna in Santa Catarina and Colônia do Sacramento on the River Plate, which were intended as primarily military outposts to assert Portuguese claims to possess the territory. In 1739 the sub-captaincy of Santa Catarina was created and in 1760 the sub-captaincy of Rio Grande do São Pedro, which was renamed Rio Grande do Sul in 1807.

The 'Golden Age'

In 1695 deposits of gold were discovered in Minas Gerais. After almost two centuries of fruitless exploration for precious metals it seemed that Brazil had at last become another *el dorado*. The mining frontier attracted a massive influx of migrants seeking to make their fortunes. During the eighteenth century up to 300,000 Portuguese left Portugal to join the gold rush. A contemporary observer, Father André João Antonil, noted in 1711: 'Every year great numbers of Portuguese and foreigners come in the fleets bound for the mines. From the cities, villages, inlets, and hinterland of Brazil there go whites, browns, blacks, and many Indians who are in the service of the Paulistas. The mixture is of every kind and condition of person: men and women, young and old, rich and poor, nobles and commoners, laymen, priests, and monks of all orders, many of whom have neither convent nor chapter in Brazil.'[9]

After being virtually uninhabited by Europeans the population of Minas Gerais rose to 30,000 in 1709 and to 300,000 in 1775, a figure that amounted to 20 percent of the colony's estimated population. The large demographic growth reflected the fact that Minas Gerais had displaced the Northeast as the economic center of the colony. Minas Gerais was also used as a base for further exploration and settlement as prospectors moved on to make new discoveries of gold and diamonds in Mato Grosso in 1719 and Goiás in 1725. Initially most of the prospectors traveled to the mining region on arduous journeys lasting for weeks and months via the inland routes from São Paulo or along the River São Francisco from the Northeast, but the preferred and fastest route became the 'New Road' from the mining administrative center of (Vila Rica do) Ouro Preto to the port of Rio de Janeiro. This greatly enhanced the growing geographical and economic importance of Rio de Janeiro and contributed to the decision to transfer the capital from Salvador to Rio de Janeiro in 1763.

The opening up of the West resulted in a major reorganization of colonial government and the vigorous assertion of royal authority. Minas Gerais was elevated to the status of a separate captaincy in 1721. Goiás became a captaincy in 1744 and was followed by Mato Grosso in 1748. The despatch of a large number of royal officials and soldiers proved necessary to ensure the collection of taxes, prevention of smuggling and maintenance of law and order in a region that experienced frequent food shortages and endemic violence. A particular cause of social unrest was the attitude of the *paulistas* (people from São Paulo), who made up the bulk of the first wave of prospectors. They contemptuously referred to the later arrivals as '*emboabas*' ('foreigners' or 'outsiders'). From 1708 to 1709 the conflict resulted in a brief period of open hostility and violence known as the 'War of the *Emboabas*.'

The disturbance provided the Crown with a justification to enforce its authority in the mining region. Roads were constructed for the safe transport of gold and were guarded by a network of military garrisons. The direct interference of royal officials was most pronounced in their attempts to supervise and record the production of gold in order to secure payment of the tax known as the *quinto* ('the royal fifth'). Local resentment turned into a brief armed revolt at (Vila Rica do) Ouro Preto in 1720 that was brutally repressed. Royal authority was even more strictly enforced in the Diamond District (*Distrito Diamantina*) in northern Minas Gerais. Whereas the Crown had been reactive in its policy towards the gold strikes, it acted speedily on learning of the discovery of diamonds in 1729. The Diamond District was declared to be royal property and restrictions were placed on the movement of people entering and leaving the area. The extraction and sale of diamonds were strictly regulated. The industry was eventually declared to be a royal monopoly in 1771. Nevertheless, smuggling could not be eliminated and was often conducted with the collusion of local officials. In contrast to the usual lax

[14] enforcement of Portuguese rule in Brazil, however, the diamond industry provided an example of the attempted implementation of the mercantilist system in which treasure was extracted from the colony for the benefit of the mother country.

Pombal

The policy of strictly regulating the mining industry during the eighteenth century reflected the ambitions of the Portuguese monarchy under João V (king from 1706 to 1750) and José I (king from 1750 to 1777) to assert its absolutist powers. For the colonies the result was increasing interference in their affairs by officials sent from Portugal. This was particularly evident during the period from 1750 to 1777 when Sebastião José de Carvalho e Melo, marquis of Pombal, served initially as foreign minister and later as the prime minister of King José I. Pombal impressed his contemporaries as a dynamic and ruthless statesman who was dedicated to reviving the economic fortunes and diplomatic status of Portugal. He was especially intent on reducing his country's economic dependence on England.[10] Since the end of the Iberian Union in 1640 Portugal had looked to England for diplomatic and military aid to counter the threat of Spain. In return, the Crown signed a series of treaties that granted commercial privileges to English merchants. The most important was the 1703 Methuen Treaty. Brazil was important to Anglo–Portuguese trade because the profits from the mining boom enabled Portugal to increase its imports from England. Moreover, English merchants and ships took a large share of the trade in re-exporting Brazilian goods from Lisbon. Pombal sought to reverse this disadvantageous economic relationship.

To achieve his aims Pombal sought to make the colonies more subordinate to the mother country. A major reorganization of colonial government in Brazil was effected by the abolition of the State of Maranhão in 1774. The subsequent incorporation of Maranhão into the State of Brazil meant the end of the 'two Brazils' and the creation of a single government to rule the colony. But Salvador was no longer preeminent because Pombal recognized the relative decline in political and economic importance of the Northeast. This was illustrated by his decision to establish a second and separate High Court of Appeals (*Tribunal da Relação*) at Rio de Janeiro in 1751. The first High Court had been located in Bahia. The redistribution of political and economic power was further underlined in 1763 by the transfer of the colonial capital from Salvador to Rio de Janeiro. The governor-general

at Salvador, who had been elevated to the title of viceroy in 1720, also took [15]
up residence in Rio.

Brazil was directly affected by Pombal's fiscal reforms, particularly the efforts to increase royal revenue. Stress was placed on a more efficient collection of the *quinto* in the mining region and the prevention of gold and diamond smuggling. Boards of Inspection were created in 1751 to examine and regulate the price and quality of colonial products, especially sugar and tobacco. Reflecting Pombal's mercantilist ideas, three private monopoly companies were created to stimulate Brazil's economic growth. In 1755 the Company of Grão Para and Maranhão was set up to promote agricultural development in the North and especially in the Amazon Valley. The Company of Pernambuco and Paraíba was set up in 1759 to revive the sugar industry in the Northeast. The third monopoly company was the Company for Whale Fishing that was established in 1765 to improve the coastal whaling industry. The purpose of the companies was to boost local economic production. In doing so, they would not only provide additional tax revenue for the Crown but also create a larger market for the import of Portuguese manufactured goods.

Like the Bourbon Reforms in Spanish America, Pombal's sweeping measures attracted criticism that they were too much in favor of the interests of the mother country. In Brazil, opposition mostly took the form of evading the payment of taxes and the resort to smuggling. The policy of asserting royal power notably brought conflict with the Church in Portugal and especially the Jesuit Order in Brazil. Pombal regarded the Jesuits as a special interest group that was a barrier to the success of his reforms both in Portugal and the colonies. In Brazil, many planters and settlers had long been jealous of the wealth of the Jesuits and particularly their controversial missionary role in defending the cause of the Indians. This gave support for Pombal's campaign against the Jesuits that resulted in the confiscation of their property and expulsion from Brazil in 1759.

The importance attached by Pombal to stimulating the Brazilian economy illustrated the fact that Brazil was the most economically valuable part of the Portuguese empire. But the success of his measures during his period in power was debatable. The monopoly companies did bring about an increase in the production of sugar in Pernambuco and were instrumental in stimulating the development of new crops such as rice and cotton in Maranhão and Pará. When Pombal resigned in 1777, however, the mining boom was over, exports were falling in value and the economy appeared to be in serious decline. Commercial links between Portugal and Brazil had been

[16] strengthened, but the mother country still retained a close economic relationship with England.

Territorial rivalry with Spain

Territorial rivalry was a prominent feature of diplomatic relations between Portugal and Spain in the eighteenth century. During the Iberian Union from 1580 to 1640 Portugal had extended the territory under its control into the Amazon Valley and the Far West. Although these areas technically belonged to Spain according to the Treaty of Tordesillas, the lack of actual Spanish exploration and settlement meant that they were effectively lost to Portugal by default. Spanish indifference, however, did not extend to the strategically important region of the River Plate known as the Banda Oriental. The struggle for possession began in 1680 when Portuguese military forces established a fort at Colônia do Sacramento on the east bank of the River Plate. A supply base was later set up at Laguna on the coast of Santa Catarina in 1684. The purpose was to assert Portuguese sovereignty over the region and to create a base for the profitable contraband trade, especially in the silver that came from Upper Peru to the port of Buenos Aires which was located across the river facing Colônia. In 1703 Portugal allied with England against Spain and France in the War of the Spanish Succession. The conflict had military consequences for Brazil and resulted in punitive French naval raids on Rio de Janeiro in 1710 and 1711. Colônia do Sacramento was also attacked and captured by Spanish troops and was under their control from 1704 until 1715. The town was returned to Portugal as part of the Treaty of Utrecht in 1713 that formally ended the War of the Spanish Succession. In 1723 a Portuguese fort was founded further to the west at Montevideo, but was abandoned in 1724. The Spanish quickly established their own settlements at Montevideo and used this as a military base to threaten Portuguese control of Colônia.

The territorial rivalry between Portugal and Spain was not solely confined to Brazil, but extended to the Orient and the Philippines. In 1747 both countries entered into negotiations to decide the boundaries of the two empires. The chief Portuguese negotiator, Alexandre de Gusmão, who was Brazilian-born, appreciated the economic significance and potential of Brazil. He wished to secure official Spanish recognition of Portugal's possession of the gold mining region in the West and the Amazon Valley, areas that technically lay west of the Tordesillas line. Colônia do Sacramento was regarded as expendable. After three years of difficult negotiations Portugal and Spain signed the Treaty of Madrid on January 13, 1750. Known as the 'Boundaries Treaty,' the agreement eliminated the line originally set by the 1494 Treaty of Tordesillas 'because of the difficulty of determining where to begin the dividing line on the northern and southern coasts of South America, and because of the moral impossibility of establishing a meridian line through the interior of the American continent.'[11] In its place was a new boundary decided according to the principle of *uti possidetis* which meant recognition of sovereignty over territory that had actually been physically settled and occupied to that date. This was greatly to the advantage of Portugal, whose control of the Amazon Valley and the Far West was, therefore, confirmed. In fact, Portugal was given legal title to more than half of South America and the modern territorial boundary of Brazil was virtually established. But Portugal also made some important concessions. While retaining the area in the South that would become known as Rio Grande do Sul, Portugal renounced all claims to Colônia do Sacramento and recognized Spanish supremacy over the River Plate. Beyond South America, Portugal gave up all claims to the Philippines.

The terms of the treaty of Madrid were controversial and were soon denounced by both governments. A change of monarch in Portugal in 1750 resulted in the rise to power of the Marquis of Pombal, who had not negotiated the treaty and refused, therefore, to recognize its validity. Another divisive issue was the fate of the Jesuit missions located near the River Uruguay. The Jesuits were determined to resist the provision contained in the Treaty of Madrid that their missions were to be placed under Portuguese jurisdiction. Various diplomatic efforts were made to settle the conflict over territorial boundaries and resulted in the treaties of El Pardo in 1761, San Ildefonso in 1777 and Badajoz in 1801. While a definitive boundary settlement still eluded the diplomats at the close of the colonial period, the acceptance of *uti possidetis* as the principle on which the ownership of territory would be decided was crucially important. Symbolized by the *bandeirantes*, it was the Portuguese and not the Spanish who had physically expanded into the interior of South America and their de facto possession ensured that the land would be part of Brazil.

The *Inconfidências*

At the end of the eighteenth century the conservative leaders of Portugal sought to isolate Brazil from the liberal political ideas emerging from the European Enlightenment and the later American and French Revolutions.

[18] This was achieved by ruthlessly suppressing signs of political dissent, combined with a policy of preventing the spread of ideas by prohibiting the use of a printing press and severely restricting the availability of imported books and pamphlets. While the mass of the population of Brazil remained uncritically loyal to Portugal, some of the educated élite, especially those who had traveled to Europe, were aware of the ideas of the Enlightenment and the revolutionary political changes taking place in the United States and France. This occurred at a time when Pombal's reforms had provoked latent anti-Portuguese sentiment and a growing sense of grievance that Brazil was suffering economically on account of exploitation by Portugal.

Pombal's policy of seeking to increase tax revenues most affected Minas Gerais. The decline of the mining industry at the end of the eighteenth century meant, however, that some taxes had been allowed to go into default. The report in 1788 that the Crown intended to enforce the payment of all tax arrears caused widespread alarm and was a major reason for the *Inconfidência Mineira* (Minas Conspiracy) in 1789. The conspiracy was organized in Ouro Preto by a small group of around 20 local and mostly prominent citizens, including priests, judges, landowners and even royal officials. They first met in secret in December 1788 and made plans for a coup to take place in February 1789. The aim was to assassinate the new governor, the Viscount of Barbacena, and provoke social disorder in Ouro Preto that would be used by the conspirators as a pretext to set up a provisional government and proclaim Minas Gerais as an independent republic. What would happen after that was never very clearly explained, but the plotters appear to have assumed that the neighboring captaincies of São Paulo and Rio de Janeiro would join the republic once independence had been declared. But the plot never materialized. It was betrayed by an informer and the conspirators were quickly arrested. In the intervening period before a trial could be held, white anxieties were considerably heightened by the outbreak of the French Revolution in 1789 and slave disturbances in Haiti in 1791. A show trial was eventually held in Rio de Janeiro during 1791. Five plotters were convicted and sent into exile in Angola, but the self-proclaimed leader of the conspiracy, Joaquim José da Silva Xavier, an army officer and amateur dentist, better known as 'Tiradentes' (the 'Toothpuller'), was treated as a scapegoat and publicly executed in April 1792. As an example to other would-be traitors, Tiradentes was hanged, drawn and quartered and his severed head displayed on a pole in Ouro Preto. When Brazil later became a republic the reputation of Tiradentes was rehabilitated and, instead of a traitor, he was regarded as a martyr and national hero.

The declared aim of the conspirators to establish a republic, and the later discovery of works of the French *philosophes* in their possession, indicated that the ideas of the Enlightenment, the American Revolution and political developments in France had reached the Brazilian élite despite the strict censorship policy of Portugal. The plot also demonstrated the existence of economic discontent in Brazil and that this could motivate political revolt. The *Inconfidência Mineira*, however, was not a movement for national independence. The conspirators did not attempt to contact any other groups in Minas Gerais or beyond the borders of the captaincy. Moreover, they represented a white élite that had no desire to provoke the masses into overthrowing the local political order. The Crown acted quickly to suppress the plot and found that there was virtually no public support for the conspirators, who were tried and condemned as traitors rather than liberals or nationalists.

In marked contrast to the plot in Ouro Preto, the *Inconfidência Baiana* or the 'Revolt of the Tailors' in Salvador in August 1798 had much more overtly radical aims. Influenced by the example and the ideas of the French Revolution, the conspirators placed handwritten manifestos on walls in the city advocating the violent overthrow of monarchical rule and the creation of a republic in its place. 'Courage Bahian People, the happy day of Liberty is at hand, the time when we will all be brothers, the time when we will all be equal,' declared one manifesto.[12] Among the many revolutionary ideas included in the manifestos were the abolition of slavery, an end to racial discrimination in employment, free trade with foreign countries, and the confiscation of church property. But the call to arms attracted no support. The Portuguese authorities quickly made more than 40 arrests. Although ten whites were included, the majority of those arrested were mulattos and African slaves. A mulatto tailor, João de Deus (do Nascimento), was identified as the leader. While parts of the revolutionary manifesto had some appeal for the white élite of Bahia, the proposals for an end of slavery and social equality were unacceptable and were considered to be reminiscent of the slave insurrection that had recently led to racial civil war in Haiti. The governor of Bahia reported to the Crown that slave revolt was 'dreaded' by local white society and that it was 'not natural for men employed and established in goods and property to join in a conspiracy which would result in awful consequences to themselves, being exposed to assassination by their own slaves.'[13] Severe punishment was expected for all the perpetrators of the plot. Nevertheless, mulattos and blacks were treated more harshly than their white fellow-conspirators. João de Deus and three other mulattos were singled out as the leaders of the plot and were condemned to public execution in 1799.

[20]   The two *Inconfidências* and the later 1817 revolt in Pernambuco revealed that the desire to break away from Portuguese control was present in colonial Brazil. Both the 1789 and 1798 conspiracies, however, turned out to be isolated and separate events. Despite the ambitious motives and plans they were little more than poorly organized and abortive intrigues rather than national rebellions. The white élite might have some sympathy for a relaxation of government restrictions in Minas Gerais and for the adoption of free trade in Bahia, but they were intensely suspicious of ideas of 'liberty, equality and fraternity' that they equated with violence and social disorder. Most of all, whites feared slave insurrection. The fact that the majority of the conspirators in the *Inconfidência Baiana* were mulatto only served to highlight their feelings of insecurity and ensured that white society remained loyal to the Portuguese Crown.

Economy

The brazilwood trade

The Portuguese voyages of discovery were primarily commercial enterprises designed to gain a lucrative profit by opening up direct trade with the Orient. Previously unknown lands such as Brazil that were discovered during these voyages were regarded as a windfall possession of the Portuguese monarchy. By assuming sovereign powers over the new territory, the Crown owned all its natural resources. The indigenous inhabitants were also subject to royal authority and protection. In fact, the purpose of colonial possessions was to provide wealth and treasure for the Crown and the mother country, a policy known as mercantilism. Most of all, the Portuguese hoped to secure easy access to spices, jewels and precious metals. Brazil began, therefore, as a considerable disappointment when Pero Vaz de Caminha reported in 1500 that there did not seem to be any gold or silver present. Subsequent explorers confirmed the lack of precious metals and their failure to come into contact with wealthy Indian civilizations. Consequently, Brazil did not prove to be another '*el dorado*' such as the Spaniards discovered in Mexico or Peru. It was neither inviting to settlement nor did it appear to offer the profitable trade potential of India and the Far East.

The early European explorers of Brazil returned to Portugal with Indians, exotic birds and samples of a local dyewood. Referred to as brazilwood, this was a hardwood that could be used for shipbuilding. More importantly, the wood also produced a red dye that was much prized by European textile producers. Moreover, it was reported that the wood was available in plentiful supply along the forests of the Brazilian coast. In 1502 a company of merchants organized by Fernão de Noronha was granted a royal lease to conduct the trade in brazilwood for three years. The Crown received a share of the profits in return. *Feitorias* were established and a successful barter trade was begun with local Indians who proved willing to cut and transport logs of dyewood. The wood was shipped to Lisbon and then re-exported mainly to Flanders and Holland. The Portuguese Crown claimed to monopolize the trade, but this was challenged by English, Dutch and especially French rivals whose ships visited the coast for the purpose of bartering with the Indians and securing their own supplies of dyewood.

The concentration on the production and export of a single staple commodity provided a foretaste of the future pattern of the economic history of Brazil. The brazilwood trade, however, produced only modest profits and contributed to moderate local economic activity. There was also an element of economic 'boom and bust' because the trade began to decline in value towards the end of the sixteenth century as a result of the gradual destruction of the accessible regions of coastal forest and a scarcity of labor caused by a sharp fall in the population of the Indians owing to disease and harsh treatment by Europeans. Without the cooperation of Indians, it became much more difficult and expensive to transport the logs to the *feitorias*. The emergence of alternative supplies in the other European colonies also made the trade more competitive and less profitable. Nevertheless, a modest export trade in brazilwood continued until the nineteenth century when the discovery of synthetic dyes led to its demise.

The rise of sugar

The adoption of the captaincy system during the 1530s resulted in attempts to replace the *feitorias* with more permanent Portuguese settlements that in turn required the land to be cultivated for agricultural purposes. Successful communities were founded at Olinda in 1537, Salvador in 1549, Santos in 1545, Vitória in 1551 and Rio de Janeiro in 1565. The settlements were located in natural bays and harbors at the coast and were set up primarily as ports to trade with Portugal. They were scattered along the coastline and separated by such large distances that they had little contact with each other. Internal trade within the colony was, therefore, minimal and except for the awareness of being an outpost of the Portuguese empire, there was little

[22] sense of common identity among the colonists. The development of virtually separate economies located in a particular large city or region and based mainly on exporting agricultural products would be a feature of the Brazilian economy until well into the nineteenth century.

Starting from scratch the captaincy system was faced with the enormous task of cultivating a wilderness. Only São Vicente and Pernambuco achieved a reasonable level of prosperity as a result of the establishment of plantations producing sugar for export. The most successful region of the colony was the Northeast where the coastal areas of Bahia and Pernambuco possessed a rich topsoil known as *massapé* and a tropical climate whose combination of heat and rain proved ideal for the cultivation of sugarcane agriculture. Moreover, land was available and cheap. The local river system also offered an accessible means of transporting sugar by boat to the coast where the Bay of All Saints provided an excellent harbor and port for shipping goods to and from Europe and also for importing African slaves from West Africa.

Sugar was valued in Europe as the equivalent of a spice to add as a sweetener to food. Although it was greatly in demand, it could not be easily produced locally. This had given the Portuguese the incentive to establish sugar plantations in their island colonies in the Atlantic Ocean, first in Madeira and later in São Tomé. The cultivation of sugarcane was first introduced into Brazil perhaps as early as 1518 and was certainly in evidence during the 1530s. Some members of Martim Afonso de Sousa's expedition in 1530 were known to have knowledge of sugar cultivation. Despite a chronic labor shortage plus frequent attacks from hostile Indians and European rivals, the sugar industry thrived in the Brazilian soil and climate and soon replaced brazilwood as the major economic activity in the colony. Production in 1600 reached more than 8,000 metric tons and rose to 14,000 tons in 1625. The number of *engenhos* (sugar mills) proliferated from 70 in 1550 to 115 in 1584 and from 179 in 1612 to 230 in 1627. In the process, Brazil fulfilled the mercantilist dream and in terms of revenue from taxes on trade became more economically valuable to Portugal than India. In fact, during the seventeenth century Brazil was the biggest producer and exporter of sugar in the world and provided Europe with most of its supply of this product. The sheer scale of growth and profit made the colony into Portugal's own '*el dorado.*'

The system of slavery

The cultivation of sugar as a cash crop for export dominated the economic activity of the Northeast and imposed monoculture upon the region. The natural fertility of the soil allowed an expanding plantation economy to emerge that was characterized by a wasteful system in which a plantation was created out of an area of forest that was cleared by slash-and-burn techniques, followed by intensive cultivation of sugarcane until the soil lost its fertility. At that point production moved to an adjoining piece of land where the same cyclical process was repeated. The plantation system also required a large number of laborers to work in the field and the *engenho*. The need was met by the ruthless exploitation of compulsory labor based on the enslavement first of Indians and then of black Africans. For more than three centuries slaves were forced to provide the labor that was of fundamental importance for the development of the sugar industry and the Brazilian economy.

Initially, Indian slavery predominated in the sugar plantations. But Indians were not always cooperative or willing workers. Sometimes they resisted or fled and their numbers were greatly reduced by epidemics of deadly diseases during the 1570s and 1580s. The Church also intervened on behalf of the Indians by criticizing their enslavement and harsh treatment. The case for the Indians was also helped by the belief of the Portuguese planters that Africans were physically stronger workers than Indians and that they were more easily manageable. In fact, from the 1570s onwards they sought to replace the latter with African slaves. The transition was slow because the planters at first lacked access to sufficient capital or credit to purchase large numbers of African slaves. By the 1630s, however, Africans greatly outnumbered Indians in the sugar plantations.

The slave trade was not a new development. In fact, Portugal had been involved in the traffic in human cargoes since the fifteenth century. A shipment of Africans had arrived in Lisbon in 1441. The transatlantic slave trade between West Africa and Brazil was monopolized by Portuguese merchants and proved to be a highly profitable industry. The proximity of the northeastern coast of Brazil to Africa meant that the voyage was relatively short and took from six to seven weeks on average. Moreover, Africans could be bought cheaply and invariably sold at a higher price in Brazil. From the 1570s onwards an average of around 4,000 slaves were imported each year. By 1600 there was a total African slave population of around 15,000 in Brazil. The level of imported slaves rose to 8,000 a year until 1680 when the total slave population was about 150,000. A temporary decline followed until the beginning of the eighteenth century when the discovery of gold in Minas Gerais stimulated a major revival in the slave trade. So many Africans entered the country that by the eighteenth century about half the population in

[24] the captaincies in the Northeast were slaves. In sugar-growing regions the proportion of slaves rose to almost three-quarters of the population.

Decline of sugar

The large profits to be gained from the Brazilian sugar industry attracted foreigners, notably the Dutch who took and controlled the rich plantations of the Northeast from 1630 to 1654. However, the struggle of the Portuguese to drive the Dutch from the colony severely damaged production and caused considerable destruction of local canefields and *engenhos*. Although it would remain the colony's leading industry, Brazilian sugar never fully recaptured the markets in Europe that were lost during the war against the Dutch in the middle of the seventeenth century. One reason was increased competition from European colonies in the Caribbean. Forced out from Brazil, the Dutch set up rival sugar plantations in Surinam. Similarly, the English established flourishing sugar plantations in Barbados. Supply began to outstrip demand. Consequently, the era of high profits came to an end as the rise in world production led to a fall in the international price of sugar. In addition, though sugar could be produced more cheaply in Brazil than in the Caribbean islands, the English, Dutch and French consciously pursued policies of mercantilism that favored the purchase of the sugar produced in their own islands. For example, about 80 percent of the sugar sold in London in the 1630s originated in Brazil. By 1670, that figure had been reduced to 40 percent, and further declined to only 10 percent in 1690.

Despite Brazil's falling share of the world sugar market, sugar was the country's leading industry throughout the eighteenth century and remained the most valuable export until it was supplanted by coffee during the 1830s. Although fortunes continued to be made and lost in the industry, the sugar planters were still the dominant political, economic and social force in the Northeast. The large majority of the population in the region, however, lived in poverty. Slaves were brutalized and maintained as an unskilled labor force. Free workers lived like virtual slaves on account of their dependence on seasonal employment and subsistence agriculture. The best land was invariably retained for sugar. Although some tobacco was successfully grown on land that was considered unsuitable for sugar cultivation, there was little capital available for crop diversification and technological improvements or innovation. The boom in sugar had made the Northeast the most prosperous region in Brazil during the seventeenth century. But adverse changes in the world market revealed the danger of relying too much on export-led growth. The

subsequent decline of the sugar industry brought economic stagnation and   [25]
backwardness to the region and its people.

The mining boom

In 1695 Brazil finally and truly found its '*el dorado*' when a major gold strike
was made at the River Velhas in what is today the state of Minas Gerais
('General Mines'). Although the discovery of gold occurred in a remote and
virtually unknown part of the country, the result was a mining boom which
lasted for most of the eighteenth century and displayed the pattern of 'boom
and bust' that has been such a feature of Brazilian economic development.
Moreover, the location of the mining industry in the interior of the country
also resulted in the transfer of the centre of economic activity in Brazil from
the Northeast to the Center-South. Further gold strikes were made in Mato
Grosso in 1719 and in Goiás in 1726. Diamonds were discovered in Minas
Gerais in 1729.

Despite the lack of roads and difficulties of transportation, migrants flooded
into the mining region in their thousands. Indeed, Brazil soon became the
world's leading producer of gold as official production[14] increased five times
between 1700 and 1720 and reached its highest point in 1760 when exports
amounted to £2.5 million. By 1780, however, they had fallen to below
£1 million. Rapid decline continued as the mines became exhausted. Nevertheless, the eighteenth century was truly Brazil's 'golden age' as the colony provided more than half the world's supply of the precious metal. This gave
a significant boost to the world economy because much of the gold was
exported directly to Portugal where the profits from its sale were used mainly
to finance royal extravagance or transferred to other European powers, especially England, in payment for imported manufactured goods. Indeed, the wealth
derived from Brazilian gold and diamonds enabled Portugal to purchase additional imports which helped to finance the British Industrial Revolution.

The mining boom was an unexpected windfall and had a varied impact on
the Brazilian economy. In order to evade paying the royal tax known as the
'*quinto*' on sales of gold, miners resorted to illegal production and smuggling.
Consequently, not all the profits from the mining boom went overseas. Considerable wealth had been acquired in Minas Gerais and was displayed in
the construction of impressive religious buildings and private houses, most
notably in (Vila Rica de) Ouro Preto where the population had risen to over
20,000 in 1740. The influx of thousands of prospectors created a demand
for foodstuffs that stimulated colonial agricultural production and trade. The

[26]   demand was met initially by imports transported from the southern provinces of São Paulo and Rio Grande do Sul and later by the development of local agriculture and cattle-raising in Minas Gerais. The shortage of workers in the mines also stimulated the movement of large numbers of slaves from the Northeast and a revival in the transatlantic slave trade. Indeed, more than 300,000 slaves were estimated to have entered Minas Gerais between 1698 and 1770. Moreover, the mining boom contributed to the growing importance and prosperity of Rio de Janeiro. Benefiting from its geographical location as the most convenient port for the export of gold to Europe, Rio de Janeiro flourished and grew in national importance and status.

Pombaline reforms

Although Portugal ostensibly pursued a mercantilist policy that sought to exploit Brazil, rules and regulations that were made in Lisbon were difficult to implement in a huge colony that was so far away. Brazil did export large quantities of sugar and precious metals to the mother country and also purchased Portuguese goods in return. There was also, however, widespread evasion of taxes and the resort to smuggling to obtain supplies of products that Portugal could not supply. Royal authority in economic matters had tended to be laxly enforced, but this was altered by the rise to power of the Marquis of Pombal in 1750. Pombal's objective was to make his king and country wealthy and powerful. Indeed, Brazil was the most economically valuable part of the Portuguese empire and formed a vital element in Pombal's mercantilist strategy. He was determined to increase royal revenue by improving the method of tax collection. At the same time, however, he sought to stimulate agricultural production so that the colony would produce more revenue and trade for Portugal. To achieve this he created three large private trading companies that were given extensive commercial privileges in designated regions of the colony. The Company of Grão Pará and Maranhão was responsible for the North, the Company of Pernambuco and Paraíba for the Northeast, and the Company for Whale Fishing for the development of the coastal whaling industry.

Although the trading companies were generally successful in stimulating local agricultural production, especially in rice and cotton, Pombal's tenure of office coincided with a period of general economic depression in Brazil brought about by the decline in gold production and a fall in exports of sugar. In fact, when Pombal gave up power in 1777 the value of the colony's exports had fallen to half the figure recorded in 1760. Ironically, economic prospects improved considerably shortly after Pombal left office as a growing internal market, combined with the external factor of revolutionary upheaval in North America and France, increased both the demand for and the prices of Brazilian agricultural products. After a long period of decline, sugar production was dramatically boosted in the aftermath of the 1791 slave rebellion in Haiti which resulted in the temporary removal of Brazil's biggest competitor. The number of sugar mills in Bahia notably increased from 122 in 1759 to 260 in 1798. Moreover, intensive cultivation expanded into new areas beyond the Northeast, especially in Rio de Janeiro which became a significant exporter of sugar during the 1790s. Other products also flourished. By the end of the century the North and Northeast were cultivating substantial quantities of tobacco, rice, cotton and cacao both for export and domestic consumption. Cultivation of coffee also began in this period. Although the name of 'Brazil' would become virtually synonymous with 'coffee,' the plant was actually not indigenous to Brazil. The seeds were originally introduced into Pará from French Guiana around 1727 by Francisco de Melo Palheta. By 1760 coffee was being grown in Rio de Janeiro. It soon spread westwards to São Paulo where its successful cultivation provided the great economic success story of nineteenth-century Brazil.

Society

Demography

The image of a forbidding wilderness and the lack of visible economic incentives meant that European settlement in Brazil developed slowly during the first century of Portuguese colonization. It has been estimated that by 1585 the settled areas of the colony contained 60,000 people, of whom half had originated from Europe. The remainder were Indians and African slaves. In 1700 the total population had grown to around 350,000. The number increased rapidly to more than 1.5 million in 1776 as a result of a high fertility rate and a marked rise in immigration from Europe stimulated by the mining boom in Minas Gerais. The figure for 1800 was over 2 million. Despite this considerable rise in settlement over three centuries, the density of population to total land area remained extremely low. Indeed, throughout the whole colonial period the population of Portugal was greater than that of Brazil.

During the sixteenth and seventeenth centuries the large majority of the colonial population preferred to stay close to the coast and were concentrated

[28] in the sugar-producing captaincies of Bahia and Pernambuco. Movement into the interior or *sertão* of the Northeast and along the northern coastline to the Amazon Valley proceeded slowly and involved relatively limited numbers of explorers and migrants. In the region of the Center-South, the important settlements were the port of Rio de Janeiro and the inland town of São Paulo. Further to the south, settlement was very sparse. The discovery of gold in Minas Gerais in 1695 resulted, however, in substantial migration into the mining region from the coastal areas and from overseas. Consequently, a dramatic rise occurred in the population of Minas Gerais, a region into which very few Europeans had ventured prior to the gold strike. The neighboring captaincies of Rio de Janeiro and São Paulo also significantly gained in wealth and population from the mining boom. By the close of the eighteenth century, however, the Northeast still remained the most populated region of the colony with 47 percent of the total colonial population. The combined populations of the captaincies of Rio de Janeiro and Minas Gerais amounted to 27 percent. The North, including Pará and Maranhão, possessed nearly 9 percent while the captaincy of São Paulo and the South had 13.5 percent.

The first Portuguese settlements were a string of small and isolated *feitorias* for the trade in brazilwood. During the second half of the sixteenth century ports were established, some of which attracted permanent settlements that eventually grew into towns and became cities. The leading example was Salvador (da Bahia), the capital of the colony and seat of the governor-general after 1549. The population of Salvador increased from 14,000 in 1585 to 25,000 in 1710, and to 50,000 in 1800. Olinda, the capital of Pernambuco, had a population of 4,000 in 1630, but had grown to only 8,000 in 1654. During the eighteenth century it was overshadowed by the development of its main port, Recife, which recorded a population of 7,000 in 1750 and 25,000 in 1810. Another rising port was Rio de Janeiro which was founded as early as 1565, but did not significantly expand until the mining boom at the beginning of the eighteenth century. Rio's population reached 30,000 in 1760 and increased to about 45,000 in 1800. In the next 20 years that figure more than doubled to 110,000. The designation of Rio de Janeiro as the national capital in 1763 underlined the shift in the share of population and economic power from the Northeast to the Center-South. This development was also exemplified by the city of São Paulo. In 1681 São Paulo was made the capital of the captaincy and in 1711 its status was raised from town to city. Its population grew from 20,000 in 1765 to almost 25,000 in 1800. But population decline could also occur in the Center-South. For example, Ouro Preto in Minas Gerais had a population of 20,000 in 1740.

This had been reduced to 7,000 in 1804 as a result of the decline of the [29] mining industry.

Society

Society during the colonial period was hierarchical and divided according to gender, income, occupation and race.[15] In addition, there was the crucially important distinction of whether a person was free or slave. While whites were free, most Africans, though not all, were slave. The dominant ruling class were a minority of white Europeans, mostly of Portuguese origin, who could ostensibly claim 'purity of blood' (*limpeza de sangue*) based on either being born in Europe or possessing European parents. Indians and Africans were considered to be racially inferior to whites. They suffered enslavement and discrimination and were firmly consigned to the bottom of the social pyramid. In the middle, however, were the people of mixed race. On account of their relatively large numbers, racial diversity and the fact that many possessed free status, they contributed to the modification and blurring of social barriers. People of mixed race could be either *mamelucos* or mulattos.[16] The *mamelucos* were the product of sexual unions between European fathers and Indian mothers. These had been common in the sixteenth century at a time when relatively few European women had settled in the colony. Mulattos were the product of white fathers and African mothers. In the seventeenth century there was a tendency to refer to all people of mixed race as *pardos* ('greys'). Even though many pardos were *livres* (free by birth) or *libertos* (manumitted either as a gift from their owner or by purchase), they were frequently subject to forced labor, suffered discrimination in employment and were treated with contempt by white society. The color of their skin gave *pardos* the stigma of a link with people of inferior African origin and was underlined during the eighteenth century when mulatto became more commonly used as a general term to describe non-whites.

Europeans who had been born in Portugal were known as *reinóis*. Whites born in Brazil were referred to as *mazombos* though this term was not frequently used and was eventually replaced by *branco*. Despite not being born in Portugal, whites in Brazil regarded themselves as Portuguese and, therefore, pure-blooded. Nevertheless, a certain amount of social embarrassment was caused by the fact that a number of white families, which had been formed during the sixteenth century, inevitably had an element of Indian ancestry. The sense of Portuguese identity in the colony, however, was affirmed and reinforced by continuous immigration from Portugal and the policy of mostly

[30] appointing Portuguese officials to take up administrative posts in the colonial government. Throughout the colonial period a tension persisted between *reinóis* and *mazombos*. Brazilian-born whites were particularly sensitive to the exclusiveness and arrogant attitude frequently adopted by Portuguese officials. They were also aggrieved at the economic privileges granted to Portuguese merchants that became synonymous with commercial profiteering and exploitation. At times of economic difficulty, Brazilian resentment sometimes erupted into violence as in the case of the 'War of the Peddlers' (*Guerra dos Mascates*) in Pernambuco in 1711. But friction did not quite develop to the same degree that came to exist between *creoles* and *peninsulares* in some parts of Spanish America. In fact, whites in Brazil felt a common bond with each other because they were free-born and lived as a privileged racial minority in a society in which, during the colonial period, the majority of the population, amounting to 75 percent, were non-white.

The leaders of white society were the wealthy male landowners and cattle-ranchers consisting initially of the donataries, their descendants and those who had acquired *sesmarias* (grants of land) and large amounts of landed property. Affluent merchants, who mostly lived in the large cities, also enjoyed social prestige and influence. The colony, however, lacked a traditional aristocracy with inherited titles and rank because few aristocrats (*fidalgos*) chose to leave Portugal for Brazil. In their place emerged a colonial oligarchy whose most prominent local figures were the *senhores de engenho* ('lords of the mill') and the *fazendeiros*. These were financially wealthy individuals who owned extensive sugar plantations and landed estates (*fazendas*), employed retainers and controlled large numbers of slaves. In their particular localities they were not only the leaders of society but also possessed considerable political and economic power over the local community, often taking the form of an extended family (*parentela*). In addition, their retainers and slaves could be mobilized into a substantial militia that served as a local police force. 'To be a *senhor de engenho* in Brazil,' remarked one contemporary observer, 'is considered like having a title among the nobles of Portugal.'[17] The rest of the white population consisted of small landowners and farmers (*lavradores*) and peasants in the rural areas and of merchants, artisans and a proletariat of laborers in the towns and cities. Though not all *lavradores* were wealthy, the *lavradores de cana* (sugarcane farmers) formed an élite group among the farmers. Similarly some artisans, especially blacksmiths, were valued for their skills. The majority of the white rural population, however, were peasant farmers (*moradores*) who might own land either by purchase or settlement but also worked as sharecroppers and laborers and generally lived at a subsistence level. Just as the middle-class *lavradores* were often financially dependent on the *senhores de engenho*, a similar client relationship existed between the *lavradores* and the peasants. In addition, the low social status of the rural peasants and urban proletariat was reinforced by poverty, illiteracy, and in some cases the fact that they were originally *degredados*, individuals who had been deported from Portugal to avoid imprisonment or execution.

While whites maintained a strong sense of racial unity and solidarity, this was not so apparent among the people of mixed race. A major difference existed between those who were free and slave. There was also the sensitive issue of different shades of color.[18] As the product of white fathers, most mulattos were free. Although they were regarded as illegitimate offspring and rarely accepted as equals in white society, mulattos did feel superior to black slaves. On the other hand, slaves could achieve freedom by purchase or by manumission from their owner. In the granting of manumission owners were more generous to women and children than to males. Distinctions also existed among slaves. Those who were Brazilian-born were called *crioulos*. Newly-arrived slaves from Africa were referred to as *bocal* or *bocais*, while those who had been in the colony for some time were known as *pretos* or *ladinos*.

The Indians

The land that was to become known as Brazil had been inhabited by indigenous peoples for several centuries before the Portuguese arrived in 1500. The exact Indian population is unknown, but has been estimated at between 3 and 5 million. The Indians were widely scattered and were divided into several disparate tribes which were based upon separate language groups. The coastal peoples in Bahia, who were the first to come into contact with the Portuguese, spoke the Tupí language and included the Tupinambá and the Tupiniquin. The Tapuia were non-Tupí speakers and inhabited the interior beyond the coast.

In contrast to Spanish America, there were neither highly-developed civilizations nor large concentrations of settlement in Brazil similar to the Aztecs in Mexico or the Incas in Peru. Moreover, the apparent lack of precious metals in Brazil resulted in the Portuguese showing little interest in exploring the land and making contact with its people. Initial relations were generally friendly and revolved around the barter trade in brazilwood. The establishment of the captaincy system during the 1530s, however, turned temporary trading posts into permanent Portuguese settlements and began the process of

[32]   dispossessing the Indians of their territory. Moreover, the subsequent development of sugar plantations during the second half of the sixteenth century created a growing requirement for field laborers that European immigration could not satisfy. The planters looked, therefore, to the local Indian population to provide the necessary manual labor.

The Portuguese proceeded to impose a system of compulsory labor upon the Indians that was equivalent to enslavement. The planters justified the use of violence and compulsion by arguing that the Indians were uncivilized savages and could be treated like beasts of burden. Like the Spaniards in the Caribbean islands, the Portuguese were also genuinely puzzled by the apparent diffidence of the Indians towards physical work and their lack of interest in acquiring money and material possessions. 'These Indians, Sir,' complained Governor Diogo de Meneses in 1610, 'are a very barbarous people having no government and being unable to govern themselves, and they are so lacking in this regard that even in their sustenance they will not save for tomorrow that which is in excess today.'[19] Some members of the Religious Orders in Brazil, especially the Jesuits, adopted the contrary view that Indians were human beings and had natural rights. The Jesuits echoed the views of the Spanish missionary, Bartolomé de Las Casas, and argued that Indians could become Christians and should not be enslaved. In a famous sermon delivered in Maranhão in 1653, Father Antonio Vieira fiercely condemned the purchase of Indians as slaves: 'What a cheap market! An Indian for a soul! That Indian will be your slave for the few days that he lives; and your soul will be a slave for eternity, as long as God is God. This is the contract that the devil makes with you. Not only do you accept it but you pay him money on top of it.'[20]

Mindful of the sense of religious mission that had motivated the *Reconquista* and the establishment of overseas colonies, the Portuguese Crown accepted that it should assist efforts to convert the Indians to Catholicism. It also approved legislation designed to prevent the enslavement of Indians. But slavery was permitted in cases where Indians were deemed rebellious and resisted religious conversion or were captured after running away. In practice, the laws were interpreted in such a way that the planters could have the workers that they wanted for their plantations. The passage of stricter legislation in 1595 and 1609 to protect the Indians from exploitation reflected an element of genuine sympathy for their plight but also indicated that the shortage of Indian laborers was no longer such a pressing issue. The main reason for this was the importation of increasing numbers of African slaves who were regarded as a superior and more reliable labor force. At the same time the supply of healthy Indian workers was steadily diminishing. From the 1570s onwards the health of Indians in Brazil had been gravely affected by the outbreak of a series of epidemics of serious diseases such as smallpox, measles and influenza. The mortality rate was extremely high because Indians had no natural immunity to these imported diseases. The result was demographic disaster in which it is estimated that the Indian population of the coastal region declined by as much as three quarters.

Portuguese efforts to impose compulsory labor on the Indians did provoke some resistance. A general rebellion erupted in 1567 in the main sugar-growing region surrounding Salvador, known as the Recôncavo. Organized revolts, however, were rare because the Indians belonged to different tribes and were often in conflict with each other. Like Cortés in his conquest of Mexico, Portuguese settlers were able to exploit local tribal rivalries and division to their own advantage. In fighting the Portuguese, the Indians were also hampered by shortage of weapons and lack of military organization. Some tribes chose to move away into the *sertão* or eventually escape as far away as the Amazon jungle. Those who stayed in the coastal region were forced to submit to Portuguese authority and exploitation. Religious Orders such as the Jesuits offered protection and resettled Indians in village communities known as *aldeias*. The Jesuits, however, stressed conversion to Catholicism and, in their determination to impose European values and discipline, pursued policies of coercion and social control that showed little sympathy for Indian traditions and culture. Towards the close of the colonial period, in 1755, a law was finally passed that liberated Indians from slavery. During the preceding two centuries, however, the Indian population of Brazil had been virtually destroyed by forced labor, religious persecution and, most of all, by disease.

The African slaves

The drastic decline of the Indian population in colonial Brazil contrasted with the steady rise in the number of black Africans who were involuntarily brought into the country as slaves. The Portuguese colonists turned to Africa for slave labor because the expansion of the sugar industry in Bahia and Pernambuco required a large number of laborers which the local Indian population could not supply. The decision to look to Africa was natural because slavery had existed there for some time. Indeed, Portuguese merchants had been trading in slaves from that continent since the middle of the fifteenth century. Initially, the high costs of transportation made Africans

[34] relatively expensive, but planters reckoned that, in terms of working capacity, one African was equivalent to three or four Indians. Africans also proved to be less vulnerable to the diseases that were decimating the Indian population. Moreover, the issue of African slavery did not attract the moral and theological controversy that had been provoked by the enslavement of the Indian. Indeed, as the Jesuit theologian, Luís de Molina, stated in 1592, African slavery was justified in natural and Roman law and had a long history dating back to the classical world.

The first shipments of African slaves began arriving in Brazil during the 1540s. By the end of the sixteenth century there were an estimated 15,000 in the colony, making up 25 percent of the colonial population. That percentage had doubled by 1680 when slaves numbered around 150,000. In 1800 there were more than 1 million slaves. The rise in population was considerable, but was not a result of natural increase. In fact, the annual number of deaths of slaves usually exceeded births. This was explained by the higher ratio of male to female slaves, usually averaging four to one. Moreover, owners invariably imposed a harsh and unhealthy working environment in which cruelty and mistreatment were common. Lack of health care also significantly contributed to high rates of infant mortality and a short life expectancy for adults. In fact, the average working life of a male field laborer after his arrival from Africa was usually no more than seven years.[21] A sugar plantation expected that every year from 5 to 10 percent of its slaves would die from overwork or ill-health. The planters willingly accepted the high mortality rate because the transatlantic slave trade offered a constant supply of relatively cheap new workers. Between 1540 and 1800 Brazil received in excess of 2 million African slaves, a figure that represented more than one third of the total number of slaves imported from Africa into the Americas during that period. The continuation of the transatlantic slave trade, therefore, ensured an increase in the slave population. Moreover, the numbers were so large that African slaves not only formed the main labor force but they also came to constitute a majority of the colonial population. In effect, the institution of slavery was the distinguishing feature of society in colonial Brazil. It was also considered by whites as the essential, if not indispensable, element that underpinned the colony's economic growth and their own prosperity.

Slaves were bought and sold and were regarded as personal possessions by their owners. They were economically exploited and subject to a strict discipline that frequently included the use of violence. The *pelourinho*, a stone whipping post prominently located in the central square of towns and villages, was frequently used for the public punishment of slaves and criminals and represented a symbol of white authority and cruelty. Like the colonized Indians, slaves were forced to submit to a life of labor. For most of the colonial period the large majority worked in agriculture, especially in the sugar industry of the Northeast that relied extensively on physical labor. During the mining boom of the eighteenth century slaves were taken to Minas Gerais to extract gold and diamonds. A small percentage of slaves performed menial tasks as servants in the home (*casa grande*) of their master or mistress. Slaves also worked as domestics in the towns and cities. Though formal marriage was rarely allowed, slaves often formed family units. Families, however, experienced disruption when slaves, especially males, were sold and moved. In such cases female slaves were left with the responsibility of looking after other family members, including children. This reinforced the matriarchal nature of the slave family.

The mistreatment of slaves could provoke resistance that took several forms including assault and even murder of their overseers or owners, an action that invariably resulted in brutal punishment and reprisals by white society. Slave revolts occasionally occurred, but were not usually well-organized and were quickly isolated and suppressed. Protest and discontent were usually shown in less overt and confrontational ways such as feigning illness, non-cooperation, sabotage of machinery, and in extreme cases by suicide. Slaves also ran away. The existence of a sizeable free black population often made apprehension difficult. Some fugitives formed or joined organized communities known as *quilombos* (or *mocambos*) in which they survived by subsistence farming and banditry. The *quilombos* of Campo Grande and Ambrósio in Minas Gerais attracted up to 10,000 members each. The most famous *quilombo* was the 'kingdom of Palmares' in Alagoas that at one time had 20,000 inhabitants. It was attacked several times by government soldiers and was finally destroyed in 1695.

The Church

In pursuing its historic duty and mission to spread and maintain the Catholic religion, the Church exercised a pervasive influence throughout all groups of society in colonial Brazil. As in Spanish America many impressive religious buildings were constructed in Brazil, but they disguised the fact that the Brazilian Church was never as economically or politically powerful as its Spanish-American counterparts. While colonial Brazil had only one archbishopric at Salvador, five archbishoprics were created in Spanish America. Moreover, the Brazilian Church was unable to acquire its own

[36] source of independent wealth. Except for occasional visitations from the Inquisition that were designed to identify and punish heretics, the Portuguese Crown enjoyed almost complete authority over the Catholic Church in Brazil. In order to reward and assist the *Reconquista* to convert the Indians, the Papacy had given the Portuguese Crown almost complete authority over the Catholic Church in Brazil. This meant that the Church was subordinate to the Crown in the matter of ecclesiastical appointments. In fact, the Portuguese king held the office of the 'Grand Master of the Order of Christ' and personally appointed all senior clergy, including bishops. His approval was even required for the publication of papal bulls in Brazil. In addition, royal interference significantly extended to financial matters. Parishioners traditionally contributed a tithe (*dízimos*) of their earnings, but the money was collected by the Crown and only partially returned to the Church.

The Church played a major role in promoting learning in the colony by establishing schools. These varied from priests providing basic education to Indians, both children and adult, in makeshift schools in the *aldeias* to more formal 'colleges' in the cities that were attended by the children of Brazilian-born whites. Among the Religious Orders, the Jesuits were particularly prominent in establishing schools. Their most successful colleges were located in Salvador, Olinda, and Rio de Janeiro. The Church was also a valuable adjunct of the Crown in pacifying and acculturating the Indians. However, the attempts of some priests, especially the Jesuits, to protect the Indians from enslavement and mistreatment by their owners provoked controversy. Sugar planters resented the removal of Indians to *aldeias* and argued that this deprived them of a vital source of labor. In remote regions of the interior, *bandeirantes* refused to recognize *aldeias* as places of sanctuary. Claiming to be in pursuit of fugitive slaves, they seized and took away Indians for slave labor. The Crown generally supported the Church, but this support was withdrawn during the period of Pombal's reforms. The loss of royal favor contributed to the celebrated expulsion of the Jesuits from the colony in 1759.

Social conditions

With the exception of the small élite of wealthy landowners, sugar planters and merchants, the vast majority of people living in Brazil during the colonial period were poor and experienced harsh conditions of life. Whether free or slave, they routinely suffered economic exploitation, social discrimination and institutional and non-institutional violence. Living in the countryside their lives revolved around a daily grind of physical labor and subsistence agriculture. Employment opportunities and working conditions were marginally better for the small number of people who lived in the cities. All suffered, however, from frequent epidemics of serious diseases. With the notable exception of hospitals and homes for the poor and orphans that were established by the voluntary religious brotherhoods (*irmandades*), there was virtually no provision for health-care or social welfare.

The general level of educational attainment was also very low. In fact, the provision of education had never been a feature of Portuguese colonial policy and was left to the Church. Just as mercantilism aimed to prevent the colony from ever becoming an industrial competitor of the mother country, the Crown similarly sought to stifle intellectual development. While books and pamphlets could be imported from Portugal, they were subject to strict censorship. The colony was not even allowed to have a printing press, and when one was set up in Rio de Janeiro in 1749 it was immediately confiscated. Despite a succession of petitions, the monarchy also refused to permit the establishment of a university in the colony. Consequently, Brazilian-born whites who wished to have a university education had to leave Brazil and travel to Europe to attend universities in Portugal, Spain or France. The most popular was the University of Coimbra where an estimated 600 students from Brazil were enrolled during the period from 1772 to 1808. As a result, the Brazilian élite were inculcated with Portuguese values and culture. 'One of the strongest unifying bonds that keeps the dependency of the colonies,' summed up a government document in 1768, 'is the need to come to Portugal for higher studies.'[22]

CHAPTER 2

THE EMPIRE

Politics

The royal family in Brazil

After lasting for three centuries, the Portuguese and Spanish colonial empires in the New World collapsed at the beginning of the nineteenth century. While the liberation of the Spanish colonies involved fifteen years of civil war from 1810 to 1825, the same outcome in Brazil occurred much less traumatically in barely one year of fighting. This relatively peaceful and speedy transition owed much to the influence of diplomatic and military events in Europe beginning with the unexpected transfer of the royal family from Portugal to Brazil in 1807. Under Dom João, the prince regent[1] and future King João VI, Portugal adopted an ambivalent stance in the succession of wars that afflicted Europe after the 1789 French Revolution. In 1806, however, the French emperor, Napoleon, devised the Continental System, a strategy of economic warfare that aimed to prohibit all trade between continental Europe and Britain. Portugal was given an ultimatum to comply, but prevaricated. Dom João's characteristically indecisive response reflected a fear of France mixed with reluctance to damage his country's close commercial relationship with Britain. In retaliation, French forces, under the command of General Andache Junot, invaded Portugal in November 1807.

Faced with the imminent prospect of capture by the French invading army, Dom João chose to leave Lisbon and seek temporary exile in Brazil. The idea of the royal family residing in the tropics appeared radical but was not entirely new. In the eighteenth century, the veteran diplomat, Luís da Cunha, had predicted that the economic and political importance of Brazil would eventually result in the relocation of the seat of royal government to the New World. The idea suddenly became a reality in 1807 as a matter of expediency rather than careful consideration or planning. The evacuation was also strongly backed by the British minister in Portugal, Lord Strangford, who coordinated British naval assistance. From November 25 to 27, 1807, as French troops drew close to Lisbon, approximately 15,000 people departed for Brazil in a total of more than forty ships. The scale of the evacuation was remarkable. The prince regent was accompanied by his mother and the royal family, his court and government officials including ministers, judges, army and naval officers, and senior clergy. The machinery of government was also transported in the form of the royal treasury, the government archives, a printing press and various libraries, which would form the nucleus of the National Library of Rio de Janeiro.

The embarkation was attended with great confusion. Many difficulties were encountered during the voyage. A storm split up the fleet. Overcrowded ships fell short of food and water. An infestation of lice required the women to shave their heads. On January 22, 1808, part of the fleet in which the prince regent traveled reached Bahia. When Dom João came ashore at Salvador, he was the first crowned European ruler to put his foot on the soil of the New World. His short stay in Salvador was memorable for the transaction of an important item of official business. Conscious that commercial links with Portugal were now cut off as a result of the French military occupation of the country and Britain's decision to impose a retaliatory naval blockade of Portuguese ports, the prince regent issued a decree on January 28, opening the ports of Brazil to trade with friendly nations. The measure was momentous in that it signified the official end of the mercantilist system that had endured for three centuries. The fact that British merchants stood to gain most from a relaxation of barriers to trade made the decision appear as a payment for British naval assistance in facilitating the evacuation from Portugal. While Dom João was grateful for British aid, his decision to open the ports was largely an emergency response that was influenced by the pressing need to raise revenue from customs duties and prevent local merchants from resorting to smuggling on a large scale. Moreover, the measure was pleasing to local Brazilian interests, especially those that produced sugar and cotton for the export trade.

Although Dom João was gratified with the warm welcome that he received in Bahia, he made it known that he intended to travel on to Rio de Janeiro and establish the royal residence there. He eventually arrived in Rio de Janeiro on March 7. The court and officials of the government traveled with the prince regent so that his decision to reside in Rio de Janeiro meant that the city instantly became the capital and center of the Portuguese empire.

[40]   Government ministries were quickly established along with a military academy, medical school, printing press and financial institutions. The growing prestige and significance of Brazil was underlined in December 1815 when Dom João issued a decree that elevated Brazil from its subordinate colonial status of 'state' (*estado*) to the same category of 'kingdom' (*reino*) that was enjoyed by Portugal. The implication was that Brazil and Portugal were at last equals.

While Dom João showed a personal liking for life in the tropics, there was considerable friction in relations between Portuguese and Brazilians. The highest political, administrative, military and legal offices were jealously guarded by the Portuguese courtiers and officials who had accompanied the prince regent on his voyage from Lisbon. Some aristocratic titles and honors were bestowed upon local landowners and civil servants, but no one born in Brazil was appointed as a government minister or a member of the Council of State, the prestigious body that advised the king on matters of state. Nevertheless, despite their political and economic privileges, many Portuguese courtiers and especially Queen Carlota Joaquina yearned to return to Portugal. They openly expressed their contempt of Brazil and Brazilians and provoked anti-Portuguese sentiment at all levels of Brazilian society. Resentment against Portuguese arrogance and influence was a feature of the 1817 Pernambucan Revolt, the one serious separatist revolt that occurred during the period of Dom João's rule. The rebellion began in Recife in March 1817 with a proclamation of a republic and demands for greater local autonomy including the expulsion of all Portuguese from the province. The movement attracted broad support among the élite including some army officers, landowners, merchants and so many priests that it became known as the 'revolution of priests.' Although the Pernambucan Revolt sent agents to Buenos Aires, the United States and Britain to gain support, it never expanded beyond the Northeast. Portuguese troops soon regained control of Recife in May 1817. The leaders of the revolt were captured and severely punished.

The evacuation of the royal family to Brazil had always been regarded as a temporary measure. The prospect of a safe return to Portugal emerged as early as 1811 when French troops were forced on to the retreat in the Iberian peninsula. Even after the final defeat of Napoleon in 1815 and despite the wishes of many of his courtiers, Dom João was personally reluctant to undertake the long sea journey from Rio de Janeiro to Lisbon. His prolonged absence, however, stimulated growing political unrest in Portugal. Influenced by events in Spain which had led to the liberal Spanish Constitution of 1820, Portuguese liberals enacted their own political revolution with an uprising in

Oporto in August 1820. A national *Côrtes* (parliament) was convened in January 1821 which prepared a new liberal constitution and demanded the immediate return of the king to Lisbon. Dom João feared that he might lose his throne if he did not return to Portugal. Along with 4,000 Portuguese he sailed from Brazil on April 26, 1821 leaving his son, the 23-year-old Pedro, as prince regent. A legend exists that Dom João believed that Brazil would soon seek to be independent. In that eventuality, he advised his son to take control: 'Pedro, if Brazil breaks away, let it rather do so for you who will respect me than for one of those adventurers.'[2]

The king's return to Lisbon in July 1821 did not deflect the determination of the *Côrtes* to restore the colonial relationship between Portugal and Brazil. The *Côrtes* proceeded to vote to deprive Brazil of its status as a kingdom and to demand that the heir to the throne, Prince Pedro, return to Portugal. In anticipation of colonial resistance, detachments of troops were prepared for dispatch to Rio de Janeiro and Pernambuco. Obedience to the *Côrtes* would be assured by placing every province under the control of a military governor who would be directly accountable to instructions from Lisbon.

Independence

The confrontational attitude taken by the *Côrtes* aroused criticism and opposition in Brazil. The Brazilian élite represented by the big landowners, leading planters and urban merchants were similar to their counterparts in Spanish America in opposing the attempted reimposition of metropolitan control from Europe, which they feared would include the restoration of former commercial privileges and monopolies. The residence of the court in Rio de Janeiro had not only elevated the prestige and status of Brazil but had also provided economic benefits that the Brazilian élite were reluctant to lose. A refusal to submit to the authority of the *Côrtes* raised, however, the question of separation from Portugal and the establishment of an independent Brazil. Prior to 1821 the Brazilian élite had equated the idea of national independence with the excesses of the French Revolution. It now appeared to be the preferable, if not the only, alternative to a humiliating return to colonial status.

Brazilian resistance to legislation passed in Lisbon was greatly aided by slowness of communications caused by geographical distance and the inability of Portugal to coerce Brazil with overwhelming military force. There was also the actual presence in Brazil of Prince Pedro, a member of the royal family and heir to the throne. The Brazilian élite, who led the movement for

[42]   independence, urged him to reject the demand of the *Côrtes* that he should return to Portugal. In a famous statement made on January 9, 1822, Pedro responded to a petition from the Municipal Council of Rio de Janeiro that he stay in Brazil with the famous word *'fico'* ('I am staying'). Although born in Portugal himself and preferring the company of Portuguese rather than Brazilians, Dom Pedro further pleased local opinion by appointing the Brazilian-born José Bonifácio (de Andrada e Silva) to act as his chief political advisor with the title of 'Minister of the Kingdom.' Educated at the University of Coimbra and a statesman of considerable intellect and political insight, José Bonifacio would become known as the 'patriarch of independence.' Guided by José Bonifacio, the prince decreed in May that no act of the *Côrtes* would have legal force in Brazil without his approval. Dom Pedro also assumed the title 'Perpetual Defender of Brazil.' The wording was significant in that the use of 'perpetual' implied that the prince intended to remain in Brazil. On September 7, en route from Santos to São Paulo, he received news that the *Côrtes* regarded him as a traitor and was insisting on his immediate return to Portugal. A letter from José Bonifacio explained that compromise was impossible: 'From Portugal we can expect only enslavement and horror. Come back and make a decision; irresolution and temperate measure cannot help. In view of this merciless enemy, one moment lost is a disgrace.'[3] Close to a stream called the Ipiranga, Dom Pedro unsheathed his sword and defiantly gave his answer to the *Côrtes* as 'independence or death.' The 'cry of Ipiranga' (*grito de Ipiranga*) proclaimed the independence of Brazil after more than three centuries as a colony of Portugal. The date of September 7 would be celebrated annually as Brazil's Independence Day.

While Brazilian independence was achieved much more quickly and with considerably less violence and destruction than in Spanish America, there were some pockets of entrenched loyalist opposition and an attitude of resistance especially in the North and Northeast to central control from Rio de Janeiro that required the use of substantial military force to overcome. The most violent clashes occurred close to Salvador, where a large Portuguese garrison of 13,000 eventually surrendered in June 1823 to Brigadier General Francisco de Lima e Silva. Garrisons further to the north and west in Maranhão, Pará, and Amazonas were isolated and subdued by the naval forces led by the bold and resourceful British naval captain, Lord Thomas Cochrane. The British mercenary was rewarded with the title of Marquis of Maranhão. All resistance in the North was suppressed by August 1823. In the South a Portuguese garrison remained in Montevideo until November when the city was evacuated and handed over to Brazilian forces. Although no major pitched battles

took place in the fight for Brazilian independence, the actual fighting on land [43]
required the deployment of a fairly large number of troops including local
militia units and volunteers.

The First Empire, 1822–1831

The dramatic cry of 'independence or death' had not been intended as an
appeal to the people of Brazil to rise up in arms and overthrow Portuguese
tyranny. In effect, Dom Pedro was essentially affirming that he intended to
stay in Brazil and govern the country in the same way that he was already
doing. The stress, therefore, was on continuity and not revolution. Consequently, the formal transition from a Portuguese kingdom to an independent empire was effected peacefully on December 1 1822 when Dom Pedro
was crowned in Rio de Janeiro as Pedro I, the 'Constitutional Emperor and
Perpetual Defender of Brazil.' The title of emperor was chosen in preference
to king so as not to offend his father, King João VI of Portugal, who was
still remembered with affection in Brazil. The country was also so huge that
it was considered to be more like an empire than a kingdom.

In marked contrast to the countries of Spanish America the newly-independent Brazil became a monarchy and an empire rather than a republic.[4] In
fact there was no serious consideration of adopting the republican political
system, which the Brazilian élite associated with political instability and social
disorder. The presence in the country of a royal prince who was willing and
able to rule made monarchy not only the logical choice but also simple to
implement. Moreover, Dom Pedro was not a usurper and had been prince
regent of Brazil since the departure of his father in April 1821. In addition,
he was able to benefit from the fact that since 1808 Brazilians had become
accustomed to regarding the king and his court in Rio de Janeiro as the seat
of political and legal authority. Although long-standing political and administrative ties with Portugal had been severed, the creation of the empire also
brought little immediate change. Indeed, the Brazilian élite was pleased
that the government and the economy continued to function as before. The
principal difference was that Brazilians had begun to replace Portuguese in
senior political and administrative posts.

1824 Constitution

Following the example of his father and other European monarchs, Dom
Pedro was in favor of ruling as a constitutional monarch. The task of drawing

[44]   up a constitution for the new state was assigned to a Constituent Assembly whose 90 members, chosen by indirect elections, convened in Rio de Janeiro on 3 May, 1823. The result, however, was a series of long debates over the exact powers to be accorded the executive and legislative branches of government. Supporters of Dom Pedro favored 'centralism' and argued that a powerful executive, in the form of the emperor, was the best means of maintaining law and order and preserving national unity. A group who subscribed to 'liberal' views feared that centralism would lead to the establishment of an absolutist ruler who would dominate and control the legislative power. The failure to reach agreement contributed to the resignation of José Bonifacio from the government in July 1823. When it appeared that the delegates were likely to produce a document that was too restrictive of the emperor's powers, Dom Pedro ordered troops to dissolve the Constituent Assembly on November 11. In his typically intemperate language, the emperor explained that a faction of the delegates that he likened to a 'revolutionary volcano' had taken control of the Assembly and were conspiring to take up arms and ruin the country.[5] José Bonifacio and his brother, the former finance minister, Martim Francisco (de Andrada e Silva), were identified as leaders of the revolutionary faction. They were arrested and sent into exile. Acting like an absolute ruler, Dom Pedro proceeded to appoint a Council of State which, under his guidance, drew up a constitution that was promulgated by imperial decree on March 25, 1824.

The 1824 Constitution divided the country into eighteen provinces to be ruled by a national government. The executive power was represented by the emperor. The legislature was composed of a two-chamber General Assembly consisting of a Senate and a Chamber of Deputies. Senators served for life-terms and were chosen by the emperor from a list of nominees made by each province. Deputies served for four-year terms and were elected from a restricted franchise. A Supreme Court was created to preside over the judicial branch. Despite liberal rhetoric guaranteeing freedom of the individual, the constitution reflected the existing colonial social structure by restricting political and voting rights only to adult males who could meet high property and income qualifications. Women and slaves were deliberately excluded. Moreover, the powers accorded to the emperor were so substantial that he was able to dominate the legislative and judicial branches. For example, he had the authority to name and dismiss members of the Senate as well as appoint high court judges and the presidents of the provinces. In addition, article 98 of the Constitution gave the emperor the 'moderating power' (*poder moderador*):

The Moderating Power is the key to the entire political organization and it is delegated exclusively to the Emperor as the Supreme Chief of the Nation and its First Representative so that he constantly can watch over the maintenance of the independence, equilibrium, and harmony of the other Political Powers.[6]

By making use of the 'moderating power' the emperor could, if he judged that the political circumstances warranted, dissolve the Chamber of Deputies and call new elections. The only tangible restraint on the emperor was the requirement that he consult with the Council of State in the use of the moderating power. The Council, however, was composed of councillors who were personally appointed by the emperor.

While the landowning and business élites of the provinces of Rio de Janeiro, São Paulo and Minas Gerais approved a political system that promised stability and order, similar interest groups in the Northeast were concerned at the centralization of political and governmental power. They also felt more directly affected by the break with Portugal. During the colonial period the cities and ports of the North and Northeast had easier and more direct communications with Lisbon than with Rio de Janeiro. Pernambuco was again the leading focal point of regional resistance. 'In the more northern Provinces,' reported the British chargé d'affaires in Rio in May 1824, 'a strong spirit of Republicanism exists and has existed for a considerable period.'[7] In July 1824 a separatist movement emerged in Recife in the form of an attempt to set up an independent republic called 'the Confederation of the Equator.' Government forces led by General Lima e Silva and Admiral Cochrane quickly suppressed the revolt.

Abdication of Pedro I

In 1822 Dom Pedro had been regarded as a hero in Brazil. Subsequently, his popularity steadily declined. Public admiration for his bravery and dashing personality was tempered by his controversial treatment of his popular wife, Leopoldina.[8] A similar high-handedness and insensitivity to the opinion of others had been exemplified in his unilateral closure of the Constituent Assembly in November 1823. On the other hand, Dom Pedro was notoriously averse to any criticism of his own behavior, a feature that was noted by the British merchant, John Armitage, who observed that 'men of integrity were as much as possible excluded from [the emperor's] presence; and the plain and simple language of truth and soberness, was superseded by the vilest adulation.'[9] The emperor had the reputation of being a brave and

[46] outstanding soldier, but his military competence was called into question as a result of the unsuccessful campaign in the Cisplatine War where the failure to defeat Argentina meant the loss of territory which Brazil had controlled before the conflict. Public discontent against the emperor was also increased by the enforced military conscription to raise soldiers for the campaign.

Pedro's difficulties were compounded by the steady increase in the cost of living that occurred during the late 1820s as a result of the inflationary effects of the government's issue of copper coinage combined with a fall in the foreign exchange value of the currency. Traditional nativist resentment was quick to blame Portuguese merchants for profiteering at the expense of the Brazilian people. Indeed, growing criticism was directed specifically at Dom Pedro for showing too much favor to Portuguese interests. Although Portugal's recognition of Brazil's independence in 1825 had been welcomed, it was known that the agreement had included a secret undertaking to pay Portugal £2 million in compensation for the loss of royal properties in Brazil. Moreover, Dom Pedro had never officially abdicated his own claim to the throne of Portugal, and his interest in dynastic developments in his home country notably increased after the death of João VI in 1826. The perception that the emperor was essentially a foreigner rather than a Brazilian was also emphasized by his personal preference to be surrounded by Portuguese companions and advisors.

In 1830 suspicion that Dom Pedro planned a coup to overthrow the constitution and establish himself as absolute ruler provoked demonstrations of public protest and violence in Rio de Janeiro that would continue intermittently for more than a year. Prominent among the emperor's critics were radical liberals known as *exaltados* (exalteds or zealots). The *exaltados* were particularly hostile to the influence of the Portuguese-born and advocated an end of the monarchy and the establishment of a federal republic in which all the regions would possess local autonomy. The argument for radical political change was considerably strengthened by news from France of the overthrow of the French king, Charles X, by the July Revolution of 1830. While the institution of monarchy was not in serious danger of being overturned in Brazil, political pressure built up for the emperor to appoint more Brazilians to ministerial office. Eventually, in March 1831, Dom Pedro appointed a cabinet of Brazilian-born moderate politicians. On April 5 he dramatically reversed his decision and summarily replaced the Brazilians with his personal favorites. Public protests were held in Rio de Janeiro on April 6 demanding the dismissal of the 'ministry of marquises' and the reinstatement of the former cabinet. The army proved reluctant to intervene and some troops even joined the demonstrators. Dom Pedro, however, refused to restore the former cabinet because this would mean the surrender of his constitutional power to name ministers. 'I will do everything for the people and nothing by the people,' was his famous reply.[10] He was not prepared, however, to order the army to crush the demonstrations. In fact his pride was stung, and rather than suffer personal humiliation, he resolved to abdicate in favor of his five-year-old son, Pedro de Alcântara. The emperor's decision was communicated to the Brazilian people on April 7:

> I prefer to descend from the throne with honor rather than to go on reigning as a sovereign who has been dishonored and degraded. Those born in Brazil no longer want me for the reason that I am Portuguese . . . My son has the advantage over me in that he is a Brazilian by birth. The Brazilians respect him. He will have no difficulty in governing, and the constitution will guarantee him his rights. I renounce the crown with the glory of ending as I began — constitutionally.[11]

Shortly afterwards Dom Pedro embarked on a British warship, and left for Europe a week later. He was never to return to Brazil, and died in Portugal in September 1834.

Regency period, 1831–1840

The dramatic abdication and sudden departure from the country of Dom Pedro came as a shock. In the resulting confusion, however, there was little support for a radical change of political system. While the political élite in Rio de Janeiro had criticized the emperor's trend towards absolutism and his Portuguese bias, they did not want an end of the monarchy. To preserve their own privileges and maintain social order, they followed Dom Pedro's wish and pledged loyalty to his son as 'the constitutional emperor, Dom Pedro II.' According to article 121 of the 1824 Constitution, however, the younger Pedro, who had been born in December 1825, could not rule until he became 18 years of age in December 1843. In the meantime, a regency acting in the emperor's name would govern the country. The members of the General Assembly who were present in Rio de Janeiro met to choose an interim council of three regents for this purpose. The full General Assembly convened in June and formally elected a regency composed of General Francisco de Lima e Silva, José da Costa Carvalho from Bahia and João Bráulio Moniz from Maranhão. But the experiment of a triumvirate proved unwieldy and indecisive. By default, the cabinet assumed the leading role of governing

[48] the country. In fact, the three-man regency was abandoned in 1834 when it was decided to reduce the number of regents from three to one and to hold elections every four years. In April 1835 Father Diogo Antônio Feijó, a priest and liberal from São Paulo, was elected as the first single regent.

Although outwardly still a monarchy, Brazil was actually a republic in all but name during the period of the regency from 1831 to 1840. For the first time in its history Brazilians held the highest offices in the state. The ruling élite, however, was still dominated by the landed oligarchy and the urban mercantile interests. Although they were sympathetic to liberal ideas, the élite described themselves as 'moderates' ('*moderados*') and emphasized continuity with the past. The most prominent political figure and leader of the moderates was Father Diogo Antônio Feijó, the priest from São Paulo and regent from 1835 to 1837. As Minister of Justice from 1831 to 1832, Feijó vigorously suppressed rebellion against the national government. He was, however, a strong supporter of federalism and the devolution of political power to the provinces. This was exemplified by the passage of the Additional Act (*Ato Adicional*) in August 1834. The measure was intended to amend the 1824 Constitution by 'adding' legislation that enabled the provinces to establish their own local assemblies which could control taxation and expenditure. The important power to appoint and remove local officials was also devolved to the provincial governments. Furthermore, the act abolished the Council of State, which was seen as a symbol of authoritarian and centralized rule.

Instead of promoting political stability and public order, decentralization stimulated greater rivalry and competition among political factions within the provinces. The resulting local disorder often extended to the lower classes, both free and slave, and released their deep-seated grievances against economic and social exploitation by the white ruling élite. The outbreak of regional violence not only became a challenge to the authority of the provincial governments but also threatened to break up the nation into separate countries like Spanish America. This created a political dilemma. Although the liberal sentiments of the ruling élite in Rio de Janeiro meant that they approved the idea of federalism, they also wished to maintain national unity and hold on to their control of the political system. The landed oligarchy in general despised and feared the masses. They were especially concerned when regional revolt posed a threat to the existing social order and interfered with the institution of slavery.

The first attempt to test the resolve of the regency arose from unrest in the army, notably a serious mutiny in Rio de Janeiro in July 1831 that lasted for ten days. The national government refused to make concessions and, after

suppressing the mutiny, pursued a policy of steadily reducing the size of the
military forces. The army numbered just over 12,000 men in 1831 and had
fallen to 6,000 in 1837. A National Guard was established in 1831 to provide a 'citizens' army' to act as both a supplement and a counterweight to the
regular army. While tension in the national capital was reduced, however,
a number of disorders broke out in the provinces beginning with the War
of the *Cabanos* in southern Pernambuco in 1832. The proclaimed aim of the
rebels known as '*cabanos*' was initially the overthrow of the regency and the
restoration of Dom Pedro I. As more slaves and Indians joined the revolt,
however, a greater emphasis was placed on securing economic improvements
and racial equality. The *cabanos* were unable to capture Recife and operated
in the countryside, where their steadily diminishing numbers engaged in
guerrilla warfare for three years. The death of Dom Pedro I in 1834 removed
one of the principal reasons for the revolt's existence. The *cabanos* were
demoralized and eventually suppressed in 1835. Just as the War of the *Cabanos*
came to an end in 1835, another major conflict erupted further to the north
in Belém where a political quarrel over the presidency of the province of
Pará was transformed into a widespread revolt of the rural poor, both free
and slave, against the white ruling oligarchy. Known as the *Cabanagem*, the
revolt lasted until 1840 and claimed up to 40,000 lives or 20 percent of the
population of the province of Pará. Violent disorders also occurred in Bahia.
In January 1835 an uprising occurred of Muslim slaves and freedmen known
as the Revolt of the *Malês* (Muslim slaves). Two years later in November 1837
the city of Salvador experienced the *Sabinada*, a revolt in which more than
1,000 died. Named after its leader Sabino Barroso, the *Sabinada* gained mass
support from the urban poor in their fight to reduce the wealth and influence
of local Portuguese merchants. Salvador was blockaded from the sea and
captured in March 1838 by government forces after a siege lasting four months.

The *Balaiada*, named after Francisco dos Anjos Ferreira, one of its leaders
who had the nickname of '*balaio*' ('the basket-maker'), broke out in Maranhão
in December 1838. Like the *Sabinada* in Bahia, the *Balaiada* consisted at first
of random outbreaks of violence that were mainly directed against the wealth
and privileges of the local Portuguese mercantile élite. The movement soon
evolved, however, into a major rebellion as a large rebel army was formed
from the *mestiço* and slave population of the countryside. The army came to
number more than 10,000 and captured the city of Caxias in July 1839. In
the process, what initially appeared to be an unimportant incident occurring
in an extremely remote part of the country, became regarded by the government in Rio de Janeiro as a serious danger to the unity of the nation. In 1840

[50] Colonel Luís Alves de Lima e Silva, the son of General Francisco Lima e Silva, was dispatched with 8,000 troops to restore order. His successful campaign earned him a reputation as an outstanding military commander and also the title of Baron de Caxias from the name of the city where he had defeated the rebels.

The provincial revolt that lasted longest and posed the most likely prospect of achieving secession was the War of the *Farrapos* or *Farroupilha* Revolution which started in Rio Grande do Sul in 1835. The rebels were derisively called '*farrapos*' ('ragamuffins') by their enemies even though wealthy local landowners and cattle-ranchers were active in the movement. Despite their uniforms of rags, the *farrapos* were powerful enough to take control of Porto Alegre in September 1835, and a year later announced the formation of a Riograndense Republic. After successfully invading neighboring Santa Catarina, they proclaimed the Republic of Piratini. In contrast to the uprisings in the North and Northeast, the rebels had the backing of influential local landowners and were able to maintain their independence from the national government until 1845.

End of the regency

During the period of the regency, regional revolt was endemic in Brazil. Nevertheless, Brazil survived intact as a united nation. One reason was the support given to the government by the landed oligarchy and the urban élite, especially from the provinces located in the Center-South. These interests joined together because they did not want to lose the political and commercial privileges that had been gained at both the national and local level since the winning of independence in 1822. They were also keen to suppress regional uprisings, which represented revolt from below and contained the threat of racial war and disturbance of a social hierarchy that was based upon maintaining the institution of slavery. The strength in numbers of the rebels was at times impressive, but was diminished by lack of effective military leadership and organization. They were also divided among themselves and unable to fight as a cohesive military force for very long.

With the exception of the *farrapos* in Rio Grande do Sul, the failure of the revolts to gain any sustained military success proved fortunate for the national government in Rio de Janeiro. Indeed, the response of the government to regional revolt was constantly hampered by military and financial weakness. In addition, the regent, Diogo Feijó, suffered from ill health and endured persistent political criticism from his opponents. Feijó eventually resigned as regent in September 1837. 'I am eagerly awaiting an occasion to resign,' he had written shortly before his resignation, 'I cannot bear the ingratitude, injustice and knavery.'[12] Feijó was making particular reference to the opposition of the Conservative Party which had been formed in 1836 from a coalition of moderates, centralists, and the supporters of the restoration of Dom Pedro I. In fact, the resignation of Feijó in 1837 signaled a reversal of decentralization and a return to centralization, a policy known as the 'regresso' ('regression'). The Regressos or Conservatives gained a notable political success in April 1838 when their candidate, the Speaker of the Chamber of Deputies, Pedro de Araújo Lima, the future Viscount of Olinda, was elected regent. In 1840 the Conservatives secured passage of the Interpretive Law which sought to 'interpret' the 1834 Additional Act to reduce regional autonomy and restrict the power of the provincial governments to appoint local officials. Another important centralist measure was the reform of the criminal code in 1841 by which the national government regained the authority to appoint all judges and police chiefs.

The political ascendancy of the Conservatives produced an unexpected challenge from the Liberals in the form of a successful maneuver to raise Dom Pedro II to the throne at the age of 14. The action contravened the 1824 Constitution which stated that Dom Pedro could not be emperor until he was 18 years old, but was justified as necessary to maintain the survival of the nation against the threat of separatist revolts currently taking place in the North, Northeast and South. Like his father, the boy emperor was regarded as a national symbol around which Brazilians would unite and disavow rebellion. Moreover, the public image of Dom Pedro was favorable and admiring. He had been raised under the guidance of eminent tutors, including José Bonifácio, and was reported to be well educated and unusually mature for his age. This aspect was stressed by Liberal politicians, including the Andrada brothers, who hoped that, once the emperor was established in power, he would reward them for their support. Despite the political calculations, however, the fact that politicians felt compelled to turn to the boy emperor to rule the country was an admission that the regency period of parliamentary rule had signally failed to provide effective government. This was underlined by the sequence of events in July 1840 in which Araújo Lima resigned as regent and the General Assembly offered Dom Pedro the crown. His acceptance brought an end to the period of the regency.

The coronation of the first Brazilian-born emperor in 1841 marked the beginning of the Second Empire. It also signified the continuation of the monarchy and the unity of the nation. Moreover, the ensuing decade saw

[52] the close of the period of regional revolt that had begun with the Pernambucan Revolt in 1817. By means of a combination of military force and astute diplomacy, Caxias ended the *Balaiada* in Maranhão in 1840, new federalist armed uprisings in São Paulo and Minas Gerais in 1842, and the revolt of the *farropos* in the South in 1845. The influence of political disturbances in Europe known as 'the 1848 Revolutions' affected Brazil in 1848, notably the *Praieira* revolt in Pernambuco. Named after the Rua da Praia ('Beach Street') in Recife, the uprising favored federalism and land reform. The failure of the rebels to take control of Recife in 1849 marked their defeat and represented an end of the movements for separatism. Despite the brief experiment during the regency of decentralization of political power to the provinces, the authority of the national government located in Rio de Janeiro was, therefore, successfully reaffirmed during the 1840s.

The political system during the Second Empire

The political system during the period of the Second Empire from 1841 to 1889 was a parliamentary constitutional monarchy based upon the model of Britain. Brazil, however, provided a contrast to Britain in the greater use that the emperor made of his moderating power to decide which political party should control the national government. For most of his reign Dom Pedro's position was further enhanced by his personal popularity and the support that he received from the landowning oligarchy. In return, he appointed favored members of the élite to the Senate and the Council of State, which was restored in 1841. Although his political powers were substantial, Dom Pedro II did not display the autocratic tendencies associated with his father. Scholarly and well-meaning by nature, his intention was to be a benevolent ruler of all his subjects. In political matters, he duly consulted the advice of the Council of State. Stressing the need for 'justice and tolerance,' Dom Pedro avoided becoming entangled in party politics, but took a close interest in government business. He saw his role as an active executive and insisted on regular meetings with the president or 'prime minister' of the Council of Ministers. 'I judge that the head of the executive power, in order to direct the use of that power,' he noted, 'has the right to *watch actively over* the conduct of the ministry.'[13] Where use of the moderating power was judged necessary, it was employed primarily as a means of alleviating conflict and avoiding serious political crisis.

Although they represented loose coalitions of separate interest groups rather than organized and disciplined political parties, a two-party political system consisting of Conservatives and Liberals came into being during the Empire. The Conservatives drew their principal support from the landed oligarchy of the Northeast and the coffee planters of Rio de Janeiro. They could also count on the backing of the influential Portuguese-born merchants in Rio de Janeiro and most of the senior officials who served in the national government. Like the Conservatives, the Liberals were identified with the interests of the landowners and planters, though these tended to be located in São Paulo, Minas Gerais and Rio Grande do Sul and to derive their wealth from coffee rather than sugar. The urban middle class and Brazilian-born merchants also tended to favor the laissez-faire ideas advocated by the Liberals.

In terms of national political policies, Conservatives loyally supported the monarchy and favored a strong central government. They also wished to maintain the institution of slavery, a stance that reflected the views of the sugar planters of Bahia and Pernambuco. During the 1830s the Liberals had been identified with the policy of federalism and the devolution of political power to the provinces. This was reversed in 1840 when the Liberals were instrumental in raising Dom Pedro to the throne and thereby instituting the Second Empire. Liberal politicians subsequently approved measures to reduce provincial autonomy. The evident inconsistencies were glossed over because Liberals and Conservatives had much in common. Both parties were essentially élitist in their distrust of the masses and fear of social upheaval and revolution. The similarities were so marked that it was a standing joke that 'nothing so much resembles a Conservative as a Liberal in power.'[14]

The Liberals took control of the cabinet on Dom Pedro's acceptance of the crown in July 1840. Contrary to some expectations, however, the young emperor did not turn out to be a political pawn of the Liberals. Within less than a year, he requested Conservative leaders to form a new government. He later dissolved the Chamber of Deputies and called for elections to ensure that the party of the government which he had appointed was returned with a comfortable majority of votes in the Chamber. This pattern of events was repeated subsequently on several occasions so that Dom Pedro alternated the parties in power eleven times during his reign. In doing so, he also prevented the rise of powerful national political leadership. Changes of prime minister were very frequent and resulted in 36 cabinets over the 49-year period of the Empire. The cabinet that lasted longest was that of José Maria da Silva Paranhos, Viscount of Rio Branco, from March 1871 to June 1875. The shortest ministry was that of Zacarias (de Góes e Vasconcelos) which lasted for six days in May 1862.

[54]   Despite the frequent changes of government, Brazilian politics during the period of the Second Empire were more stable and peaceful than in the rest of Latin America. The Brazilian élite boasted that, just as in Britain and France, they enjoyed freedom of speech and that political issues were fully debated in parliament, in the press and, where necessary, put to the voters to decide in national elections. In fact, real political debate was muted by the lack of differences between the Conservatives and the Liberals. This was underlined by their leaders joining together to form a cabinet of 'conciliation' from 1853 to 1857. Elections for the Chamber of Deputies were held at fairly regular periods, but restrictions on the franchise and control over the casting of votes in the provinces by rural political bosses known as *coronéis* ('colonels') meant that the results were predetermined in favor of the ruling party. The electoral process was, therefore, a sham. One politician described how 'the system' operated: 'The opposition struggled furiously in the election here, with lots of means. We defeated them completely because we're in the government; if they were in the government they would have won completely.'[15] In reality, however, the national political system continued to revolve around the emperor. This made him vulnerable to the charge of political manipulation and abuse of power because the holding of elections was regarded not as a means of stimulating public debate or seeking 'the will of the people' but a calculated ploy to secure the election of deputies to support the new government that he had already appointed.

The religious question

The significance of Dom Pedro II's central role in the politics of the Second Empire was demonstrated by the 'religious question' that resulted from the outbreak of conflict between church and state. The clash was not over the religious faith of the people. Indeed, Roman Catholicism was the state religion of Brazil, a fact that had been recognized and fully affirmed in the 1824 Constitution. In terms of appointments of clergy and distribution of resources, the Catholic Church in Brazil had been historically very much under the control of the Crown. Although Dom Pedro II was a member of the Catholic Church, he showed little personal interest in religious affairs. But he was concerned over the implications for Brazil of the attempt of Pope Pius IX to reassert the universal authority of the Vatican during the 1860s. In Brazil, the clash occurred over the issue of Freemasonry, a fraternal order that was popular in Brazil and included Dom Pedro as a member. Indeed, the emperor's open practice of Freemasonry conflicted with Pope Pius IX's

papal bull denouncing the Masonic Order as atheistic. Dom Pedro refused, [55]
however, to approve the publication of the papal bull in Brazil.

Direct conflict between church and state was precipitated in 1872 when
Dom Vital Maria Gonçalves de Oliveira, Bishop of Olinda, instructed the
clergy and religious brotherhoods in Pernambuco to abjure their Masonic
oaths and expel any members who were known to be Masons. Brotherhoods
that resisted were suspended by the bishop. With the emperor's full support,
the Conservative government intervened and ordered the suspension to
be rescinded. The bishop refused. In 1874 Dom Vital was prosecuted for
defying the government and sentenced to four years in prison. Antonio de
Macedo Costa, Bishop of Pará, was involved in a similar case and suffered
the same fate. Both sentences were later commuted to simple detention. The
issue, however, had stimulated considerable political controversy resulting in
a division within the cabinet, leading eventually to the resignation in 1875 of
the prime minister, the Viscount of Rio Branco. The change of prime minister
was part of a compromise agreed upon by the emperor and the Vatican. The
pope revoked prohibitions against Masons in Brazil. In return, the two
bishops were granted amnesty. By manipulating the political system, Dom
Pedro had eventually prevailed in the 'religious question,' but, in the process,
his authority had been publicly challenged and his support within the clergy
had been reduced.

The Paraguayan War

Just as he showed little interest in church affairs, Dom Pedro attached little
importance to his relations with the Brazilian military. Indeed, he was the
model of the nineteenth-century 'citizen king' in his rejection of the *caudilho*
tradition that was such a characteristic of so many Spanish-American rulers.
He was indifferent to military insignia and medals and made no effort to cultivate the support of high-ranking military officers. Only a tiny number of
military men were appointed as senators or members of the Council of State.
In fact, Dom Pedro held anti-military views and was content to leave the
army and navy in a relatively weak and undeveloped condition.

Standing military forces were necessary, however, not only to maintain
public order but also to defend the national territory. The region of most
strategic concern was the River Plate where traditionally Brazil had vied with
Argentina to assert control over the Banda Oriental. Despite the creation of
the Republic of Uruguay in 1828, Brazilian–Argentine rivalry continued and
was further complicated during the 1850s by Paraguay's growing military

[56] power and interest in the region. Francisco Solano López, who succeeded to the dictatorship of Paraguay in 1862, formed an alliance with the *Blanco* Party that ruled Uruguay. Skirmishes fought between the *Blancos* and their rivals in the *Colorado* Party spread across the border into Rio Grande do Sul. In August 1864 Brazilian troops entered Uruguay with the aim of aiding the *Colorados* to take power. In October López retaliated by seizing a Brazilian ship in the River Paraguay and then sent troops to invade Mato Grosso. In March 1865 he dispatched troops to Uruguay even though this would mean their crossing Argentine territory. The Argentine government refused permission. On 1 May 1865 the governments of Brazil, Argentina, and Uruguay joined in a Triple Alliance and declared war to fight the aggression of 'the tyrant López.' In fact, Paraguayan troops never took the offensive in Uruguay so that the resulting Paraguayan War or 'War of the Triple Alliance' was actually fought in Paraguay. The contemporary press likened Paraguay to David in his fight against Goliath.

Brazil was ill-prepared to fight a major continental war. The navy had maintained a small number of effective warships which achieved naval supremacy after defeating the small Paraguayan navy at the battle of Riachuelo in June 1865. But ultimate victory required the defeat on land of the large Paraguayan army. The Brazilian army, however, had suffered from a long period of political neglect and inadequate budgets. Numbering only 18,000 at the beginning of the war, it was neither trained nor equipped to wage an offensive military campaign. Recruitment faced many difficulties. Indeed, the draft was so unpopular and inefficiently administered that the military authorities were compelled to appeal to slaves to volunteer and to promise them their freedom in return.

Mobilization was so slow that the army to invade Paraguay was not ready until April 1866. In the first major military action of the war, Brazilian forces suffered a reverse at the battle of Curupaití in September. Morale significantly improved, however, when Caxias took personal command of the Brazilian army in October 1866 and began the siege of the strategically important fortress at Humaitá in July 1867. The capture of Humaitá in August 1868 opened the way for a successful assault on the capital of Paraguay. In what became a campaign of annihilation of the enemy, Brazilian troops had to overcome fierce Paraguayan resistance, including large numbers of women and children, and eventually entered Asunción on 5 January 1869. The death of López on 1 March 1870 brought an end to the war.

Brazil mobilized an army of 200,000 men to fight the war. More than half saw service in the war zone and at least 30,000 fatalities were recorded.

Brazilian forces made up around two thirds of the number of allied soldiers so that Brazil's share of the war effort was much greater than that of the other two allies. The cost of the war was considerable and stimulated a rise in inflation and a large increase in the foreign debt. More politically controversial, however, was the growth in size and prestige of the army and the resulting problem of postwar demobilization. There was also a question of politicization of the military, especially among the army officer corps that had increased in numbers during the war from 1,500 to 10,000. Dom Pedro II had supported the war and wished to inflict a heavy defeat on Paraguay. His well-known anti-military views, however, caused unease among officers who were suspicious that the government invariably placed political calculations above the country's national interest. This was increased in 1868 by the forced resignation of the Liberal prime minister, Zacarias de Góes e Vasconcelos, whose cabinet had provided effective civilian direction of the war effort in its final stages. Discontent, however, was alleviated by the personal loyalty shown to Dom Pedro by the duke of Caxias, who enjoyed great prestige and respect within the officer corps. The death of Caxias in 1880 removed one of the most important pillars of support for Dom Pedro and the institution of monarchy.

Slavery and abolition

The controversy over slavery was the issue that caused most political disharmony throughout the Second Empire. When Dom Pedro was crowned emperor in 1841, Brazil was one of only a handful of countries in the Western Hemisphere that had not abolished slavery. Even though the Brazilian élite was proud to claim that their country was a constitutional monarchy, they still retained the colonial mindset that regarded the institution of slavery as an economic necessity and an essential element for a society that was stratified in terms of class and race. Many of the élite owned slaves and were, therefore, self-interested members of the 'slavocracy.' The right to own slaves was also prized by Brazilians of much more modest means. A British visitor to Rio de Janeiro in 1828 noted that 'slaves form the income and support of a vast number of individuals, who hire them out as people in Europe do horses and mules.'[16] Slaves represented not only a capital investment but also a way of gaining social prestige. Pressure for abolition from critics, whether domestic or from overseas, only served to harden the determination of slave-owners to maintain Brazil's version of the 'peculiar institution.' 'Brazil lives upon slave labour,' concisely summed up the British chargé d'affaires at Rio de Janeiro, James Hudson, in 1846.[17]

[58]   During the first half of the nineteenth century, the controversy concerned not so much the issue of domestic slavery but the continuation of the trans-atlantic slave trade from Africa. In deference to Britain, Brazil had signed a treaty in 1826 to abolish the trade within three years. The General Assembly passed a law to this effect in 1831, but enforcement was so lax that the annual inflow of slaves more than doubled after a decade. Opinion on the slave trade, however, noticeably changed during the 1840s. The new arrivals from Africa were seen as contributing to the growing incidence of slave unrest and rebellion in the Northeast that was such a worrying feature of the 1830s and 1840s for the landowning élite. The outbreak of deadly epidemics of cholera and yellow fever were also linked in the public mind to the slave trade. Yellow fever, unknown since 1686, broke out in Rio de Janeiro in 1849, claiming more than 6,000 deaths in three years. Furthermore, there was a renewal of British diplomatic and naval pressure culminating in British warships entering Brazilian territorial waters to seize slaveships. The result was the passage in 1850 of the Eusébio de Queiroz law that outlawed the importation of slaves into Brazil and included enabling legislation to ensure that the measure was enforced.

The restrictions contained in the 1850 law applied only to the slave trade. Nevertheless, they provided an important boost to the morale of the anti-slavery movement in Brazil. Although the idea of immediate abolition of slavery was regarded as too extreme, there was steadily growing support for the proposal to introduce gradual emancipation over a fixed period of time. The moral arguments condemning slavery as vicious and cruel were strength-ened by events in the United States where the American Civil War brought about the end of slavery. As a result, Brazil gained the odium of becoming the largest slave-owning country in the Western Hemisphere and the world. The poor performance of the army at the start of the Paraguayan War reinforced the sense of national inadequacy. Slavery was not only increasingly perceived in Brazil as a major national embarrassment but also as a reason for the country's economic and military backwardness when compared with Europe and the United States.

The movement for abolition found its strongest support in the cities. The most prominent leader was Joaquim (Aurélio Barreto) Nabuco (de Araújo), a celebrated writer and member of the élite from Pernambuco who became president of the Brazilian Anti-Slavery Society in 1880. In Rio de Janeiro, the journalist and orator, José (Carlos) do Patrocinio, constantly reiterated the cry that 'slavery is theft,' and was particularly effective in public debate. The abolitionists were also assisted by the political machinations of 1868 that brought about the forced resignation of the Liberal prime minister and so angered the Liberals that they issued a public manifesto demanding various radical political reforms including abolition. Even though Dom Pedro publicly stated his approval for the abolition of slavery in 1867, he failed to provide positive leadership on the issue. He favored the gradualist solution and hoped that the question would be settled with the passage in September 1871 of a compromise measure known as the Rio Branco law or the Law of the Free Womb. This stated that all future children born to slave mothers would become free. The slave-owner would look after the child until the age of 8 when he would receive financial compensation from the government. If the compensation was declined, the owner could require the child to work until the age of 21. In addition, slave-owners were required to allow any slave to purchase his or her freedom at the prevailing market price.

In effect, the 1871 law guaranteed the maintenance of the status quo for at least 21 years. Nonetheless, although the measure had few immediate practical results, it placed a time limit beyond which slavery could not survive. The political question, therefore, became whether the time limit should be shortened. During the 1880s a vigorous public debate ensued in which Conservatives continued to favor gradualism while Liberals wanted a speedy end to the institution. Abolitionists pointed out that current slaves could remain enslaved for life so that slavery might theoretically continue for at least another 60 to 70 years. In fact, the political debate appeared increasingly academic as the number of slaves was steadily reduced by manumission and a growing groundswell of opinion that slavery was not only morally wrong but that slaves were also more expensive and less flexible than wage or 'free' labor. In 1884 the provinces of Ceará and Amazonas declared emancipation of their slaves. The passage of the Saraiva–Cotegipe law in 1885 freed all slaves over 60 years of age. Abolitionists especially in São Paulo began to incite slaves to run away to freedom. The result was not individual flight but often the abandonment of whole plantations. 'They flee in all directions,' reported the minister of agriculture in the province of São Paulo, 'and, transporting themselves on the railroads, they take refuge in the city of Santos, where they consider themselves immune and free from any legal compulsion from their masters.'[18] Army units were called out, but proved reluctant to intervene and return fugitives to their plantations. By 1887 the total number of slaves had shrunk to less than 1 million and represented only 5 percent of the national population.

On May 13, 1888, while Dom Pedro was away from the country convalescing in Europe, the Princess Regent Dona Isabel gained the title of the

[60] 'Redemptress' when she signed the 'Golden Law' that had been passed by the General Assembly. All Brazil's remaining slaves, estimated to number 650,000, were given immediate and unconditional emancipation. The passage of the measure gained the monarchy some brief popularity, but a feeling lingered that Dom Pedro had been too passive and had not provided adequate leadership. There was criticism that he had acted against the interests of his traditional supporters among the slavocracy who had influence within the Conservative Party. Although some former slave-owners would retaliate by joining the Republicans, the general response was muted because most slaves had already been freed by 1888 and it was evident that the institution of slavery could not be maintained any longer in Brazil.

Republicanism

The desire to establish a republic had been present in the *Inconfidências* of 1789 and 1798, the revolts in Pernambuco of 1817 and 1824, and later during the regency period. The idea of republicanism, however, remained tainted with treachery and violent revolution. Moreover, Brazilians had only to look to the neighboring countries of Spanish America to associate republicanism with political instability. The idea suddenly attracted a new interest in 1868, however, when the emperor's action in bringing about the downfall of the Liberal cabinet angered Liberals into suggesting the replacement of the monarchy with a republic. As in 1830, news of events in France also exerted an influence. In 1870 the Emperor Napoleon III fell from power and the Third French Republic was established.

In November 1870 a small group of Liberals, mainly teachers, doctors, and lawyers, organized a Republican Club in Rio de Janeiro. A 'Republican Manifesto' was published in December 1870. The manifesto articulated traditional Liberal ideas in opposing centralization of political power. 'Provincial autonomy is for us Republicans,' the document emphasized, 'a cardinal and solemn principle which we inscribe on our banner.'[19] But the Manifesto went further in advocating an end of the monarchy and the establishment of a federal republic based on the successful model of the United States. Though they refrained from proposing the abolition of the monarchy while Dom Pedro was alive, the republicans argued that the monarchical system was obsolete and that it hampered Brazil's development as a modern nation, especially in the growth of industry. Republican ideas in Brazil owed much to the writings of the French philosopher, August Comte. Known as 'positivism,' Comte's philosophy stressed the importance of rational thought and the application of science to produce a formula that would be used to organize society and achieve 'order and progress.'

Consistent with their advocacy of federalism and provincial autonomy, Republicans avoided forming a national party and preferred to organize separate clubs, mostly in the cities of the Center-South. The strongest clubs were in São Paulo where a state-wide organization, the *Paulista* Republican Party (*Partido Republicano Paulista* or PRP), was founded in 1873. Though republican activities were most developed in the cities, it was notably in São Paulo that the movement attracted the support of a number of landowners and planters. This reflected the feeling in São Paulo that the province was contributing much more in taxes to the national budget than it was receiving in return. 'When we want to progress,' the *paulista* politician Martim Francisco Ribeiro de Andrada complained in 1884, 'the centralization web envelops us; our political offices are filled with people alien to our way of life, to our interests, and to our customs.'[20] *Paulistas* were attracted to the idea of a federal republic which would allow provinces to control their own finances and decide such topical questions as the admission of immigrants from Europe. The Republicans, however, were a minority movement. Lacking funds, organization and patronage, they did badly in national elections. But a strong base of support arose in São Paulo. In 1884, that province elected three Republican deputies to the General Assembly, including Prudente (José) de Morais (e Barros) and (Manuel Ferraz de) Campos Sales. They were the first republicans to sit in the General Assembly.

The military question

The ideas of republicanism and positivism had a special attraction for some members of the army officer corps. A new generation of junior officers had emerged after the Paraguayan War who differed from their predecessors in possessing a broader education and in showing less attachment to the mon-archical system. They felt particularly frustrated by the failure of the imperial government to improve military pay and conditions, especially after the substantial sacrifices that the army had made during the Paraguayan War. A desire to reform the political system evolved and was stimulated by the teach-ings of officers who had visited France and had returned to Brazil imbued with the ideas of positivism. The most prominent example was Lieutenant Colonel Benjamin Constant (Botelho de Magalhães), an instructor at the Praia Vermelha military academy in Rio de Janeiro. Constant was both a positivist and a republican. His students idolized him.

[62]   To promote reform required involvement in political activity. Military regulations stated, however, that army officers must avoid making public statements on political issues. The regulations were openly breached in 1879 by the publication of critical comments made by officers about a proposal in the General Assembly to reduce the size of the army. On this occasion, however, the regulations were not enforced against the officers. When similar incidents occurred during the 1880s, the government acted to reprimand and discipline the officers concerned. The resulting state of tension between the government and the army became known as the 'military question.' While the majority of officers remained loyal to the emperor and the government, growing concern was felt that the army was being unjustly treated and that its 'honor' was being impugned. In a show of solidarity, senior officers sprang to the defense of their junior colleagues. The leading spokesman of the military was Marshal (Manoel) Deodoro (da Fonseca), a veteran of the Paraguayan War who had been promoted to field marshal in 1884. His popularity among fellow-officers was underlined in 1887 when he was elected as the first president of the Military Club (*Clube Militar*), a society that was founded to represent and speak for military interests.

In a personal letter of protest to Dom Pedro in February 1887, Deodoro warned that insults to the military were a 'very serious matter' and would result in a future 'storm' if the 'injustice' was not rectified.[21] The letter also indicated that the unquestioning support of the military for the government should not be taken for granted. While Deodoro was known to be personally loyal to the emperor, other officers such as Benjamin Constant argued in favor of taking the next logical step and replacing the Empire with a republic. In fact, Republican politicians had been active in cultivating friendly relations with army officers. Conscious of their own limitations, Republicans recognized that radical political change was unlikely to happen by means of elections or votes in the General Assembly and that the army had the organization and power to effect a coup and bring about a republic. Such an outcome, however, was contingent upon senior commanders agreeing to become political activists.

1889 coup

The 1870s and 1880s appeared as a twilight period for the Brazilian monarchy. Suffering from diabetes, Dom Pedro II steadily deteriorated in health and he appeared increasingly frail and prematurely aged. In contrast to his earlier years he also became noticeably detached from government business and, at times, seemed to be indifferent about political developments and the future of the country. 'The emperor [is] everyday more forgetful of current matters and remote from political questions,' remarked a Conservative senator in April 1889.[22] It was even suggested that Dom Pedro believed that Brazil would become a republic after his death. The question of succession to the throne was also clouded by the absence of a male heir. Princess Isabel was the emperor's daughter and, therefore, the legal heir, but in a male-dominated country, there was considerable apprehension over the prospect of a woman as the reigning monarch. There was also some concern that her husband, the Count d'Eu, was a foreigner. Moreover, Isabel had become a controversial political figure as a result of her ardent support for the abolition of slavery.

The decline in the prestige and popularity of the monarchy was linked to a similar disenchantment with the political system that was increasingly perceived as undemocratic and unrepresentative. In particular, there was growing criticism that the emperor and the non-elected members of the Council of State and the Senate possessed too much power, while inadequate representation was accorded to the rising wealth of the provinces of the Center-South, especially São Paulo. The pressure for radical political change was evident in June 1889 when the new Liberal prime minister, the Viscount of Ouro Preto, wrote to Dom Pedro 'that in some of the provinces there is agitated and active propaganda for a change in the form of government.' He added an ominous warning that 'this propaganda bodes no good for the future, for it wishes to expose the country to institutions for which the country is not prepared.'[23]

Ouro Preto was referring to calls for a republic to which he was resolutely opposed. His strategy was to counter the Republicans with his own radical reforms such as reducing the power of appointed officials in the Council of State and the Senate and the transfer of their power to the General Assembly and the provincial presidents. The proposed reforms, however, were defeated by the General Assembly. The emperor thereupon dissolved the Chamber and called for new elections in November. The replay yet again of the 'old' politics confirmed that the Empire would not reform of its own volition. In the intervening period before the scheduled elections Republicans alerted army officers to alleged secret plans prepared by the government to disperse the army throughout the country. At a meeting on November 9 the Military Club in Rio de Janeiro delegated Benjamin Constant to prepare a coup to overthrow the emperor. Constant worked closely with prominent Republican leaders such as Quintino (Antonio Ferreira de Sousa) Bocaiúva and Rui Barbosa,

[64] but his most important success was in persuading Marshal Deodoro that the government was seeking 'to annihilate' the army[24] and that, in the circumstances, the creation of a republic was preferable to the continuation of the Empire. Moreover, Deodoro agreed to be the leader of the coup and thereby guaranteed that it would have the backing of the troops stationed in the capital.

Meanwhile, the government had complacently ruled out the likelihood of a coup. It was assumed that the principal military figures in Rio de Janeiro. Deodoro and the Adjutant General, Marshal Floriano (Vieira) Peixoto were loyal to the emperor. When troops under Deodoro's command surrounded government buildings before dawn on November 15, the action came as a complete surprise and there was minimal resistance. A decisive moment occurred later when Marshal Floriano Peixoto refused to comply with orders from Ouro Preto to attack the rebels. In response to the prime minister's comment that Brazilian troops had obeyed orders without question in the Paraguayan War, Floriano stated that 'there we faced enemies and here we are all Brazilians.'[25] At first, it was believed that the aim of the coup was simply to force a change of cabinet. In the afternoon, however, Deodoro declared the overthrow of the monarchy and the establishment of a republic.

During the afternoon of November 15 Dom Pedro traveled by train to Rio de Janeiro from his summer palace at Petrópolis. On the next day he was told that a republic had been declared and that the royal family would have to leave the country within 24 hours. Like his father in 1831, Dom Pedro decided to choose exile rather than risk civil war. On November 17, the royal family sailed to exile in Portugal and France. Dom Pedro's farewell words were emotional and dignifed: 'In departing, therefore I with all the persons of my family, shall always retain the most tender remembrances of Brazil in offering ardent prayer for its greatness and prosperity.'[26] Like the transition from colony to empire in 1831, the switch from monarchy to republic in 1889 took place peacefully. Foreign diplomats in Rio de Janeiro expressed surprise not so much at the fact that a successful coup had occurred but at the almost total absence of support for the monarchy. The American minister, Robert Adams, viewed the turn of events as: 'the most remarkable ever recorded in history. Entirely unexpected by the Government or people, the overthrow of the Empire has been accomplished without bloodshed, without riotous proceedings or interruption to the usual avocations of life.'[27] There was no doubt that the monarchy had declined in prestige and that issues such as abolition of slavery and the religious question had undermined its traditional support among the landed oligarchy and the Church. But the crucial factor in explaining the success of the 1889 coup was the role of the army. As the Republicans had realized, it was the army that possessed the organization and force to implement a radical change of the political system. Once the senior army commanders were convinced of the need to act, the coup was implemented and the Empire was brought to an end.

Economy

Relations with the world economy

The arrival of the Portuguese royal family in Brazil in 1808 produced an unexpected stimulus for the Brazilian economy. On January 28, 1808 the prince regent, Dom João, issued a decree opening the ports of Brazil to trade with friendly nations. Though smuggling had been a common practice during the colonial period, the 1808 decree signified an official end of the exploitative mercantilist system that had lasted for three centuries. Not only could Brazil trade openly with the outside world but it would also be allowed to expand its internal economic activity beyond agriculture and mining. Throughout the colonial period Portugal had sought to prohibit the development of manufacturing and industry in Brazil to prevent the colony from becoming an economic competitor of the mother country. After 1808 government policy was substantively altered as Dom João proceeded to revoke decrees that had previously restricted the establishment of factories in Brazil. Subsidies were also provided to develop local resources, especially the wool, silk, and iron industries. The invention and introduction of new machinery for manufacturing goods was encouraged by exemptions from customs duties.

The opening of the ports to the world economy was beneficial to Brazilian landowners and planters who produced sugar and cotton for the export trade. The subsequent boost to foreign trade, however, was mostly to the advantage of British merchants, especially when competition from Portuguese shipping was temporarily removed by the French occupation of Portugal and imposition of the Continental System. The British regarded the opening of the ports as a great business opportunity and by August 1808 it was estimated that up to 200 British merchants were resident in Rio de Janeiro alone. The port of Rio de Janeiro quickly became the principal commercial centre for the trade in British manufactured products, not only for Brazil but also with the rest of South America. The advantageous position enjoyed by British merchants was confirmed by a commercial treaty signed in 1810 that fixed the duty on goods imported from Britain at 15 percent. This was 1 percent lower than the duty on goods imported in Portuguese ships. A general tariff of around 24 percent applied to products from other countries. British goods, therefore, enjoyed a distinct tariff advantage until the expiry of the 1810 treaty in 1844.

Britain was the world's leading economic power and the main trading partner of Brazil during the nineteenth century. A triangular trade emerged in which British merchants supplied the bulk of the manufactured goods, especially textiles, hardware and machinery that were imported into Brazil. The British merchant ships that carried these goods to Brazil then carried a large proportion of Brazilian produce to the United States, where they loaded American goods for export to the European market and, in some cases, for re-export to Brazil. While Britain did not seize or occupy Brazilian territory, its economic influence on the country was extensive and pervasive.

Independence did not alter Brazil's dependent relationship with the world economy. In effect, Brazil found that Portuguese mercantilism was replaced by British imperialism. The Brazilian Minister in London, Sérgio Teixeira de Macedo, summed up in 1854 that: 'the commerce between the two countries is carried on with English capital, on English ships, by English companies. The profits, . . . the interest on capital, . . . the payments for insurance, the commissions, and the dividends from the business, everything goes into the pockets of Englishmen.'[28] British merchants, bankers and shipping companies not only dominated the export trade, but were also the main source of private investment for Brazil's industrial development. In 1855 the House of Rothschild was appointed as the Brazilian government's sole financial agent, and regularly floated loans in London. By 1880 British investments in Brazil were estimated to amount to almost £40 million. The access to international capital markets and the resulting inward investment was regarded as vital for Brazil's economic development. The abolitionist leader, André Rebouças, gave a positive welcome to the 'capital which comes principally from London,' a place he described as 'the treasury of the whole world.'[29]

British economic preeminence in Brazil was challenged during the last quarter of the nineteenth century when the United States became Brazil's largest single export market. The American share of Brazilian exports doubled from just over 20 percent in the 1840s to more than 40 percent during the 1880s. The growth was largely due to increased sales of coffee. Americans not only showed a distinct preference for the quality and flavor of Brazilian coffee, but they were able to import it into the United States free of customs duty. The trade, however, was very one-sided because Americans had little to sell in return. While annual Brazilian exports to the American market during the 1870s and 1880s ranged from $40 to $50 million, imports from the United States were less than $10 million a year. During the same period the value of British exports to Brazil was considerably higher and in excess of £30 million a year. Consequently, at the end of the Second Empire in 1889, Britain still remained the leading foreign exporter to Brazil and the principal source of investment and financial services.

The export economy

At the start of the nineteenth century sugar was the country's most valuable export. The economic dislocation caused by the French Revolutionary Wars severely damaged the production of sugar in the Caribbean islands and boosted the demand for Brazilian sugar in Europe. By 1821 sugar made up 40 percent of Brazil's annual export earnings. But Brazil quickly lost its competitive advantage when full-scale sugar production resumed in the islands of the Caribbean. Further competition arose from Cuba, the United States, and in Europe, where the cultivation of beet sugar rapidly developed. During the decade of the 1830s sugar fell to around 25 percent of Brazil's annual exports and was overtaken by coffee as the country's leading export. In fact, sugar never regained its leading position. During the second half of the nineteenth century production actually increased, but was directed to the domestic market rather than overseas. By the 1890s sugar made up only 6 percent of exports. Brazil's share of the world sugar market also declined from 10 percent during the 1840s to less than 5 percent by the end of the nineteenth century. Moreover, earnings were also reduced by a fall in world prices during the 1870s and 1880s.

By contrast, coffee was the outstanding economic success story of the nineteenth century. Cultivation of coffee had started in the late eighteenth century and soon became concentrated in the valley of the Paraíba do Sul River in the provinces of Rio de Janeiro and São Paulo where the climate and the naturally fertile soil (*terra roxa*) proved ideal for slash-and-burn cultivation on a large scale. Brazil's share of world coffee production rose from 20 percent in the 1820s to over 40 percent in the 1840s, and to more than 60 percent in the 1880s. During the decade of the 1830s coffee became the country's leading export and made up 40 percent of annual export earnings. This figure rose to more than 60 percent during the last decade of the Second Empire.

Only a small number of provinces were significantly involved in the cultivation of coffee. These included Rio de Janeiro, Minas Gerais and most

[68] notably the northern and western areas of São Paulo, which were producing more than half the nation's coffee by the end of the Empire. São Paulo forged ahead during the second half of the nineteenth century because it possessed naturally fertile soil, an abundant and steady stream of relatively low-waged immigrant labor from Europe, and railways linking the plantations to the port of Santos. Just as coffee displaced sugar as the most valuable export during the 1830s, the Center-South overshadowed the Northeast as the most prosperous and dynamic economic region of the country during the Empire. This was further underlined and emphasized by the correspondingly faster growth of population, employment and economic infrastructure, consisting of ports, banks, utilities and transportation, which were concentrated in the Center-South. By the middle of the nineteenth century per capita income levels in the Center-South had passed those of the Northeast.

Along with sugar and coffee, cotton was the third principal item of export during the imperial period. During the first half of the nineteenth century Brazilian cotton found it difficult to compete with American cotton in the large British market. The severe dislocation caused by the American Civil War from 1861 to 1865 provided a sudden stimulus for Brazilian exports so that cotton became the second most valuable export during the 1860s. But this boom was short-lived and exports soon declined in quantity and value. The subsequent development of the cotton industry began to depend not so much on exports but the growth of internal demand arising from the domestic textile market.

The fastest-rising product in the late nineteenth century was rubber. Wild rubber (*hevea brasiliensis*) was natural to the Amazon region, but was not in international demand until the discovery of the vulcanization process by Charles Goodyear in 1839. Brazil quickly became the world leader in the production and export of rubber. From an initial shipment of 31 tons in 1827, exports rose to nearly 1,500 tons in 1850, 3,000 tons in 1867 and 7,000 tons in 1880. By the 1880s rubber provided 8 percent of total annual revenue from exports. Almost all the rubber originated in the provinces of Amazonas and Pará, where the 'rubber boom' stimulated a doubling of population and a five-fold expansion of exports during the second half of the nineteenth century.

Economic growth during the nineteenth century

The monetary and fiscal policies pursued by the imperial government during the nineteenth century were supportive of export-led growth and generally had an inflationary impact. In addition, the expenditures of both the royal court from 1808 to 1821 and the later imperial governments were usually in excess of annual income. Shortfalls were met by various means including expansion of the money supply, raising taxes especially on foreign imports, allowing depreciation in the foreign exchange value of the unit of currency, the *milréis*, which fell from 43 pence in 1833 to 27 pence in 1847,[30] and the resort to overseas borrowing. Though these policies tended to promote economic growth they were also inflationary. For example, the shortage of currency during the First Empire was alleviated first by the minting of a large quantity of copper coins and then the issue of paper money drawn on the Bank of Brazil (*Banco do Brasil*), which had been created in 1808. This soon resulted, however, in widespread counterfeiting and large rises in the cost of living, particularly in the cities, and contributed to the collapse of the Bank of Brazil in 1829. The experience of rapid inflation was relatively novel and was referred to by contemporaries as '*inchação*' ('swelling').[31]

Economic conditions improved during the 1830s as a result of increased exports of sugar and coffee. A similar rise in foreign imports was beneficial to government finances because more than 50 percent of revenue was derived from the tariff on imported goods. In contrast to taxes on land or individuals, customs duties were mostly paid by foreigners and were relatively easy to administer and collect. Their share of annual government revenue increased to more than 70 percent after the expiry in 1844 of the Anglo–Brazilian commercial treaty that ended the preferential tariff on imports of British goods. Brazilian customs duties were quickly lifted to an average level of more than 30 percent. Except for a brief period during the 1850s, average tariff levels steadily increased throughout the Second Empire and were in excess of 50 percent in 1888. The money raised was used to finance the policy of running budgetary deficits and to pay for exceptional expenses such as the costly Paraguayan War.

The government also regarded the tariff as a means of protecting the development of particular sections of Brazilian industry, especially textiles and clothing. Direct government intervention to aid industry, however, was very selective and provoked controversy. The educated élite was receptive to European ideas of economic liberalism and laissez-faire that argued that state interference in business was inherently damaging and counter-productive. The landed oligarchy was anti-business for different reasons. They stressed the vital economic importance of agriculture and regarded industry as a competitor for both labor and capital. Indeed, throughout the nineteenth century 90 percent of the working population were employed in agriculture. Less than 10 percent worked in industry.

[70]   Industry was slow to develop in Brazil for many reasons. The winning of independence did not alter the state of internal communications, which remained extremely poor. The development of internal markets and trade was hampered by the often precarious, expensive and slow transportation of goods. The bulk of the labor force, both slave and free, was illiterate, lacked industrial skills and was denied economic opportunity. Wages were so low that the domestic market for manufactured goods was severely limited in size. Moreover, Brazilian manufacturers lacked access to adequate sources of domestic capital and credit. Raw materials and capital goods were lacking and had to be imported. In addition, there was severe competition from cheap British products that enjoyed tariff advantages until 1840.

Communications began to improve markedly during the Second Empire. This reflected not so much a conscious change in the attitude of the imperial government towards industry as a straightforward response to the rapid growth of the world economy. Throughout South America governments were seeking to modernize their economies by encouraging the construction of telegraph lines and providing financial subsidies for steamships and railroads. Brazil was no exception. The first telegraph line was introduced in Rio de Janeiro in 1852. Connecting lines were established with Europe in 1874, Montevideo in 1879 and Buenos Aires in 1883. By 1889 Brazil possessed around 7,500 miles of telegraph lines. Communications over water were improved by the establishment of a steamship line between Rio de Janeiro and the Northeast and the formation in 1852 of the Amazon Steam Navigation Company to assist the development of the Amazon region.

The most dynamic growth was in railroads. In 1854 the first railroad was opened in Brazil for the 10-mile journey from Guanabara Bay in Rio de Janeiro to Petrópolis. Railroads soon proved to be a major attraction for foreign investors, especially the British, who placed more than half their total investments in Brazil in this particular sector of the economy. Foreign investors were impressed by the political stability of the Second Empire and the offer of financial subsidies by the government towards the cost of railroad construction and fixed guarantees for future earnings. The result was a boom in railroad development that saw an increase in railroad track from 800 miles in 1864 to 6,000 miles in 1889. The best-known railroad was 'The Dom Pedro Segundo' (renamed 'The Brazil Central Railroad' in 1889) which was completed in 1877 and connected Rio de Janeiro and São Paulo. Another important line linked São Paulo with Santos and started operations in 1868. This line made Santos the major port for the export of coffee and thereby exemplified the fact that railroads were primarily intended to facilitate and improve the movement of exports to the ports. Development was piecemeal

because an integrated national system was not envisaged. Nonetheless, railroads had wider economic benefits such as reducing the cost of transportation of goods and opening up previously inaccessible areas of the countryside
to agricultural cultivation and settlement.

The growth of industry was assisted by the establishment of a number of
financial institutions during the nineteenth century. Although it lasted for
only just over two decades, the first Bank of Brazil was created in 1808. The
Rio de Janeiro Stock Exchange was formed shortly afterwards to organize
commercial and industrial companies. The educated élite, however, tended
to regard finance and business as tainted with speculation and fraud. Indeed,
a career in business was frowned upon and definitely lacked social prestige.
Nevertheless, a number of successful entrepreneurs emerged during the
Second Empire. The most celebrated was Irineu Evangelista de Sousa, Viscount
of Mauá, who was instrumental in achieving the financing of Brazil's first
railway in 1854. Mauá acquired extensive interests in almost every aspect of
Brazil's economic activity including commerce, banking, mining, shipping,
and railroads. Moreover, his ambitions and interests extended beyond Brazil
to owning ranches in Uruguay and setting up commercial offices in London,
New York and Buenos Aires.

A financial crisis in 1875, however, brought about the collapse of Mauá's
financial empire followed by bankruptcy in 1878. Mauá's mercurial career
repeated the pattern of 'boom and bust' and appeared to confirm the preju-
dices of his contemporary critics who had argued that he was reckless and
irresponsible. However, his contribution, and that of other Brazilian entrepreneurs, played an important part in helping to modernize the Brazilian
economy. At the end of the Second Empire in 1889, agriculture was still
the dominant economic activity in the country, but the signs of industrial
development were evident especially in the cities. This was illustrated by the
fact that the number of factories, mainly involved in manufacturing textiles,
had increased from 50 in 1850 to 636 in 1889, while the number of industrial workers was estimated at more than 50,000.

Society

Demography

At the beginning of the First Empire in 1822 Brazil's population numbered
4.7 million. Fifty years later the first official census in 1872 recorded a
doubling of population to 9.9 million. In 1890 the figure was more than

14 million. The growth of population throughout the nineteenth century represented an annual rate of increase of approximately 1.7 percent. The rise was the result of natural increase and immigration including large numbers of African slaves during the first half of the century, and a substantial influx of European immigrants later in the century. The pattern of settlement continued to be similar to the colonial period in that the majority of people lived in the countryside and, with the exception of Minas Gerais, were not very distant from access to the sea. The Northeast remained the most populated region with more than 40 percent of the population. The most populated province, however, was Minas Gerais in the Center-South, which had just over 2 million inhabitants in 1872. The second was Bahia with 1.4 million. Pernambuco was third. A notable feature of the last half of the century was the rapid growth of São Paulo, which had risen to become the fourth largest populated province in 1872. Rio de Janeiro was in fifth place.

Only a few large cities were evident in 1822. The biggest was Rio de Janeiro with a population in excess of 110,000. Second was Salvador with 60,000. Recife and São Paulo had about 25,000 each. Most provincial capitals were relatively small cities with populations of less than 10,000. The national capital of Rio de Janeiro, however, was a significant city and was similar in population to large European and North American cities. Indeed, Rio de Janeiro experienced dramatic growth during the nineteenth century. Part of the reason was its geographical location as a major international port and center for commerce and finance not only for the mining industry but for the rising coffee trade of the Paraíba Valley. In addition, there was the impact of the arrival of the royal court and thousands of courtiers and bureaucrats in 1808. One result was the construction of new and impressive buildings to make the city more suitable as a royal residence. As the center of national government there was also a major expansion in administrative employment.

At the end of the Second Empire the number of large cities had not greatly changed from the beginning of the nineteenth century. Rio de Janeiro, however, had greatly outstripped the others in size. In 1890 its population had risen to 520,000 inhabitants. Salvador remained the country's second city with 175,000. Recife was third with 112,000. Benefiting from the boom in the rubber trade, Belém had jumped from a population of 40,000 in 1875 to almost 100,000. São Paulo was fifth with 64,000 inhabitants but its population was growing rapidly at well above the national average. São Paulo recorded a rate of increase of 3 percent per annum between 1872 and 1886 and of 8 percent per annum between 1886 and 1890.

Society

In 1822 the composition of the population was fairly equally divided between whites, slaves, and free persons of mixed race. The main change from the colonial period was that slaves were no longer a majority of the population. The trend continued throughout the nineteenth century. In the 1872 census persons of mixed race, who now became more commonly referred to as mulattos, formed 42 percent of the population, while whites comprised 38 percent and slaves were less than 20 percent. The abolition of slavery in 1888 meant that the category of slave was removed from the figures showing the racial composition of the population in 1890. In that year whites were in a majority and made up more than 44 percent of the population, while mulattos were just over 41 percent and blacks were around 15 percent. The higher proportion of whites was explained mainly as a result of increased immigration from Europe.

The nature of the Brazilian economic and social élite hardly changed during the Empire. Although the landed wealth based on sugar experienced a relative decline, the landowning oligarchy not only remained preeminent but was also strengthened by the rise of coffee. Like sugar, the new industry was characterized by the development of large estates that both required and conferred considerable economic and political power and privileges upon the plantation owners. The highly-concentrated pattern of landholding in Brazil, therefore, was very different from the United States where homestead legislation was designed to distribute public lands to the landless. Land laws in Brazil, however, continued the system started by the grant of *sesmarias* during the sixteenth century and promoted the consolidation and acquisition of massive estates by large landowners.

A feature of the Second Empire was the increase in the political influence of the landed oligarchy at the local level. This was known as *coronelismo*, a name that originated from the courtesy title of *coronel* or 'colonel' that many landowners held and which was derived from their service in the National Guard. The *coronel* (plural *coronéis*) acted like a rural boss and provided the provincial president and the political party that he endorsed, either Conservative or Liberal, with the votes necessary to win municipal and national elections. In return, the local influence and prestige of the *coronel* were bolstered by the receipt of jobs, favors, and legal and military protection from his patron in the provincial capital and the political leaders in Rio de Janeiro. In turn, the *coronel* distributed patronage to his own clients. The strength of *coronelismo* reflected the fact that the vast majority of Brazilians still lived in the countryside

[74]   where economic, social and political activities were dominated and controlled by their dependent relationship with the local *coronel.*

For the mass of free Brazilians, most of whom were mulattos, the establishment of an independent nation did not materially affect their customary desperate living conditions. They remained landless and tied to subsistence agriculture. The high rate of infant mortality, lack of health-care and frequent epidemics of serious diseases such as cholera and yellow fever meant that life expectancy was short. Although racial and gender prejudice remained a major barrier to advancement, employment opportunities and living conditions were marginally better in the cities than in rural areas. But cities also possessed notorious reputations for violent crime and disease. In Rio de Janeiro it was estimated that at least 25 percent of the city's population lived in tenements. A distinctly unflattering impression of the national capital was gained by William E. Curtis, who briefly visited the city in 1885 as the secretary of the United States Latin American Trade Commission: 'Viewed from the deck of a ship in the harbor, the city of Rio looks like a fragment of fairyland — a cluster of alabaster castles decorated with vines; but the illusion is instantly dispelled upon landing, for the streets are narrow, damp, dirty, reeking with repulsive odors, and filled with vermin-covered beggars and wolfish-looking dogs.'[32]

Slavery

The institution of slavery remained an integral feature of society for almost the whole of the nineteenth century. At the start of the First Empire in 1822 there were more than 1 million slaves in Brazil, making up around 30 percent of the national population. In fact, Brazil possessed the largest slave population in the world. By the middle of the nineteenth century the number of slaves had more than doubled to over 2 million. This reflected not so much the rate of natural increase but the continued importation of African slaves via the transatlantic slave trade. Even though it was legally prohibited in 1831, the traffic in slaves actually increased from an average of less than 20,000 a year in the 1830s to over 50,000 a year during the late 1840s. After the ending of the slave trade in 1850, the slave population gradually declined and numbered 1.5 million in 1872 or the equivalent of 15 percent of the national population. Slavery was finally abolished in 1888.

The rise of the coffee economy and its growing demand for labor significantly changed the distribution of the slave population during the nineteenth century. Between 1821 and 1851 more than 80 percent of slaves arriving from Africa were sent directly to the Center-South. As a result there was a marked growth in the slave population of the provinces of Rio de Janeiro, Minas Gerais and especially São Paulo. In addition, there was a growing internal slave trade as sugar planters in the Northeast compensated for the declining fortunes of the sugar industry by selling their slaves to the coffee planters of the Paraíba Valley and São Paulo. 'Every coasting vessel brings its ten to thirty slaves for sale at Rio, for the supply of labor in this vicinity and on the coffee plantations,' reported the American minister at Rio, James Watson Webb, in 1862, 'and the cry is heard from the provinces of Pará, Maranham, Piaui, Parahiba, Pernambuco, and even Bahia, that they are being depopulated for the benefit of the southern provinces, by the inevitable law of demand and supply.'[33] By 1872 more than half the slave population was concentrated in the three main coffee-producing provinces. Just as slave labor had been the engine behind the growth of the sugar industry, it fulfilled the same function later for the dramatic rise of the coffee industry. The 1872 census also revealed that not every slave was a field laborer or was involved in agricultural work. In fact, as many as 30 percent of all slaves worked in towns and cities. The range of occupations was large and included domestic servants, porters, street vendors, factory workers, barbers and undertakers.

The treatment of slaves in Brazil continued to be inherently cruel. Conditions on coffee plantations in the Paraíba Valley were just as harsh as on the sugar plantations of the Recôncavo. 'Many inhuman *fazendeiros*,' observed Father Caetano da Fonseca in 1863, 'force their slaves with the lash to work beyond physical endurance. These wretched slaves, using up their last drops of energy, end their days in a brief time.'[34] An unfavorable comparison was even made with the United States. On his visit to Bahia in 1866 Professor Louis Agassiz of Harvard University noted that 'the institution [of slavery] from a moral point of view has some of its most revolting characters in this country, and looks, if possible, more odious than it did in the States.'[35] The viciousness of the system, however, was somewhat moderated by the '*brecha camponesa*' ('peasant breach'), a practice in which slave-owners, especially on coffee plantations, allowed their slaves to grow agricultural produce for their own personal consumption and even for sale. Slaves, therefore, became similar to free peasants (*moradores*) and had rights to the goods that they had produced. In this sense a 'breach' was made in the system of slavery. Another mitigating factor was the increasing incidence of freedom by manumission. The 1872 census revealed that more than 70 percent of the black population was free. The passage of the Law of the Free Womb in 1871 boosted the number of manumissions to more than 130,000 between 1871 and 1885.

[76]   The inevitability of the end of slavery was finally accepted by the General Assembly in 1888. Indeed, the simple passage of the 'Golden Law' was deemed sufficient to extirpate the evil institution from Brazil. No financial provision was made for the future, either in the form of compensation for slave-owners or assistance for freed slaves. For the latter, the fact that they were legally free was of little benefit in the competition for jobs with white workers.

Immigration

With the exception of the long-established immigration from Portugal and the Portuguese Atlantic Islands, few European countries sent emigrants to Brazil. Before the advent of the steamship the sea passage was slow and expensive. Moreover, Europeans were more attracted to North America than to Brazil, whose image was extremely negative in terms of an oppressive climate, prevalence of tropical diseases, the lack of free land and few employment opportunities. The existence of slavery in Brazil also deterred immigration. During the early nineteenth century, however, there were some initiatives taken by the imperial government to support schemes to attract immigrants from Germany and Switzerland. They particularly wanted small farmers to help to colonize rural areas in the South. From 1823 to 1830 about 10,000 Europeans migrated to Brazil of whom 6,000, mostly Germans, settled in Rio Grande do Sul. The most successful German colony was founded in 1824 in São Leopoldo near Porto Alegre. The large majority of settlements, however, were soon abandoned and ended in failure. An attempt to use German and Swiss immigrants as plantation workers was made in 1847 by the *paulista fazendeiro* Nicolau (Pereira) de Campos Vergueiro. Persistent complaints about both working and living conditions in São Paulo resulted, however, in damaging publicity that discouraged further immigration from Europe. The governments of Prussia and Russia even advised their citizens against settling in Brazil.

A major wave of European immigration began during the 1870s. Brazil shared in this worldwide movement of people. From an average of around 10,000 immigrants per year in the 1850s, the figure doubled in the 1870s and continued to rise in the 1880s. One reason was the growing pressure for the abolition of slavery that caused landowners and especially the coffee planters of São Paulo to turn to Europe for an alternative supply of labor. But developments in Europe were also important. These included agricultural depression and improvements in transportation, particularly the railroad and steamships. The provincial government of São Paulo actively countered the

negative image of Brazil by agreeing to pay the sea passage for families
from Italy, and also set up an immigration agency to publicize the available
employment opportunities. The policy was vindicated in 1887 when immigration to Brazil from Europe reached the record level of 55,000. During the
following year it more than doubled to 133,000. Moreover, it was notice-
able that 90 percent of the immigrants were from Italy while more than half
were destined for São Paulo.

Education

Just as the transfer of the court to Brazil in 1808 opened the ports to world
trade, it also brought an end to the Portuguese policy of imposing cultural
isolation on the colony. An important symbol of intellectual liberation
occurred in May 1808 when a printing press was finally established in Rio
de Janeiro. A second press soon followed in Salvador. The colony's first
newspaper, the *Gazeta do Rio de Janeiro*, began publication in September
1808. Though royal approval was necessary for publication until 1821,
many books and pamphlets were printed and openly distributed. Literary
societies were formed by the educated élite. The royal library brought from
Lisbon was used to provide the foundation for a national library.

Although no university was established in Brazil, a number of colleges
were opened including in 1810 a military academy in Rio de Janeiro, and
during the 1820s medical schools in Rio de Janeiro and Salvador and law
schools in Olinda and São Paulo. The law school at Olinda was transferred to
Recife in 1854. The aim of the colleges was to provide an education for the
sons of the élite and to train future army and navy officers, doctors, lawyers
and government civil servants. The gaining of a law degree known as the
bacherel was regarded as a mark of achievement and often led to a career in the
government bureaucracy. Like the University of Coimbra, the law schools in
Brazil facilitated the formation and continuation of an administrative élite of
government officials, magistrates and judges who served at both the national,
provincial and local levels. Their common social and educational backgound
made a notable contribution to maintaining the political stability of the
Second Empire and promoting a sense of national unity.

Although the 1824 Constitution guaranteed free primary education to all
citizens, the Empire followed the practice of the colonial period and did little
to promote public education. This was left to the Church, charitable organizations and private initiative. The central government could act positively, as
exemplified by the opening in 1838 in Rio of a public secondary school, the

[78] Colégio Dom Pedro II. Two years earlier, however, the responsibility for providing primary and secondary education had been transferred to the provinces. The lack of adequate funding meant that results were extremely mixed. During the 1850s an estimated 60,000 pupils attended primary schools and 3,700 secondary schools. The 1872 census showed an increase to 150,000 pupils at the primary level and 10,000 at the secondary level. However, out of a population of almost 10 million this meant that only 17 percent of children between the ages of 6 and 15 were attending school and usually for no more than two years. Moreover, the census revealed that 80 percent of the population was illiterate. A study by a commission of the Senate in 1882 discovered that there was only one public school for every 200 children of school age in 1878. The chairman of the commission, Rui Barbosa, gloomily concluded: 'The report of our commission cannot fail to leave us grief-stricken for the state of our primary instruction.'[36]

Diplomacy

Independence

Brazil suddenly became an adjunct to the Napoleonic Wars in 1807 when the prince regent, Dom João, chose to escape from imminent French imprisonment by transferring his court from Lisbon to Rio de Janeiro. But Napoleon made no attempt to pursue the Portuguese royal family or to plan a military campaign to attack Brazil. European diplomats typically regarded Brazil as too remote and peripheral to their interests. The notable exception was Britain, who wished to support its Portuguese ally and to develop commercial contacts with a potentially lucrative market. Indeed, British diplomacy played an important role in persuading Dom João to seek exile in the New World. British warships ensured that the royal convoy reached its destination safely, and effectively guaranteed that Brazil would be protected from French military reprisals. The traditionally close relationship between Portugal and Britain was underlined when Dom João issued a decree in January 1808 opening the ports of Brazil to foreign trade. British merchants benefited most from this action. Their growing hold over Brazilian trade was strengthened by the conclusion of a new commercial treaty in 1810 that gave a preferential tariff advantage to British goods imported into Brazil. The preeminent commercial position that Britain enjoyed in Portugal as a result of the 1703 Methuen Treaty was, therefore, replicated in Brazil.

The winning of independence in 1822 further strengthened diplomatic and commercial relations between Brazil and Britain. British mercenaries, notably Lord Cochrane, made a significant contribution to military victory. Moreover, the threat of British naval power deterred the European powers of the Holy Alliance from giving military assistance to the kings of Spain and Portugal to reconquer their former colonies.

Even though Brazil was spared external military intervention, it faced a difficulty in securing formal diplomatic recognition by the European powers. Such recognition was considered necessary by Dom Pedro and José Bonifacio. Even prior to the 'Cry of Ipiranga,' they had issued a 'manifesto to friendly nations' on August 6, 1822. Diplomatic agents were sent to Europe to argue that Brazil had enjoyed the status of a kingdom since 1815 and should be treated as an equal of the European monarchies. Recognition was also valuable for domestic political reasons because it would confer legitimacy upon the new regime. However, in what would be a recurring theme for the future, Brazilian diplomats found that they possessed little influence at the courts and the foreign offices of the great European powers. Those governments attached much more importance to the attitude of the Portuguese king than the supplications of Brazilian envoys. Dom João's outright refusal to recognize Brazil's independence essentially prevented the other European monarchs from establishing diplomatic relations. Indeed, the members of the Holy Alliance led by the Tsar of Russia were very reluctant to endorse the overthrow of a legitimate monarch and the creation of an 'empire' that revived memories of Napoleon and his imperial ambitions.

Dom Pedro and José Bonifácio pragmatically looked for support from neighboring states. In Argentina and the United States, Brazilian diplomats were even instructed to suggest forming a defensive military alliance to oppose a Portuguese invasion. No such alliance materialized. Dom Pedro, however, was particularly pleased at the decision in May 1824 of the American president, James Monroe, to receive José Silvestre Rebelo as Brazilian chargé d'affaires. Although Monroe was opposed to the principle of monarchy, his action meant that the United States became the first foreign country to recognize the independence of Brazil.[37] The emperor also responded positively to Simón Bolívar's invitation to send a Brazilian delegate to a Pan-American conference to be held at Panama. A delegate was named, but did not attend. The British chargé d'affaires at Rio de Janeiro reported that 'the nomination may be considered as having been announced to the public more for the sake of saving appearance than for any other effect.'[38]

[80]   The diplomatic support of the United States and Spanish-American nations was useful, but exerted limited influence on the European powers. Following the same strategy that Portugal had pursued during the eighteenth century, most Brazilian diplomatic effort was directed at cultivating close relations with Britain. 'With England's friendship we can snap our fingers at the rest of the world,' a Brazilian diplomat reported from London in July 1823 and, once this was secured, he concluded that 'it will not be necessary to go begging for recognition from any other power for all will wish our friendship.'[39] Fortunately, the mutual national interests of Brazil and Britain coincided. The British government was in favor of according recognition and was pleased that Brazil would remain a monarchy. The British foreign secretary, George Canning, wished to maintain the commercial privileges contained in the 1810 treaty and was aware that the treaty expired at the end of 1825 and would have to be renewed. He was also conscious of growing diplomatic and economic rivalry with the United States, a threat that was underlined by the announcement of the 'Monroe Doctrine' and American diplomatic recognition of Brazil.

Brazilian diplomats were correct in believing that the mediatory role of Britain would be the decisive factor in persuading Portugal to abandon its intransigent attitude. In 1825 the British diplomat, Charles Stuart, visited Lisbon for discussions with the Portuguese government. He then traveled to Rio de Janeiro where he was able to conclude an agreement on August 29, 1825 in which Portugal recognized the independence of Brazil. But the cost of securing recognition was high. Brazil was required to make a number of concessions including a secret payment to Portugal of £2 million. Brazil also agreed not to attempt to unite with any other Portuguese colony. This provision was intended to prevent the incorporation of Angola into the Brazilian Empire and effectively frustrated any ambition to develop political links with Africa. In addition, Stuart negotiated a separate commercial arrangement with Brazil that renewed the preferential tariff on British goods contained in the 1810 treaty. Another treaty was concluded in which Brazil agreed to abolish the slave trade from Africa within three years of the agreement taking effect. Both treaties with Britain were provisional and required some renegotiation. The slave trade treaty was eventually ratified in 1826 and the commercial treaty in 1827. In the meantime, Britain recognized the independence of Brazil in January 1826. Similar action was soon forthcoming from the leading European powers, including Austria, France, and Prussia. Among the Spanish-American countries, Mexico granted recognition in 1825, Argentina in 1827 and Colombia in 1828. Despite having to make commercial concessions and to consent to abolish the slave trade, Brazil was accepted as an independent nation state without suffering any punitive loss of territory. Full diplomatic relations were quickly established with the leading European powers. During the First Empire Brazil sent diplomatic representatives to 24 foreign capitals, twice as many as Colombia and Peru and three times the number dispatched by Argentina.

The treaty system

Brazilian diplomats found that they had no part to play in the power politics of Europe. George Canning delivered a pointed rebuke in 1825 when he referrred to 'an opinion on the part of the Brazilian Government, not only that Brazil is on a footing with all other Governments in the world, but it is somewhat superior to them.'[40] The interest of the European powers and the United States in the Brazilian Empire was concentrated on trade, so that diplomatic relations mostly revolved around commercial and consular business. A treaty system emerged in which the 1827 commercial treaty with Britain provided a model for similar agreements that the First Empire concluded with France, Austria, Prussia, Denmark, the United States, and Holland. Eventually treaties were signed with 19 countries. Each treaty contained a most-favored-nation clause that granted not only tariff reductions on imported goods but also gave special legal privileges to foreign nationals. This allowed foreigners extra-territorial rights in that they could appeal to their own consular and diplomatic representatives in Brazil and claim immunity from Brazilian laws. Dom Pedro and his ministers justified the concessions as necessary to secure diplomatic recognition and to assist Brazil's economic development. Nevertheless, there was considerable criticism that the treaties conferred only a spurious equality and actually exposed Brazil to political humiliation and economic exploitation.

Brazil's vulnerability to external diplomatic pressure was most visibly demonstrated by the issue of the transatlantic slave trade. A desire to abolish the slave trade was a prominent feature of British foreign policy throughout the first half of the nineteenth century. In response to British pressure, Dom João agreed to a treaty in 1817 that prohibited the slave trade north of the Equator. Exploiting Brazil's desire for diplomatic recognition, Britain secured a new arrangement that was ratified in 1827 and aimed to end the transatlantic slave trade within three years. The British navy was also given authority to stop and search ships suspected of transporting slaves on the high seas. Although the Brazilian General Assembly passed a law in 1831 declaring

[82] that all slaves entering Brazil would be automatically freed, the slave trade was allowed to continue openly. The 1831 law was a public relations act designed 'to show the English' ('*para ingles ver*') and was never adequately enforced. All attempts at abolishing the trade proved ineffective so long as the Brazilian export economy needed slaves and looked to Africa to supply them. In 1845 the British parliament retaliated and unilaterally passed a Slave Trade Act, known in Brazil as 'the Aberdeen Bill' after the British foreign secretary, Lord Aberdeen, which authorized the British navy to treat suspected slave ships as if they were pirates and, if necessary, pursue those ships into Brazilian ports. The implementation of the Aberdeen Bill led to the violation of Brazilian sovereignty and was bitterly resented in Brazil. Even an ardent abolitionist such as Joaquim Nabuco considered the bill 'an insult to our dignity as an independent people.'[41] Despite increased British naval action, the slave trade actually flourished in the 1840s and only declined during the following decade as a result of political and economic changes within Brazil rather than direct pressure from Britain.

The controversy over the Aberdeen Bill coincided with Brazil's refusal to renew the 1827 Anglo–Brazilian commercial treaty in 1844. A similar agreement with the United States had also been allowed to lapse in 1841. No longer earnestly seeking diplomatic recognition, the Brazilian government felt more confident in its dealings with foreign powers. It politely declined to enter into discussions for a renewal of the treaties and welcomed the gradual ending of a system that was considered to have been inherently unequal and humiliating. Moreover, the preferential tariffs came to an end with the termination of the treaties and, in effect, gave the imperial government full control over its own customs duties for the first time. A tariff policy was now instituted in which duties on imports of foreign goods were raised as a means of increasing government revenue and to protect domestic industry from foreign competition.

Brazil could also openly resist British pressure. In December 1862 the British minister at Rio de Janeiro, William Christie, high-handedly ordered British warships to blockade the port for six days in retaliation for the arrest of British sailors. Dom Pedro II responded to the crisis by stating that Brazil must stand for its rights as a sovereign nation and where necessary adopt 'a policy of its own.'[42] When the British government refused to make an official apology and pay compensation for damage to Brazilian property, the Brazilian government broke off diplomatic relations. In a similar incident in 1864, Brazil protested to the United States government over the seizure by an American warship of a Confederate cruiser at dock in Salvador da Bahia. The Brazilian government resolutely declared that the national flag had been insulted and demanded that the United States make an official apology. In both cases, Brazil's firm stand was successful.

Rivalry in the River Plate

While both Dom João and Dom Pedro I were prepared to be accommodating to the great European powers and the United States, a different attitude was projected in relations with the neighboring nations of South America. Conscious that their nation was not only historically and culturally different from the Spanish-American countries but also much larger in terms of geographical area, population and natural resources, Brazilian diplomats fondly believed that it was the leading power in the continent. The very fact that Brazil was a monarchy was regarded as a positive advantage. 'What a picture unhappy [Spanish] America shows us!' commented José Bonifácio in 1823. He added: 'For fourteen years its peoples have torn themselves to pieces, because, after having known a monarchical government, they aspire to establish a licentious liberty. And, after having swum in blood, they are no more than victims of disorder, poverty, and misery.'[43]

The outbreak of the movements for independence in Spanish America created opportunities for Brazilian territorial expansion. Taking advantage of the political instability in Buenos Aires, Dom João sought to extend Portuguese control over the Banda Oriental and gain access to the River Plate. A military expedition was dispatched in 1811 to occupy the region. British diplomatic pressure compelled the withdrawal of the troops in 1812, but another expedition was sent in 1816 that defeated the local forces led by José (Gervasio) Artigas. In 1821 the Banda Oriental was officially incorporated into Brazil as the Cisplatine Province.

Though hampered by internal disorder and the cost of the war against Spain, the newly independent Argentine nation was intent on driving the Portuguese from the Banda Oriental and restoring the former boundaries of the Spanish viceroyalty of the Plate to include not only the Banda Oriental but also Paraguay and Upper Peru (Bolivia). A battle for regional hegemony began between Brazil and Argentina that would last throughout the nineteenth century. 'The entire possession of the eastern bank of the River Plate,' stated the British chargé d'affaires at Rio de Janeiro, Henry Chamberlain, in July 1818, 'is absolutely necessary for the safety of Buenos Ayres and the interior Provinces.' As a result, he predicted that 'Brazil could never hope to enjoy quiet possession of the Montevidean territory.'[44] The anticipated hostilities

[84] in the Banda Oriental erupted in April 1825 when a group of rebels known as 'the Thirty-Three' refused to accept the 1824 Brazilian Constitution. They declared war on Brazil and advocated union with Argentina. In October Argentina annexed the Banda Oriental. Dom Pedro I replied by formally declaring war on Argentina in December 1825. In the ensuing Cisplatine War Brazilian forces experienced a series of set-backs both at sea and on land. But Argentina failed to achieve a decisive military victory. Consequently, both sides became war-weary and accepted Britain's offer to help end the conflict. 'Lassitude, exhaustion, internal added to external differences, a growing conviction on both sides of the impossibility of a complete triumph on either,' explained the British Foreign Secretary, Lord Dudley, in April 1828.[45] With the assistance of British diplomatic mediation, a compromise was reached in August 1828 which ended the fighting and resulted in the Banda Oriental becoming the new independent state of (The Oriental Republic of) Uruguay in 1830.

The creation of an independent 'buffer state' finally resolved a territorial dispute that had begun with the creation of the Portuguese settlement at Colônia do Sacramento in 1680. The arrangement, however, marked a set-back for Brazilian expansionist ambitions though this was tempered by the agreement of all parties to the free navigation of the River Plate, thereby allowing access for all shipping to the interior of the continent via the Paraná and Paraguay rivers. In fact, Brazilian diplomacy stressed a desire to be friendly in its dealings with its Spanish-American neighbors and to avoid interference in their domestic affairs. Partly this was a reflection of domestic weakness arising from the abdication of Dom Pedro I in 1831 and the outbreak of a series of regional uprisings during the 1830s and 1840s. Brazilian diplomats were also conscious that their country shared common borders with nearly all the new South American states. With the notable exception of the River Plate region, most of these borders were located in remote and virtually uninhabited regions so that there was little actual friction between rival settlements. Nevertheless, throughout the Empire Brazilian governments stressed a desire to resolve border questions peacefully by negotiation on the basis of the principle of *uti possidetis* that had been contained in the 1750 Treaty of Madrid.

Conflict returned to the River Plate region during the 1840s when the Argentine dictator, Juan Manuel Rosas, attempted to expand his control into Uruguay and Paraguay. Brazil would not allow Argentina to dominate the region and supported Uruguay in its military action against Rosas. Despite the overthrow of Rosas in 1852, Brazil remained actively involved in the internal politics of Uruguay. A new factor entered the strategic balance when the Paraguayan dictator, Francisco Solano López, sent troops to Uruguay in 1864. Paraguayan forces also invaded a small portion of Brazilian territory in Mato Grosso. Brazil responded to the threat to its regional influence by joining with Uruguay and Argentina to form the Triple Alliance against Paraguay. In the resulting Paraguayan War from 1865 to 1870, Brazil contributed most to the victory of the allies and demonstrated that it was the major military power in the region. Instead of promoting regional peace, however, the defeat of Paraguay only stimulated rivalry between Brazil and Argentina. This was evident in their disagreement over the postwar settlement, especially the transfer of the former Paraguayan territories of the Chaco and the Misiones. Tensions were also increased by Argentina's determination to redress its perceived military imbalance with Brazil.

Although Dom Pedro II had been willing to pursue a strategy seeking total victory against Paraguay, his general indifference to military matters meant that Brazil did not seek to use its substantially-enlarged army to expand its territory at the expense of neighboring states. In fact after 1870 Brazil became preoccupied with domestic issues, especially the abolition of slavery and the rise of republicanism. By contrast, foreign affairs were not given much attention. An important development, however, was taking place in the Western Hemisphere as a result of the rising economic and political power of the United States and a corresponding decline in the influence of Britain. The growing interest of the Brazilian élite in the 'colossus of the north' was exemplified by Dom Pedro's visit to the centennial exhibition held at Philadelphia in 1876. There was also awareness that the United States had become Brazil's largest market for exports of coffee. Consequently, the imperial government proved receptive to the unexpected suggestion made in 1887 by the American president, Grover Cleveland, that the two countries should conclude a commercial treaty. The decision to enter into negotiations signified a reversal of a policy maintained since 1844 of not negotiating commercial treaties with countries beyond the neighboring states of South America. Brazil also agreed to accept the invitation of the United States to attend a Pan-American conference scheduled to be held at Washington in October 1889. In marked contrast to the 1826 Panama Congress, a Brazilian delegation actually attended the Conference. Just as Brazilian foreign policy was entering into a new active phase, however, the Second Empire came to an abrupt end in November 1889.

CHAPTER 3

THE FIRST REPUBLIC, 1889–1930

Politics

The Federal Republic

The leaders of the 1889 coup had seized political power in Rio de Janeiro by the use of military violence. They proceeded quickly to assert their authority by constituting themselves as a temporary or 'provisional' government and decreeing the establishment of a federal republic. A series of executive proclamations were issued which sought not only to inform the people about what had happened but also to justify and legitimize the new regime. Despite the authoritarian procedure, a desire for popular approval and legitimacy existed and was demonstrated by the prominence given to the claim that the armed services had carried out the coup on behalf of 'the people' throughout the whole of the country. The *pronunciamento* on November 15, 1889 unilaterally stated that 'the people, the army, and the navy' had overthrown the monarchy and displaced it with a provisional government 'whose principal mission is to guaranty by public order the liberty and rights of citizens.'[1] The proclamation was signed by the leader of the coup, Marshal Deodoro da Fonseca. Although Deodoro had effectively replaced the Emperor Dom Pedro as head of state, he preferred to style himself modestly as 'chief of the provisional government.' Other signatories publicly declaring their support for Deodoro included Rui Barbosa, Quintino Bocaiúva, and Benjamin Constant. All three were duly rewarded with important positions in the new government. Rui became finance minister, Quintino headed the ministry of foreign relations, while Constant was appointed as war minister.

Despite endeavoring to reassure the people that political conditions were stable and peaceful and that they should continue their daily lives as normal, the provisional government was intent on emphasizing that the monarchy had been definitely abolished and that the old imperial regime was overthrown. [87] This was reinforced by important symbolic changes which sought to redefine the nation as a modern federal republic. The name of the country was altered from the 'Empire of Brazil' to the 'The United States of Brazil.' A new national flag depicting a positivist motto that stressed 'order and progress' shortly followed. The separation of church and state was decreed. Of practical necessity, however, the enactment of a new constitution to replace the existing 1824 Constitution took much longer. A committee of five jurists was appointed on December 3 to prepare a draft document that would be presented for approval to a constituent assembly scheduled to meet on November 15, 1890, the first anniversary of the overthrow of the Empire. The drafts were completed and submitted for scrutiny and editing to Rui Barbosa. The final document reflected Rui's personal admiration for the constitution and political system of the United States and also the prevailing mood among the political, intellectual and business élites that Brazil should rise above its imperial and slavocratic past and become transformed into a modern democracy and industrial society.

The Constituent Assembly convened in Rio de Janeiro on schedule in November 1890. Its work lasted for just over three months and the constitution was officially promulgated on February 24, 1891. The actual constitutional debate proceeded fairly smoothly because a large majority of the members of the assembly were carefully chosen liberals and army officers who supported republicanism and favored the adoption of a federal political system. Moreover, they acknowledged that the transfer of political power from the center to the regions, which had been promised in the Republican Manifesto of 1870, had been a prime motive of the 1889 coup. Prominent among the advocates of decentralization and greater autonomy for the state governments were the influential coffee interests, especially from São Paulo. The legacy of the Empire persisted, however, in the desire to retain a central executive authority and a national legislature that would be located in Rio de Janeiro. Indeed, liberals preferred a strong central government as not only modern and efficient but also the best means of maintaining Brazil's political and territorial unity. Support was also forthcoming from business interests who believed that centralism would promote industrial growth by directly assisting the development of a national market.

The discussion on executive power was resolved in favor of a presidential system of government that was meant to be broadly similar to that of the United States in which the federal government was separated into executive, legislative, and judicial branches. Although the position and title of emperor

[88] were abolished, the office of chief executive was retained in the form of the president of the republic. Unlike the hereditary monarch, however, the president and vice-president would be elected by direct popular vote for non-renewable four-year terms. The president was, therefore, chosen by the people and ineligible to succeed himself. Although no mention was made of the moderating power, the president possessed substantial executive powers. The fact that he appointed his cabinet ministers and that they were responsible only to him was designed to promote administrative efficiency but resulted in presidential rather than congressional government. Furthermore, the potential for presidential preponderance was facilitated by the provision of emergency powers in which the president could unilaterally declare a state of siege and order federal military intervention 'in case of foreign attack or serious internal disturbance.'[2]

A desire existed for parliamentary checks on the presidency and was reflected in the delegation of legislative power to a National Congress. A separate judiciary was also established consisting of a Supreme Court and lower federal courts. Both the National Congress and the Supreme Court would be located in Rio de Janeiro. The organization of the National Congress was similar to the imperial General Assembly in being divided into a Senate and a Chamber of Deputies. Irrespective of their size or population, each state would be equally represented by three senators. In contrast to the Empire, however, senators would no longer possess automatic right of tenure for life and would have to submit themselves for re-election every nine years. In the Chamber of Deputies, deputies would serve three-year terms and would be elected on the basis of population, a provision that was politically advantageous to the more populated states. As part of its function to check and balance the executive, Congress had the power to impeach the president and could ultimately secure his removal from office. Another important congressional power was control over the tariff on foreign imports and the resulting income derived from import duties.

The aspect of the work of the Constituent Assembly that attracted most contemporary comment was the granting of significant constitutional powers to the state governments. The twenty provinces of the Empire plus the newly-created Federal District comprising the city of Rio de Janeiro were regarded as equal members of the federal union and became essentially self-governing states with their own constitutions, popularly elected governors, legislative assemblies and courts of law. In addition, they possessed virtual financial autonomy that notably included the authority to raise revenue from duties on goods exported from the state. While the majority of states had

little external trade, the export tax was an important and profitable privilege   [89]
for those with large and flourishing export economies such as São Paulo and
Minas Gerais. Moreover, states were given the right to maintain their own
militias (*forças públicas*). In practice, these took the form of police forces and,
in the particular case of São Paulo, resulted in a state 'army' that was equivalent if not superior in manpower, training and equipment to the federal army.
The maintenance of independent military forces highlighted and reinforced
the decentralized nature of the 1891 Constitution. It also demonstrated a
basic inequality in that some states possessed greater wealth and would be
correspondingly more powerful than others.

Military rule

Foreign observers were surprised not so much by the fact that a successful
coup had actually taken place in 1889 as by the almost total absence of
public support for the monarchy when the long-anticipated event finally
materialized. The British minister at Rio de Janeiro, Hugh Wyndham, wrote
that he could 'hardly realise' that the emperor had been driven from the
country 'for which he has done so much.'[3] The apathetic public mood
appeared to extend to the process of drawing up the new constitution. In fact,
élitism and conservatism dominated political life in the Republic just as they
had during the Empire. Despite talk of positivism, democracy and liberal
reforms, the masses were still not allowed to participate directly in the Brazilian political system. Although universal manhood suffrage was adopted in
theory, the passage of a literacy requirement effectively deprived the majority of the population of the right to vote. The political reality was that an
army clique had seized power by force in 1889 and was firmly in control of
the provisional government and the distribution of its material resources.
Consequently, the principal beneficiaries were army officers who were
rewarded with generous increases in salary and appointment to lucrative and
influential posts in the federal and state governments. The size of the army
rose accordingly from 13,500 in 1889 to 18,000 in early 1893.

There was no organized national opposition to military political supremacy.
The coup had created a republic, but had not resulted in a major political
realignment. Ill-prepared and surprised by the sudden collapse of the Empire,
civilian politicians were divided amongst themselves. Many of those who had
held office during the Empire chose to withdraw into temporary political
isolation. A more positive response was forthcoming from prominent political leaders such as Rui Barbosa and Quintino Bocaiúva who wished to

[90] cooperate with the army and readily accepted Deodoro's invitation to join the provisional government. Nevertheless, a clash of personalities and policies was soon evident. Deodoro was a distinguished career military officer, who was authoritarian rather than democratic by temperament and training. Despite his initial personal reluctance to lead the coup against the emperor, once in office he showed an increasing desire to stay in power both for reasons of personal vanity and a sense of patriotic duty. In essence, Deodoro believed that the army had created the republic and was required to defend and preserve the new political order from internal and external enemies. As a result the army took over the constitutional role of the emperor and established what was effectively a military dictatorship known as the 'Republic of the Sword' which, instead of being a brief transitional regime, held on to power and ruled Brazil for the first five years of the republic.

On January 21, 1891 Deodoro da Fonseca's high-handedness finally provoked the resignation of the whole cabinet over a controversy arising from a public works contract. The focal point of criticism of Deodoro, however, was in the Constituent Assembly, which became officially known as the National Congress after the promulgation of the constitution on February 24, 1891. The constitution also brought a formal end to the provisional government and instructed the Congress to elect the first president of the republic for a term of office to last until 1894. As the army's preferred and only choice, the election of Deodoro appeared to be a mere formality. However, his opponents chose to register a mark of protest by nominating Prudente de Morais as a rival candidate. Prudente was the current president of the Constituent Assembly and a former governor of São Paulo. More pertinent, however, was the fact that he had expressed views critical of the army's interference in politics and was regarded as an anti-military candidate. On February 25, 1891 Deodoro secured victory by 129 to 97 votes and became the first president of the Republic. Another army general, Marshal Floriano Peixoto, was elected vice-president with a more substantial majority. Deodoro's margin of success was smaller than anticipated and illustrated the extent of his personal unpopularity. It was also a hollow victory in that the threat of military intervention had hovered over the election process and it had been expected that, if Deodoro should be defeated, the army would immediately proclaim his dictatorship and dissolve Congress. In the circumstances, Prudente secured therefore an impressive number of protest votes.

Resentment against Deodoro was made worse by the growing economic crisis known as the *Encilhamento* that was widely attributed to financial speculation and scandal. Discontent erupted at the opening session of the new

Congress in November 1891. The government was accused of corruption and there were even hints that the president might be impeached. Deodoro reacted by arbitrarily decreeing the dissolution of Congress and proclaiming a state of siege. The assumption of virtual dictatorial power was controversial and resulted in bitter criticism of the president in the press and a marked decrease of support for him within the armed services. This was exemplified by Vice-President Floriano Peixoto who secretly conspired with disaffected naval officers. On November 23, 1891 Admiral Custódio (José) de Melo seized control of warships in Guanabara Bay and threatened to bombard the city of Rio de Janeiro if Deodoro did not reconvene Congress. Deodoro accepted the will of the armed services. He dutifully resigned and handed over power to Floriano Peixoto. The disconsolate 'founder of the republic' retired immediately from the army and public affairs and died in August 1892.

Although Floriano Peixoto and Deodoro da Fonseca had both been born in the northeastern state of Alagoas and had risen to the highest military rank of marshal, Floriano conspicuously lacked the military bearing and manners of Deodoro. Floriano possessed, however, a greater personal affinity with ordinary people. By reinstating the dissolved Congress, he reinforced this image and appeared as the champion of constitutional rule. Nevertheless, Floriano faced a difficult time in office and reacted in a similar dictatorial style to Deodoro, thereby earning himself the nickname of the 'Iron Marshal.' Shortly after coming to power Floriano's legal right to act as head of state was queried on the grounds that Deodoro had not completed the required two years of office and that, according to the constitution, a special presidential election was necessary to choose his successor. The stubborn side of Floriano's character was demonstrated when he simply retained the title of vice-president while resolutely resisting calls from civilian politicians to submit himself for election. Persistent critics were arrested and several were exiled to the remote Amazon region. The most serious challenge to his authority, however, emerged from the navy, which had been growing increasingly resentful of the army's political prestige and national prominence. Floriano's attempts to appease senior admirals such as Eduardo Wandenkolk and Custódio de Melo with political office and favors were unsuccessful. In addition, the authority of the federal government was also challenged by riots and disturbances in several states stretching from Pernambuco and Ceará in the Northeast to the separatist movement in Rio Grande do Sul where endemic regional violence had developed into a full-scale civil war in February 1893.

The problem of civil disorder was made worse by the Naval Revolt at Rio which began in September 1893. Condemning Floriano Peixoto as a 'tyrant,'

[92] Admiral Custódio de Melo once again took command of the fleet of Brazilian warships in Guanabara Bay and threatened to bombard the capital. De Melo confidently expected Floriano to resign as Deodoro had done in identical circumstances almost two years earlier. But Floriano refused to stand down and denounced the naval rebels as mutineers and traitors. In contrast to his predecessor, Floriano was able to retain the full loyalty and support of the army while his naval opponents were not only divided amongst themselves but also seriously damaged their cause by appearing to wish a restoration of the monarchy. By July 1895 the Naval Revolt and the rebellion in Rio Grande had been successfully overcome. Floriano was praised as the 'consolidator' of the Republic. Curiously, however, this success did not lead to a perpetuation of military government. In fact, even while the Naval Revolt was in progress and a rebel army from Rio Grande was reportedly marching towards São Paulo with the aim of joining forces with the naval rebels, Floriano approved the holding of a national presidential election on March 1, 1894 in accordance with the schedule laid down in the 1891 Constitution.

For Floriano to refuse to allow the election would have lent substance to the charge of his critics that he was intent upon establishing a personal dictatorship. Moreover, pressure for an election came from the ruling élite of São Paulo who were giving the vice-president important political, financial and military support in his struggles against the naval rebels and the separatist movement in Rio Grande. The *paulistas* valued Floriano because his rule brought national order that assisted financial development and helped to attract foreign investment and immigration to their state. São Paulo was also politically well-organized and controlled by the *Paulista* Republican Party. The discipline of *paulista* deputies was exemplified in the National Congress where their leader, Francisco Glicério, provided political backing for Floriano with the creation in July 1893 of the Federal Republican Party (*Partido Republicano Federal* or PRF), a political coalition consisting of senators and deputies from several states. But the *paulistas* did not want military rule to continue indefinitely. Ideally they wished to place one of their own senior political leaders at the head of the federal government. This was evident at a convention of the PRF in September 1893 which nominated Prudente de Morais for the presidency. Floriano was not considered because he was constitutionally ineligible to be a presidential candidate. In the election that followed on March 1, 1894, Prudente polled 277,000 votes to 38,000 votes for Afonso (Augusto Moreira) Pena, the candidate from Minas Gerais. The margin of Prudente's victory was impressive in that he gained 84 percent of the total vote. However, a mere 2.2 percent of the total population

actually voted. The low turn-out was only partly explained by the fact that [93]
a state of siege existed in Rio and that civil disorder prevented the holding
of elections in three southern states. More significant was the enforcement of the literacy requirement that narrowly restricted the franchise and
ensured that local planters and landowners exercised the ultimate political
control.[4]

The *paulista* presidents

Despite speculation of a military coup to keep Floriano in office, the inauguration of Prudente de Morais as the first civilian president of the republic
took place on schedule in November 1895. Five years of uninterrupted military government, therefore, came to a peaceful end. The return of the army
to barracks reflected not only their obedience to the constitution but also a
desire to withdraw from active involvement in political questions. There was
also the factor of Floriano's serious illness and his subsequent death on June
29, 1895, which deprived the army of a national figurehead and experienced
political leadership. The navy still remained jealous of the army, but its senior
officers were demoralized by the humiliation of the abortive Naval Revolt
and were no longer receptive to political intrigues. By contrast, the election
of Prudente was widely interpreted as a positive sign and demonstrated, for
the first time since the beginning of the republic, that civilian politicians were
able to offer a practical alternative to military rule.

During his first year in office Prudente was a fortunate beneficiary not only
of the disarray of the military but also of the final termination of both the
Naval Revolt and the separatist movement in Rio Grande do Sul. Although
the restoration of political order in Rio Grande was a significant boost to the
concept of federal union, the generous terms of amnesty offered to the rebels
by Prudente aroused criticism that he was too lenient. Particular concern was
expressed over alleged monarchist conspiracies. Brazilians had lived under
the Empire for so long that they found it difficult to believe that monarchy
had been ended forever. The most outspoken defenders of the republic were
extreme nationalists who were located in Rio de Janeiro and known as
'Jacobins.' They had organized 'patriotic battalions' to defend the federal
capital during the Naval Revolt and continued to accuse the former rebels in
Rio Grande of holding strong monarchist sympathies. The Jacobins openly
admired the repressive measures adopted by Floriano and argued that, unlike
the 'Iron Marshal,' Prudente did not fully appreciate the seriousness of plots
to restore the monarchical system.

[94]   Apprehension that the republic was in acute danger suddenly turned into alarm bordering on panic in 1896 as news reached Rio de Janeiro about developments in the remote 'backlands' (*sertão*) of the Northeast where a charismatic preacher, Antonio Vicente Mendes Maciel, popularly known as *Conselheiro* ('the Counselor'), had established a large and growing millenarian community at Canudos, a hamlet 200 miles north of Salvador, Bahia. A dispute with local government officials in 1896 had resulted in the rout of a state police force sent to quell the disturbances. Governor Luís Viana of Bahia responded to the set-back by requesting the assistance of federal troops. Viana stressed that the armed cowboys (*jagunços*) of the backlands and supporters of Conselheiro were not only vicious criminals but also politically motivated in wishing to overthrow the republic and restore the monarchy. Consequently, a local dispute became transformed into the 'War of Canudos' (*Guerra de Canudos*), a national question concerning the future of the infant republican system of government. The ensuing dispatch and humiliating defeat of two federal army expeditions to Canudos created near hysteria in Rio and served to justify the organization of an even larger military force consisting of more than 10,000 soldiers equipped with cannon and machine guns and personally directed by the minister of war, Marshal Carlos Machado Bittencourt. After Canudos had been besieged for more than three months the mission was eventually accomplished on October 5, 1897 with a ruthless display of overwhelming force that destroyed the 'mud-hut Jerusalem' and massacred the large majority of its 15,000 inhabitants including men, women and children. The soldiers discovered that Antonio Conselheiro had died two weeks prior to the final assault.[5]

The federal government claimed that the rule of law required the assertion of severe military measures and that the destruction of Canudos represented a decisive defeat of a dangerous monarchist conspiracy. But the ability of Conselheiro and the *jagunços* to defy and successfully resist the federal army for so long was a severe blow to the image and prestige both of the army and the president of the republic. Prudente was roundly accused of being weak and acting unworthily in allowing the army to bear the stigma of defeat in the backlands. His unpopularity was demonstrated by an attempted assassination on November 5, 1897 in which the minister of war, Marshal Bittencourt, tried to protect the president and was stabbed and killed. The assailant was a young soldier, Marcelino Bispo, who was later revealed to have been given weapons and encouragement from the editor of the Jacobin newspaper, *O Jacobino*. Far from removing the president from office, the failed assassination plot actually gained Prudente considerable public sympathy and seriously damaged his critics. Moreover, Prudente seized the opportunity to impose a state of siege in the Federal District and to order the symbolic closure of the Military Club in Rio de Janeiro, a well-known meeting place of army officers and stronghold of Jacobin sympathies. Prudente's 'November coup' was politically significant in showing the extent of presidential power available under the 1891 Constitution. Despite criticism that he was a weak and ineffective executive, Prudente served his full four-year term of office and provided a successful transition from military to civilian rule. As the first *paulista* to become president, he inaugurated the period of *'paulista* presidents,' a development that also highlighted the growing national political ascendancy of his own state.

The political influence of São Paulo was reaffirmed in 1898 by the electoral victory of another *paulista* statesman for the presidency. At the invitation of São Paulo in July 1897 the political leaders of São Paulo, Minas Gerais, Pernambuco and Bahia had met to nominate the current governor of São Paulo, Campos Sales, for the presidency. In doing so the governors bypassed the National Congress and affirmed their right to nominate the president. The Federal Republican Party and the Jacobins reacted by proposing Lauro Sodré, the former governor of Pará, as an opposition candidate. But the PRF was a national party in name only and unable to organize an effective campaign. Proclaiming his own long-standing republican credentials as the candidate of the 'family of the Republican Party'[6] and with the secure backing of the most populated states, Campos Sales subsequently won the election in March 1898 by the huge majority of 420,000 to 39,000 votes. Prudente de Morais duly handed over the presidency to Campos Sales in November 1898. Although the Republic had been in existence for less than a decade, the tradition of civilian rule appeared to be already well established. In contrast to four years earlier, there were no rumors of a military coup to prevent the inauguration from taking place.

The stated aims of the new president were the maintenance of public order and especially the promotion of financial stability. In the period of inter-regnum before assuming the presidency, Campos Sales had visited Europe where he negotiated the 1898 Funding Loan with the British bankers, the Rothschilds. The purpose of the loan was to finance what had become a large federal budgetary deficit resulting in high inflation and a depreciating currency. At the same time Campos Sales undertook to deflate the economy by raising federal taxes while sharply reducing government expenditure. The resulting austerity measures were extremely unpopular and their implementation required the approval and continuing support of the legislature. Campos

[96] Sales secured this not by lobbying individual congressmen but by dealing directly with the state governors and regional landed oligarchies to persuade them to join in what was effectively a national political consensus on fiscal and monetary policy. The adherence of the governors was vital because the first loyalty of congressmen was to their state political leader and party. Consequently, the governors essentially controlled the votes of their delegations (*bancadas*) of state representatives in the National Congress. In return for what was virtually a guaranteed majority vote in the Chamber of Deputies, Campos Sales carefully avoided interfering in the domestic affairs of the states. 'The Union thinks what the States think,' he summed up.[7] This mutually beneficial arrangement became known as the 'politics of the governors' (*política dos governadores*).

State governors and landed oligarchies approved the 'politics of the governors' because it allowed them to govern their states with minimal federal interference. To make the arrangement function effectively they undertook to guarantee electoral victory. This was achieved by the system of *coronelismo* in which the governors provided jobs and favors to the local *coronéis* in return for the delivery of votes at municipal and federal elections. The governors also took a close interest in the person who headed the federal government because they recognized, as both Floriano Peixoto and Prudente de Morais had recently demonstrated, that the president of the republic was crucially important in terms of distributing federal jobs and patronage. Moreover, state autonomy had been directly impinged upon by presidential proclamations of states of siege and the subsequent deployment of federal military forces. The best opportunity for gaining influence over the president was to take an active involvement in his selection that, according to the 1891 Constitution, would occur every four years. As exemplified by the nomination of Campos Sales in 1897, the process consisted of preliminary discussions among governors to choose an 'official' candidate and then their collaborative effort to secure his election by delivering the necessary number of votes. The process also became an integral element of the 'politics of the governors' and was dominated by the leaders of the most powerful states, notably São Paulo and Minas Gerais. These two states were not only the wealthiest, but their populations contained a higher number of literate males and consequently more voters than the other states. In addition, they possessed well-organized state political parties operating at the local level and in the National Congress. Working together for mutual political and economic benefits their informal understanding was popularly referred to as 'coffee with milk' (*café-com-leite*), a description reflecting São Paulo's association with coffee

production and Minas Gerais' with milk. Amongst the other states, the most   [97]
politically influential were Bahia, Rio Grande do Sul, Pernambuco and Rio
de Janeiro State.

Elections were just as one-sided as during the Empire. The 'politics of the
governors' and *coronelismo* were successful in virtually guaranteeing certain
victory in state and federal elections for the candidates chosen by the élites
and bosses. In terms of the presidential elections the margin of victory was
invariably overwhelming and often represented more than 90 percent of the
popular vote. The political system was openly corrupt and repressive. The
turn-out at elections was low because the franchise was narrowly restricted
and registers of voters were carefully monitored by the *coronéis*. Moreover,
there was no secret ballot and votes were usually cast publicly. Where opposition emerged, it was often suppressed by fraud and violence. The closed
nature of the political system facilitated the growth of one-party state political machines, a development that further stifled political participation and
acted as an obstacle to the formation of national political parties with competing ideologies and programs. The power of the state machines was also
evident in the National Congress whose members were selected mainly
for their loyalty and obedience to their particular state party. Congressional
credentials committees verified election results and, in consultation with the
president, sifted out potential dissidents, a process so ruthless that it was popularly referred to as the '*degola*' ('beheading'). In effect, the 'politics of the
governors' brought political stability and ensured the continuation of civilian
rule, but the exclusive nature of the political system was undemocratic and
showed little qualitative change from the earlier period of military rule beyond
greatly increasing the role and influence of the oligarchies representing the
big states.

Even though his administration successfully restored the national finances
and, for the first time since the creation of the republic, presided over a
four-year period of relative domestic peace and order,[8] Campos Sales was an
unpopular president. This was partly explained by his tight fiscal policy and
the resulting steep rise in the cost of living. Moreover, acknowledged as
the architect of the 'politics of the governors,' Campos Sales was blamed by
liberals for the failure of the Republic to institute democratic reforms. Nevertheless, the 'politics of the governors' was successful once again in 1901 in
securing the selection of a third *paulista* for president. Discussions between
Campos Sales and the governors of Minas Gerais and Bahia resulted in the
nomination of the current governor of São Paulo, (Francisco de Paula)
Rodrigues Alves. Although Campos Sales was insistent that Rodrigues Alves

[98]   be selected, the fact that the latter was a fellow-*paulista* was not decisive. More pertinent was the proven administrative experience of Rodrigues Alves and his reputation for financial expertise. Consequently, Campos Sales was confident that Rodrigues Alves would provide continuity of monetary policy.

The choice of Rodrigues Alves attracted some adverse comment because of his conservative political ideas and particularly his well-known pro-monarchist background. During the Empire Dom Pedro had awarded him the title of Counselor. Moreover he had never been a member of the republican movement, nor had he played any part in the overthrow of the Empire in 1889. On the other hand, Rodrigues Alves had quickly accepted the Republic by becoming a member of the Constituent Assembly and subsequently served as minister of finance under Floriano and Prudente. Whatever doubts existed over his past monarchist associations, they proved immaterial because the 'politics of the governors' was successful in securing his election by 592,000 votes to less than 43,000 for his opponent, the long-standing republican, Quintino Bocaiúva.

In keeping with the traditions of the Empire, the administration of Rodrigues Alves displayed an aristocratic ethos that was evident in its proclaimed determination to govern the country fairly and competently. The president appointed to the cabinet a number of highly talented individuals drawn from several states including Leopoldo de Bulhões of Goiás as minister of finance, José Joaquim (J.J.) Seabra of Bahia as minister of the interior, Lauro Müller of Santa Catarina as minister of transportation and public works, and José da Silva Paranhos, the baron of Rio Branco, as minister of foreign affairs. In terms of domestic policy, the most celebrated undertaking was the start of a major effort to transform the national capital, Rio de Janeiro, into a modern city with emphasis on beautification, eliminating health hazards and improving commercial and port facilities.

Struggle for the presidency

For his successor, Rodrigues Alves preferred the current governor of São Paulo, Bernardino de Campos. The prospect of a fourth successive *paulista* president, however, was controversial and revealed an inherent weakness of the 'politics of the governors'. The system worked well so long as the governors of Minas Gerais and São Paulo agreed on the candidate as they had done in 1897 and 1901. The failure to reach a consensus in 1905 resulted, however, in the emergence of bitter regional tensions and rivalries. The ensuing political uncertainty gave an opportunity for the senator from Rio

Grande do Sul, (José Gomes) Pinheiro Machado, to assert a powerful influence on the process to select the president. The rise of a *gaúcho* (cowboy, horseman) politician to national influence reflected the growing economic wealth and political status of Rio Grande do Sul. In 1906 the *gaúcho* state surpassed Bahia in terms of possession of presidential votes and was third in this respect to Minas Gerais and São Paulo. Moreover, in the absence of national political parties, Pinheiro enjoyed the signal advantage of being backed by a well-organized and disciplined state party whose leader, Antonio Augusto Borges de Medeiros, remained governor of the state continuously from 1898 to 1928. This gave Pinheiro the secure political base to become vice-president of the Senate in 1902 and to acquire a position of great influence on the credentials committee which allowed him to build up a large personal following of congressmen known as the 'Bloc' (*'Bloco'*). Delegations from the relatively weaker northern and northeastern states often felt isolated and neglected in the National Congress. By accepting Pinheiro's leadership they gained strength in numbers and were rewarded with political jobs and favors. For more than a decade the *gaúcho's* strong and colorful personality pervaded congressional and national politics. In the opinion of the American chargé d'affaires at Rio de Janeiro, Pinheiro 'may even be said to entirely dominate the political situation in Brazil.'[9]

Pinheiro Machado's growing reputation as the 'kingmaker' was illustrated in 1905 when he swung the support of the Bloc to the *mineiro* leader, Afonso Pena, and, in so doing, prevented a *paulista* from being nominated as presidential candidate. Rodrigues Alves accepted that it was politically impossible to elect another *paulista* and that the selection of a *mineiro* was appropriate, if not overdue. It was, however, the first time that an incumbent president was unable to secure the nomination of his choice of successor. The course of events also marked a visible set-back to São Paulo by bringing an end to the period of *paulista* presidents that had lasted since 1894. On the other hand, the 'politics of the governors' continued to function smoothly in that the 'official' candidate, Afonso Pena, secured almost 98 percent of the votes cast and won by 288,000 votes to 5,000.

Despite having had the endorsement of Pinheiro Machado in the presidential election, Afonso Pena regarded the *gaúcho* leader as too conservative and obstructive a force in the National Congress. Their awkward relationship was expressed in conflict over the choice of the next president. For the 1910 election Pena wanted the nomination of a fellow-*mineiro* and eventually chose his finance minister, Davi Campista. In an attempt to assert his own political influence over the president and also to enhance the national

[100] political standing of Rio Grande do Sul, Pinheiro backed the candidacy of Marshal Hermes (Rodrigues) da Fonseca. Hermes was a native of Rio Grande do Sul and the nephew of Deodoro da Fonseca. A career soldier, he became minister of war in the Pena administration and introduced a number of reforms to reorganize and strengthen the armed services. In particular, he sponsored legislation providing for future military conscription and made a well-publicized visit to Germany in 1909 to observe the training and maneuvers of the German army.

In May 1909 Hermes da Fonseca received the endorsement of Pinheiro Machado and the Bloc for the presidency. He accepted the nomination and resigned from the cabinet. The support of leading *mineiros* for Hermes was confirmed shortly afterwards by the selection of Venceslau Brás (Pereira Gomes) as vice-president. President Pena, however, continued to favor Campista and gained the adherence of the *paulista* élite who believed that the finance minister could be best relied upon to continue the policy of the Pena administration to promote exports and to provide federal financial aid for the valorization of coffee. But the death of Pena in June 1909 deprived Campista of his main support. His candidacy was effectively ended when the new president, Nilo (Procópio) Peçanha, endorsed Hermes. After dominating federal politics for so long, the *paulistas* were finally out-maneuvered. Their response was to turn to an 'outsider,' Rui Barbosa, the celebrated statesman from Bahia. After some years in the political wilderness, Rui Barbosa had attracted national attention and acclaim by his speeches brilliantly defending the rights of small nations at The Hague Conference on International Peace in 1907. On his return to Brazil, 'the eagle of The Hague' determined to fight for the political rights of the Brazilian people. Rui denounced the corrupt rule of the regional oligarchies and bosses and was scathing of their calculated efforts to obstruct liberal reforms. He was particularly apprehensive over the choice of Hermes as a presidential candidate and interpreted this as a calculated attempt to revive military influence in government and politics. According to Rui, the election represented a straightforward choice between civilian and military rule. Should Hermes da Fonseca win, Rui predicted that 'Brazil will plunge forever into the servitude of the armed forces.'[10] *Paulista* support for Rui Barbosa was reflected in the choice of Governor Manuel Albuquerque Lins of São Paulo as his running mate.

The lack of consensus among the state governors combined with Rui Barbosa's intervention meant that, for the first time in the history of the Republic, a truly contested election for the presidency occurred in 1910. There were even overtones of the famous American presidential election of 1896 as

Rui acted like the 'underdog,' William Jennings Bryan, and traveled large distances spreading the message of liberal reform to the people in rural as well as urban areas. The partisans of Marshal Hermes, however, were confident of victory because they had the backing of the leading state political machines. Only São Paulo and Bahia were opposed. Moreover, annoyed at Rui Barbosa's overtly anti-militarist campaign, army officers were much more willing to campaign than in previous elections and openly supported Hermes. The tried and tested ability of the governors and *coronéis* to deliver the votes needed for victory was evident in the final result which registered 233,000 votes for Hermes to 126,000 for Rui. Hermes even won in Salvador, the capital of Bahia, Rui's home state. 'A stupendous victory,' enthused Pinheiro Machado.[11] Moreover, both Pinheiro and Hermes could take satisfaction in having defeated not only Rui but also the *paulistas*, who had dominated presidential elections since 1894. Nevertheless, their delight was moderated by the fact that Hermes had recorded only just over 64 percent of the popular vote, the lowest percentage for a winning candidate up to that date.

The administration of Hermes da Fonseca bore certain similiarities with those of the two first military presidents. Each was confronted by a naval revolt in the harbor of Rio de Janeiro. For Hermes, the revolt occurred only a few days after assuming office in November 1910. The rising was not on the scale of 1893–94, but the mutiny by the crews of the nation's two most powerful battleships was humiliating to the federal authorities and signified that a decade of relative domestic peace had come to an end. Although the naval mutiny was overcome, civil disturbances subsequently sprang up in various parts of the country, sometimes erupting into violence that required the intervention of federal troops.

In marked contrast to his civilian predecessors, Hermes was more disposed to use his presidential powers and interfere directly, with military force if necessary, in the internal political affairs of the states. To an extent this was a deliberate policy formulated in consultation with Pinheiro Machado and designed not only to punish the regional élites who had backed Rui in the 1910 election but also to ensure that compliant regimes were put in their place. However, the junior army officers who carried out the interventions often possessed a very different rationale. In seeking to justify the overthrow of entrenched political machines and oligarchies, they talked of the 'politics of rescue' or 'salvation' (*política da salvação*) that ironically meant purging the republic of the same backward and reactionary vested interests that Rui had castigated in his campaign for the presidency. Prominent examples of 'salvation' took place in the northeastern states of Pernambuco and Bahia. In

[102] the latter case, federal forces bombarded the city of Salvador from the sea and invaded by land in January 1912. Fighting also occurred in Ceará and revolved around the activities of a charismatic and unfrocked priest, Padre Cícero (Romão Batista) who, like Antonio Conselheiro, had attracted thousands of devoted followers to his headquarters at Juazeiro in the backlands of the Northeast. In 1913 federal forces remained neutral while Padre Cícero successfully asserted his independent authority and organized an army that marched on Fortaleza to bring down a state government that was opposed to President Hermes. After 1912 a major disturbance also broke out in the South where the preachings of Miguel Lucena Boaventura, known as José Maria 'the Monk,' resulted in the establishment of a millenarian community very similar to Canudos in the 'Contestado,' a disputed region claimed by both the states of Paraná and Santa Catarina. In contrast to Antonio Conselheiro, José Maria died very early in the movement. His followers believed, however, that he would return from the dead. After the humiliating repulse of several federal army expeditions, federal forces eventually crushed the rebels in October 1915.

Although President Hermes da Fonseca and Pinheiro Machado remained close political allies and confidants, the pursuit of the 'politics of salvation' actually posed a serious threat to the political influence of the *gaúcho* leader. Indeed, many of the regional oligarchies that were challenged were allies of Pinheiro and had joined his new political party, the Republican Conservative Party (*Partido Republicano Conservador* or PRC), which he had formed in November 1910 to replace the Bloc. In addition to the fragmentation of the PRC, Pinheiro also faced the continuing hostility of the *paulista* political élite that was determined to prevent him from succeeding Hermes as president in 1914. The obvious alternative candidate was Rui Barbosa, but his chances of success were regarded as slim so long as he was opposed by the military. The uncertainty was broken by the *mineiros* who proposed the nomination of their former state governor and current vice-president of the republic, Venceslau Brás. The *paulistas* responded by announcing their support for Brás, thereby reviving the *café-com-leite* arrangement and, in the process, dashing Pinheiro's personal hopes for the presidency. Pinheiro realistically accepted defeat and endorsed Brás. In return, he was compensated with the selection of his preferred choice, Senator Urbano Santos of Maranhão, as vice-presidential candidate. The outward show of unity was impressive and resulted in Brás securing more than 90 percent of the popular vote. The American ambassador at Rio de Janeiro reported that the election 'passed off so quietly that the public was scarcely aware of it' and added that it 'has been carried out on the habitual lines and the wishes of the people have been subordinated, as usual, [103] to those of the dominant political group.'[12]

The nomination of Venceslau Brás demonstrated that the coalition of state parties formed by Pinheiro Machado and backed by Rio Grande do Sul could not prevail over the wishes of a *mineiro–paulista* alliance. Moreover, Pinheiro's personal political power had definitely waned and he was no longer regarded as the 'kingmaker.' This was confirmed by the new president's choice of cabinet, which included a number of the *gaúcho's* political enemies. The likelihood of a political counter-attack from Pinheiro was ruled out by his assassination in September 1915. The fact that no politician in the National Congress was able to take Pinheiro's place was testimony to his remarkable political skills. Moreover, a vacuum in leadership meant that the PRC, like the PRF before it, never became a viable national political party. Consequently, the next presidential succession in 1918 was dominated by the *mineiros* and *paulistas* and proceeded very much according to plan. The former president, Rodrigues Alves, was nominated to succeed Venceslau Brás and in the ensuing unopposed election he won 99 percent of the popular vote.

'Coffee-with-milk'

Chronic illness, however, prevented Rodrigues Alves from taking office and he died in January 1919. The choice of successor was complicated by a division between Minas Gerais and São Paulo, in which each state favored its own governor. Among the other alternative candidates, Rui Barbosa was the best-known but also the most controversial. The stalemate was broken when Epitácio (Lindolfo da Silva) Pessôa, a senator from Paraíba, emerged as an acceptable compromise. Although he represented a small northeastern state, Pessôa had impressed the *paulistas* when he had served as minister of justice under Campos Sales. He had also recently attracted favorable publicity and national attention as head of the Brazilian delegation at the Versailles Peace Conference. Notwithstanding Pessôa's personal merits, Rui Barbosa protested that the oligarchies were blatantly seeking to impose their personal choice upon the people. He decided, therefore, to contest the special presidential election scheduled for April 1919. When the election was held Pessôa was en route home from Paris and was not even present in Brazil. Nevertheless, the result was very similar to 1910. Although Rui Barbosa gained almost 30 percent of the vote, the 'official' candidate recorded a comfortable victory with almost 286,000 votes to just over 116,000.

[104]   Epitácio Pessôa eventually assumed the presidential office on July 28, 1919. In his choice of cabinet members, the new president displayed an unexpectedly independent streak in putting civilian politicians instead of military figures in charge of the war and navy departments. Senior officers in both the army and navy judged the appointments to be deliberately provocative and offensive. Relations with the military deteriorated further when the president vetoed the military budget. A leading critic of Pessôa was the former president, Hermes da Fonseca, who had recently returned to Brazil after residence in Europe and had been elected president of the Military Club in Rio. Pessôa was also subject to political criticism over his ambitious program of federal financial assistance for irrigation projects in the drought-ridden Northeast. Around 15 percent of the federal budget was allocated for this purpose in 1921–22. In effect, Pessôa was using the patronage of the presidency to aid his own region and reward his political supporters. While this policy boosted his prestige and influence in the northeastern states, those same states lacked sufficient presidential votes to make Pessôa a serious candidate for the 1922 presidential election.

Pessôa recognized that he was only an interim president and made no objection in 1921 when the *mineiro* and *paulista* political leaders nominated Artur (da Silva) Bernardes, the governor of Minas Gerais, as the official presidential candidate. But the clear intention of the *mineiros* and *paulistas* to control and monopolize the presidency by rotating it between their two states once again provoked growing dissatisfaction. In retaliation, the states of Bahia, Pernambuco, Rio de Janeiro and Rio Grande do Sul joined together to form an opposition known as the 'Republican Reaction' (*Reação Republicana*) and backed the former president Nilo Peçanha as an opposition candidate. The campaign mounted by Nilo Peçanha and the Republican Reaction condemned the 'imperialism' of Minas Gerais and São Paulo and complained that the regions were unfairly neglected.

The Republican Reaction realized that they lacked sufficient votes to defeat the *mineiro–paulista* alliance, but hoped to attract support from the military by exploiting the latter's known disaffection with Epitácio Pessôa. This was forthcoming at the very start of campaigning in October 1921 with the publication in a Rio newspaper of leaked letters allegedly written by Bernardes that referred to Nilo Peçanha as a mulatto, described Hermes da Fonseca as 'that overblown sergeant'[13] and accused senior army officers of bribery and corruption. At first the 'Bernardes Letters' were widely believed to be authentic, though some months later they were acknowledged as forgeries. In the meantime, however, Hermes and many senior officers accepted their authenticity and consequently endorsed Nilo. Though both sides claimed [105] victory in the ensuing election, Bernardes was given a clear majority with 56 percent of the popular vote. Despite demands for a recount from Nilo's supporters, Bernardes was officially declared the winner. The outcome demonstrated yet again that Brazil's presidents were chosen by an oligarchical élite and that the 'official' candidate never lost an election.

The poor relations between Pessôa and the army had been a prominent feature of the electoral campaign and continued to deteriorate after the election. An increasingly divisive issue was the frequent deployment by the president of federal troops to interfere in disputed state elections. Although the practice had been common under Deodoro and Floriano and had been revived by Hermes, officers complained that Epitácio Pessôa was using the army as a purely political instrument. The grievance was expressed in a telegram sent from Hermes to the commander of the federal army garrison of Recife, Pernambuco, stating that 'politics passes, the army stays.'[14] The comment was interpreted to mean that presidential orders for the military to intervene in local politics should be resisted. When Pessôa learnt of the telegram in July 1922 he judged it to be a deliberate act of insubordination and immediately ordered the house arrest of Hermes and closure of the Military Club for six months. Two days later on July 5, 1922 the garrison at Fort Copacabana and several hundred cadets at the nearby Realengo Military Academy in Rio de Janeiro revolted. The ostensible purpose was to protest the arrest of Hermes, but there was also a vague plan to mount a coup similar to that of 1889 which would place the military in power and thereby prevent Bernardes from becoming president. The revolt was essentially a spontaneous gesture of protest that was rapidly and easily overcome by loyal government forces. However, there was heroic resistance from a group of eighteen junior officers who emerged from Fort Copacabana determined to fight to the death on the beach. Five died and the survivors became national heroes. Despite the defeat of the revolt, it was subsequently regarded as a glorious and heroic episode.

Despite its failure, the 1922 Revolt was historically very significant in providing the first manifestation of a movement led by junior army officers, mainly lieutenants (*tenentes*), and known as *tenentismo*. The *tenentes* represented only a minority of the officer corps but their ideas were highly influential within the military. They wanted a strong and prosperous Brazil, but had little confidence in the Republic and its civilian politicians whom they regarded as corrupt, vain and inefficient. Given the closed nature of the political system, the *tenentes* were prepared to advocate the use of force to bring about a change of government. But the *tenentes* wanted more than just a change of personnel at the top. They called for radical economic and social reform to alleviate and eventually eliminate poverty in the cities and the countryside. *Tenentismo* never developed into an organized political movement with a coherent program, but its revolutionary ideas had wide appeal and posed a direct threat to the power that the regional oligarchies and bosses had wielded for so long.

With his reputation already severely damaged by accusations of fraudulent election and the legacy of the 'Letters,' Bernardes took office in November 1922 amid growing economic and political crisis. Subsequently, he became even more controversial and unpopular because of his frequent proclamations of states of siege and interventions in state politics, ostensibly to maintain law and order but also aimed at asserting presidential authority and installing his own political supporters in positions of power. Moreover, the president's reputation for being personally vindictive appeared to be reinforced by censorship of the press and the refusal to grant amnesty to the officers involved in the 1922 Revolt. A policy of strict fiscal conservatism also made Bernardes appear unsympathetic to business and industry. Particularly controversial was his decision to withdraw federal financial support for the valorization of coffee and for the irrigation projects that his predecessor had initiated in the Northeast. So unpopular did Bernardes become that for some time he remained confined within the presidential palace and would not make public appearances.

Despite his concern for his personal safety, Bernardes was not a weak president and vigorously resisted challenges to his authority. The major crisis occurred on July 5, 1924, the second anniversary of the revolt at Copacabana, when a serious military rising erupted among federal army units in São Paulo. The rebels condemned the excessive use of presidential authority and demanded the restoration of constitutional liberties. With the support of the *paulista força pública*, the rebels were able to retain control of the city for 22 days before deciding to evacuate under pressure of a massive assault from greatly superior numbers of government troops. The federal army remained loyal to Bernardes and proceeded to repress smaller revolts that had broken out in Sergipe, Amazonas and Rio Grande do Sul. Led by Captain Luís Carlos Prestes, a group of rebels moved north from Rio Grande and eventually linked up with the soldiers who had fled from São Paulo. In March 1925 they began a march into the interior with the intention of mobilizing the peasants in violent revolution against Bernardes. For almost two years the force, numbering around 1,500 and known as the 'Prestes Column' (*Coluna Prestes*), covered 15,000 miles across the North and Northeast. Several battles and skirmishes were fought before the Prestes Column reached Bolivia in February 1927, where they decided to disband. The march did not succeed in establishing a permanent base of operations nor in mobilizing the peasantry as a political force, but it captured the public imagination and drew attention to the issues of massive rural poverty and deprivation. Prestes was so influenced by his experiences that he declared himself a Marxist in 1929. He visited the Soviet Union in 1931 and later became leader of the Brazilian Communist Party. Few *tenentes* followed his example, but *tenentismo* noticeably became more concerned with stressing the vital importance of economic development as a means of promoting fundamental social and political change.

While the Prestes Column fought its way across the backlands, national politics proceeded in their customary and élitist fashion. According to the *café-com-leite* arrangement, Bernardes would be succeeded by a *paulista*. Indeed, the *paulistas* felt that a president from their state was long overdue. Although Rodrigues Alves had been elected in 1918, he had not actually taken up office, so that there had not been a serving president from São Paulo since 1906. A convention of state governors met in September 1925 to nominate the governor of São Paulo, Washington Luís (Pereira da Sousa), for president. Fernando de Melo Viana of Minas Gerais was selected for vice-president. The *café-com-leite* slate was unopposed. The death of Rui Barbosa in March 1923 had removed the one individual who possessed the national reputation and standing to launch a contested election. The campaign was conducted against a backdrop of public apathy and cynicism. Washington Luís duly won the election with more than 98 percent of the popular vote. The result had been a foregone conclusion. As part of the various deals that had been struck by the candidate with the governors, a number of political bosses were appointed to the cabinet, one of which was the rising *gaúcho* politician, Getúlio (Dornelles) Vargas, who became minister of finance at the age of 43.

The 1930 revolution

Washington Luís was a more affable and congenial personality than Bernardes and this was reflected in his greater public popularity. In addition, he lifted a number of states of siege and relaxed restrictions on the press. His period in office, however, was increasingly dominated by economic problems. The financial priority of the administration was to achieve a budgetary surplus and to maintain the value of the currency. Initially the policy was highly successful, but the worldwide economic crash occurring in 1929 brought about a collapse in foreign trade and investment leading to a sharp

[108]   fall in the value of the currency. The coffee plantation owners were particularly affected by the sudden economic downturn.

Concerned to secure continuity of economic policy, Washington Luís
selected Júlio Prestes (de Albuquerque), the then governor of São Paulo, as
his successor. Not only did Washington Luís have confidence in the financial
competency of Prestes but he also believed that São Paulo was the nation's
most wealthy and successful state and, therefore, merited a longer hold on
the presidency. The choice, however, upset the *café-com-leite* arrangement.
The governor of Minas, Antonio Carlos (Ribeiro de Andrada), was distrustful
of Washington Luís and had already clashed with the president over the direction of economic policy. To thwart the *paulistas*, Antonio Carlos persuaded
Getúlio Vargas to contest the election. Vargas had resigned as finance minister
in the Washington Luís administration to become governor of Rio Grande
do Sul in January 1928. The states of Rio Grande do Sul, Minas Gerais and
Paraíba formed a coalition known as the Liberal Alliance (*Aliança Liberal*)
to conduct his campaign. João Pessôa, governor of Paraíba and nephew of
ex-president Epitácio Pessôa, was nominated as vice-presidential candidate.

The presidential contest in 1930 was hardly equal. The 'official' candidate,
Júlio Prestes, enjoyed the backing of the incumbent president and a political
alliance led by São Paulo that consisted of the large majority of the state
political machines. By contrast, only the three states of Minas Gerais, Rio
Grande do Sul and Paraíba officially endorsed Getúlio Vargas and the Liberal
Alliance. The origins of the Liberal Alliance lay in anti-*paulista* sentiment and
especially the personal resentment of the *mineiro* governor in being passed
over for the presidency. But the Liberal Alliance also attempted to present a
broader appeal. This was demonstrated in the only public speech that Vargas
delivered outside Rio Grande do Sul. In Rio de Janeiro on January 2, 1930 he
not only criticized the selfish policies of the oligarchies but also sought to
appeal to the urban middle classes and industrial workers by undertaking to
improve health, education and welfare benefits. Despite his radical rhetoric,
Vargas was essentially conciliatory and non-confrontational. In terms of
political ideology he was more a liberal democrat than a revolutionary. This
was recognized by the pro-Marxist, Luís Carlos Prestes, and was used to
justify his own refusal to endorse Vargas for the presidency. Moreover, few
workers played an active or visible role in Vargas's electoral campaign.

In March 1930 Júlio Prestes secured victory over Vargas with almost 58
percent of the popular vote. Electoral fraud had no doubt occurred, but this
applied to both sides. Pernambuco, for example, was typical of states backing
the 'official' candidate in giving Prestes almost 90 percent of the popular vote

while Vargas received just over 10 percent. In Rio Grande do Sul, however, the state's 'favorite son' was awarded almost 300,000 votes while Prestes was given less than 1,000. Although Vargas publicly accepted the result, discontent simmered and some of his supporters, led by his closest aide, Osvaldo (Euclides de Sousa) Aranha, secretly plotted a coup to prevent Prestes from being installed as president. Undertakings of military support for Vargas were forthcoming from the commander of the federal forces in Rio Grande, Colonel (Pedro Aurélio de) Góes Monteiro, and prominent *tenentes* in the Northeast such as Juarez (do Nascimento) Távora and João Alberto. Meanwhile, tensions were visibly heightened in May when the National Congress, under instructions from Washington Luís, refused to recognize the election of opposition deputies from the states of Minas Gerais and Paraíba. In July Vargas's running mate, João Pessôa, was murdered in Recife. Although the murder was caused by a local political feud, speculation was rife that it was a calculated act of political revenge in which President Washington Luís was implicated. The murder dramatically revived the Liberal Alliance and provided it with a martyr.

The idea of using force to overthrow an elected government was boosted by a successful military coup in Argentina on September 6. Vargas's caution was finally put aside and he gave instructions for the revolt to proceed. The military uprising began simultaneously in Rio Grande do Sul, Minas Gerais, and Paraíba on October 3. The proclaimed aim was to 'restore' liberal democracy and promote economic recovery by overthrowing the government of Washington Luís. The president was unprepared militarily and appeared confused by the turn of events. Moreover, the federal army showed a distinct reluctance to fight and several units defected to the rebels. When the government lost control of several Northeastern state capitals and a large rebel army from the South marched steadily closer to São Paulo, the attitude of senior army officers in Rio de Janeiro became critically important and ultimately decisive. In a manner reminiscent of Dom Pedro's exercise of the moderating power, they judged that Washington Luís was unable to defeat the rebels and that the installation of President-elect Júlio Prestes was impossible. Army chief of staff General Augusto Tasso Fragoso explained that 'agitation had erupted everywhere' and posed the threat of a 'national revolution such as had never been seen.'[15] In order to restore peace, the president was placed under arrest on October 24. Shortly afterwards he left the country. As it had been in 1889, the army was directly instrumental in bringing down the government in 1930. A military junta temporarily assumed the executive powers of government and one week later handed over power to Vargas. On November 3 Vargas

[110]   formally took office as 'chief of the provisional government.' On November 11 he suspended the 1891 Constitution and thereby brought an end to the 'First' Republic.

Economy

Crisis and recovery

During the last quarter of the nineteenth century Brazil was a principal beneficiary of the massive flow of people, capital and goods associated with the rapid growth of the world economy and was bracketed with Argentina and Chile as one of the leading economic nations of South America. This standing was scarcely affected by the sudden change from empire to republic in 1889. In fact, the last imperial government headed by the Viscount of Ouro Preto was notably in favor of economic expansion. To alleviate the damaging economic effects of the abolition of slavery in 1888, it had sought to aid the former slave-owners by increasing the money supply and making substantial loans to private banks. The results were gratifying in that economic confidence was boosted and the foreign exchange value of the *milréis* rose to the high level of 27 pence. Consequently, the provisional government, in which Rui Barbosa was finance minister, came into being in November 1889 at a propitious time. Despite his lack of practical experience in financial administration, Rui subscribed to the economic theory that government should play a positive role in encouraging economic activity. He was determined, therefore, to continue the measures undertaken by Ouro Preto to increase the money supply. This policy was considerably facilitated by the Banking Act of January 1890 that allowed private banks to issue substantial amounts of new paper currency that could be redeemed with Treasury bonds rather than gold.

The act of removing regulations in order to promote economic activity and enterprise fitted in very well with the desire of liberal politicians and intellectuals who saw the change of regime in 1889 as a historic opportunity to reject the imperial past and transform Brazil into a modern economy. The policy also contained many political attractions and financial rewards for the power élite. In the short term, printing substantial quantities of paper banknotes certainly gave a boost to the economy as the amount of money in circulation doubled in 1890 and grew by 125 percent in the period from 1889 to 1891. The biggest gain, however, was in financial services. Several new banks were created and trading on the stock market reached new record levels in response to the floating of a host of joint-stock companies seeking to raise capital. The stock market boom was referred to by the popular racing term of *Encilhamento* ('saddling-up') and suddenly ended in late 1891 with a spectacular crash and a wave of bankruptcies. The rest of society, especially urban workers, was not spared and suffered from inflation and rising unemployment. Furthermore, the symbolic indicator of the health of the national economy, the foreign exchange value of the *milréis*, collapsed to less than one third of its former value. Instead of producing a strong and prosperous economy, the inflationary policy of the provisional government had been a failure. In addition, it had seriously damaged Brazil's international image and credit reputation. The *Encilhamento* had a political impact too and contributed to the overthrow of Deodoro da Fonseca in November 1891. Though no longer finance minister, Rui was blamed for financial imprudence and the *Encilhamento* permanently tarnished his political reputation.

Although the *Encilhamento* revealed the risks of government intervention in the economy, it also highlighted the serious shortcomings of private enterprise and, therefore, served to justify an increase rather than a reduction in the interventionist role of the federal government. Despite the decentralized nature of the republic, central economic direction and regulation became accepted as necessary to achieve financial stability. For example, after the *Encilhamento* the federal government felt compelled to monitor the money supply more carefully and withdrew the authority of private banks to issue new banknotes in December 1892. Successive presidential administrations throughout the 1890s pursued a policy of deflation and stressed the importance of balancing the federal budget by increasing taxes and reducing expenditures. Raising additional government revenue during the Republic, however, was just as difficult as it had been during the Empire because there was considerable political and social resistance to increasing taxes on land and property. Moreover, the other main source of income, the export tax, had been transferred to the states. During the administration of Floriano Peixoto considerable attention was directed to levying duties on foreign imports, a policy which was also justified as tariff protection for Brazilian manufactures against the competition of cheap foreign goods. In fact, the federal government continued to derive around 70 percent of its annual income from this source.

Floriano found it impossible to restrain money supply and balance the budget because he had to meet unexpected financial costs arising from serious internal disturbances such as the Naval Revolt and the civil war in Rio Grande do Sul. Consequently, the foreign exchange value of the *milréis* fell to 10 pence

[112]   in 1892. The devaluation of the *milréis* not only damaged Brazil's international reputation and ability to raise foreign loans, but it also had the practical effect of making it more expensive to service the foreign debt because the payments were usually made in gold. The low point was reached in 1898 just after the election to the presidency of Campos Sales when it was estimated that servicing of the foreign debt would absorb more than half the federal budget. Even after stringent economies were taken into account, a deficit of £4 million was forecast. A vicious economic circle had been created in which the *milréis* steadily dropped to 5 pence and the country's gold reserves were seriously depleted.

Effectively bankrupt, Brazil was saved from financial disaster by the 1898 Funding Loan. This was an arrangement that the Brazilian government negotiated with the British bankers, the House of Rothschild, for a loan of £8.5 million to 'fund' Brazil's budgetary deficit and promote the country's economic recovery. The terms were favorable in that interest payments were deferred for three years and a further moratorium of ten years was placed on the repayment of the original capital sum. The loan, however, was conditional on President Campos Sales undertaking to balance the federal budget and setting targets to reduce the amount of paper money in circulation. Despite criticism that the administration was too subservient to foreign bankers, Campos Sales and his finance minister, Joaquim (Duarte) Murtinho, firmly believed that a strict deflationary policy was absolutely necessary to achieve financial stability and economic growth. Moreover, a balanced budget would reduce inflation and help Brazil regain the confidence of foreign investors. This would improve the value of the *milréis* and make it easier to service the foreign debt. Despite the occurrence of a severe banking crisis in 1900, the deflationary policy demonstrated success in 1901 when the *milréis* reached more than 10 pence in value and the government was able to make repayments of the foreign debt in gold. During the administration of Rodrigues Alves from 1902 to 1906 the *milréis* climbed in value from 12 to 16 pence. The Brazilian Treasury was also able to build up a sizeable holding of gold reserves in London. Confidence in Brazil was demonstrated by the relatively easy raising of foreign loans to finance public works programs, especially for the improvement of the city and port of Rio de Janeiro.

King Coffee

Although republican Brazil remained essentially an agrarian economy with the large majority of the population living in the countryside and working on the land, the agricultural sector was overshadowed by the flourishing export economy, which was regarded as the mainstay of the national wealth. Brazil was traditionally a large exporter of staple agricultural products, especially sugar. By the end of the nineteenth century, however, the principal exports were coffee and rubber. These two commodities accounted for over 80 percent of the country's foreign trade and underpinned a regular surplus in the national balance of payments until World War I.

The discovery and exploitation of wild rubber in the Amazon region had made Brazil the world leader in rubber production. Many large fortunes were made from the ensuing 'rubber boom' but not as much as from coffee, which was 'king' in Brazil and provided more than two thirds of total export earnings by the end of the nineteenth century. The cultivation of coffee and its export enjoyed spectacular growth during the 1890s as a result of the expansionist monetary policy of the provisional government and buoyant world demand, especially in the United States. By the first decade of the twentieth century Brazil far outranked other producers and possessed around 80 percent of the world coffee trade. Among the states of Brazil, São Paulo was by far the largest producer. In fact, the tax on coffee exports made São Paulo the wealthiest state in the Republic, which both released and attracted further funds for investment into the industry and its infrastructure.

During the 1880s Brazil's output of coffee averaged 5 million bags a year. The lure of high profits resulted in the planting of millions of new trees, leading to a bumper crop of 16 million bags in 1901. The inelasticity of world demand for coffee meant, however, that abundant supplies inevitably depressed both prices and profits. Moreover, the deflationary policy associated with the 1898 Funding Loan resulted in a higher foreign exchange value that reduced the amount of *milréis* earned from coffee exports. Depressed profit margins and the prospect of further massive annual crops in excess of 20 million bags prompted the governments of Rio de Janeiro State, Minas Gerais and São Paulo to hold a convention at Taubaté, São Paulo, in 1906. Discussion centered upon how to reverse the trend of falling prices. Although some consideration was given to means of curbing production, the *paulistas* preferred not to interfere with cultivation. They favored the prior purchase and storage of coffee in order to withhold supplies from the world market. In this way coffee would be increased in value or 'valorized.'

The idea of manipulating the international price of coffee aroused little initial enthusiasm from the federal government even though a *paulista*, Rodrigues Alves, was currently serving as president of the republic. Nor were the other state governments sympathetic to the proposed scheme. Not only

[114] was 'valorization' regarded as enormously expensive but it was also criticized as designed primarily and selfishly to serve the sectional interests of the *paulistas*. Nevertheless, as the largest coffee producer, the state of São Paulo felt compelled to implement the scheme on its own. But prices did not immediately recover, so that the state government was soon burdened with large debts and huge stocks of coffee amounting to several million bags. State bankruptcy was only forestalled by a reversal of federal policy in 1907. So important was the welfare of the coffee trade to the national economy and Brazil's financial reputation that President Afonso Pena was persuaded to guarantee foreign loans contracted by São Paulo for the purpose of valorization. 'I am not inclined, as you know, towards government intervention in commodity markets,' Afonso Pena wrote to Rodrigues Alves, 'but in view of the exceptional situation in which we find ourselves, I believe the aid requested completely justified.'[16]

Federal support was tardy and reactive to events, but it enabled São Paulo to enter into arrangements with foreign merchants and bankers to finance the storage of its surplus coffee stocks. The price of coffee duly rose and earnings from exports were increased. Rising prices for domestic consumers, however, attracted unfavorable comment especially in the United States, where an anti-trust action was launched by the Justice Department in 1912. This forced the sale and disposal of valorized stocks of coffee held in the United States. Although the first valorization scheme was wound up in 1913, Brazilians believed that it had been successful in mitigating the problem of coffee overproduction by securing price stability. Consequently, similar federal intervention to support coffee prices was repeated during World War I. In response to the wartime decline in coffee exports a large loan was made to the state government of São Paulo in 1917 to aid the purchase of more than 3 million bags of coffee.

World War I

The significance attached to international commodity prices and the level of demand for Brazilian products in overseas markets highlighted the close relationship between Brazil and the world economy based on Western Europe and North America. Foreigners were particularly attracted to Brazil's export economy and invested heavily in port facilities, railways and banking services. In 1889 the total amount of foreign investment in Brazil was around $600 million, and rose to over $2.5 billion in 1930. In terms of public debt, Brazil had the largest in Latin America, rising from $564 million in 1912 to just over $1 billion in 1928. When exports boomed, sufficient foreign [115] exchange was earned to service the debt. At times of contracting world trade, however, the federal government often resorted to large foreign loans to fund anticipated budgetary deficits and protect the export economy. But foreign loans exacted more than just the repayment of capital and interest. As the 1898 Funding Loan demonstrated, foreign bankers frequently insisted that the federal government give an undertaking to pursue conservative and deflationary financial policies.

The adverse consequences of stressing export-led growth and reliance on inflows of foreign capital were demonstrated by World War I. The war broke out in 1914 at a difficult time for the Brazilian economy. A collapse in the world price of rubber in 1911 had been followed by the loss of overseas markets to the more efficient rubber producers of the Far East. The ensuing 'rubber crisis' combined with a simultaneous fall in coffee prices to result in a deficit in the balance of payments for the first time since the 1880s. The American ambassador, Edwin Morgan, even feared that 'national bankruptcy' was imminent.[17] Despite appeals from the state governments of Pará and Amazonas for federal financial support, there was however no political disposition to 'valorize' rubber. Instead, as it had done in 1898, the federal government intended to meet the financial shortfall by borrowing in London. Hostilities in Europe disrupted negotiations, but a large loan was eventually arranged with the Rothschilds in October 1914. Subsequently, however, the war temporarily closed Brazil's traditional source of foreign capital in Europe.

Meanwhile, the federal deficit was further increased by the loss of customs revenue arising from the contraction of the import trade with Europe. Exports were also adversely affected as British naval power gradually curtailed all commercial contact with the Central Powers of Germany and Austria, thus depriving Brazil of its second largest coffee market. No alternative outlets materialized because coffee was not considered an essential commodity by the Allies and was, therefore, not given an adequate allocation of shipping for export purposes. As the war continued, further obstacles were placed in the way of trade by the imposition of Allied wartime regulations prohibiting British and French commercial dealings with allegedly pro-German Brazilian firms. The result was a sharp decline in Brazilian exports from £40 million in 1913–14 to £27 million in 1914–15. Business revived in 1915, owing to increased Allied orders for sugar and other staple agricultural products, but it was not until the postwar boom of 1919 that Brazilian exports recovered to their 1913 levels.

[116]   On the other hand, the 'external shock' of World War I had a constructive influence on the growth of the Brazilian economy. Up to 1889 the development of Brazilian industry had been sparse because economic resources were concentrated on the export sector. In addition, the large majority of manufactured and capital goods were traditionally imported from overseas. However, led by cotton textiles, flour mills and food processing, industry took advantage of monetary inflation, tariff protection and a depreciating *milréis* to take a bigger share of the domestic market during the 1890s and continued to grow, though at a more modest rate, during the following decade. The outbreak of World War I damaged Brazilian exports, but it conversely stimulated local industry by reducing the volume of imported consumer goods from Europe. In the case of well-established domestic industries such as textiles and clothing, the switch from handicraft to factory production was accelerated and Brazil became almost self-sufficient in these products. Another successful wartime industry was iron and steel. Starting virtually from scratch, the production of pig iron increased from 3,500 tons in 1915 to 11,700 tons in 1918. Although the economy was still dependent on foreign imports for coal, chemicals, machinery and capital goods, the advance of national industrial development during World War I was indicated in the census of 1920 that listed 13,336 firms, of which 5,936 or 44 percent had been created between 1915 and 1919. Most firms, however, employed a relatively small number of workers. It was estimated that industrial workers numbered 374,000 in 1920, amounting to 4 percent of the total work force.

The world war also altered Brazil's pattern of overseas trading by weakening established European interests and presenting a signal opportunity for the extension of United States commercial influence throughout Latin America. The United States already provided Brazil's biggest export market and its position was considerably strengthened as it took not only a greater percentage of coffee, but also almost all the manganese, and the largest single share of hides, cocoa, and rubber. American businessmen sought to take full advantage of Europe's commercial disarray. In April 1915 the British minister at Rio de Janeiro reported that 'the United States are making great efforts.'[18] He jealously noted the frequent arrival of commercial missions, the opening of an American branch bank in the capital, and the proposal to establish a direct steamship line with New York. The process was, therefore, under way in which the United States replaced Great Britain as the major source of new capital investment in Brazil. While British investment grew by approximately $252 million between 1913 and 1929, American investment rose by $426 million during the same period.

The 1920s

Although industrialization continued throughout the 1920s, output grew at a slower annual rate than during the previous decade. Development remained concentrated on light manufacturing, especially textiles, shoes and food processing. Brazilian industry also continued to import substantial amounts of machinery and capital goods. Indeed, foreign investment was generally perceived as beneficial in creating new factories and employment. A celebrated example was the success of the Ford Motor Company, whose São Paulo plant assembled 2,000 motor vehicles in 1919 and increased this to 45,000 in 1925. More contentious was the concern of nationalists that foreigners were buying up substantial amounts of national territory and gaining control of valuable economic resources. The schemes of the American entrepreneur, Percival Farquhar, to exploit the vast iron-ore deposits located at Itabira in Minas Gerais excited particular suspicion and stimulated a debate over the future control of the country's iron and steel industries.

The most important economic activity, however, was still the export of agricultural products and especially coffee. Indeed, the fluctuating fortunes of the coffee industry were the prominent feature of the Brazilian economy during the 1920s. Wartime restrictions had temporarily reduced coffee exports so that their value slumped to merely one third of the nation's annual export total. The end of the war and the sudden release of pent-up consumer demand in North America and Europe resulted, however, in a surge of coffee exports in 1919. But the postwar boom was short-lived. A glut of coffee drove down prices and profits. Other Brazilian exports were similarly affected and contributed to a deficit in the balance of payments in 1920. Moreover, the foreign exchange value of the *milréis*, which had remained above 12 pence during the war, plunged to 8 pence. To prevent the currency from falling further in value, the federal government was persuaded to give financial support to a renewed valorization scheme designed to arrest the decline in coffee prices. 'The defense of coffee,' explained President Epitácio Pessôa in October 1921, 'thus constitutes a national problem, the solution to which is vital for a sound economic and financial policy in Brazil.'[19]

The international price of coffee recovered in 1922 and soon increased to its highest level for more than a decade. At the same time Brazilian exports of coffee boomed and represented more than 70 percent of the value of the country's annual export trade. Although the 1921 valorization undoubtedly contributed to the revival of prices, the most influential factors were the lack of serious international competition and especially the sustained demand for

[118] coffee in the economically prosperous North American market. In fact, the prosperity of the coffee industry enabled President Artur Bernardes to reject *paulista* proposals for the federal government to underwrite a continuous and systematic policy known as the 'permanent defense' of coffee. Bernardes had come to office in 1922 determined to balance the federal budget and maintain the foreign exchange value of the *milréis*. While recognizing the efficacy of valorization during periods of acute overproduction of coffee, he wished to avoid an expensive federal commitment to a permanent policy of price support. There was also awareness that the issue of valorization exerted a negative influence in the negotiation of foreign loans because overseas bankers and their governments were suspicious of concerted efforts to manipulate international prices. Domestic critics cynically suggested that, as a *mineiro*, Bernardes was merely displaying the characteristic sense of rivalry between his own state and São Paulo, but the view that valorization should be the responsibility of the coffee-producing states had been held by previous presidents, including the *paulista*, Rodrigues Alves. Consequently, as it had done in 1906, the government of São Paulo recognized that action had to be taken independently and in December 1924 established a state agency, the Institute for the Permanent Defense of Coffee or 'Coffee Institute,' to organize the financing and direction of valorization. Minas Gerais and Rio de Janeiro State created similar state agencies.

In 1926 President Washington Luís succeeded Bernardes as president and inherited an outwardly stable economy that was enjoying the benefits of export-led growth. Both the balance of payments and the federal budget were in surplus in 1927, for the first time since 1908. Brazil appeared highly prosperous, an impression that was projected by the beginning of the construction of two major highways linking Rio de Janeiro with São Paulo and with Petrópolis. But a familiar crisis emerged in 1928. Once again the coffee industry was blighted with serious overproduction. This time, however, the cycle coincided with falling world demand. Further turmoil was created by the New York stock market crash in October 1929 and the ensuing collapse in the international price of coffee, which fell by a half in less than a year. The *paulista* Coffee Institute raised foreign loans to implement valorization, but the scale of the unfolding crisis was so great that Brazilian warehouses were glutted with stocks of unsold coffee. Despite his *paulista* background, Washington Luís firmly refused the suggestion that the money supply be increased to drive up the price of coffee. The president was quoted as saying that 'the planters are on their own.'[20]

Although Washington Luís was concerned over the emerging deficit in Brazil's balance of payments arising from the decline in coffee exports, he believed that a revival in trade was more likely to result from a lower rather than an artificially-created higher international price. His stated priority was to defend the value of the *milréis* and to meet financial shortfalls by arranging a large foreign loan as Campos Sales had done in 1898. Washington Luís, however, had not reckoned on the sheer severity of the world economic crisis which delivered an external shock to Brazil that was even greater than that associated with World War I. The result was a vicious circle in which the fall in the value of coffee exports meant not only a worsening of the balance of payments but also lower earnings of foreign exchange to service what had become the largest foreign debt in Latin America. In addition, the onset of world economic depression prevented the negotiation of a large funding loan from foreign bankers. Meanwhile, the country's gold reserves were steadily depleted and in March 1930 the Treasury abandoned its efforts to support the *milréis* in the foreign exchange market so that its value dropped to a new low, the equivalent of 5 pence. A major financial crash had contributed to the overthrow of the first president of the republic in 1891. An even greater economic disaster seriously weakened the government of Washington Luís and stimulated not only his personal downfall but also the collapse of the Republic in October 1930.

[119]

Society

Demography

The national population grew steadily during the Republic. The 1890 census recorded 14 million people in Brazil. Growing at an annual average of more than 2 percent, the number increased by 50 percent every two decades to reach 22 million in 1910 and over 33 million at the end of the Republic in 1930. The rise reflected natural population growth supplemented with substantial immigration from Europe. It was also very similar to the experiences of Argentina and the United States, the two other nations of the Western Hemisphere that also received a large net influx of foreign immigrants. Compared with Brazil there was a slightly higher rate of increase in the population of Argentina from 4 to 11 million, while the United States demonstrated a smaller proportional increase from 63 to 123 million.

Despite the more than doubling in the number of people during the period from 1890 to 1930, such was the territorial vastness of Brazil that the density of population remained low. In terms of geographical distribution there was still a marked preference for people to settle in the same narrow

[120] band of land close to the sea and running from Pará in the North to Rio Grande do Sul in the South, while large tracts of the interior were uninhabited or contained only small pockets of population. Within the area of settlement, however, the historical trend of internal migration from the North to the South continued after 1889. While the 1872 census indicated that the population of each section was broadly equal, the 1900 census showed that the South had 3 million more people than the North. The difference steadily widened in the twentieth century. The southern states that gained most population were São Paulo and Rio Grande do Sul. This pattern was illustrated in the change in the rank ordering of states according to population. At the beginning of the Republic Minas Gerais was the most populated state followed by Bahia, São Paulo, Pernambuco and Rio Grande do Sul. In 1930, however, the order had changed with São Paulo possessing the largest population followed by Minas Gerais, Bahia, Rio Grande do Sul and Pernambuco.

Internal migration was not just from the North to the South. Pulled by the attraction of work in the booming rubber industry and pushed by the destructive impact from a succession of droughts, especially the 'great drought' (*sêca*) of 1877–79, an estimated 150,000 migrants (*retirantes*) from the Northeast were drawn westwards to the Amazon during the 1890s. But they found that wages and living conditions in the Amazon region were scarcely better than in the Northeast. Another attractive destination for people from the North was the Federal District of Rio de Janeiro. From 1872 to 1920 Rio received more internal migrants than the state of São Paulo.

A prominent feature of Brazil's population growth during the Republic was immigration from Europe. The dramatic upsurge in the level of immigration from an annual average of 20,000 to more than 50,000 actually predated the 1889 coup and had started in the 1880s in response to the growth in the world economy, the increased mobility of labor in Europe and improved ocean-going transportation. Among the nations of the Western Hemisphere, Brazil was not so attractive a destination as the United States or Argentina, but its flourishing coffee industry offered employment opportunities. As a result almost 3 million immigrants arrived in Brazil during the period from 1889 to 1930. The peak year was 1891 when 215,000 immigrants entered the country. In fact, the 1890s recorded the highest levels of immigration in Brazilian history. The numbers began to decline after 1897, but another boom occurred in the years leading up to the outbreak of World War I in 1914. This wave of immigration peaked in 1913 with 192,000 arrivals, the second highest annual figure recorded for Brazil. Immigration collapsed during the world war, but recovered in the 1920s. The highest point in this wave of immigration was in 1926 when 121,000 immigrants entered [121] the country.

The flow of foreign immigration into Brazil was closely entwined with the growth of the economy of the state of São Paulo. Not only did the state absorb two thirds of all foreign immigrants to Brazil but, during the decade of the 1890s, more Europeans chose to emigrate to São Paulo than to Argentina. The influx of so many foreigners was evident in the 1920 census which showed that, while only 5 percent of the national population was foreign-born, the corresponding figure for the state of São Paulo was 18 percent. Italians were the largest single national group in São Paulo and numbered more than 1 million. So many chose to live in the city of São Paulo that it began to seem quite different from anywhere else in Brazil and was popularly referred to as 'the city of Italians.' The second-largest group in the state were the Portuguese, followed by the Spaniards. Immigrants from Italy, Portugal and Spain made up 80 percent of the foreign-born population and, in terms of language and culture, were easily assimilated. Not all immigrants, however, were from Europe. The first shipment of immigrants from Japan arrived at Santos in 1908. Just over a decade later the 1920 census revealed 24,000 Japanese-born residents of the state. After São Paulo, the Federal District and Rio Grande do Sul were the most favored destinations for foreign immigrants. Minas Gerais provided a stark contrast. Despite its ranking as the most populated state in the nation, only 1.5 percent of the population was classified as foreign-born in 1920. In the wave of immigration from 1908 up to World War I, statistics showed that Minas Gerais attracted only 6,600 immigrants while São Paulo received 363,000. Indeed, many Europeans who initially arrived in Minas Gerais decided to leave and move on to São Paulo.

Another notable aspect of demographic development during the Republic was the considerable increase in the population of Brazil's largest cities. From 1890 to 1920 Rio de Janeiro grew from 520,000 to over 1 million, Salvador from 175,000 to 283,000, Recife from 112,000 to 239,000 and São Paulo from 64,000 to 580,000. Although no more than 10 percent of Brazilians might be described as living in urban areas, cities attracted considerable contemporary discussion and admiration and were regarded as symbols of national progress. For this reason the *mineiros* began to build a new state capital at Belo Horizonte in 1897. On his visit to the Amazon in 1914 the former American president, Theodore Roosevelt, noted significant urban developments and cited Manaus and Belém as 'very striking examples of what can be done in the mid-tropics.' Manaus, the rubber capital of the world, was judged by Roosevelt to be 'a remarkable city,' which had been transformed in half

[122]   a century from 'a nameless little collection of hovels' into 'a big, handsome modern city, with opera house, tramways, good hotels, fine squares and public buildings, and attractive private houses.'[21] Cultural achievement was also evident in São Paulo where the Modern Art Week Show was held from February 11 to 17, 1922. The event formed part of the centennial celebrations of national independence and displayed striking evidence of Brazil's artistic and creative energy to the world.

The most celebrated example of urban change and modernization during the Republic occurred in the national capital of Rio de Janeiro. From 1903 to 1906 under the direction of the City Prefect, (Francisco) Pereira Passos, several narrow streets and tenements (*cortiços*) of the 'old' city were demolished and replaced with Parisian-style boulevards and avenues in the latest European *belle-époque* style. Considerable publicity was attached to the official opening in November 1905 of the impressive Avenida Central (later renamed Avenida Rio Branco) and its continued construction to link with the Avenida Beira Mar to provide a picturesque boulevard stretching for six miles along the bay. Visiting foreigners were greatly impressed by the transformation of Rio de Janeiro. 'No nation can show a more conspicuous example of modern energy and enterprise than is seen in the new federal capital of Brazil,' stated an American visitor. 'The marvellous changes in Rio' earned the fulsome praise of a British journalist, who added that the capital 'is the most beautiful and now one of the cleanest cities in the world.'[22]

Society

The architectural changes and beautification of Rio de Janeiro were directly linked with significant changes in the provision of public health. The campaign to improve sanitation and sewerage systems was organized by Dr Osvaldo (Gonçalves) Cruz and was designed to rid the city of endemic deadly diseases such as yellow fever, bubonic plague, malaria and smallpox. The improvements were welcomed by the élite and the middle classes, but their immediate impact was not so beneficial for the poor. Especially controversial was the attempt to eradicate mosquitoes and the implementation of a program of compulsory smallpox vaccination in 1903 and 1904. Protests against the arbitrary and insensitive actions of public health inspectors and police erupted into a full-scale riot in the centre of Rio de Janeiro in November 1904.

The violence in Rio de Janeiro reflected the long-standing discontent of an urban poor who suffered from low living standards, rising food prices and increasing interference, harassment and violence perpetrated by government officials. There was also suspicion that the changes introduced in Rio de Janeiro and other major cities had an ulterior motive in seeking to promote 'racial' progress. The Brazilian élite traditionally felt a sense of racial and cultural inferiority to Europe and sought to compensate for this by adopting European styles of behavior, dress and architecture. They were also very receptive to fashionable racial theories that sought to prove the supremacy of the Aryan race and could be used to advocate a 'whitening' (*branqueamento*) of the national population. Although the policy of actively encouraging immigration from Europe was motivated primarily by a desire to gain cheap labor, it was also calculated to increase the number of 'white' Europeans in the Brazilian population. By contrast, a definite discriminatory bias was shown towards Asians and Africans, who were regarded as a degenerative racial influence and a barrier to modernization. The results of what amounted to the operation of a 'white immigration policy' were illustrated in the 'whitening' of the national population. Whereas almost 44 percent of the population had been identified as white in the 1890 census, by 1940 the figure had risen to 63 percent.[23]

The popularity of ideas of racial 'regeneration' or 'eugenics' illustrated the growing racial consciousness in favor of white supremacy and black inferiority that was a feature of élitist attitudes during the Republic. The belief was exemplified by the Brazilian diplomat and historian, Manoel de Oliveira Lima, when he attributed the economic and cultural decline of the Northeast to 'the almost complete absence of European elements.'[24] Despite the abolition of slavery in 1888, there was no government policy to improve the financial and material conditions of the ex-slaves. Although importance was attached to educational qualifications and family connections, employment in professional and clerical posts was frequently subject to a color bar. Senior positions in the government, the military and the Church were visibly reserved for whites. The image of Brazil overseas was important to the Foreign Minister, the Baron do Rio Branco, who insisted that Brazilian diplomats sent to Europe should be 'tall, well groomed, and personally attractive,' and that their wives should be, 'if not always beautiful . . . white or near-white in appearance.'[25] The reference to 'near-white' showed, however, the absence of an absolute color line and the continued existence of a degree of social mobility that enabled some mulattos to advance in employment and in society.

Movements in favor of social change and reform did exist during the Republic, but they tended to be small in numbers and lacking in political

[124]   influence. Positivism aimed to assist the urban poor by advocating government assistance to stimulate industry and create jobs. *Tenentismo* was led by junior army officers, mainly lieutenants (*tenentes*), and emerged after 1922 to promote radical economic and social reform to alleviate poverty in the cities and the countryside. Other examples of notable radical movements were the establishment of the Brazilian Communist Party in 1922 and the founding of the Democratic Party of São Paulo in 1927, the feminist *Federação Brasileira para o Progresso Feminino*, and the *Centrol Dom Vital* of the Catholic Right. Support across political and class lines was attracted to national campaigns to improve public health after investigations in the interior of Brazil revealed shocking rates of endemic diseases such as malaria and hookworm. Little was achieved, however, to counter the validity of the embarrassing description of Brazil as 'an immense hospital.'

The rural poor

An even more rigid class structure was evident in the countryside. Despite the contemporary attention given to the growing cities, the large majority of the population still lived in the country, so that Brazil remained a traditional and essentially a rural society during the Republic. In Brazil's most populated state, Minas Gerais, the 1920 census classified 95 percent of the population as rural. The same census also confirmed that land ownership was still highly concentrated throughout Brazil. It was estimated that 300,000 landowners owned three-quarters of all the land. Rural society continued, therefore, to be dominated and controlled by an oligarchy consisting of the big landowners, planters and ranchers. The mass of society were mostly sharecroppers and laborers who lived and worked at a subsistence level. Opportunities for economic and social improvement were minimal. There was little provision of public education, so that illiteracy was rife. Hygiene was poor and disease endemic. Infant mortality was high and the average life-expectancy was less than 35 years.

The unsympathetic and frequently brutal attitude of the Brazilian élite towards the rural poor was illustrated in the 'War of Canudos' (*Guerra de Canudos* described earlier) in 1896–97. Fleeing from poverty and oppression, thousands of peasants had established a sizeable millenarian community at Canudos in the remote 'backlands' (*sertão*) of the Northeast. Government officials and leading politicians in Bahia and Rio de Janeiro showed no disposition to attempt to understand the desperate economic and social circumstances of the peasants. Their spirited resistance against the local police was simply interpreted as the deliberate defiance of the rule of law. Canudos was

considered to be a den of vicious outlaws (*jagunços*) and religious fanatics [125]
who were acting outside the law and living on the margin of civilization. The
Brazilian élite was firmly convinced that order must be restored. The result
was the dispatch of large federal military forces equipped with artillery and
under orders not only to suppress but, if necessary, to exterminate the community and all its civilian inhabitants including women and children. The
mission was accomplished in 1897.

The Indians faced a similar struggle for survival. Reduced in numbers
to less than a million in 1900, some had chosen to be acculturated and to
abandon their traditional way of life. Most had withdrawn, however, to the
isolation of the remote jungles of the Amazon region. Although few Brazilians
had actually ever come into personal contact with the Indians, they generally
subscribed to the extremely negative view that the Indians were wild savages
who belonged to an inferior race which was doomed to extinction. The lack
of sympathy was illustrated by the 1891 Constitution that neither specifically mentioned Indians nor recognized their rights to tribal lands. The Indians
were not only despoiled of their lands by the new state governments, but
they were also directly threatened by the Amazonian rubber boom and its
advancing horde of rubber tappers (*seringueiros*). During the 1890s Colonel
Cândido (Mariano da Silva) Rondon advocated integration rather than
exclusion and emerged as the foremost friend and champion of the Indians.
Partly Indian by descent, Rondon argued that government and white society
should adopt measures to improve and civilize the Indians so that they could
become productive workers and good citizens. In 1910 Rondon was appointed
the first head of the newly-created federal Indian Protection Service (*Serviço
de Proteção aos Indios* or SPI). The colonel's ability and sincerity were not in
doubt. In his journey in the Amazon region, Theodore Roosevelt noted that
Rondon had 'an exceptional knowledge of the Indian tribes' and had been
able to persuade some of them to begin 'to tread the road of civilization.'[26]
The SPI attempted to build on Rondon's pioneering work by sending out
officials to establish contact with remote Indian tribes, but was able to do
little to halt the decline of Indian population caused by violence and the spread
of disease arising from the invasion of the region by whites in search of jobs
and land.

The industrial poor

The Brazilian working class did not have to face the threat of extermination,
but they also experienced unsympathetic treatment from employers and
government. Although industrial workers made up only a small minority of

the total labor force, they numbered more than one million by 1920. The rise resulted from the growth of manufacturing industry which stimulated an influx of European immigrants and the movement of peasants from the countryside to the cities in search of employment. Unskilled and semi-skilled jobs were generally available, but pay was low and working conditions in factories were bad. In fact, the relatively abundant supply of labor kept wages down and hampered efforts to persuade employers to improve working conditions. European immigrants, many of whom possessed socialist and anarchist backgrounds, were instrumental in organizing trade unions, mostly of skilled workers, to campaign for higher pay and better treatment from employers. In 1906 the first national congress of trade unions was held and was followed two years later by the establishment of the Brazilian Labor Confederation (*Confederação Operária Brasileira* or COB). The high visibility of radical and foreign-born workers in the leadership of the new trade unions gave the labor movement a lasting foreign image and a revolutionary reputation that disturbed the Brazilian élite but also had the effect of making it difficult to recruit Brazilian workers and mobilize them for industrial action. Consequently, membership remained relatively small and generally restricted to skilled workers.

The economic dislocation arising from World War I, however, stimulated labor militancy and boosted the role and membership of trade unions in Brazil. The labor movement was prominent in organizing demands for increased wages to compensate for the high inflation, especially in food prices, caused by the war. A wave of strikes occurred from 1917 to 1920 including the first successful general strike in Brazilian history, which broke out in São Paulo in July 1917 and involved up to 40,000 workers. Although the scale of the 1917 strike forced concessions from the employers, the gains were short-lived. The bargaining position of both workers and trade unions was inherently weak so long as employers could resort to a large pool of unemployed and under-employed workers including women and children, and immigrants who were prepared to work for lower wages and assist in breaking strikes. Consequently, the living conditions of most industrial workers did not improve during the Republic. Like the peasants in the countryside, industrial workers suffered from low wages and dangerous working conditions. The plight of the poor was sympathetically referred to in the press as the 'social question,' but there was little prospect of real material change. For example, attempts to form trade unions encountered the fierce hostility of employers and government. Trade union activities and officials were frequently subject to institutional violence in the form of interference and

harassment by the police. Foreign-born leaders were singled out for arrest   [127]
and often deported, while native-born officials were compelled to move to
remote regions of the country such as Amazonas or Mato Grosso.

Diplomacy

Recognition and reciprocity

The end of the Empire in 1889 did not directly threaten Brazilian national
security. The Emperor peaceably accepted exile and there was no immediate
attempt either by his supporters or foreign powers to restore the monarchy to
power. In fact, the independent nations of the Western Hemisphere were
pleased that Brazil had finally joined them in adopting the republican system
of government. 'Nothing so grand or so excellent has ever been achieved in
the history of any nation,' enthused the American senator, John T. Morgan.[27]
Within two weeks of the coup, Uruguay and Argentina had established
full diplomatic relations with the provisional government of Deodoro da
Fonseca. Other countries maintained unofficial relations, but delayed granting formal recognition because of concern for diplomatic propriety and legal
technicalities. The United States decided to recognize the Republic in January 1890, while France was the first of the European powers to grant official
recognition in July 1890. Britain waited until after the promulgation of the
constitution in 1891.

In contrast to 1825, Brazil was not required to make any specific concessions in return for the granting of diplomatic recognition. Nor did Britain
play the same leading role. The most important relationships were with
Argentina and the United States, the two nations that would be at the center
of Brazilian diplomacy during the Republic. In fact, Argentina had been one
of the first South American nations to recognize the Republic and had proclaimed a national holiday to celebrate the change of regime. The provisional
government was grateful and readily agreed to Argentina's proposal to enter
into discussions to settle the long-standing Misiones boundary dispute. To
expedite agreement, negotiations were conducted by telegraph on January 5,
1890. Details were glossed over and within two hours the contested territory
was divided almost equally between the two countries. The Brazilian foreign
minister, Quintino Bocaiúva, traveled to Buenos Aires to sign a treaty defining
the boundary and to affirm what appeared to be a new era of Argentine–
Brazilian cooperation and friendship. But the provisional government had

[128]   not reckoned on the degree of domestic Brazilian hostility to the proposed treaty. A century of fierce rivalry to control the Plate region could not be easily set aside. Street demonstrations protesting the loss of national territory to Argentina occurred in Rio and were a prelude to congressional rejection of the settlement. Both governments acknowledged defeat and decided to submit the boundary question to the arbitration of the President of the United States. Argentine opportunism, seeking to exploit the change of political regime in Brazil, had been foiled.

The selection of the American president as arbitrator was further confirmation of the prestige and leading influence that the United States now held in the international affairs of the Western Hemisphere. While the provisional government recognized the importance of maintaining good relations with the European powers, it was particularly interested in cultivating closer political and commercial links with the 'great northern republic.' This had been evident shortly after the 1889 coup when the Brazilian minister at Washington actually informed the American Secretary of State that speedy American diplomatic recognition was vital if the new Republic was to survive. There was also the knowledge that the United States represented the largest single market for Brazilian exports. A commercial reciprocity treaty was signed on January 31, 1891 to promote further trade. In return for the free entry of Brazilian sugar into the American market, the Brazilian tariff was either removed or reduced on the importation of various American goods. The granting of preferential rates, however, provoked criticism not only from foreign but also from Brazilian merchants. Like the Misiones boundary settlement with Argentina, the political cost of altering the tariff was much greater than initially envisaged by the provisional government. Moreover, the value of the reciprocity treaty was thrown into question in May 1891 when it was learned that the United States had concluded an identical arrangement with Spain so that Cuban sugar would also have free entry into the United States. Nevertheless, the treaty proved financially advantageous for Brazil. The expectation of dominating the American sugar market was dashed, but this was more than offset by a substantial increase in coffee sales to the United States.

The signing of the reciprocity treaty in January 1891 marked a high point of cooperation between the United States and the new Brazilian republic. As Brazil subsequently became preoccupied with its own internal political concerns and showed little desire to be involved actively in foreign affairs, diplomatic relations between the two countries diminished in significance. The Naval Revolt of 1893–94 provided a brief exception, but the defeat of the revolt owed more to the determined personality of Floriano Peixoto and the divisions among his enemies than to external factors. Nevertheless, Floriano was so grateful that he ordered July 4, 1894 to be observed as a Brazilian national holiday. But a few months later, the Brazilian government was not so pleased by President Cleveland's unilateral abrogation of the 1891 reciprocity treaty. More important however was Cleveland's decision in the eagerly-awaited arbitration of the Misiones boundary dispute with Argentina. In February 1895 Brazilians were delighted by the announcement of an award that gave their country virtually all of the disputed territory. The result was regarded as a personal triumph for the negotiating skill of Rio Branco, who had presented his country's case in Washington. The annoyance over President Cleveland's abrogation of the reciprocity treaty soon became a distant memory in the light of what was interpreted as a conclusive demonstration of American friendship for Brazil. In December 1895 the Brazilian Senate seized the opportunity to send a message of congratulations to Cleveland for his handling of the Venezuela Boundary Crisis. In 1898 Brazil adopted a conspicuously friendly attitude towards the United States during the Spanish–American War. Two warships were sold to the American navy and ships of the United States fleet were allowed to take on fuel and to refit in Brazilian ports.

Approximation with the United States

Such positive action was uncharacteristic of Brazilian diplomacy during the late 1890s. In South American affairs Brazil was overshadowed by Argentina and Chile, who were engaged in a diplomatic battle for regional prestige and influence. Moreover, a lack of interest was shown by the Brazilian government in the diplomatic activities of the wider world. This was exemplified in the decision to refuse an invitation to attend the First Peace Conference at The Hague in 1899. 'Brazil has of late years unwisely allowed herself to drop out of international society,' remarked the British minister at Rio de Janeiro.[28] A major change, however, occurred at the beginning of the twentieth century when Brazil once more became a regional power of significance and sought to assume an international role commensurate with its size and aspirations. A remarkable element of continuity in the conduct of diplomacy was provided by Rio Branco, who served continuously as Foreign Minister from December 1902 until his death in February 1912. The Ministry of Foreign Affairs, popularly known as 'the Itamaraty,' became famous for its professionalism and diplomatic skill as Rio Branco masterminded a conspicuous effort to promote a positive image of his country and its people to the wider world. Several new missions were established, so that Brazil was represented in 39 countries. Of all the diplomatic appointments, the selection of Joaquim Nabuco as Brazil's first ambassador to the United States in 1905 was undoubtedly the most successful.

Rio Branco came to office at a time of heightened Latin American anxiety over the spread of European imperialism arising from the resort to 'gunboat diplomacy' of Britain, Italy and Germany in their attempt in 1902–03 to coerce Venezuela to resume payments of its foreign debt. The new Foreign Minister stressed a policy of cooperation rather than confrontation with the great powers. Indeed, as a result of its adherence to the terms of the 1898 Funding Loan, Brazil was on good terms with its foreign creditors. Nevertheless, rumors persisted of European designs upon Brazilian territory. In Rio Branco's opinion, internal divisions prevented the Latin American nations from effectively uniting against external danger. The obvious counterpoise was provided historically by the United States, who had checked European territorial ambitions in the Western Hemisphere by the Monroe Doctrine. In contrast to most of his Spanish-American colleagues, Rio Branco argued that Latin America should look to Washington for protection against external interference. He considered that far from being a danger, the rising military power of the United States was a force for hemispheric peace and stability because it served as a restraint upon European aggression.

Rio Branco's views were not purely altruistic and reflected an element of Brazilian self-interest. American diplomatic goodwill had contributed significantly to the favorable resolution of Brazil's boundary dispute with Argentina over the Misiones in 1895 and aided Rio Branco in securing Peruvian recognition of Brazil's legal title to the Acre territory in 1904. There were also significant economic benefits. 'The United States,' noted Rio Branco, 'are the principal market for our coffee and other products.'[29] The extension of commercial relations with the United States would, therefore, increase Brazil's wealth and reduce financial dependence upon Europe. Rio Branco concluded that American friendship and support would be assured if Brazil aligned its own foreign policy as closely as possible to that pursued by the United States. The concept was not completely original. But the baron's talk of shifting the 'axis' of Brazil's foreign relations from Europe to the United States sounded different and justified the new description of his policy as the strategy of rapprochement or 'approximation' (*aproximação*).

The first tangible sign that Washington had become diplomatically as important as London, Paris, or Berlin was the upgrading of relations between

Brazil and the United States from ministerial to ambassadorial rank in 1905. Brazil's status was further enhanced by the choice of Rio de Janeiro in preference to Caracas or Buenos Aires as the venue for the 1906 Pan-American Conference and the decision of Secretary of State Elihu Root to head the American delegation. Root's presence in Rio gave considerable prestige to the meeting because it was the first time that a serving Secretary of State had left the United States on an overseas mission. The high point of approximation appeared to be reached as Root left Brazil with the parting words that the two countries 'acting together, would form a single and eternal guarantee for the integrity of America.'[30] Elated by the apparent selection of Brazil as the preferred partner of the United States, Rio Branco was able to indulge his dreams of Brazilian leadership of the southern continent.

Brazil's diplomatic achievements provoked hostility from Argentina and, consequently, contributed to the build-up of diplomatic tension in South America. During the 1890s Brazil's internal disorders had muted the traditional rivalry between the two South American giants, but the reemergence of a stable and prosperous Brazil disturbed the balance of power in the River Plate. Argentina was alarmed not only by the success of Rio Branco's policy of approximation but also by the increase of Brazil's territorial boundaries in the Acre region and the extension of Brazilian political influence into Uruguay and Paraguay. Another cause of anxiety was the decision of the Rodrigues Alves administration in 1904 to purchase powerful warships from Britain as part of a strategy to modernize the Brazilian navy. The naval build-up merely complemented Rio Branco's plan to promote Brazil's international stature. However, it also threatened to upset the existing South American balance of power in which Argentina enjoyed naval superiority over both Chile and Brazil. Rio Branco turned to Washington for diplomatic support. While Root was genuinely friendly towards Brazil, he had no intention of interfering in the quarrel between the two neighbors. By its unwillingness to side with Brazil against Argentina, the United States government revealed the limits of the strategy of approximation and thereby exposed the precariousness of Rio Branco's pretensions to South American leadership.

Further diplomatic discomfort was experienced at the Second Peace Conference held at The Hague. In 1899 the Campos Sales administration had demonstrated Brazil's lack of active interest in international affairs by declining to attend the First Peace Conference. By contrast, only a few years later the invitation to the Second Peace Conference was quickly accepted. Rio Branco grasped the opportunity for Brazil to make its debut on the international stage and appear as one of the powers contributing to the cause of

[132]   world peace. A prominent role was envisaged and was underlined by the appointment of one of the largest delegations, comprising twelve officials. At its head was the distinguished senator and orator, Rui Barbosa. The conference, however, was dominated by the great powers of Europe, who accepted the United States as an equal but assigned Brazil to the category of a minor nation. Rui bridled against this treatment and became the sensation of the conference when he delivered a celebrated speech that asserted the principle of equal representation.

The euphoria of the 1906 Pan-American Conference was, therefore, short-lived. Root's visit brought hemispheric prestige, but this had only a modest impact on Brazil's standing in the wider world as the conference at The Hague demonstrated. Moreover, it soon became apparent that Brazil lacked the political authority and material resources to lead the southern continent. The hollowness of this pretension was exposed in the contested presidential election of 1910 that appeared to signal a return to the chaos of the early years of the Republic. Just as Brazil's prestige was declining, Argentina enjoyed the glory of hosting the Pan-American Conference in 1910, followed shortly afterwards by elaborate celebrations to mark the centenary of Argentine independence. The gloom and jealousy of the Brazilian élite was heightened as the world praised their rival's achievements and proclaimed Buenos Aires as the Paris of South America.

Both Rio Branco and his successor, Lauro Müller, responded by allowing the strategy of approximation to recede into the backgound. Soon after he became Foreign Minister in 1912, Müller publicly stressed the importance of developing close relations with Argentina and Chile. But the subsequent emergence of the informal association of the three countries, popularly known as the 'ABC,' was not meant to imply the formation of an anti-American alliance. Müller wished to remain on good terms with the United States and was delighted to make two visits to that country in 1913 and 1916. Indeed, in marked contrast to the Spanish-American republics, Brazil was much less critical of American 'dollar diplomacy' in Central America and the Caribbean region. When it seemed that war was about to erupt as a result of the Vera Cruz Crisis in April 1914, the United States turned to Brazil to look after the affairs of its embassy in Mexico City. The Brazilian ambassador at Washington, Domício da Gama, proudly explained that Brazil was chosen because it was the 'most important American nation' represented at the Mexican capital.[31] Müller complied with the American request for diplomatic assistance, but he also sought to exert a moderating influence upon both the United States and Mexico by joining with Argentina and Chile to propose their joint

mediation of the dispute. Müller's critics pointed out the inherent contradiction of a policy that sought both to support and oppose American actions
in Mexico. The Foreign Minister explained that the ABC initiative was not
intended as a condemnation of American aggression but was a sincere and
necessary attempt to prevent the Mexican crisis from escalating into a war
that would be harmful to all the nations of the Americas. While the explana-
tion was statesmanlike and reassuring, it could not hide the dilemma facing
Brazilian diplomacy of trying to cultivate good relations simultaneously with
both the United States and Argentina.

World War I

The Brazilian government was peripheral to the events that brought about
the outbreak of war in Europe in 1914, and responded by declaring a policy
of neutrality and nonintervention. Although Brazil had long maintained
friendly relations with all the belligerents, it was evident from articles in the
press and public meetings that there was more public sympathy with the
Allied powers of Britain and France, especially the latter. 'Brazil is a Latin
country with a great admiration and friendship for France,' noted a British
report, 'and this is at the root of her partiality.'[32] The educated Brazilian élite
was particularly outraged at the German invasion of Belgium. The unpro-
voked and callous attack upon the sovereignty of a neutral nation was
regarded as indefensible. Moreover, the image of German barbarism was
reinforced in the Brazilian mind by skillful British and French propaganda.
On the other hand, Brazil had good reason to maintain friendly relations
with Germany. The foreign minister, Lauro Müller, was a conspicuous
example of the success of the large community of German immigrants who
had settled in southern Brazil. Trade between the two countries had also
grown to such an extent that in 1914 Hamburg ranked second only to New
York in its share of the Brazilian coffee trade. Indeed, almost 2 million bags
of valorized coffee originating from São Paulo were stored in German ports
at the beginning of the war. The local sale of this coffee was quickly completed, but the proceeds amounting to £6 million were retained by the
Bleischroeder bank of Berlin. The release of this money became a preoccupation of Brazilian diplomacy and provided a powerful argument for adopting
a conciliatory attitude towards Germany.

Brazil found the pursuit of neutrality to be inherently difficult. Bordering
the Atlantic and possessing large international trading interests, it could
neither remain immune from the economic dislocation caused by the war nor

[134]   avoid becoming directly involved in the controversy over maritime rights. The controversy arose as a result of Germany's use of the new weapon of the submarine to sink not only enemy but also neutral ships. After vigorous protests from the United States, the German government sought to avoid a rupture of relations with the neutral nations over the issue, but reversed this policy in January 1917 when it decided to implement unrestricted submarine warfare. Several merchant ships of all nations were subsequently sunk, including four Brazilian ships. Brazil's sovereignty was directly challenged and the government retaliated, first by breaking off diplomatic relations on April 11 and then by formally declaring war on Germany on October 23. The latter decision replicated that of the United States, who had joined the war in April, but contrasted markedly with the attitude of Argentina, whose government was currently organizing a diplomatic conference to enable the nations of Latin America to remain neutral. Brazil's ambivalent response to the Argentine initiative and later its decision to declare war effectively sabotaged the conference and rekindled the traditional suspicion and rivalry between the two countries. Argentine diplomats believed that Brazil was seeking to revive the policy of approximation and use American support to pose as the champion and leader of South America. 'It was her proud boast,' observed the British minister at Rio, 'that she [Brazil] was the first among the Latin American republics to support the United States.'[33]

The deliberate sinking of Brazilian merchant ships by German submarines was the principal reason and justification for Brazil's decision to go to war in 1917. But Germany did not directly threaten Brazil's national security, so that Brazil's actual military contribution to the Allied war effort was slight and was restricted mainly to the dispatch of a small naval squadron which arrived too late in Europe to experience active wartime service. In fact, financial considerations had been uppermost in the decision to join the war. The Brazilian government expected that wartime association with the Allies, and especially the United States, would alleviate the damaging economic effects of the war. In particular, there was a desperate need for increased imports of American coal. Another aim was to boost sales of coffee, which as a luxury product had seen its demand substantially reduced by the war. But American officials refused to grant any special favors. The great battles to decide the outcome of the war were being fought in Europe, and their plans for victory did not include diverting either scarce shipping or important strategic materials to Brazil. Although supplies of coal were eventually made available, the purpose was not to please the Brazilian government but to ensure that the

Brazilian railways were able to transport strategically important minerals such [135] as manganese for export to the United States.

While the decision to join the war as a co-belligerent produced disappointing economic returns, it appeared to be vindicated in 1918 by the fact that Brazil had backed the winning side and could proudly claim to be one of the victorious powers that had defeated Germany. Elated by victory, the Brazilian élite looked forward to the exciting prospect of Brazil's inclusion in the great postwar peace conference to be held at the Palace of Versailles in France. Although its actual involvement in military operations had been small, Brazil hoped for a position of some distinction at the conference table. Brazil learned, however, that it would be allowed only one delegate. After the intervention of the American president, Woodrow Wilson, this was increased to three. In effect, the world of international diplomacy remained firmly divided into 'greater' and 'lesser' powers. The 'Big Four' of Britain, France, Italy, and the United States dominated the conference proceedings and reserved the important committee appointments for themselves. Smaller nations were treated with little consideration. Far from enjoying a position of honor and influence, Brazil had to be content with a place on the commission assigned to draw up the covenant of the League of Nations.

Brazil's international reputation was damaged rather than enhanced by the Versailles Conference. At The Hague in 1907 Rui Barbosa had argued eloquently for the rights of small nations. In sharp contrast, the Brazilian delegation at Versailles became preoccupied with what appeared to be a mercenary assertion of national interests. An unseemly debate arose over the amount of financial compensation due on the payment of the coffee money that had been frozen in German banks during the war. The conference committee on finance recommended that Germany should pay compensation but that this should be in marks at the prevailing rate of exchange. Depreciation of the mark since 1914 meant, however, that Brazil stood to lose a substantial sum. The same committee also proposed that the various merchant ships confiscated from Germany be allocated to the victors in proportion to maritime losses suffered during the war. This would allow France to retain the ex-German ships that had been interned in Brazilian ports in 1914 and later chartered to the French government in 1917. Both proposals were vigorously contested by the Brazilian delegation. The question of the coffee money degenerated into a squabble over interest percentage points, while the matter of the ownership of the ex-German ships aroused heated discussions until the French delegates conceded that they were the property of Brazil. Brazilian diplomacy was eventually successful but at the cost of appearing selfish and overly concerned with financial gain.

The League of Nations

The establishment of the League of Nations in 1920 alleviated the bruised feelings arising from the Versailles Conference. Brazil was recognized as a founding member of the new world organization and accorded one of the four non-permanent seats on the League Council. The Brazilian élite was flattered at the attention bestowed by Europe upon their country and showed no disposition to follow the example of the United States and retreat into isolationism. Indeed, the American decision to remain outside the League served to enhance Brazil's sense of international status and influence. As the only Latin American nation initially represented on the Council, Brazil was able to outshine Argentina and irritated the latter by claiming the leadership of the American continent.

Unlike the great European powers, Brazil's membership of the League Council was non-permanent and subject to election by the League Assembly. According to the American ambassador in Brazil, Edwin Morgan, the securing of permanent status soon became 'the principal aspiration' of the Itamaraty.[34] Britain and France were unsympathetic. They were prepared to broaden membership of the Council, but their thoughts centered on bringing in the absentee great powers such as the United States and Germany. Although Brazil's particular claims were politely ignored, concerted pressure from the other Latin American members resulted in a decision to enlarge the Council in 1923 by including a second Latin American country. But both seats were still classified as nonpermanent and would be subject to reelection every three years. The Assembly subsequently elected Brazil and Uruguay.

The lukewarm reception given to Brazil's desire for a permanent seat was not entirely due to the insensitivity and selfish calculation of the great European powers. In fact, the idea of a special status for Brazil had never been acceptable to the other Latin American governments. During the early 1920s traditional Spanish-American suspicions were heightened by Brazil's evident determination to strengthen and modernize its army and navy, notably by the contracting of foreign military missions from France and the United States. The Argentine foreign minister, Estanislau Zeballos, reacted in 1922 by publicly describing Brazil as a 'serious menace.'[35] Relations between the two rivals became even more tense in 1924 when the Bernardes administration announced a substantial naval program designed to replace Brazil's obsolete

warships. The Spanish-American nations used the League of Nations as a means [137]
of expressing their displeasure and proposed that the two Council seats
reserved for the hemisphere should rotate annually among all the Latin American countries. The adoption of this scheme was clearly intended to deprive
Brazil of the Council seat it had uninterruptedly held since 1920.

The question of membership of the League came to the forefront of world
affairs in 1925 as a result of the Locarno agreement that established postwar
boundaries in Europe and paved the way for admitting Germany to membership of the League Council. Brazil was not a party to the agreement made at
Locarno and was not bound by its provisions. In fact, the Bernardes administration regarded it as a signal opportunity to press once again for Brazil's
own permanent seat. At a time, however, when the country suffered from
serious domestic political unrest, the implied claim that Brazil was an equal
of Germany provoked only indignation and ridicule in Europe. A series of
clumsy diplomatic maneuvers, including the use of the veto to prevent German
membership, further isolated Brazil and proved counter-productive in reviving
the charges made at the Versailles Conference that Brazilian diplomacy was
selfish and unyielding. Not only was a permanent seat on the Council definitely ruled out, but Brazil also faced the prospect of being defeated in the
elections for the nonpermanent seats. To avoid further diplomatic humiliation,
Brazil announced on June 11, 1926 that it would formally leave the Council
and the League.[36]

The association with the new world organization had encouraged the
pretensions of the Brazilian élite to think of Brazil as a world power. 'Now,
we have become a nation,' one diplomat proudly boasted, 'that reaches beyond
its continent to take part and be heard in the deliberations that concern the
world.'[37] In reality, those 'deliberations' had little relevance for Brazil and
were essentially peripheral to Brazilian national interests. Nevertheless, by
openly pressing for a permanent seat on the Council the Bernardes administration raised public awareness of the League and correspondingly suffered a
severe blow to its prestige when Brazil felt compelled to declare its intention
to leave the organization in humiliating fashion in 1926. Reeling from the
shock of the debacle of Geneva, Brazilian diplomacy abandoned its pursuit
of international status and turned instinctively to the policy of cultivating
friendly relations with the United States and Argentina, the countries that
mattered most to Brazil.

The strategy was sensible, but it contained the perpetual dilemma for
Brazilian diplomacy during the Republic of how to be on good terms simultaneously with both the United States and Argentina. The problem loomed

[138]   acutely at the Pan-American Conference held at Havana in 1928. By refusing to join the general condemnation of American military intervention in the countries of the Caribbean and Central America, the Brazilian delegation inevitably came to be seen as siding with the United States. So long starved of tangible diplomatic successes, the Itamaraty could not resist the temptation to boast that a special understanding existed between the two non-Spanish powers. This was further displayed in the visit of President-elect Herbert Hoover to Rio de Janeiro in December 1928. Brazilians were delighted at the international attention paid to their country and its capital city. They were flattered to receive a visit from the next president of the United States and were determined to surpass Buenos Aires in their show of lavish hospitality to their distinguished guest.

In reality, however, Brazilian diplomacy during the late 1920s was similar to that of the late 1890s in being generally reactive and negative. Not only did Brazil pointedly refuse to sign the Kellogg–Briand Peace Pact, but it also resisted being directly associated with American efforts to mediate the Chaco territorial dispute between Bolivia and Paraguay. As 1930 approached, Brazilian politics became almost totally absorbed with the question of presidential selection. The subsequent struggle to overthrow President Washington Luís was conducted without resort to appeals for assistance from any foreign power. Despite the prevailing political and economic crisis in 1930, Brazilian national security was not threatened. Indeed, the new government of Getúlio Vargas, which came to power in 1930, concentrated on consolidating its hold on government and, in contrast to 1822 and 1889, attached no great significance to securing diplomatic recognition by foreign nations.

CHAPTER 4

ERA OF GETÚLIO VARGAS, 1930–1964

Politics

Consolidation of power

In a manner reminiscent of its predecessor more than 40 years earlier in 1889, the 'provisional government' that came into power in November 1930 and created the 'Second Republic' was imposed on the people of Brazil by military force. The public response was similarly passive. One notable difference, however, was that the head of the new regime, Getúlio Vargas, was a civilian politician rather than a general.[1] Moreover, Vargas possessed markedly greater public appeal and political acumen than Deodoro da Fonseca and held on to power for a much longer period of time. In fact, he dominated Brazilian politics for the next quarter of a century and his influential legacy endured after his death in 1954. Such a prospect seemed most unlikely in 1930 because Vargas not only came to office at a time of considerable political uncertainty and economic crisis but he was also relatively little known and untested in terms of national politics. The Liberal Alliance had chosen the *gaúcho* governor to be its leader principally because he was neither a *mineiro* nor a *paulista*. He was also valued more for his conciliatory personal style and background for political moderation rather than any flamboyant or radical tendencies. Indeed, Vargas had served as finance minister in the Washington Luís administration and was, therefore, directly associated with the politics of the First Republic.

Moreover, Vargas's rise to power was far from triumphal. He had failed to win the 1930 presidential election and, consequently, lacked an electoral mandate. In fact, the actual timing of the overthrow of President Washington Luís in October 1930 was a result of a decision taken by senior army commanders rather than the outright military success of Vargas's forces. The military junta had also transferred power with reluctance and their attitude towards the new government and its leader remained ambivalent. In addition, Vargas's source of political power appeared extremely fragile. The Liberal Alliance that had been formed to fight the 1930 presidential election was not an organized political party, but consisted primarily of a temporary coalition of disaffected political 'outsiders' who were brought together by their opposition to Washington Luís and his determination to flout the '*café com leite*' arrangement and impose his successor as the next president. Preoccupied with defeating '*paulista* imperialism' and pursuing their own personal political goals, the members of the Liberal Alliance were unable to formulate a coherent and systematic political program to put into effect, should they come to power.

Vargas quickly dissipated the mood of crisis and disharmony by showing in his first days in office that he was determined to assert and consolidate his position as undisputed leader of the provisional government. The old political system was publicly repudiated and declared redundant as all legislative bodies at federal, state and municipal levels were immediately dissolved. No mention was made of organizing future elections. Instead, Vargas proclaimed his intention to act as a dictator and rule by decree. But this effective abandonment of liberalism did not lead to a personal tyranny. To the Brazilian people 'Getúlio' was never a totalitarian ruler such as Hitler or Stalin but a typical *caudilho* (chief) from the South whose paternal ways were made acceptable, if not popular, by an affable and modest personality. In politics, too, the wily *gaúcho* conformed to the traditional customs. While always ensuring that he would take the final decision on matters of state, Vargas preferred that a consensus be reached wherever possible. His skill in the art of political manipulation and distribution of patronage was evident as politicians and military figures who had backed the Liberal Alliance were rewarded with jobs and promotions, while opponents were arrested and punished. Osvaldo Aranha entered the cabinet as Minister of Justice, while Góes Monteiro became a full colonel and was later promoted to the rank of general. However, the 'politics of the governors' was not restored. Indeed, the new regime turned away from the federalism of the First Republic and stressed the concentration of power in the hands of the central government and especially the chief executive. The resulting policy of direct federal interference greatly undermined the prestige and power of the state party political machines. Federal interventors, mostly *tenentes* drawn from the army, were appointed to replace state governors. Only the governor of Minas Gerais was permitted to retain his office. In addition, Vargas sought to weaken the power of the *coronéis* by decreeing that the federal government would appoint all mayors and supervise municipal budgets and local police forces.

Despite his patent authoritarianism, Vargas sought to convey the impression of a 'revolutionary' federal government that was acting on behalf of all the people of Brazil in its determination to implement the platform of the Liberal Alliance by promoting what he described as 'national reconstruction.' The term was deliberately vague, but it was widely interpreted to mean a definite break with the past and the development of a modern and 'new' Brazil in which the power of the landed oligarchies would be diminished while the political significance of new forces representing the urban middle-class, business and the industrial workers would be enhanced. An improvement in economic and social welfare was also an essential feature of 'national reconstruction' and would be the task of the Ministry of Education and Health and the Ministry of Labor and Industry, two newly created departments of the federal government. While Vargas's desire for reform was genuine, he was not an advocate of either class conflict or a major redistribution of wealth. His emphasis on 'national' reconstruction was a calculated appeal for the backing of all elements of the nation ranging from the landowners to the workers and peasants. Under his leadership they would fight together to root out political and financial corruption, an objective that all patriotic Brazilians would approve. Indeed, the essential moderation of the '1930 Revolution' was underlined by the fact that it studiously avoided the controversial issue of land reform. The federal government did attempt to redistribute national income by increasing wages of industrial workers, but these benefits were limited and conditional upon trade unions being placed under strict governmental supervision and regulation.

During his first two years of government Vargas was particularly influenced by the views of the *tenentes*, the junior army officers who pressed not just for the overthrow of the corrupt state political machines but for a 'revolutionary' restructuring of the nation in political, economic and social terms. The *tenentes* wished not only to build a strong and modern Brazil but also advocated aid to the masses of poor people living in the interior by effecting fundamental economic and social reform. Although they acted more as a pressure group rather than an organized political party, the *tenentes* had backed the Liberal Alliance and hoped that this would give them an important executive role in Vargas's fight against the entrenched state oligarchies. Their long-standing suspicion of civilian politicians as self-serving and incompetent made them advocates of centralized government and authoritarian rule. In their view, dictatorship was preferable to democracy because it was more likely to bring about major reform. The influence of the *tenentes* on Vargas, however, began to wane in 1932 as criticism mounted that, in their role as state interventors, they were often too politically radical and insensitive to local opinion. Lacking popular support, they quickly became more of a political liability than an asset.

Another factor that contributed to Vargas's successful consolidation of personal power was the public perception that the political system of the First Republic had been defective and that change was necessary. This was exemplified in the support given to Vargas in 1932 to defeat a *paulista* revolt that was widely interpreted in the rest of the country as an attempt to restore the old political order. Discontent in São Paulo arose from Vargas's use of *tenentes* to interfere in the government of the state. *Paulistas* were long accustomed to enjoying a position of national prestige and leadership so that their pride was particularly stung by the appointment as interventor in their state of Lieutenant João Alberto (Lins de Barros), a *tenente* from the Northeast. João Alberto was condemned as a 'foreigner' and a Communist after he decreed a large wage increase for factory workers and ordered land to be distributed to supporters of the 1930 Revolution. Although João Alberto only held office for a relatively short period from November 1930 to July 1931, local resentment against the federal government continued to simmer and erupted into the 'Constitutionalist Revolution' from July 9 to October 2, 1932.

Commanded by General Bertoldo Klinger and backed by 40,000 troops mostly drawn from the state *força pública*, the rebels declared their aim of leading a national movement to overthrow Vargas's dictatorship and restore constitutional government. But the revolt was poorly planned and ill prepared. Crucial military support that was confidently expected from Minas Gerais and Rio Grande do Sul did not materialize. Indeed, the federal army remained loyal to Vargas and adopted a strategy of attrition in which the state was surrounded by large land forces eventually numbering more than 75,000 while also being subjected to a blockade by sea and attacks from the air. The rebels prepared to defend the city of São Paulo stubbornly, but their capacity to resist was steadily eroded by increasing federal military pressure and their own conspicuous failure to attract sufficient numbers of *paulista* workers and peasants to their cause. In part this was because the revolt appeared to be a reactionary attempt by the *paulista* oligarchy to restore the First Republic and thereby regain its former privileges and power. The rebels finally surrendered on September 29. The episode represented a victory for the federal government and especially for Vargas, who characteristically imposed a conciliatory peace. The *paulista* rebels had fought bravely, but they were branded as

'disloyal' and found that the political prestige and influence that their state   [143]
had long enjoyed in national affairs was severely damaged.

The constitutional interlude

Despite Vargas's success in defeating the rebellion of São Paulo, there was growing public pressure for the period of dictatorship to end and for elections to be held to restore constitutional government. Indeed, contrary to the advice of the *tenentes*, Vargas publicly acknowledged the 'provisional' nature of his regime and had even given an undertaking in February 1932 to take steps to 'reconstitutionalize' the nation. Elections eventually took place in May 1933 to select a Constituent Assembly whose function would be to approve a new constitution and elect a president of the republic. The Constituent Assembly met in November 1933. A new constitution was prepared and promulgated on July 16, 1934, thereby formally ending the provisional government that had been in power since November 1930. The 1934 Constitution was not a radical document and did not differ greatly from its 1891 predecessor. Its purpose was essentially to legitimize the new regime by grafting on to the 1891 Constitution various decrees passed since 1930. For example, the new constitution included measures introduced in 1932 and implemented in 1933 to increase popular participation in the political system by enforcing a secret ballot in elections and extending the franchise to 18-year-olds and to working women. It also codified the responsibilities that the federal government had assumed for economic and educational policies. The National Congress with its two houses was reinstated, but a notable addition was the provision of 50 appointed 'class representatives' mainly drawn from trade unions to join the elected 300 deputies. The concept of specifically appointing rather than electing representatives indicated a lack of confidence in elections and pointed the way to the creation of an anti-democratic 'corporate state.' The new constitution provided, however, for the direct popular election of the president of the republic, though the first president would be chosen by the Constituent Assembly. Like the 1891 Constitution, the president was to serve for a four-year term and was ineligible to succeed himself. On July 17, 1934, the day after the promulgation of the constitution, the assembly proceeded to elect Vargas as the nation's constitutional president to serve for a four-year term. Vargas won comfortably with 175 votes against 59 for the ex-governor of Rio Grande do Sul, Borges de Medeiros, who was put forward by Vargas's critics as a token opposition candidate. Elections for state legislatures took place in October 1934.

[144]   The return to constitutional government in 1934 encouraged a marked revival of political activity and saw the appearance for the first time in republican Brazil of two well-organized national parties competing against each other. Both drew inspiration from overseas and aimed to overthrow the existing political system. In the process, they effectively polarized Brazilian politics between the left wing and the right wing. On the left was the Brazilian Communist Party (*Partido Communista Brasileiro* or PCB) that had been founded in 1922 and, except for a few months during 1927, was declared an illegal organization until 1945. Weakened initially by internal conflict and police repression, it gained public attention and political influence during the 1930s as a result of the growing discontent in Brazil caused by the world economic depression. The party's prestige was boosted in 1935 after the secret return of the celebrated leader of the 'Prestes Column,' Luís Carlos Prestes, from Moscow. Called by his admirers 'the Cavalier of Hope,' Prestes remained in hiding, but his speeches denouncing Vargas and advocating socialist revolution were read out by his supporters in an orchestrated publicity campaign. At the same time, under instructions from the Comintern in Moscow, the PCB sought to attract and mobilize broader political support by taking a leading role in the movement for a 'popular front' of left-wing organizations known as the National Liberation Alliance (*Aliança Nacional Libertadora* or ANL). The foremost opponent of the ANL was the right-wing Brazilian Integralist Action (*Acão Integralista Brasileira* or AIB) formed in 1932 as a deliberate imitation of the fascist parties of Benito Mussolini in Italy and Antonio de Oliveira Salazar in Portugal. Led by the journalist Plínio Salgado, the party proposed an 'integral' state under a single authoritarian head of government. Dressed in a uniform of green shirts and jackboots, the private militia forces of the Integralistas were a prominent feature of massive public rallies and demonstrations which declared support for the basic moral and traditional values of 'God, Country, Family.' The largest rallies took place in cities and frequently erupted into violent clashes with members of the ANL. Despite their admiration for European fascism, the Integralistas were strongly nationalistic and could be very critical of foreign influences on the country's economy and culture. Their pronounced hostility to 'godless' Communism attracted considerable support from the middle class and the Catholic Church, one of whose priests enthusiastically described the Integralistas as 'soldiers of Christ.'[2]

The *Estado Nôvo*

In contrast to European authoritarian leaders such as Mussolini and Hitler, Vargas did not exploit the patronage of the presidency to form his own

political party machine or create a popular movement that would reflect and
propagate his personal views and ideology. In fact, during his first period in
power from 1930 to 1945, he remained an enigma, seemingly determined
to hold on to the country's highest office and preferring to operate behind
the scenes while seeking to avoid becoming identified with any one particular
political faction or party. Nevertheless, his personal sympathy for Integralism
and aversion to Communism was clear. While he approved of the spirit of
nationalism and discipline of the Integralistas, he showed concern over the
growing militancy of the National Liberation Alliance, especially its association with International Communism and the implied threat to resort to
armed struggle to overthrow the capitalist order. In April 1935 Vargas
welcomed the passage in Congress of a National Security Law that was
designed to give the executive special powers to suppress subversive
elements. In July the Act was used to declare the ANL an illegal organization.
The threat of Communist violence actually became a reality in November
1935 when armed uprisings led by small groups of pro-Communist soldiers
occurred in Natal, Recife and Rio. Although the soldiers talked of replacing
Vargas with Prestes, their actions were motivated more by discontent over
low pay and poor living conditions than revolutionary ideology. Moreover,
the risings were not coordinated and were quickly suppressed by federal
troops. Nevertheless, the example of violence and disloyalty, especially the
murder of army officers, gave Vargas the opportunity to use the 'Bolshevik
threat' to suspend the 1934 Constitution and justify what amounted to
a reimposition of dictatorial rule. A 'state of war' applying to the whole of
the country was declared for 90 days and repeatedly renewed by Congress
until June 1937. With the backing of the military, the Church and the
middle class, the federal government launched a vigorous and brutal anti-
Communist campaign directed by the chief of the federal police, Felinto
(von Strubling) Müller. Several thousand suspected members and supporters
of the Brazilian Communist Party were arrested and either imprisoned or
deported. The most celebrated arrest was that of Prestes, who was eventually
captured in Rio de Janeiro and sentenced to a term of 16 years' imprisonment.

Vargas's authoritarian tendencies and distrust of democracy were further
demonstrated by his ambivalent attitude during the campaigning in 1937 for
the national presidential election scheduled for January 1938. According to
the 1934 Constitution Vargas was ineligible for election. This allowed new
political figures to emerge as candidates for national office. The front-runner
was the governor of São Paulo, (Armonado) Sales de Oliveira, who campaigned
as a liberal constitutionalist pledged to reduce the authority of the federal
government and return power back to the states. José Américo de Almeida

[146] from the Northeastern state of Paraíba offered the radical ideas of the *tenentes* and described himself as 'the people's candidate,' while Plínio Salgado represented the Integralistas. Vargas, however, was convinced that he should remain in power, a strategy that became known as '*continuismo*' (continuism). Although an element of personal ambition was, no doubt, present in his calculations, he also genuinely feared that the election of a new president would mean a return to the divisive political intrigues of the First Republic and represent a set-back for national economic and social development. But Vargas did not attempt to engage openly in the electoral process so that he could inform the people about his concerns and appeal for their support. The experiences of fighting against the Washington Luís administration in 1930 showed him that election results were unpredictable and that the backing of the military was absolutely crucial to secure his political objectives. Consequently, he plotted with his senior generals, notably Army Chief of Staff Góes Monteiro and Minister of War Eurico (Gaspar) Dutra, to foment a state of internal crisis that could be used to justify a coup and thereby pre-empt the presidential election.

The generals were sympathetic because Vargas had carefully cultivated the military throughout his period in office, providing them with generous financial appropriations and promotions. It was no accident, therefore, that military forces had almost doubled from 38,000 in 1927 to 75,000 in 1937. Moreover, senior officers genuinely feared the threat of Communism and did not forget that military units had been subverted in the 1935 risings, an event described by Góes Monteiro as 'the most terrible crisis in its [Brazil's] history.'[3] The public disclosure by Dutra on September 30 of a document discovered very conveniently by army officers in Rio de Janeiro which outlined the 'Cohen Plan,' an alleged Communist plot to assassinate prominent members of the federal government and unleash an orgy of violence, resulted in Congress voting to declare the country once again under a state of war. Amid a mood of mounting political uncertainty and rumors of an imminent military coup, the National Congress was surrounded by troops and closed on November 10, 1937. Later that day Vargas made an address over the radio announcing that he was declaring a state of national emergency to save the nation from the political instability and danger of imminent civil war that was being caused by the campaign for the presidency. Those elections would be cancelled. Vargas also announced the immediate adoption of a new constitution for what he called the *Estado Nôvo* (New State), a term copied from the Salazar regime that had seized power in Portugal in 1933. In effect, the Second Republic and the brief period of liberal constitutional government were terminated. In

their place, Vargas was re-establishing his personal dictatorship and creating
'the Third Republic.'

Unlike its predecessors in 1891 and 1934, the 1937 Constitution was not the product of a special committee or a constituent assembly but the work of Francisco Campos, a lawyer from Minas Gerais who had been assigned the task of secretly preparing the document for the November coup. Although provision was made for a plebiscite to demonstrate popular approval of the new constitution, this never occurred. The 1937 Constitution was, therefore, imposed on the country. Its stated aims were to provide order, maintain unity and promote national economic development through the creation of a strong federal executive in which the president of the republic possessed virtual dictatorial powers. The presidential term of office was extended from four to six years so that Getúlio would remain as president until 1943. The authoritarian tone of the document was considerably influenced by European fascism and represented a rejection of the liberal constitutionalism of the 1934 Constitution. It also marked a decisive defeat for the idea of decentralizing political power and allowing the state governments a large degree of autonomy. Even more than during the Second Empire, the states were placed directly under the control of the central government.

Vargas ensured that there was no effective opposition to his dictatorship by decreeing the dissolution of Congress, the abolition of all political parties and the imposition of strict censorship of the press. In fact, the November coup and the restrictions on political activity provoked little visible protest. The Communists and left-wing factions belonging to the National Liberation Alliance were already decimated by police repression. The liberal constitutionalists found themselves effectively outmaneuvered and made redundant by the sudden cancellation of the presidential election. By contrast, the Integralistas greeted the coup and the establishment of the *Estado Nôvo* as a welcome adoption of their own fascist ideas. Contrary to his expectations, however, Plínio Salgado was not given either high political office or accorded a position of influence. Moreover, the decree proscribing political parties was also applied to the Integralistas. A small group of Integralistas retaliated in May 1938 by attacking the presidential palace with the intention of kidnapping the president. Vargas and his daughter, Alzira, armed themselves with pistols and successfully resisted the rebels. In doing so, they were acclaimed as public heroes. The plot was so clumsily executed, however, that it was widely suspected of having been prepared by pro-government agents to provide an excuse to suppress the Integralistas. Indeed, Vargas seized the opportunity to denounce the Integralistas as 'Nazis' and to order mass arrests.

[148]   Salgado was forced to leave the country and seek exile in Portugal. Like the Communists, the Integralistas were effectively destroyed as a national political force.

The resort to repression and censorship was explained and justified on the grounds that it was necessary to preserve the country from internal and external enemies. During the *Estado Nôvo* thousands of political opponents of the regime were placed under police surveillance and suffered arrest, torture and imprisonment. Although Vargas undoubtedly preferred dictatorship to democracy, he also recognized the importance of gaining and holding the allegiance and support of a wide spectrum of interest groups including the military, business leaders, the middle classes and organized labor. To achieve this he still sought to continue the policy of 'national reconstruction,' but now publicly redefined his goal as the creation of 'a corporate state' that would bring economic and social benefits for all citizens. The concept of 'corporatism' not only sought to build a prosperous and stable Brazil but also a country that was economically independent and militarily strong, two objectives that particularly appealed to the nationalism of the military and the middle classes. Corporatism also reflected the belief that a high degree of national planning and investment were required at the federal level in order to promote development throughout all the country and not just on a narrow regional or class basis. For example, federal assistance and encouragement were given to migrants to settle and cultivate land in the sparsely-inhabited western regions of Brazil, a policy described as 'the march to the West.' The federal government also sought to stimulate industrial growth by bringing employers' organizations and trade unions within the corporate state. In the case of trade unions (*sindicatos*) of skilled workers, the Ministry of Labor possessed veto power over the selection of union officials and set up government-appointed tribunals to deal with disputes between employers and trade unions. Another feature of the corporate state was the bureaucratic growth of the federal government, a development that increased the number of officials and expanded the patronage available to those politicians who supported Vargas and the *Estado Nôvo*.

The fall of Vargas in 1945

Just as the threat of International Communism served to increase the authority of central government, Vargas's prestige and role as head of the federal government was similarly strengthened by the growing international crisis in Europe and the Far East that resulted in the outbreak of war in Europe in

1939. When Brazil entered the war on the Allied side in August 1942 he was
able to appeal to Brazilian patriotism. He also gained from the national pride
that Brazilians felt in the accomplishments of their troops fighting in Europe,
especially the exploits of the 25,000 men of the Brazilian Expeditionary
Force (*Força Expeditionário Brasileiro* or FEB) in Italy. In fact, contrary to the
advice of some of his senior generals, Vargas had insisted that Brazilians take
on an active combat role in Europe. Indeed, Brazil was the only Latin American country to do so.

Ironically, however, Brazil's participation in the war effort also had the
opposite effect of weakening Vargas's position as dictator by highlighting
the contradiction of a country under an authoritarian regime that was simultaneously fighting to liberate people in Western Europe from the tyranny of
similarly repressive political systems.[4] Criticism, however, was stifled so long
as political parties were prohibited and strict censorship of the press was
enforced. Nevertheless, protest could not be completely repressed. A manifesto
published in Minas Gerais in October 1943 was the first public indication of
unrest. It was signed by 90 prominent *mineiros* and appealed to the rest of the
nation to press for the restoration of liberal constitutionalism. 'If we fight
against fascism at the side of the United Nations so that liberty and democracy may be restored to all people,' the *mineiros* argued, 'certainly we are not
asking too much in demanding for ourselves such rights and guarantees.'[5]
Vargas vigorously denounced the manifesto as not only unpatriotic but also
damaging to the national war effort. Indeed, he used the fact that the country
was at war to justify the cancellation of the presidential election due in 1943
when his six-year term expired. Shortly afterwards, however, he stated that
elections would be held after the war had ended, a concession which implied
that 'reconstitutionalization' could not be perpetually postponed.

The prospect of elections was further enhanced by the course of the war in
Europe where it became clear at the end of 1944 that the democracies were
certain to achieve a smashing victory over their fascist enemies. Consequently,
the public pressure for the adoption of democratic forms of government and
an end to fascist-style dictatorship swelled in Brazil and throughout Latin
America. Ominously for Vargas, the Brazilian military was in favor of an
opening of the political system. To a considerable extent, this reflected the
growing admiration for the United States that resulted from the close cooperation during the war between Brazilian and American officers. Leading generals
such as Goés Monteiro and Dutra, who had been primarily instrumental in
ensuring the success of the 1937 coup, privately informed Vargas that his
period of dictatorial rule would have to end. The question became not whether

[150] elections would be allowed, but when exactly they would take place. Indeed, from 1943 onwards Vargas seemed to be making advance preparations for his own future campaign for the presidency. In marked contrast to the 1930s, he began to exploit the patronage of the presidency and the resources of the federal government in order to present himself not as a dictator but as 'a man of the people.' This 'populist' strategy was similar to that of Juan Domingo Perón in Argentina, especially in seeking to cultivate a close relationship with trade unions and their working-class members. Information was disseminated which placed particular emphasis on the many benefits such as the introduction of the minimum wage, improved pensions and medical care that industrial workers and their families had gained under the *Estado Nôvo*.

The momentum in favor of holding elections was stepped up in February 1945 by the publication in the daily press of an interview with José Américo in which the 1938 presidential candidate argued that the presidential election must shortly be held and that Vargas's candidacy should not be permitted. The fact that the interview actually escaped censorship was interpreted as a sign that the period of political repression and Vargas's long personal rule was drawing to a close. In March Eduardo Gomes, an air force brigadier and survivor of the 1922 Revolt of the *tenentes*, publicly announced that he would be a candidate for the presidency. Gomes enjoyed wide support from junior military officers. His criticism of the 1937 coup also made him popular among the liberal constitutionalists and the various political factions that opposed Vargas and wanted to see the dictator overthrown. Moreover, the long period of dictatorship had prevented the rise of national political figures so that a military candidate was likely to be better known to the public and, therefore, stood a better chance of winning a presidential election than a civilian.

Meanwhile, Vargas had decreed a constitutional amendment stating that direct elections for the presidency, the Congress and state legislatures would take place. In the case of the presidency this would be the first direct election since 1930. At first, Vargas would not rule out his own candidacy, but in a speech in March he implied that he could not be a candidate and intended to go into retirement after the elections. The war minister, General Dutra, subsequently emerged as the 'official' candidate and was assumed to be the president's chosen successor. In May Vargas confirmed that elections for the presidency and the National Congress would be held in December. A new political party, the Social Democratic Party (*Partido Social Democrático* or PSD), which had been formed in April, endorsed Dutra's candidacy. The PSD had the backing of the majority of state interventors who remained loyal to Vargas. The liberal constitutionalists and anti-getúlismo forces pledged to support

Eduardo Gomes and formed the National Democratic Union (*União Democrática*   [151]
Nacional or UDN) to organize his national campaign for the presidency.

Despite the fact that an official electoral campaign was under way between
Gomes and Dutra, the behavior and intentions of Vargas soon became the
principal topic of discussion and speculation in the press. Rumors abounded
that he would attempt a 'continuist' coup to hold on to power just as he had
done in 1937. Corroborating evidence for this was found in his studiously
ambiguous attitude as to whether he would actually be a candidate. The confusion was increased rather than decreased by the creation of the Brazilian
Labor Party (*Partido Trabalhista Brasileiro* or PTB), a new political party which
was actually organized within the Ministry of Labor and had named Vargas
as its 'honorary president.' There was also the sudden appearance of a group
of private citizens known as the '*Queremistas*' who adopted the slogan '*queremos
Getúlio*' ('We want Getúlio'). The *Queremistas* organized a mass rally that
paraded outside the presidential palace in Rio de Janeiro on October 3 to
mark the 15th anniversary of the start of the 1930 Revolution. Their proclaimed object was the cancellation of the presidential election. They wanted
elections still to be held in December but, as had occurred in 1933, they would
be limited to the election of a constituent assembly. Vargas, therefore, would
remain as president until a new constitution was promulgated.

Vargas's attempt to manipulate the political process in 1945 proved
unsuccessful and ultimately self-defeating. Statements that he intended to
retire clashed with rumors of a 'continuist' coup, the formation of the PTB
and the emergence of the *Queremistas*. The result was confusion and distrust.
Moreover, the electoral campaign in 1945 was markedly different from 1937
in that Dutra and Gomes were both military figures and could not be so easily
put aside as the civilian candidates had been eight years earlier. Indeed, the
senior military commanders were not openly sympathetic to Vargas in 1945.
'If President Vargas loses the support of any substantial portion of the Army,'
an American diplomatic official had predicted in January 1945, 'his government is not likely to survive.'[6] In 1937 the military and Vargas had been united
in their alarm over the Communist threat. In 1945, however, senior army
officers expressed concern over his decision to resume diplomatic relations
with the Soviet Union and especially the granting of an amnesty in April to
imprisoned Communists and the subsequent legalization of the Communist
Party. There was even suspicion that the president had entered into a secret
accord with Luís Carlos Prestes because, after his release from prison, Prestes
had made a number of public speeches stating that Vargas should remain as
president. The generals were also perturbed by current events in Argentina

[152]   and feared that Vargas intended to imitate the Argentine leader, Juan Perón, and establish a populist regime that would deliberately stir up class conflict and social unrest in Brazil. Perón's return to power in Argentina on October 17 was widely attributed to the prevarication of the Argentine military. The lesson was not lost upon the Brazilian generals, who grasped that quick action was necessary to overthrow Vargas. On October 29 troops surrounded the presidential palace and an ultimatum was presented to Vargas to resign. Like Dom Pedro II in 1889 and Washington Luís in 1930, Vargas was taken by surprise and recognized that resistance was futile. A bloodless coup took place in which Vargas formally resigned the office of president and left Rio de Janeiro to return as a private citizen to his ranch in Rio Grande do Sul. In farewell statements he claimed that his time in office had been devoted to working for the people of Brazil and that he would be exonerated by events. In what was regarded as a calculated attempt to maintain good relations with the military, he remarked: 'I have no grounds for ill will against the glorious armed forces of my country, whose prestige I have always sought to enhance.'[7]

The 1945 election

The intervention of the military in 1945 was not designed to impose a change of government upon the country. It was quite different from the action taken in 1937 in that the intention was to ensure that the forthcoming presidential election should take place on schedule rather than prevent it. Nevertheless, the coup was highly significant because it overthrew Vargas, ended the *Estado Nôvo* and inaugurated a 'Fourth' Republic whose political system would be democracy and not authoritarianism. This was demonstrated by War Minister Goés Monteiro entering into discussions with the two presidential candidates, Dutra and Gomes, on how to fill the vacant office of president. They decided that a leading member of the judiciary should act as interim president. The chief justice of the Supreme Court, José Linhares, agreed to serve in this office until the new president was inaugurated on January 31, 1946.

The presidential and congressional elections that took place in December 1945 were the first national elections since 1934. Elections for state legislatures followed in 1946. Over 6 million voters voted in the 1945 presidential election, a record figure which was more than three times the number that had voted in 1930. For the first time, urban workers participated fully in the electoral process. In addition, the electoral process was regarded as having been fairly conducted. While the operation of the secret ballot reduced

intimidation and corruption, the manipulative influence of the state political
machines and the *coronéis* remained powerful especially in rural areas. This
factor undoubtedly aided Dutra, who was the 'official' candidate and possessed
the backing of the federal government and most of the state interventors who
had been appointed during the *Estado Nôvo*. Dutra polled just over 3 million
votes, against 2 million for Gomes. The margin of victory was considered
narrow, although Dutra had gained 55 percent and therefore could claim an
overall majority of the total popular vote. The third candidate in the election
was Yedo Fiúza, the former mayor of Petrópolis. Though a non-Communist
he was sponsored principally by the Brazilian Communist Party as an anti-
military candidate and surprised political commentators by gaining more than
half a million votes.

Although ostensibly in retirement in Rio Grande do Sul, Vargas still
exercised an influence on the election. Despite speculation that he might take
revenge on those who had overthrown him and endorse the left-wing Fiúza,
Vargas eventually issued a public statement in favor of Dutra. The endorsement, however, came only one week before the election and was heavily quali-
fied. 'I shall be at the people's side against the President if the candidate's
promises are not fulfilled,' he remarked.[8] While the ex-president took no
active steps to put his own name forward, it was placed on the ballot, usually
as a candidate for the Brazilian Labor Party, for deputy or senator in a number
of states. To the dismay of his civilian and military critics, Vargas's national
popularity was decisively re-affirmed as both Rio Grande do Sul and São Paulo
elected him to the Senate, while six states and the Federal District chose him
to be one of their congressional deputies.

For the first time in Brazilian history, the respective performances of the
new national political parties in the elections attracted serious contemporary
analysis. The Social Democratic Party was pleased with the results. Not only
had its presidential candidate achieved victory, but the party gained 151 deputies and 26 senators so that it possessed a clear majority in both houses of
Congress. By contrast, the National Democratic Union was extremely disap-
pointed. The UDN had confidently predicted victory for Gomes, but found
that the removal of Vargas from office suddenly deprived them of the single
issue that had been their main target of criticism and principal vote-winner.
In terms of congressional seats the UDN won only 77 deputies and 10 senators. The Brazilian Labor Party fared even worse and gained only 22 deputies and 2 senators. On the other hand, the PTB was a relatively small party
whose strength and appeal were limited to trade unions and the urban working
class.

[154]   The political party that made the most striking advance in 1945–46 was the Brazilian Communist Party. Its presidential candidate had entered the campaign only two weeks before the election, but had still achieved the respectable total of half a million votes. In the congressional elections, Prestes was elected to the Senate from the Federal District and 14 Communists were chosen as deputies, giving the PCB the best electoral results of any Communist party in Latin America. Success was mostly attributed to the popularity of Prestes, who was, after Vargas, the second best-known political figure in Brazil. In fact, the long years of imprisonment from 1936 to 1945 had embellished rather than tarnished his heroic past. In addition, as in Western Europe just after the end of World War II, Communist parties throughout Latin America benefited from the improved international image of the Soviet Union as a brave ally in the fight for freedom against fascism. While suspicion of Communism remained latent in Brazil, it seemed that the PCB had finally begun to recover from the stigma attached to its leading role in the abortive 1935 revolt.

The Dutra administration

Eurico Dutra was sworn in as president on January 31, 1946. A competent career officer and administrator, he had served as Minister of War from 1936 to 1945. Dutra, however, was not an experienced politician. Nor was he an effective public speaker. Indeed, his bland personality had contrasted unfavorably with that of Gomes during the campaign for the presidential election. Despite his former self-confessed admiration for Nazism, Dutra promised not to return the country to dictatorial rule. Above all, he wanted 'tranquillity' and a peaceful transition from the authoritarian past to democracy. Although Dutra was closely identified with the PSD, to promote 'tranquillity' he was prepared to act in a bipartisan manner and to offer posts in the cabinet to members of the UDN.

The new president awaited the preparation and ratification of a new constitution. The National Congress assembled in February 1946 and appointed a commission of legal experts to draw up a new draft constitution. This was debated in Congress and promulgated on September 16. The 1946 Constitution essentially reinstated the political system contained in the 1934 Constitution by re-affirming the role and powers of the National Congress. Although curbs were placed on the authority of the president, his power to intervene in the affairs of the states was recognized. The presidential term of office was fixed at five years and the position of vice-president was restored.

A president could not succeed himself. Although elections and civil rights [155] were guaranteed, the franchise was still restricted to literates. In addition, enlisted men in the armed services were not eligible to vote.

Dutra's uninspiring leadership and generally passive approach gave the impression that he was performing the role of an interim president. The one issue in which he acted decisively was suppression of Communism. In part, this reflected the traditional hostility of the senior military towards Communism. This was heightened by concern that Communism was growing in strength in Brazil, a fact illustrated by the electoral success of the PCB and reinforced by warnings from the United States government and its political and military representatives in the country. As soon as Dutra assumed office a purge was begun of Communists in federal employment. In 1947 the image of Communism was damaged by a serious industrial strike in São Paulo and a remarkable statement from Prestes that he would personally support the Soviet Union in the eventuality of a war between the Soviets and Brazil. Later in the year the PCB was declared illegal under a clause of the 1946 Constitution prohibiting 'anti-democratic' organizations. In January 1948 Prestes and the 14 Communist deputies were expelled from the National Congress. Despite the tough line taken against the PCB, the repression of the late-1940s was not as brutal as that of a decade earlier. The PCB, however, never regained the electoral influence and success that it briefly achieved in 1945–47. Though it would continue to exercise a powerful influence especially upon trade union officials and Brazilian intellectuals, the ideology of Communism remained limited in its popular appeal especially when faced with the hostility of powerful enemies in the military, the Catholic Church, and the political and business élites.

Vargas returns to power

Although Brazil's adoption of democracy in 1945 stimulated the appearance of a number of new political parties at national and state level, politics still largely revolved around personalities. In this respect, the most important was Getúlio Vargas. After his election victories in 1945, Vargas chose to take up his seat as PSD senator for Rio Grande do Sul. He made, however, only occasional appearances in the Senate. As always, he remained an enigma and his political future and intentions were subject to endless speculation. While Vargas had not actually submitted himself to a direct presidential election since 1930, his potential to win votes was considered to be formidable. Not only did he retain the backing and allegiance of many groups and individuals

[156] who had benefited from the *Estado Nôvo* but he was also able to attract wide popular support, particularly among the new urban voters. As the presidential election of 1950 approached, Vargas embarked upon a political campaign delivering speeches that expounded the philosophy of '*trabalhismo*' ('Laborism') and were deliberately 'populist' in tone. In particular, they stressed his image as the 'father of the poor' and cited the achievements of the *Estado Nôvo* in promoting economic benefits and social welfare for the masses.

Vargas's strategy to win the presidency in 1950 was not just to present himself as a populist. He also negotiated the private arrangements that had long been customary for aspiring presidential candidates ever since the beginning of the Republic. The most important was to maintain good relations with the military. Vargas duly gained assurances from Goés Monteiro that they would not prevent his candidacy or accession to office, if elected. Close contact was also maintained with leading members of the PSD, though Vargas eventually accepted the nomination of the PTB. At the same time, he entered into a private understanding with Adhemar de Barros, the leader of the Progressive Social Party (*Partido Social Progressista* or PSP) and a rising populist politician who had been elected governor of São Paulo in 1947. São Paulo was regarded as a critical factor in winning the election because it possessed more eligible voters than any other state. In return for the support of the PSP, Vargas gave an undertaking of future support for Adhemar's presidential ambitions. In addition, he accepted as his vice-presidential running mate the PSP nominee, João Café (Filho), even though the latter was a former member of the National Liberation Alliance and had been exiled to Argentina for his criticism of the *Estado Nôvo*.

While Vargas was endorsed by the PTB and the PSP of São Paulo, the opposition was divided. The UDN renominated Gomes and the PSD selected the relatively little-known *mineiro* politician and former mayor of Belo Horizonte, Cristiano Monteiro Machado. During the ensuing campaign Vargas concentrated on presenting a scathing indictment of Dutra's 'conservative' administration and promised substantial federal aid to industry and an increase in wages for workers. The note of populism was evident in a famous statement that he made in Rio de Janeiro: 'If I am elected on October 3, as I take office the people will climb the steps of Catete with me. And they will remain with me in power.'[9] In marked contrast, Gomes favored a traditionally liberal laissez-faire approach to economic policy and even advocated repeal of the minimum wage legislation that had been passed during the *Estado Nôvo*. Machado preferred to limit his campaigning to his native state of Minas Gerais. The

election result illustrated the extent of Vargas's national popularity and
political skill. He won 17 states plus the Federal District with 3.8 million
votes or 48.7 percent of the total vote, almost an overall majority. Gomes
gained 2.3 million votes, while Machado took third place with 1.7 million. A
new record of more than 8 million votes was recorded. The crucial contribution of the state of São Paulo towards Vargas's victory was indicated by the
fact that its voters provided a quarter of his total vote. Indeed, Vargas had
become something of a folk hero for ordinary Brazilians so that many voted
for him as an individual rather than for the parties that had nominated him.
The PTB won only 51 seats in the Chamber of Deputies, while the PSP
had 24. The largest parties were the PSD with 112 deputies and the UDN
with 81.

Even though Vargas was gratified by his victory, which he regarded as
a personal vindication by the Brazilian people, the position he had won was
that of a popularly-elected president and not a dictator. Instead of ruling by
decree as he had done for most of his previous period of power, he would
now have to develop a working relationship with the politicians in the National
Congress in order to pass laws. The task was made extremely difficult by the
country's lack of experience in democratic procedures. Moreover, several
political parties existed and none possessed an overall majority. While Vargas
enjoyed good relations with the PSD and the PTB, he encountered sustained
hostility from the UDN. Leaders of the UDN even tried to persuade the military not to allow Vargas's inauguration on the grounds that the 1946 Constitution required a president to achieve an absolute majority of the popular
vote. While the military dismissed the UDN claim as belated and spurious,
it was evident that they were themselves divided over their opinions of the
new president.

In his electoral campaign Vargas had promised positive action to overcome the serious economic problems facing the nation. A national policy was
unveiled in the Five-Year Plan announced in September 1951 by Finance
Minister Horácio Lafer. The 'Lafer Plan' was formulated and implemented by
a group of technocrats including engineers, economists, and civil servants.
Their purpose was to direct investment into basic industries and pay particular attention to improving transportation and supplies of energy. An important requirement for the success of the Lafer Plan was the continued inflow of
foreign capital. The extent of foreign involvement in the economy was, however, a very sensitive political issue. Although Vargas had long stressed the
importance of Brazil's achieving 'economic independence,' he had generally
welcomed foreign investment during the *Estado Nôvo*. For example, foreign

[158]   financial assistance had been essential to develop the steel industry located at
Volta Redonda. After 1945, however, he became increasingly strident in his
advocacy of economic nationalism. Foreign bankers and corporations were
condemned for their selfish and systematic exploitation of Brazil's industry
and economic resources. The issue was symbolized by growing controversy
over oil. Following on from the announcement of the Lafer Plan, a bill was
introduced into Congress in December 1951 proposing the creation of a mixed
public–private corporation to explore and develop the country's oil resources.
The government would be the majority share-holder in the new company,
which would be known as *Petrobrás* (*Petróleos Brasileiros*). Under the terms of
the original bill, a role for private capital in the oil business was still envisaged because existing refineries would not be affected by the proposed legislation. The bill, however, provoked a fierce debate. Influenced by the politics
of the Cold War, Brazilian Communists condemned any arrangement with
the international oil corporations, who were regarded as agents of the capitalist governments of the West. Economic nationalists pointed out the exor-
bitant profits made by foreign corporations in the oil business and demanded
that strategically-important industries such as oil must be nationalized and
resulting profits retained for Brazil. The nationalist argument was countered
by business interests which stressed the vital importance of attracting foreign
capital and maintaining good relations with overseas trading partners, especially the United States. Elements within the military were also eager not to
disturb the close professional links that had been established with the United
States. Conditioned by ideas emanating from the *Escola Superior da Guerra*
(Higher War College or ESG), the nation's prestigious military staff college
that had been established in 1949, they believed that Brazil must ally with
the West in the battle against International Communism. While Brazilian
opinion strongly favored the West, it was aroused and excited by the appeal
of economic nationalism. Indeed, the slogan of '*o petroléo é nosso*' ('the oil is
ours') gripped the public imagination and persuaded Congress in October
1953 to approve a measure providing for the full nationalization of the oil
industry.

After initially taking a moderate approach to the *Petrobrás* issue, Vargas
had become more radical in response to growing political and public pressure.
A similar move to accommodate public opinion was evident in the debate
over a proposed increase in the minimum wage. In part, this reflected Vargas's
electoral strategy to build up support among the workers and their unions for
the forthcoming congressional elections in October 1954. But substantive
action was also required to deal with the destructive impact of rampant

inflation that had cut the real wages of workers in 1953 to only 53 percent of   [159]
the 1943 figure. In June 1953 two important appointments were made to the
cabinet. One was Osvaldo Aranha, Vargas's long-time close political associate, who became Finance Minister. The other was João (Belchior Marques)
Goulart who was appointed Minister of Labor. Goulart's father had been a
friend and neighbor of Vargas in Rio Grande do Sul. His son, João or 'Jango,'
as he was popularly known, had been so close to Vargas that he was even
rumored to be the president's illegitimate son. Despite his affluent background,
Goulart built his political career on close links with trade unions and rose to
become Vice-President of the PTB. His promotion to the cabinet was controversial because it indicated that Vargas was seeking to appeal to the
workers. The military were especially wary of Goulart. Some suspected him
of Communist sympathies, but the biggest concern was that he intended to
use the unions as a paramilitary force and establish a syndicalist regime
('*república sindicalista*') of the kind that Perón had created in Argentina.

The new ministers had diametrically opposed views. While Aranha
launched the 'Aranha Plan,' a programme of economic austerity designed to
reduce inflation, Goulart argued that there should be a large increase in the
minimum wage to reduce poverty and suffering among the working class.
The middle classes objected to the proposed increase on the grounds that it
would be inflationary and discriminatory. More ominously for the government was the publication in February 1954 of a 'Colonels' Memorandum,' a
manifesto signed by 80 officers which complained that military salaries had
been depressed for so long that Goulart's proposal would actually give some
workers a higher wage than junior officers. The protests coincided with fierce
criticism of Vargas and the government by Carlos Lacerda, a prominent member of the UDN. Over the radio and in his influential newspaper, *Tribuna da
Imprensa*, Lacerda relentlessly assailed the government for incompetence and
corruption and alleged that Vargas was planning a coup to reimpose dictatorial rule. Particularly damaging to the administration was the exposure of a
financial scandal in which the Banco do Brasil made unsecured loans to the
journalist, Samuel Wainer, for the purpose of setting up a pro-government
daily newspaper, *Ultima Hora*.

The 1954 crisis

The announcement of Goulart's resignation on February 22, 1954 seemed
to imply that Vargas supported Aranha's austerity program. Enigmatic as
always, the president subsequently delivered a speech at Petrópolis in May

[160]   in which he dramatically announced a doubling of the minimum wage. His speech also contained an unambiguous appeal for the support of the workers: 'With your votes you can not only defend your interests, but you can influence the very destiny of the nation. As citizens your views will bear weight at the polls. As a class, you can make your ballots the decisive numerical force. You constitute the majority. Today you are with the government. Tomorrow you will be the government.'[10] The tone of the message was out of political character because Vargas had always preferred to reach a consensus on policy matters and to avoid conflict wherever possible. By appealing directly to the class consciousness of the workers, he alienated the middle classes and upset the military.

The most fierce criticism of Vargas appeared in the radio and press campaign orchestrated by Carlos Lacerda. On August 5 an attempt was made in Copacabana to assassinate Lacerda. While Lacerda was merely wounded in the foot, stray shots killed his volunteer bodyguard, Air Force Major Rubens Florentino Vaz. The air force was incensed and demanded a military inquiry that traced the planning of the assassination attempt to the chief of the presidential guard, Gregório Fortunato.[11] The investigation also uncovered a wide variety of questionable financial activities in which several of Vargas's aides were involved, including widespread bribery and fraud and connections with organized crime. Dismayed by the revelations and the ammunition that they would supply to Lacerda, Vargas lamented: 'I feel like I am standing in a sea of mud.'[12]

'There is no longer any doubt that the continuation of democratic institutions in Brazil is dependent upon the removal of Senhor Getúlio Vargas from power,' summed up an editorial in the *Diário Carioca*.[13] Enormous pressure, including daily public demonstrations outside the presidential palace, was exerted for the president to resign. Vargas pointed out, however, that he was not personally implicated in the murder of Vaz and that there was, therefore, no compelling legal reason why he should give up his office. After some hesitation, senior military commanders eventually decided to demand his resignation. At 70 years of age Vargas felt that he had little room for political maneuver and had privately warned that he would rather die than suffer a repetition of the personal humiliation of being driven from office as had occurred in 1945. He was true to his word, and shot himself in the heart on August 24. A political testament was discovered at his bedside that explained that his decision to commit suicide was caused by 'international economic and financial groups.' He concluded: 'I fought against the looting of Brazil. I fought against the looting of the people. I have fought bare-breasted. The

hatred, infamy, and calumny did not beat down my spirit. I gave you my life. [161]
Now I offer my death. Nothing remains. Serenely I take the first step on the
road to eternity and I leave life to enter history.'[14] The act of suicide and
the accompanying testament, which was regarded as a personal farewell to
the nation, not only saved Getúlio from the imminent humiliation of a second
deposition by the military but also made him a martyr and promoted his post-
humous reputation as the 'father of the poor.'[15] His critics were temporarily
silenced. Lacerda went into hiding. Some offices of foreign financial institutions were the target of popular wrath and suffered damage from street
demonstrations. The violence, however, did not last for long. The suicide
had been a shock, but it did not leave a lasting bitterness within society.

The election and presidency of Kubitschek

Vargas's death elevated Vice-President João Café Filho to the presidency.
A new cabinet was quickly formed to which Café appointed several leading
members of the UDN, including the twice-defeated presidential candidate,
Eduardo Gomes. The elevation of the UDN to a position of power, however,
did not materially affect government policy. Café Filho considered himself
a substitute president who did not have a popular mandate to introduce
significant political changes. Moreover, the congressional and state elections
were only a few weeks away. He had no intention of attempting a continuist
coup and saw his task as maintaining order so that the elections could
proceed on schedule on October 3.

The elections duly took place in orderly fashion. The results, however,
hardly affected the composition of the National Congress. The PSD remained
the largest single party. Once again, the UDN recorded a disappointing
performance. In individual contests João Goulart lost his bid to become a
senator for Rio Grande do Sul, but any joy among the anti-getúlistas was
muted by the victory of Goulart's brother-in-law, Leonel (de Moura) Brizola,
for the Chamber of Deputies. Considerable publicity was given to the victory
of Jânio Quadros (da Silva) over Adhemar de Barros for the governorship of
São Paulo. In the previous year Quadros had won the election for mayor
of the city of São Paulo. Although he did not belong to any of the major
political parties, his reputation for honesty and integrity and his pledge to
fight corruption in government had rapidly made him a leading political figure
in São Paulo.

Presidential elections followed on schedule in 1955. The PSD nominated
the popular governor of Minas Gerais, Juscelino Kubitschek (de Oliveira).

[162] The unusual surname denoted that Juscelino was the grandson of a Czech immigrant. An astute politician, he sought to complement the strong influence of the PSD in rural areas by entering into an electoral alliance with the PTB to gain the latter's urban votes. In return, however, he accepted the controversial João Goulart as his vice-presidential running mate. General Juarez Távora, a *tenente* and long-time critic of Getúlio, was the UDN presidential candidate while Adhemar de Barros was nominated by the PSP.

In the ensuing electoral campaign Kubitschek echoed the policies associated with Vargas and appeared much more energetic and imaginative than his opponents. Using the slogan 'fifty years' progress in five' to great effect, he stressed the vital importance of economic growth and promised massive investment to transform Brazil into a modern, industrial nation that would gain international respect and admiration. He also underlined his commitment to promote advances in social welfare and made a point of reviving the idea of moving the federal capital from Rio to the West in order to stimulate the neglected interior region of the country. The idea had a long history dating back to Tiradentes in the eighteenth century, but had never been seriously entertained by national politicians.

The result of the presidential election held on October 3, 1955 was a narrow victory for Kubitschek with almost 3.1 million votes to 2.6 million for Távora. Adhemar de Barros was a close third with just over 2 million votes. Indeed, Adhemar's success in winning the largest number of votes in his home state of São Paulo significantly contributed to Kubitschek receiving only 34 percent of the total popular vote, a much smaller share than Vargas in 1951 and Dutra in 1945 and well short of an absolute majority. João Goulart won the vice-presidential contest in a victory that was interpreted as another popular vindication for Vargas and his populist policies. Goulart's critics alleged, however, that he maintained secret links with Communists. The fear of Communists infiltrating the federal government prompted Carlos Lacerda and some members of the UDN to join with sympathetic military officers in an attempt to block Kubitschek and Goulart from taking office. A complicated series of events took place in November 1955 in which the war minister, Marshal Henrique (Batista Duffles Teixeira) Lott, ordered army units to occupy key positions in Rio de Janeiro and thereby prevent the conspirators from establishing themselves in government.[16] Senior military commanders believed that they had a legal obligation to adhere to the results of the presidential election and that Kubitschek and Goulart should be formally installed as president and vice-president on January 31, 1956. For example, General Távora later recalled that many officers were worried that Communism would

grow in influence under Kubitschek, but he considered that 'they did not feel
they had the right to block his inauguration by violence.'[17]

Juscelino Kubitschek's presidency from 1956 to 1961 was a period of such
political calm that it seemed to contemporaries that the long-delayed national
experiment in democracy was finally being implemented successfully. With
the exception of two short-lived and abortive coups organized mainly by
disgruntled air force officers, relations between the new president and the
military were cordial. In addition, there was dynamic economic activity as
Kubitschek sought to deliver his campaign promise of 'fifty years' progress
in five.' His administration placed particular emphasis on central economic
planning and generating massive investment both from internal and external
sources. The most notable and visible success was the rapid development
of the automobile industry located mainly in São Paulo. While industrial
production boomed and profits rose, Kubitschek did not neglect the workers
and introduced a large increase in the minimum wage in 1958.

As part of a program of national economic development the Kubitschek
administration established regional development agencies of which SUDENE
(*Superintendência para o Desenvolvimento do Nordeste* or 'Superintendency for
the Development of the Northeast') was the largest and most famous. Major
projects were started to improve road transportation and construct hydro-
electric dams to provide power in remote rural areas throughout the country.
The foremost example of Juscelino's ambition and achievement was, however, the building of a new federal capital at the geographical center of
the country in the state of Goiás, more than 600 miles northwest of Rio de
Janeiro. The city was named Brasília and was formally opened as the new
federal capital on April 21, 1960. The event symbolized national unity and
was particularly gratifying to Brazilians because it also attracted considerable
worldwide interest. Not only had Brazilians built a city from virtual scratch
in the space of only a few years, but its futuristic architecture and original
airplane design were a topic of international discussion and admiration.

Kubitschek gave Brazilians pride and confidence in their country, but he
fell short of achieving 'fifty years' progress in five.' Not for the first or the last
time for governments in modern Brazilian history, his administration found
that pursuing a policy of sustained high government spending brought rapid
economic growth but at the price of stimulating rising inflation. Economies
were introduced as early as 1958 in order to combat the rise in prices. The
result, however, was a slowing down of economic growth that provoked
criticism of government policy from political opponents, business and trade
union leaders. At the same time foreign bankers grew apprehensive that

[164] Kubitschek would resort simply to printing new money to finance anticipated future budgetary deficits. In his search for a substantial inflow of foreign investment Kubitschek suggested in May 1958 that the United States lead a major economic recovery program, which would be known as 'Operation Pan-America' ('*Operação Pan-Americana*') because it would seek to aid all the economies of Latin America. The proposal was studiously ignored by the Eisenhower administration, although a similar idea was formulated by President John F. Kennedy in 1961 and was called the 'Alliance for Progress.' In 1958 American officials were preoccupied with what they considered was Kubitschek's reckless financial profligacy, and supported the International Monetary Fund's reluctance to agree to Brazil's request for a loan of $300 million. In June 1959 Kubitschek abruptly broke off negotiations with the IMF and angrily retorted: 'Brazil has come of age. We are no longer poor relatives obliged to stay in the kitchen and forbidden to enter the living room. We ask only collaboration of other nations. By making greater sacrifices we can attain political and principally economic independence without the help of others.'[18]

The rise and fall of Quadros and Goulart

Kubitschek's emotive defiance of the IMF and foreign bankers was highly popular in Brazil because it appealed to traditional patriotic and nationalist sentiment. During the final year of his presidency he was able, therefore, to avoid externally-imposed austerity measures and continue instead with his inflationary policy of stressing economic growth. Indeed, dealing with the awkward problem of inflation would be passed to his successor because the 1946 Constitution laid down that a president could not succeed himself. Consequently, Kubitschek could not be a candidate in the 1960 election, though no doubt his populist policies were intended to enhance his chances in the next presidential election scheduled for 1965. In the event, the president was careful to play a minimal role in the political battle to find his successor.

In 1960 the candidates for the presidency were Henrique Lott, Jânio Quadros and Adhemar de Barros. Lott was an army officer who had risen to the high military rank of marshal and had served competently as War Minister under Café Filho and Kubitschek. Nominated by the PSD, he was regarded as the 'official' government candidate. Support from the PTB was also ensured by the selection of João Goulart as his vice-presidential running mate. But Lott lacked political experience and was not an effective campaigner. In marked

contrast, Jânio Quadros possessed a charismatic presence and was regarded
as a political 'phenomenon.' A former governor of São Paulo, Quadros had
enjoyed a meteoric political rise during the 1950s capitalizing on the fact
that he was a political outsider dedicated to providing honest and efficient
government. His symbol during the 1960 election was a broom with which
he promised to sweep the rogues and rascals from political office. Quadros
accepted the nomination of the UDN, but he constantly played down the
importance of party affiliation. The custom of making secret political deals
and arrangements was anathema to him. He cherished his independence and
wanted to appear as 'a free citizen, rather than a prisoner in the presidency.'[19]
The third candidate in 1960, Adhemar de Barros, was endorsed by the PSP
and, though expected to win a considerable number of votes in the state of
São Paulo, he was not considered likely to do well beyond his home state.

Despite the great public excitement caused by his candidacy, Jânio Quadros
worked hard to ensure victory. He flew over 150,000 miles and delivered
hundreds of speeches. The 'phenomenon' was rewarded with almost 6
million votes, a total which came close to the votes of Lott and Adhemar combined. But split-ticket voting was also a feature of the election so that the
PSD–PTB candidate, João Goulart, won the vice-presidential contest for the
second time. Although Quadros did not quite win an absolute majority of
the popular vote, the result was regarded not only as a smashing personal
triumph but also as a victory for the democratic will of the people and a
resounding defeat for the professional politicians.

Quadros's success also brought the UDN to power. Despite securing
several appointments to cabinet office, however, the UDN was able to exercise
little influence on an independently-minded president who felt that he owed
little to the party for his election. Ensconced and isolated in the newly constructed Alvorada Palace in Brasília, Quadros's awkward personal style of
doing business and especially his sensitivity to criticism resulted in poor relations with all the political parties in Congress. While the new president was
clearly determined to attack corruption in all branches of the federal government, he lacked a coherent political program. Proclaiming the defeat of
inflation as the priority of his administration, a confused economic policy
was introduced which imposed austerity measures to cut back federal spending
and reduce economic growth while seeking to stimulate the economy with
the aid of large loans from the IMF and the Alliance for Progress. Foreign
policy aroused particular controversy as Jânio placed less importance on
Brazil's relations with the United States and sought to strengthen links with
the Third World, especially the newly-independent nations of Africa. But it

was his desire to improve relations with Communist countries that caused most concern. In 1960 Jânio had accepted an invitation to visit Cuba. The famous revolutionary leader, Ché Guevara, visited Brazil in August 1961 and was awarded the Order of the Southern Cross (*Cruzeiro do Sul*), an action that was publicly condemned by the UDN leader, Carlos Lacerda. The president's critics were also concerned by his decision to send Vice-President Goulart on a trade mission to the Soviet Union and the People's Republic of China.

The nation was stunned on August 25, 1961 when Quadros suddenly announced his resignation in a written message that was read out in Congress. In words reminiscent of Getúlio Vargas's last testament in 1954, the message referred to 'foreign' and 'terrible forces' that had deliberately and persistently thwarted efforts 'to lead this nation onto the path of its true political and economic liberation, the only path that would bring the effective progress and social justice which its noble people deserve.'[20] The reasons for the resignation have never satisfactorily been explained, but it seems very likely that Quadros expected his action to provoke a political crisis in which the military would assume power for a brief period during which public pressure would build up for his reinstatement in office with greatly expanded executive authority. A crucial element in this scenario was the assumption that the military would refuse to allow Vice-President Goulart to succeed to the presidency. Indeed, Goulart's suitability was not helped by the fact that he was in a Communist country, the People's Republic of China, at the time of the resignation.

Quadros, however, had seriously miscalculated. His swift departure from the country to Europe only two days after his resignation meant there was no figurehead to rally support around. Indeed, Quadros's open disdain for the political establishment meant that Congress showed little hesitation in accepting the resignation and appointed the president of the Chamber of Deputies, Pascoal Ranieri Mazzilli, as acting-president. The public also showed little sympathy and felt that Quadros had acted selfishly and precipitately in giving up the presidency after less than seven months in office. Moreover, the trade unions and left-wing political groups were pleased with the prospect of Goulart becoming president and had little reason to support the unpredictable Jânio. The military were openly divided. War Minister Odílio Denys was highly suspicious of Goulart's Communist associations and appeared determined to prevent his succession. 'The situation obliges us to choose between democracy and Communism,' declared Denys.[21] General (José) Machado Lopes, the commander of the Third Army based in Rio Grande do Sul, however, was strongly in favour of Goulart. The prospect of civil war loomed as the Vice-President made his way back to Brazil. A characteristically Brazilian compromise was reached, however, in which the military agreed to Goulart becoming president on condition that his authority was considerably restricted. Congress, therefore, amended the constitution to create a parliamentary system in which the cabinet became a Council of Ministers and was headed by a prime minister who would share executive powers with the president. Goulart signified his acquiescence and was formally elevated to the presidency on the day of national independence, September 7, 1961.

The compromise of 1961 averted civil conflict, but it was basically unworkable because neither the president nor Congress believed in the efficacy of the arrangement. Goulart soon made clear his intention to remove the restrictions. There was little opposition because public opinion was receptive to the idea that he had been unfairly treated. Indeed, his supporters pointed out that Goulart had behaved responsibly as vice-president since 1956 and throughout the 1961 constitutional crisis. Moreover, at a time of growing economic crisis it was argued that the country needed strong executive government. The logic for revoking the constitutional amendment was also accepted by the military. Consequently, the issue was put to the people in a plebiscite on January 6, 1963. Out of a total of 12 million votes more than 9 million expressed a preference for the restoration of full presidential powers.

Goulart interpreted the result of the plebiscite as a personal triumph and a popular mandate to proceed with a program of economic and social welfare that he referred to as 'basic reforms.' In effect, he was continuing the policies associated with Getúlio Vargas. Like Vargas, Goulart was outwardly congenial and conciliatory. But he lacked the political astuteness of his mentor and was also judged by contemporaries to be weak and indecisive. This was partly due to the fact that, despite his long political career dating back to the 1940s, Goulart had mostly served as a 'second-in-command' and had never held executive positions such as the mayor of a major city or the governor of a state. In addition, the attempt to implement radical reforms coincided with a period of increasing economic, social and political crisis. When congressional elections took place in 1962, they merely re-affirmed the fragmented state of the political system in which the PSD remained the largest single party but was well short of holding an overall majority in Congress. Discontent and impatience with Congress showed itself in the growing incidence of strikes and political demonstrations.

In January 1963 Goulart responded to the economic crisis by announcing the adoption of an ambitious and optimistic 'Three-Year Plan,' drafted by the economist Celso Furtado. The Plan promised to deliver a high rate of growth

[168]   combined with falling levels of inflation. In effect, the government was essentially continuing the expansionist policies of Kubitschek in the belief that economic growth would by itself ultimately defeat inflation. In the short term, however, economic production lagged and inflation continued its relentless rise. Furthermore, the deficit in the balance of payments widened and the foreign debt rose. The Goulart administration sought to alleviate the financial deficit by raising extra loans from the United States and the IMF, but found itself severely hampered by its identification with economic nationalism and fiscal irresponsibility. Goulart frequently blamed foreign corporations for contributing to the country's economic woes and approved the introduction of stringent regulations on remittances overseas of profits made by foreigners in Brazil. External confidence in the government, however, was shaken by its decision to increase the salaries of civil servants and military officers by 70 percent in 1963, a figure well above the guideline of 40 percent originally included in Furtado's Three-Year Plan. As a result, inflation soared to an annual figure of more than 80 percent during 1963, while foreign investment in Brazil sharply declined.

In contrast to his presidential predecessors, including Vargas, Goulart sought to implement radical social reforms, notably the expropriation of large amounts of agricultural land and its redistribution to local peasants. This reflected a combination of personal conviction, electoral calculation and a response to the increasing violence and disorder that was erupting in the countryside and was especially evident in the Northeast where Francisco Julião had organized *Ligas Camponesas* (Peasant Leagues) to mobilize the peasants into armed action. A bitter dispute between the president and Congress arose over the Agrarian Reform Bill presented in March 1963. Landowners claimed that the bill was a direct attack on the principle of private property. Confronted with congressional intransigence, Goulart chose not to resign like Quadros but to issue a direct appeal to the people, thereby arousing 'popular forces' to overthrow the reactionary forces blocking reform. The strategy was unveiled on March 13, 1964 with much fanfare in Rio de Janeiro at the first of a series of mass rallies. The event in Rio attracted an audience of 150,000, plus millions more watching on television. With prominent left-wing leaders, including Communists, at his side, Goulart declared the expropriation of 'under-utilized' properties adjoining federal highways and properties and asked for public support for 'great structural changes.' More powerful and charismatic, however, was the earlier speech of his brother-in-law, Leonel Brizola, which warned ominously that, if Congress did not agree to the proposed reforms within 30 days, the people would 'know what to do.'[22]

In seeking to mobilize 'popular forces,' Goulart appeared to be copying [169] the populist policy pursued by Vargas after 1943. There were significant differences, however, in that Vargas's preference for political consensus was rejected in favor of a strategy aimed at deliberately provoking political polarization. However, as Justice Minister Abelardo Jurema later explained, Goulart 'underestimated his adversaries and overestimated the strength of the masses.'[23] The landed oligarchy were alarmed by the threat of fundamental agrarian reform. The established political bosses of the PSD and UDN resented the rise in political influence of organized labor and left-wing groups. Goulart's swing to the left also worried foreign investors and especially the United States government, who feared that Communist influence was rapidly growing in Brazil. In fact, the 'popular forces' supporting the president were disorganized and lacking in numbers. On March 19, less than a week after the rally in Rio, opponents of the government held their own mass demonstration in São Paulo. More than 500,000 joined in a 'March of the Family with God for Liberty' as a mark of protest against Goulart's association with Communism and his consequent alleged betrayal of Christianity and family values.

As the political crisis escalated, the attitude of the military was once again crucial. Goulart had pursued a policy of divide and rule with the military in which he appointed to senior posts men that he considered loyal, while also cultivating a personal following among noncommissioned officers (*sargentos*) and enlisted men. His support for allowing non-commissioned officers to join trade unions and participate in politics and for enlisted men to have the vote reflected this strategy. The bulk of the officer corps was, therefore, isolated. The policy angered and alienated many officers who believed that Goulart was seeking to subvert military discipline and thereby undermine the unity and authority of the military. They also feared that the president was using trade union organizations such as the *Comando Geral dos Trabalhadores* ('General Workers' Command' or CGT) to prepare a continuist coup after which he would impose his policies on the nation by decree. Following the rally in Rio de Janeiro on March 13, the chief of staff of the army, General (Humberto de Alencar) Castelo Branco, felt it incumbent to inform senior officers that the army would not assist the government to overthrow the constitution and 'submit the nation to Moscow Communism.'[24] Confidence in the president was decisively shaken in late March when he reacted to a mutiny of sailors in Rio by dismissing the Navy Minister and granting an amnesty to the mutineers. Recognizing that the military 'had arrived at the moment of action,'[25] General Carlos Luís Guedes ordered infantry units on March 31 to march from Minas Gerais and attack Rio. The proclaimed aim

[170] of the coup was to overthrow the president and restore constitutional government. Support was quickly forthcoming from other senior military commanders and prominent political leaders. On April 1 troops met with minimal resistance as they seized the principal government offices in Rio and Brasília. Meanwhile, President Goulart had left the capital on a flight to Rio Grande do Sul. His opponents in Congress immediately responded by declaring the presidency vacant and elevated the president of the Chamber of Deputies, Ranieri Mazzilli, to the office of acting-president. Like his presidential predecessors in facing similar crises in 1889, 1930 and 1945, Goulart decided not to engage in civil war, preferring instead to leave Brazil on April 4 and seek exile in Uruguay. In so doing, he was instrumental in bringing an end to the relatively short-lived era of democratic politics that had lasted from 1945 to 1964.

Economy

Recovery and growth

The era of Getúlio Vargas began in November 1930 at a time of serious domestic and international economic crisis. Despite its proclaimed intention to 'reconstruct' the nation, the new government showed no inclination to introduce radical economic measures and indicated that it would seek to maintain financial stability. A policy of careful fiscal management was adopted with the emphasis on producing a balanced budget, servicing a foreign debt that exceeded more than $1 billion and halting the fall in the foreign exchange value of the *milréis*. Financial opinion, both at home and abroad, was reassured by the appointment as Finance Minister of a leading *paulista* banker, José Maria Whitaker. When it became difficult to service the foreign debt Vargas allowed the *milréis* to depreciate in value and followed the practice of previous governments in seeking to renegotiate a new funding loan with foreign bankers. In 1931 he agreed to the visit of the British banker, Otto Niemeyer, who completed a financial mission that resulted in a restructuring of the debt and a rescheduling of repayments.

The Vargas administration differed, however, from its immediate predecessor in deciding to give substantial financial aid to the coffee industry. This was partly a reward to the coffee planters for support during the 1930 Revolution, but it also reflected the traditional belief that the revival of the economy was closely linked with increasing export earnings, especially from coffee. Indeed, the recovery of coffee exports was deemed so important that, [171] for the first time, the federal government took over the role of the states in actively seeking to revive the industry. The *paulista* Coffee Institute was, therefore, replaced by a federal agency. In 1933 a National Coffee Department was established to supervise a program of systematically reducing the planting of new coffee trees. Large quantities of coffee were also regularly purchased and destroyed. During the decade of the 1930s an estimated 60 million bags were burned, the equivalent of two years of world consumption of coffee.

Despite the considerable efforts to ensure a healthy future for the coffee industry, 'King Coffee' did not dominate the Brazilian economy during the 1930s. While the actual quantity of coffee exports soon regained its former level, the sharp decline in world prices meant that overseas earnings in 1935 were only one third of their value in 1929. In domestic terms, while coffee remained the single most important crop, its value as a proportion of the country's agricultural exports fell from 30 percent at the beginning of the decade to 16 percent at the close. Moreover, Brazil's share of the world coffee market was reduced from 60 percent in 1932 to less than 50 percent in 1937. In contrast to the beginning of the century, the decline in market share was unlikely to be reversed due to increasingly strong competition from other Latin American countries, especially Colombia. Indeed, the rise of alternative sources of supply steadily impaired the ability of Brazil to influence the international price of coffee as it had done in the past by unilateral action such as valorization and destruction of crops.

Although overseas earnings from coffee were in decline during the first half of the 1930s, Brazil avoided a trade deficit largely on account of a sharp fall in imports from $416 million in 1929 to $108 million in 1932. This resulted from the severe contraction in international trade and the depreciation of the *milréis* that pushed up the price of foreign goods. In addition, there was a steady increase in the value of exports of other Brazilian products to compensate for the shortfall in sales of coffee. Indeed, the government sought to stimulate trade with the creation in 1934 of the Federal Council for Foreign Trade (*Conselho Federal de Comércio Exterior* or CFCE). The most successful export proved to be cotton. Unlike most other commodities, the international market for cotton remained buoyant, so much so that world prices actually rose relative to coffee. Consequently, Brazilian cotton production grew sixfold from 1932 to 1939. In contrast to coffee, however, an increasing proportion of this output was not directed to exports but was absorbed by the booming domestic cotton textile industry. In fact, throughout the 1930s

[172]   in a process that has been described as 'spontaneous industrialization'[26] domestic industrial production steadily acquired a larger share of the national gross domestic product (GDP) as Brazilian manufacturers sought to supply the demand formerly met by foreign imports. By 1938 domestic industry accounted for almost 85 percent of the supply of manufactured articles. Much of the production served the function of import-substituting industrialization (ISI) because it was designed not for export but for the local Brazilian market. In effect, economic growth was being stimulated by domestic rather than external demand.

Brazil was unusual among Latin-American countries in not being so severely affected by the world economic crisis. As early as 1933 not only was Brazil's trade balance back in surplus but industrial production had recovered to its 1929 peak. It rose a further 50 percent by 1937. During the decade of the 1930s GDP averaged annual growth of 4.3 percent, while industrial output from 1933 to 1939 recorded an average annual increase of 11.2 percent.[27] These statistics reflected a significant change in the structure of the economy as it shifted from traditional domination by agriculture to an increasing emphasis on manufacturing. The number of workers employed in industry rose by more than 10 percent each year, and almost three times as many factories were established in the 1930s as during the previous decade. Much of this new economic activity took place in the Center-South region of São Paulo, Minas Gerais, the Federal District, Rio de Janeiro State and Rio Grande do Sul. These states were responsible for more than 80 percent of manufacturing production and employed 75 percent of industrial workers. São Paulo, however, was the leader and indisputably the nation's center of industry. Possessing merely 15 percent of the national population, São Paulo employed more than 40 percent of the country's industrial workers and produced 50 percent of all manufactured goods by 1939.

Like the 'New Deal' in the United States, the federal government was increasingly supportive of the development of Brazilian industry during the 1930s. Indeed, President Getúlio Vargas came to favor the introduction of central economic planning and increased state intervention in the economy because he believed that industrial growth was essential to reconstruct Brazil into a strong and prosperous modern state. Vargas was also sympathetic to the nationalist views held most prominently by the *tenentes* and seemingly strengthened by the destructive impact of the Great Depression that foreign capitalists and corporations had for too long exercised a selfish and exploitative influence on the Brazilian economy. During the *Estado Nôvo* the federal government sought to assert the country's economic independence by

assuming an increasingly active and significant role in regulating foreign-
owned utilities such as electricity, telephone and gas and promoting efforts
to achieve self-sufficiency in products with national security implications,
notably oil and steel. The National Petroleum Council was formed in 1938
to supervise exploration for oil. In 1940 the construction of a major steel
works was begun at Volta Redonda in Rio de Janeiro State. The massive project
was intended to be a symbol of Brazilian industrial achievement.

Although some economic nationalists argued for the exclusion of foreign
participation in the construction and management of major national industries, this proved impossible because the establishment of a large-scale steel
industry required a substantial amount of capital investment that was not
available from local sources. The Brazilian government had, therefore, to turn
to foreign bankers and negotiate a $20 million loan from the U.S. Export–
Import Bank in 1939 to fund the beginning of the construction of the steelworks at Volta Redonda. Despite the swift recovery from the world economic
crisis and the achievement of steady industrial growth during the 1930s, Brazil
remained an economically underdeveloped country whose well-being required
access to export markets and foreign capital. The successful development
of manufacturing industry disguised the fact that the majority of Brazilians
were still employed in agriculture and remained poor even by Latin American standards. In 1939 GDP production per capita was only 25 percent of
that of Argentina and 60 percent of the average figure for Latin America.

World War II

The significance of external factors for Brazil's economy was again underlined by World War II. The outbreak of war in Europe in 1939 was similar
to 1914 in stimulating substantial quantities of exports of Brazilian raw
materials and minerals. A new development, however, was the marked
demand for Brazilian manufactured goods, especially cotton textiles which
rose to become the country's principal export earner during the war. Indeed,
the trade balance moved decisively in Brazil's favor on account of not only
the boom in exports but also the decrease in foreign imports caused by the
switch in the belligerent countries from civilian to war production and the
severe wartime dislocation of shipping. Brazilian manufacturing industry
also gained from the decline of foreign competition, although its growth was
restricted by the lack of capital investment, foreign machinery and a skilled
labor force. Consequently, in comparison with the late 1930s when annual
industrial growth averaged more than 10 percent, the rate of increase for the

[174] period from 1940 to 1945 was more modest and actually fell to just over 5 percent.

World War II contributed further to the expansion of the economic role and activities of the federal government. Central planning was increased by the creation of a national mobilization board to allocate economic resources for the war effort. The economic power of the government was also keenly felt in the imposition of rationing of strategic goods such as oil, the levying of direct taxes on consumer products to compensate for the loss of customs revenue, and in 1942 the issue of a new coin, the *cruzeiro*, to replace the *milréis*. The increased spending of the government combined with a persistent shortage of capital and consumer goods resulted, however, in inflationary pressures that drove up the cost of living. During the 1930s prices had risen on average by an annual figure of 6 percent. This figure rose to almost 20 percent from 1941 to 1945. Far from being a temporary aberration, the rapid rate of increase in inflation soon became a regular feature of Brazil's economic life.

Economic ties between Brazil and the other countries of the Western Hemisphere were strengthened by World War II. Trade with Argentina noticeably increased. Brazil's exports to Argentina more than doubled in value, while imports from that country rose from 12 to 17 percent of Brazil's total imports during the period from 1938 to 1943. The biggest commercial gains, however, were with the United States. During the period of the war American goods made up more than 50 percent of Brazil's foreign imports. In addition, the United States purchased almost 50 percent of Brazil's exports. American Lend–Lease aid in the form of military equipment was also substantial and was designed to cultivate a close economic, political and military relationship between the United States and Brazil.

Postwar growth and crisis

Brazil appeared economically prosperous at the end of the war in 1945. A succession of wartime trade surpluses in the annual balance of payments meant that the country had built up considerable reserves of foreign exchange amounting to $708 million. This position of economic strength persuaded President Eurico Dutra to abandon the interventionist policy of Getúlio Vargas in favor of a return to the economic liberalism of the First Republic in which prosperity once again relied on the export of staple goods led by coffee, while a policy of laissez-faire was adopted towards domestic industry. Like 1919, however, the ending of wartime economic restrictions in 1945 was followed by the similar release of pent-up consumer demand for

foreign imports which steadily depleted Brazil's foreign exchange reserves   [175]
to less than $100 million and provoked a balance of payments crisis. The
Dutra administration responded in 1947 with the imposition of import
licenses and complex foreign exchange controls designed to restrict imports
and maintain a fixed value of the *cruzeiro* at Cr$18.50 to the US dollar.

Although he personally favored a laissez-faire attitude towards industry,
by seeking to suppress foreign imports Dutra was essentially endorsing the
policy of ISI that stressed the promotion and protection of manufacturing
industry in order to provide for the substitution of imports. The strategy was
much more enthusiastically adopted by Getúlio Vargas, who returned to the
presidency in 1951. Not only did ISI aid the balance of payments and reduce
the country's vulnerability to external economic fluctuations but it also contributed to the creation of employment and the promotion of *desenvolvimentismo*
(developmentalism), an economic ideology that aimed to achieve a modern
industrial economy and was very much in vogue during the 1950s. Substantial investment in Brazilian industry was a key feature of the Five-Year Plan
announced in September 1951 by Finance Minister Horácio Lafer. Indeed,
industrial production more than doubled between 1946 and 1955. Moreover, as already exemplified by the success of the project to build the state-
owned steelworks at Volta Redonda, Vargas expanded his program begun
during the *Estado Nôvo* of cooperating with foreign capitalists and multinational corporations to develop and manage new industries, notably automobiles and durable consumer goods. In his message to Congress in 1951
Getúlio had stated that his government would 'facilitate the investment of
foreign private capital, especially in association with domestic capital, as long
as it does not damage the fundamental interests of our country.'[28] But the
issue of foreign investment still provoked Brazilian economic nationalism.
This was evident in the controversy over the creation of *Petrobrás*, a state-
owned monopoly to control the exploration and drilling for oil. The establishment of *Petrobrás* in 1953 was regarded as a major victory for economic
nationalism and a defeat for the foreign oil corporations.

A period of rapid economic development occurred during the presidency
of Juscelino Kubitschek from 1956 to 1961. Under his presidency Brazil
experienced remarkable economic growth as GDP increased by an annual
average rate of 7 percent. For the five-year period from 1956 to 1961 industrial production rose by almost 80 percent and replaced agriculture as the
leading sector of the economy. In 1960 industry made up 25 percent of
GNP compared to 22 percent for agriculture. The total number of industrial
workers also exceeded 10 million for the first time and employment was

[176] increasing twice as fast in industry as in agriculture. Indeed, Brazil seemed at last to be fulfilling its great economic potential as one of the fastest-growing economies not only in Latin America but in the world. Its achievements were symbolized by the building of the new federal capital, Brasília, and the booming automobile industry in São Paulo which was producing more than 130,000 vehicles a year by 1960.

Kubitschek's pursuit of dynamic industrial development involved a policy of high government spending and contracting large foreign loans that brought growth but also directly contributed to an inflationary rise in prices and acute exchange rate instability. Moreover, the terms of world trade moved sharply against Brazil during the 1950s so that the prices of exports of staple commodities fell in real terms compared to the cost of expensive imports of foreign capital goods and oil which were vital for Brazilian industrialization. The governments of Getúlio Vargas and Juscelino Kubitschek both resorted to short-term foreign loans to finance trade deficits. But as the foreign debt steadily grew, its servicing became more and more expensive. The result was a serious balance of payments crisis in 1957. Meanwhile, inflationary pressures provoked growing social tensions, industrial conflict and political controversy. Unable to boost exports or reduce imports by any significant amount in the short term, Kubitschek hoped to finance the balance of payments deficit by negotiating a large foreign loan. Foreign bankers, however, were critical of the president's reluctance to implement austerity fiscal measures and especially his unwillingness to impose a freeze on wages. They accused the Brazilian government of seeking to finance economic growth by the irresponsible expedient of simply issuing new banknotes and thereby increasing the domestic money supply. In 1959 Kubitschek responded to the reluctance of the International Monetary Fund to agree to Brazil's request for a loan of $300 million by abruptly breaking off negotiations.

Kubitschek's defiance of the IMF was politically popular in Brazil, but his continuation of expansionist economic policies pushed the rate of inflation to more than 25 percent during his last year in office. He bequeathed to his successors, therefore, a difficult economic legacy that was made worse by growing political instability. Consequently, neither President Jânio Quadros nor President João Goulart proved able to reduce the accelerating rate of inflation or alleviate the economic crisis. Although Quadros introduced austerity measures and negotiated a large loan from the United States, his short period in office from January to August 1961 limited his impact on economic affairs. The attitude of President Goulart was more expansionist. He chose to copy the ambitious policies of Kubitschek in the belief that the resulting economic growth would by itself resolve the problem of price inflation. But the period [177] of expansion that had begun in 1956 came to an end as the rate of GDP growth fell from 10.3 percent in 1961 to 5.3 percent in 1962. Moreover, inflation continued its relentless rise, the deficit in the balance of payments widened, and the total foreign debt rose to $2 billion. It was estimated in 1963 that the cost alone of servicing the foreign debt during the following year would absorb 45 percent of the country's annual export earnings. Confronted with the prospect of national bankruptcy, the Goulart administration attempted the traditional remedy of introducing an austerity budget while at the same time negotiating a funding loan with foreign bankers, principally in the United States and the IMF. Brazilian officials, however, found themselves hampered in the negotiations by the president's reputation for political radicalism and fiscal irresponsibility. The failure to procure a large loan from the IMF made default on the foreign debt almost certain. Meanwhile, inflation soared to an annual figure of more than 80 percent during 1963 and touched almost 100 percent in early 1964. As the country faced imminent economic collapse, the military intervened in March 1964 and overthrew Goulart.

Society

Demography

Between 1930 and 1960 the population of Brazil more than doubled from 33 to 71 million. The total in 1960 was, therefore, five times the number of people recorded in 1890 just after the proclamation of the First Republic. The rise in population reflected an annual growth rate of more than 2 percent that was maintained throughout the first half of the twentieth century and even slightly increased to 3 percent during the decade of the 1950s. Although there was a significant reduction in the influx of foreign immigrants in the period after 1930, this was more than compensated for by the combination of a rising birth rate and a decrease in the mortality rate resulting from improvements in public health, especially successful national campaigns against epidemic diseases. The pattern of rapid population growth was not peculiar to Brazil. It applied to all the countries of Latin America and much of the developing world, and was referred to as the 'population explosion.' Brazil, however, still remained the most populated country in Latin America and accounted for more than 20 percent of the total population of the region.

[178]　　　　After 1930 the distribution of the majority of the Brazilian population still continued to be located in a band close to the coast and to favor the South. The well-established pattern of relative decline of population in the North contrasted with the growing concentration of settlement in the South. The trend accelerated during the era of Getúlio Vargas. By 1960 44 percent of the population lived in the Center-South region comprising the states of São Paulo, Minas Gerais, Paraná, Rio Grande do Sul, Rio de Janeiro State and the Federal District. São Paulo's position as the most populated state was consolidated after 1930. In 1960 around 13 million or 18 percent of the national population lived in São Paulo, while 10 million or 13.8 percent resided in Minas Gerais. Bahia was the third most populated state, followed by Rio Grande do Sul and Pernambuco. The fastest growth among individual states, however, was recorded in Paraná, which doubled its population during the 1950s. With the exception of Maranhão, which attracted almost a million migrant peasants during the 1950s, the states of the Northeast and the North generally experienced only a slight rise in overall population. Significant percentage increases, however, were recorded in the West where the exhortations of Getúlio Vargas to 'march to the West' and the building of the new federal capital at Brasília resulted in a marked growth of settlement in Goiás and Mato Grosso.

European immigration was not such a prominent element of Brazil's population growth after 1930 as it had been earlier in the century. The impact of the world economic crisis that struck Brazil after 1929 resulted in a reduced demand for labor combined with political pressure to protect the jobs of Brazilian workers from competition by foreign immigrants. In 1934 restrictions were introduced in the form of immigration quotas that were based on the national origins of immigrants entering Brazil during the previous 50 years. Whereas a total of more than 700,000 immigrants arrived in the decade from 1924 to 1933, the figure for 1934 to 1943 was less than 200,000. In effect, the flow of immigration returned to the modest level that had been common during the late-Empire. After a further period of decline caused by World War II, immigration from Europe revived during the 1950s. In 1952 more than 84,000 immigrants entered the country, the highest annual figure since 1922. However, Brazil's population had risen from 30 million in 1920 to over 50 million in 1950 so that the actual numerical effect of immigration upon population growth during the 1950s was much less than during the 1920s. Moreover, since the largest national quotas were reserved for and taken up by immigrants from Portugal, Spain, Italy, Germany and Japan, foreign immigration simply reinforced rather than altered the existing national composition of the Brazilian population.[29]

Although the majority of Brazilians continued to live in the countryside, [179]
there was a steady increase in internal migration from the country to the city
during the period from 1930 to 1960. This was demonstrated by the fact
that the proportion of the national population living in cities rose from 30
percent in 1940 to 45 percent in 1960 and became an absolute majority shortly
afterwards. During the period from 1940 to 1960 Rio de Janeiro almost
doubled its population from 1.7 million to over 3.2 million, while the city
of São Paulo almost tripled its population from 1.3 million to 3.7 million. In
the process, São Paulo became the most populated city in the nation. But urban
growth was evenly spread between the North and the South and was not just
confined to Rio and São Paulo. This was demonstrated by the census of 1960
which showed that Recife remained the country's third most populated
city with a population of 790,000. However, Belo Horizonte with 680,000
people replaced Salvador in fourth place. Closely following Salvador was Porto
Alegre with 640,000. Despite its drop in the ranking order from fourth to
fifth, Salvador could hardly be described as in decline because it had more
than doubled its population from 290,000 to 655,000 during the period
from 1940 to 1960.

Society

Despite rapid urban and industrial growth from 1930 to 1960, Brazil still
remained essentially a traditional agrarian society in which from half to two
thirds of the population continued to dwell in the countryside and to work
primarily in agriculture. The hierarchical class structure also endured in
which the landed oligarchy enjoyed a disproportionate share of wealth,
political influence and social privileges, while the large majority of the rural
population experienced harsh conditions of life and work. Indeed, hardship
made the lure of the city increasingly attractive. Migration from the country
in search of economic opportunity and improvement, if not survival, was a
feature of the 1930s, especially in the aftermath of the severe drought of
1931–32. The movement of people was further boosted and facilitated in
the 1950s by major improvements in road and rail transportation and greater
employment opportunities. During that decade urban areas absorbed an
intake of migrants amounting to almost one quarter of the rural population.

The mass of migrant workers found that living conditions in the cities were
often little better than in the country because the process of urbanization was
unplanned and simply evolved with limited state regulation or concern for
public health or social welfare. The sense of national pride that the élite had
shown in the rebuilding and regeneration of the nation's rapidly growing

[180]   cities at the beginning of the twentieth century was no longer so evident. Instead, from the 1930s onwards the development of Brazil's major cities was characterized not so much by impressive new civic buildings and municipal improvements but by urban sprawl and decay. This was particularly reflected in the emergence of squalid shanty towns consisting of slums that were usually located on unstable land at the perimeter or the outskirts of cities, a process known as 'development on the periphery' ('*periferização*'). Commonly known as *mocambos* in Recife and *favelas* in Rio de Janeiro and the cities of the Center-South, they provided both a home and a refuge for large numbers of migrant families from the countryside whose daily life was dominated by the constant presence of hunger, degradation and violence.

Employment opportunities were definitely available in the cities as manufacturing industry grew and new factories were established. But workers generally suffered from low pay, poor conditions and insecurity of employment. Although trade unions existed, they represented mostly skilled industrial workers. Moreover, unions were subject to the control of the Ministry of Labor and lacked independence. In order to prevent the growth of a powerful trade union movement, the federal government permitted only one union in each trade. The Ministry of Labor also appointed leading union officials, intervened in serious industrial disputes and was invariably opposed to strike action. President Getúlio Vargas, however, was publicly sympathetic to the plight of industrial workers and during the *Estado Nôvo* sought to improve their pay and conditions by the introduction of a minimum wage in 1940. Improvements in pay, however, were constantly undermined by inflation and an abundant supply of labor especially for unskilled employment. Consequently, the mass of Brazilian workers gained little advance in real monetary terms and remained poor even by Latin-American standards.

Differences in class structure became more visible as a result of industrialization and urbanization. The ranks of the middle class were swollen by the expansion of the federal and state government bureaucracies, and the legal, educational and medical professions. The number of factory workers also considerably increased, although they were generally accorded a lower social status than white-collar clerical workers. Moreover, cities highlighted the contrast between wealth and poverty much more sharply than the countryside. Just as many of the poor migrants from the countryside thronged into the *favelas* where they endured conditions of desperate poverty and deprivation, the wealthy and the middle classes chose to live in town houses and especially in large apartment buildings which came to dominate the center and fashionable residential sections of the leading cities. Indeed, the middle

classes were attracted to the inner cities because they offered access to   [181]
municipal services such as gas, electricity and water supply. While income
levels usually determined the quality of housing in a particular part of a city,
racial segregation was not a feature of Brazilian cities. In fact, the proximity
of large numbers of relatively poor people had advantages for the affluent
because it provided a valuable supply of *zeladores* (janitors) and *empregadas*
(maids).

The economic and social status of women appeared to advance as a
result of economic and urban growth after 1930. This was symbolized by the
granting of the vote to working women in 1932. Women did fill many of the
newly-created clerical and teaching posts, but most other jobs involved
low-paid and unskilled work in textile factories or in domestic service. A study
of wages of adult workers in Rio de Janeiro in 1920 revealed that the average
daily wage for a man was 50 percent higher than for a woman. Even though
they made up almost half the total national labor force, female workers
had less legal protection and fewer financial and welfare benefits than male
workers. In fact, they were positively discouraged by the Ministry of Labor
from joining trade unions. Whenever the government issued official statements
about women it was to reinforce traditional gender roles by stressing and
praising their role as mothers and homemakers. The economic and political
contribution and potential of women was studiously ignored. In fact, the
possession of the vote had little actual significance because no direct elections were held between 1933 and 1945.

Social conditions

The constant increase in population especially in the cities exerted considerable pressure on welfare services such as health-care and education. Prior to
1930 the provision of such services had been either minimal or inadequate.
The prospect of change was heightened by the creation of the Ministry
of Health and Education in 1930. But little of substance was achieved.
Although public health programs designed to treat and prevent serious
endemic diseases were instituted from time to time, the amount of funding
for long-term health-care was relatively meager. In 1960 the average life
expectancy was estimated at 46 years, but in some parts of the Northeast it
was less than 40 years. More success was evident in the promotion of public
education, an objective that was identified by Getúlio Vargas as an essential
element of his plan to reconstruct the nation and stimulate industrialization.
It was reckoned in 1930 that 25 percent of the population was illiterate and

that as many as 50 percent had never attended school. During the 1930s more than 40,000 primary schools were established, while the number of students enrolled in secondary schools increased from 90,000 to 227,000. The impact of educational change, however, was slow and patchy especially in the states of the interior and the Northeast. A study of Goiás showed that the improvement in the literacy rate rose by only 3 percent from 1930 to 1940. In the Northeastern state of Alagoas in 1950 more than 70 percent of the population was unable to read and write.

Nationality and race

The rapid development of media communications was a notable feature of the era of Getúlio Vargas. The influence and popularity of radio broadcasting was greatly assisted by the establishment of a national radio network during the 1930s. It was estimated that there were 1 million radio receivers in the country in 1941. Ten years later this figure had increased to 3.5 million. The actual size of audiences was considerably extended by the use of loud-speakers to broadcast radio programs in the open in remote rural areas and *favelas*. The cinema was also very popular and motion picture theaters in the cities attracted large audiences. Just like the press, radio broadcasting and the cinema were subject to regulation and manipulation by the federal government. A new government ministry, the Department of Press and Propaganda (*Departamento de Imprensa e Propaganda* or DIP), was created for this purpose. Direct methods of communication were often employed. For example, during the *Estado Nôvo* a radio program, the *Hora do Brasil* (The Brazil Hour), was broadcast each night to promote the government's ideal of patriotism and the work ethic. In the manner of the 'fireside chats' of President Franklin D. Roosevelt, Getúlio Vargas also presented regular radio broadcasts to promote his image as the 'father of the poor.'

The governments headed by Getúlio Vargas astutely perceived the value of promoting popular culture to attract public support for their policies and to serve as a safety valve to defuse political discontent. A notable example was *futebol* (soccer) which by the early twentieth century had become the country's national sport. During the 1930s professional leagues were estab-lished and Brazil became recognized all over the world as a country whose people excelled at playing soccer. Government assistance was instrumental in helping to finance a national Brazilian team and in 1950 to organize the hold-ing in Brazil of the World Cup, the prestigious tournament involving the best national teams in the world. The final, in which Brazil lost narrowly to

Uruguay, was played in the new Maracaná Stadium in Rio de Janeiro, the [183] largest soccer stadium in the world. The Brazilian team later went on to win the World Cup in tournaments organized in Sweden in 1958 and Chile in 1962. The accomplishments and soccer skills of Brazilian teams and individual players such as Edson Arantes do Nascimento, who was more popularly known as Pelé, brought Brazil international recognition and admiration.

By publicly endorsing the national soccer team, successive Brazilian governments aimed not only to promote patriotism and national unity but also to gain political popularity from the success earned in international matches and tournaments. A similar motive was evident in granting financial assistance for the annual Rio Carnival (*Carnaval*). In return the samba schools were required to register with the federal government and to submit to official censorship. The government also played a leading role in the efforts to restore important historic monuments and buildings such as the Imperial Palace in Petrópolis. The idea of fostering a sense of national purpose and cultural identity was referred to as '*brasilidade*' (Brazilianization) and became one of Getúlio Vargas's declared objectives. While the pursuit of *brasilidade* was positive in its intention of assisting the policy of national reconstruction and regeneration, it also had a negative influence in its stimulation of Brazilian nationalism and anti-foreign sentiment. For example, criticism was directed against the pervasive influence of American culture in the form of Hollywood movies, consumer goods and the presence of American servicemen stationed at military bases in Brazil during World War II. A more ugly aspect of nationalism was demonstrated during the 1930s in the public and political pressure to place restrictions on immigration and hostile demonstrations against German, Japanese and Jewish ethnic minorities.

The deliberate introduction of national quotas as part of the policy of immigration restriction accorded with the process of 'whitening' the population that continued throughout the period from 1930 to 1960. Not only did the proportion of blacks decrease in the national population but they also fared relatively badly compared with whites in terms of educational qualifications and employment. Charges of racial discrimination were countered by the Brazilian élite with the contention that black Brazilians simply failed to take advantage of the available opportunities for economic advancement and social mobility. In fact, it was argued that Brazil was a 'racial democracy' in which all citizens were equal and race relations were conducted harmoniously. In this respect, Brazil was considered to be unique in the world and to contrast very favorably with the United States where racial segregation legally existed in the southern states until 1954. Particularly influential and

[184]   appealing to the white élite was the work of the social scientist, Gilberto Freyre, whose *Casa Grande e Senzala* (translated into English as 'The Masters and the Slaves') was published in 1933. Freyre directed attention to the significant contribution made by blacks in the historical development of Brazil. Rather than a transplanted piece of European society, Brazil was a 'new world in the tropics' that provided an example of a genuinely multiracial and multicultural tropical civilization composed of a mixture of Europeans, Indians and Africans. While Freyre's writings undoubtedly attracted further research and interest in the African heritage in the history of Brazil, the concept of racial democracy was belied by evidence of discrimination against blacks and eventually required the passage of civil rights legislation. The glare of adverse publicity arising from the refusal of a hotel in São Paulo to admit the internationally-renowned black American dancer, Katherine Dunham, prompted the National Congress in 1951 to pass the Afonso Arinos Law which prohibited racial discrimination in public services, education and employment.

Diplomacy

Reactive diplomacy

Foreign diplomats in Rio de Janeiro were surprised at the swift downfall of President Washington Luís in 1930, but there was no inclination to exploit Brazil's political instability by meddling in internal affairs. In fact, official diplomatic recognition of the new government headed by Getúlio Vargas was soon forthcoming from the leading foreign powers and was achieved more rapidly than in 1889. 'The provisional government fully controls the country and is supported by the people,' the American ambassador, Edwin Morgan, informed the State Department.[30] The appointment as Minister of Foreign Affairs of the experienced *mineiro* jurist, Afrânio de Melo Franco, met with approval from the foreign diplomatic corps, so that routine business continued without any significant interruption.

At a time of political disorder and economic depression throughout the world, the foreign policy of the new regime was understandably cautious and reactive. This was evident in its attitude to regional affairs. A principal object-ive was to maintain friendly relations with Argentina. Indeed, the sudden contraction of trade with traditional European markets after 1929 enhanced Argentina's importance as a major trading partner and, in particular, an outlet for surplus Brazilian exports. Moreover, diplomatic consultation and co-

operation with Argentina was valued as a result of the emergence of serious [185]
boundary disputes between Peru and Colombia over possession of the Amazon
port town of Letícia and especially the outbreak of the Chaco War in 1932
between Paraguay and Bolivia. The latter conflict attracted the close attention
of the Itamaraty and the military because it was feared that it might spill over
into Brazilian territory. Brazilian diplomats joined with officials from Argentina, other Latin-American countries and the United States in offering good
offices that were instrumental in helping to bring about a peaceful resolution
to both border disputes.

The good state of relations between Brazil and Argentina was exemplified
by the visit of the Argentine president, Augustín Justo, to Rio de Janeiro in
October 1933. In turn, Getúlio Vargas was received in Buenos Aires two years
later. The occasion was notable in marking the first visit by a serving Brazilian
president to Argentina since Campos Sales in 1900. Latent national rivalries,
however, were revived by the Chaco War and the acute consciousness of
Argentina's military superiority over Brazil. Brazilian military leaders suspected that Argentina had territorial designs on both Paraguay and Bolivia
and was even preparing secret plans for an invasion of southern Brazil. 'Our
policy has been one of cordial friendship with Argentina and abstention in
the Chaco question,' Vargas informed the Brazilian ambassador to the United
States in 1934 and added: 'We should maintain it, but we need to take
military precautions.'[31] The desire to redress Brazil's perceived military
weakness in comparison with its neighbor was heightened by the growing
tension and conflict in the wider world, especially the Italian invasion of Ethi-
opia in 1935 and the outbreak of the Spanish Civil War in 1936. These distant
wars did not directly threaten Brazilian national security, but they attracted
growing public attention in Brazil on account of the large number of
immigrants from Italy and Spain.

A close relationship with the United States was also a fundamental aspect
of Brazilian diplomacy during the 1930s. The United States was the most
powerful nation in the hemisphere and, as Rio Branco had earlier argued,
provided Brazil with a valuable counterpoise against any potential hostility
from the Spanish-American nations. In 1933 the inauguration of the new
American president, Franklin D. Roosevelt, and his subsequent proclamation
of the 'Good Neighbor Policy' were publicly welcomed by Vargas. The Brazilian government also demonstrated its support of American diplomatic aims
by signing the Kellogg Peace Pact at the 1933 Pan-American Conference
in Montevideo. The good feelings were warmly reciprocated by President
Roosevelt, who appreciated the significance of Brazil's friendship and

diplomatic support in promoting his Good Neighbor Policy throughout the hemisphere. 'Without our country,' remarked Brazilian Ambassador Osvaldo Aranha in 1934, 'the United States can do nothing in America.'[32] In November 1936 en route to the Pan-American Conference in Buenos Aires, Roosevelt made a point of stopping off at Rio de Janeiro where he lavished praise on Vargas for his adoption of social welfare policies. He even lauded the Brazilian president as his co-author in conceiving the idea of the New Deal.

The German challenge

Throughout the 1930s the United States remained Brazil's single largest export market and source of new capital investment, so that friendly relations with that country were vital in helping to bring about Brazil's recovery from economic depression. Brazil was, therefore, receptive to American commercial initiatives and was the first nation to sign a reciprocal trade agreement in 1935. The agreement was important for Brazil because it ensured that American imports of Brazilian coffee remained free of duty. But the most notable growth in Brazil's overseas trade during the 1930s was with Germany. In marked contrast to the customary trading practices of Brazil's other commercial partners, the Nazi government that came to power in 1933 required that trade be conducted in what amounted to a barter system in which Brazilian exports were paid for in a special German currency known as *aski* or compensation marks. These marks were not convertible into foreign exchange or gold and could only be used to buy German goods. The arrangement, however, was attractive to Brazil because it offered not only a signal opportunity to increase and diversify exports but also obviated the need to allocate scarce foreign exchange and gold reserves to finance foreign trade. Moreover, Germany was keen to buy Brazilian agricultural goods, in exchange for industrial products including arms and munitions that were eagerly wanted by the Brazilian military. In fact, the barter system was so successful that Brazil doubled its exports to Germany from 1933 to 1938. Germany not only purchased large quantities of coffee and rubber but also became the biggest market for Brazilian cotton and cacao. During the same period Germany's share of Brazil's import trade more than doubled from 12 to almost 25 percent.

The visible growth of German interest in Brazil was not just limited to commerce. Brazil was one of a number of Latin-American countries that the Nazi government wished to cultivate because the population contained a substantial number of immigrants of German extraction. In addition, Germany sought to revive its pre-World War I influence over the Brazilian military by [187] supplying weapons and training and issuing invitations to senior officers to attend German army maneuvers. American diplomats anxiously observed these developments that they regarded as a serious challenge to their country's political and economic influence in Brazil. Their concern was further heightened by the creation of the *Estado Nôvo* in 1937 and its close association with the ideas and practices of European fascism. A typical American reaction was summed up by *Newsweek Magazine* in an article entitled 'Getulio Vargas Makes Brazil First Fascist State.'[33]

Although it upset the United States, Germany's pro-active Latin American diplomacy possessed definite advantages for Brazil. In a policy that has been described as 'pragmatic equilibrium,'[34] the Vargas administration welcomed the increase of trade with Germany and even entered into discussions over possible German loans for Brazilian industrial development such as the projected steel mill at Volta Redonda. Despite its outward fascist sympathies, however, the *Estado Nôvo* pursued a nationalist policy of *brasilidade* and vigorously repressed pro-Nazi activities in Brazil. Moreover, Brazilian diplomacy carefully avoided becoming identified with the international ambitions of Nazi Germany and continued to seek close relations with the United States. For example, Osvaldo Aranha, who served as ambassador in Washington from 1933 to 1938 and Minister of Foreign Affairs from 1938 to 1944, constantly stressed the importance of pursuing the traditional strategy of 'wholehearted alignment' with the United States.[35] When war broke out in Europe in September 1939, Brazil declared its neutrality in the conflict and followed a policy very similar to that of the United States. Brazil attended the Pan-American conference of foreign ministers held at Panama City and subscribed to the adoption of a neutrality zone which it was hoped would protect and insulate the Americas from the war in Europe.

The attitude of the Brazilian public towards World War II was very similar to that shown at the outbreak of World War I in 1914. Although the élite generally favored Britain and France, admiration was shown at the early military successes of the Axis powers, especially the swift victory over France in 1940. There was, however, no initial diplomatic or public pressure to abandon neutrality and enter the war. Indeed, the government and military leaders were only too well aware that the country was militarily weak and ill-prepared. Nevertheless, Brazilian national security was directly affected, if not threatened, by the expanding conflict. A major concern was the inadequacy of the navy to protect the Northeastern coastline or 'bulge' from an external attack. There was also anxiety that the disaffection of pro-Axis elements

[188] in the South might induce civil unrest or even encourage an opportunistic Argentine invasion. In addition, there were adverse economic consequences caused by the establishment of a British naval blockade that virtually terminated Brazil's formerly profitable trade with Germany.

Diplomatic cooperation with the United States

Prior to 1939 Getúlio Vargas had encountered a negative response in his efforts to purchase military equipment from the United States. American diplomats had been disturbed by the prospect of assisting the emergence of a powerful Brazilian military that might threaten Argentina and upset the strategic balance in South America. Vargas's resulting annoyance was reflected in his overtures to German companies for weapons and his determination to continue to maintain friendly diplomatic relations with the Axis governments at the beginning of the war. But American perception of Brazil's strategic significance was considerably altered by the outbreak of war in Europe. The geopolitical reality was that Brazil was the largest and most vulnerable of the Latin American countries. In fact, the Roosevelt administration became concerned that Brazil might possibly align with the Axis powers or, after the dramatic collapse of France in 1940, that Germany might use the French colonies in West Africa to launch an invasion of Northeastern Brazil. Moreover, the onset of war and the resulting disruption of trade with Europe heightened Brazil's value as an important source of agricultural products, raw materials and minerals, especially rubber, iron ore and quartz crystals. Vargas was, therefore, able to conclude an attractive arrangement in which Brazil agreed to supply raw materials and provide naval bases in the Northeast in return for American arms and financial assistance including a substantial loan for the projected steelworks at Volta Redonda. American Lend–Lease aid was formally extended to Brazil in October 1941.

After the United States joined the war in December 1941, Brazil severed diplomatic relations with Germany on January 28, 1942 and formally entered the war as 'an associate power' on August 22, 1942. The actual sequence of events was influenced as much by the German submarine threat as by American pressure or blandishment. Even though Brazil was ostensibly neutral, just as in World War I, the increase in trade between Brazil and the Allies and the granting to the United States of the use of military bases on Brazilian territory signified to the German government that Brazil was effectively on the side of the Allies. From February 1942 onwards, Brazilian merchant ships experienced attacks from German U-boats operating in Atlantic waters.

A major German submarine offensive was launched in August 1942 that [189]
resulted in the sinking of six Brazilian ships within a period of less than a
week. Four were passenger ships, so that the loss of life was heavy. Mass
demonstrations erupted throughout the country demanding retaliation.
German- and Italian-owned businesses were attacked. Vargas responded by
issuing a declaration of war against Germany and Italy on August 22, 1942.[36]
A few days later in an Independence Day speech the president indicated the
vital role of public opinion: 'You asked by every form of expression of the
popular will that the Government should declare war on the aggressors, and
this was done.'[37]

World War II

Close cooperation bordering on subordination to the United States was
the main feature of Brazil's diplomacy and military policy in World War II.
Indeed, for the first time since the brief period of Rio Branco's policy of
'approximation,' Brazil enjoyed appearing as the favored Latin American ally
of the United States. Not only did this enhance Brazil's regional status ahead
of Argentina but there were immediate and substantial financial benefits.
By breaking off diplomatic relations with the Axis powers in January 1942,
Brazil had been rewarded by the Roosevelt administration with a doubling
of the amount of the Lend–Lease aid that had been initially allocated in
October 1941. American assistance was further increased after Brazil's
formal declaration of war and grew to such an extent that Brazil received
more than $350 million or 70 percent of the total Lend–Lease aid given by
the United States to Latin America during World War II. The aid was not
just limited to weapons and munitions. One highly visible element was the
arrival of substantial numbers of American military and civilian officials.
Many were assigned to the 'bulge' of the Northeast where they worked to
improve and construct local air and sea defenses against possible German
attack. The naval bases of the Northeast soon became an important staging
post for the preparation and dispatch of American troops, equipment and
supplies in the Allied invasion of North Africa in 1942.

In terms of actual military contribution to the war effort, it was assumed
by Allied and Brazilian commanders that Brazil would fulfil limited naval
duties, but would not be able to commit troops to an overseas combat role. In
1942 the army numbered no more than 60,000 soldiers and was mostly
stationed in the South to counter potentially pro-Axis activities. 'We did not
have an organization and a mobilization [plan] to fight overseas,' recalled the

[190] operations officer of the FEB (*Força Expeditionária Brasileira*), Colonel Humberto de (Alencar) Castelo Branco, 'only for combat in South America and internally.'[38] Vargas, however, wanted the army to undertake an overseas combat mission. He reckoned that this would not only assure the continuation of American military aid but would also boost the nation's hemispheric and international prestige and thereby its potential for influence in the postwar world. Consequently, against the advice of some senior generals he ordered the creation of the FEB, which would be sent to participate in the Allied invasion of Italy. The FEB was equipped, transported and supplied by the United States government and would serve under American military commanders. In July 1944 the first contingent left Rio de Janeiro for Italy where they joined the United States Fifth Army commanded by General Mark Clark. Around 25,000 Brazilian troops were sent to Italy and were in action from September 6, 1944 to May 2, 1945. The exploits of the FEB, notably their contribution to the hard-fought Allied victory at Monte Castello in March 1945, evoked great pride and patriotism in Brazil. Vargas's decision to send troops overseas was, therefore, vindicated and brought him considerable political popularity. The FEB was also significant in stimulating close professional and personal cooperation between the Brazilian and American militaries and thereby established an enduring relationship that would be a prominent feature of the postwar period. Many Brazilian officers acquired considerable respect and admiration for the United States, especially its military and technological skills. 'In the War the United States had to give us everything: food, clothes, equipment,' summed up one ex-FEB officer and he added: 'After the War, we were less afraid of United States imperialism than other officers because we saw the United States really helped us without strings attached.'[39]

Participation in World War II resulted in Brazil surpassing Argentina to become the leading military power in South America. In addition to the resulting revival of élitist pretensions to regional leadership, there was also the belief that Brazil had achieved the status of a world power and ought to acquire an influential role in the new international councils such as the United Nations Organization that were being formed to shape the postwar world. Indeed, there were high hopes that more success would be forthcoming in 1945 than at the end of World War I because Brazil had gained considerable prestige for being the first South American nation to join the war[40] and for being the only Latin-American country to have sent combat troops to Europe. Brazil's regional and international status had been underlined at a meeting between the two presidents in Natal in January 1943 when Roosevelt had stated that the United States and Brazil were equal partners in the war [191] and that Vargas would be invited to attend the peace conference at the end of the war. Later at the Dumbarton Oaks conference at Washington in 1944 Secretary of State Cordell Hull implied that Brazil might even be assigned a permanent seat on the Security Council of the new United Nations. In fact, Brazil was keen to become active in world affairs and demonstrated this by establishing diplomatic relations with the Soviet Union on April 2, 1945 and also by declaring war on Japan on June 5. With the endorsement of the Roosevelt administration, Brazil hoped for a permanent seat on the Security Council of the United Nations. But American support proved much more uncertain after Roosevelt's sudden death in April 1945. The Potsdam Conference in July 1945 was monopolized by the leaders of the 'Big Three' powers of the United States, the Soviet Union and Great Britain. The 'Big Three' were preoccupied with settling the political boundaries of Europe and displayed an attitude of indifference towards minor powers such as Brazil. Nevertheless, Brazil was able to play an active part in the formation of the United Nations and was given membership of the Security Council, though on a temporary two-year basis.

Disillusionment with the United States

During the years immediately following the end of World War II Brazilian diplomacy stressed the continuation of close relations with the United States. Brazil was gratified to host the Inter-American Conference at Petrópolis in 1947 and to receive a personal visit from President Harry Truman to close the meeting. Brazilian delegates worked effectively with American officials to secure the smooth negotiation of the Inter-American Treaty of Reciprocal Assistance, a collective security arrangement more popularly known as the 'Rio Pact.' In the same year the Brazilian government endorsed the American policy of 'containing' the threat of International Communism by outlawing the Brazilian Communist Party and severing diplomatic relations with the Soviet Union. At the United Nations where Osvaldo Aranha was elected president of the General Assembly in 1947, Brazilian delegates provided staunch support for the United States in the emerging 'Cold War' with the Soviet Union.

Although it served to gratify Brazilian diplomatic pretensions to regional leadership, postwar cooperation with the United States resulted in relatively few tangible benefits simply because Brazil no longer received preferential treatment. 'We fought in the last war and were entirely forgotten and rejected

[192] in the division of the spoils,' complained Getúlio Vargas in 1951.[41] During World War II the United States had risen from isolationism to globalism. Consequently, its geopolitical priorities had significantly altered so that the countries of Latin America, including Brazil, were generally neglected after 1945. The Dutra administration resented the difficult and protracted negotiations that were required to persuade American officials and bankers to give aid for economic development and contrasted this with the generous treatment accorded to the countries of Western Europe in the Marshall Plan. The Brazilian military were similarly aggrieved by the virtual termination of American military aid. Consequently, the decision of the Truman administration to agree to a transfer of American arms to Argentina in 1948 provoked considerable dismay. The American ambassador at Rio de Janeiro, Herschel Johnson, reported the disappointment of 'many Brazilian officers' over what they perceived as Truman's policy of 'courting Argentina and taking for granted the friendship of loyalty of Brazil.'[42]

Visible signs of disenchantment with the United States appeared during the 1950s. The decade began with Brazil's refusal to send a token expeditionary force to join the American army in the Korean War. Lack of foreign economic assistance was held to be partly to blame for military unpreparedness. 'If [Washington] had elaborated a recovery plan for Latin America similar to the Marshall Plan for Europe,' explained Foreign Minister João Neves da Fontoura, 'Brazil's present situation would be different and our cooperation in the present emergency could probably be greater.'[43] Added to the criticism of the United States was the complaint that Brazil was being treated as an inferior. A suspicion also existed that Brazilian economic and military development were being deliberately restricted. This was illustrated in the controversy over the formation of the national oil company, *Petrobrás*, and the growing resentment against the alleged exploitation of the country's economy by foreign capitalists. Nationalist sensitivities were also evident in the opposition to allowing the United States to construct and operate a missile-tracking station on the island of Fernando de Noronha.

Independent foreign policy

The American attitude of neglect and indifference motivated the gradual emergence of a more independent Brazilian foreign policy. Both the Vargas and Kubitschek administrations sought to improve political and economic relations with the countries of Spanish America. In 1958 President Juscelino Kubitschek took a major initiative and proposed 'Operation Pan America,' a program designed to stimulate the economic development of the whole of [193] Latin America. The plan failed, however, principally because no support was forthcoming from the Eisenhower administration. At the United Nations Brazilian delegates took an active part in endorsing resolutions to promote world disarmament and schemes to aid economic development. Brazilian troops were assigned to the United Nations Emergency Forces that carried out peace-keeping duties in the 1956 Suez Crisis and the later Congo Crisis.

Despite its traditional support for the principle of self-determination, Brazil was guarded over the issue of decolonization during the 1950s, partly on account of its long-standing policy of non-interference with Portuguese colonial rule in Africa. This changed with the victory of Jânio Quadros in the 1960 presidential election. Quadros publicly condemned colonialism and announced his intention to cultivate close economic and cultural links with the nations of the Third World, especially the newly-independent African countries. He pointed out that Brazil possessed historic ties with Africa and that its racially mixed society had much in common with the people of that continent.

Furthermore, in what was interpreted as a move away from his country's traditional policy of close alignment with the United States, Quadros expressed sympathy for the revolutionary regime that had been established in Cuba by Fidel Castro. Despite diplomatic pressure from the Kennedy administration, the Brazilian government refused to support American policies to isolate Cuba. Moreover, Quadros questioned whether the bipolar division of the world caused by the Cold War was relevant to Brazil. In his opinion, Brazil should relax its attitude of hostility towards International Communism and enter into political and economic agreements with Communist countries. Vice-President João Goulart was subsequently sent to the Soviet Union and the People's Republic of China on a mission to promote goodwill and trade.

Despite his brief tenure of office in 1961, Quadros was given the credit for breaking with Brazil's diplomatic past and introducing an 'independent foreign policy' ('política exterior independente'). While the emphasis on the similarity of Brazilian national interests with those of Africa, and especially the reinterpretation of the significance of the Cold War, appeared novel, if not radical, his overall diplomatic aims were hardly new. Successive governments since 1945 had recognized that Brazil needed access to overseas markets and foreign capital in order to stimulate industrial development and modernization. If these were not sufficiently forthcoming from the United States and Western Europe, then Brazil must explore alternative sources. Consequently, Kubitschek had attempted to open up new export markets in

[194] Latin America by Operation Pan-America and had negotiated agreements to sell coffee to the Soviet Union and sugar to the People's Republic of China. Moreover, Quadros's policy was continued by his successor, João Goulart. The new president made speeches critical of capitalist exploitation of the Third World. He also formally renewed diplomatic relations with the Soviet Union in November 1961 and resisted American diplomatic pressure to expel Cuba from the Organization of American States (OAS). On the other hand, just like his predecessors, Goulart sought to negotiate financial aid from the United States and repeatedly stressed his desire for close relations with the Kennedy and Johnson administrations. These efforts failed because American officials could not accept his pro-Communist leanings. The brother of President Kennedy, Robert Kennedy, visited Brasília in December 1962 and after his meeting with Goulart bluntly explained why no American loans would be forthcoming: 'When there are people in authority in Brazil who follow the Communist line, it cannot be expected that we will work with them effectively.'[44]

CHAPTER 5

FROM MILITARY TO CIVILIAN RULE, 1964–2000

Politics

The military in power

It was not a new historical development in Brazil for senior military commanders to intervene at times of grave national crisis, overthrow the head of the government and suddenly find themselves in charge of the country. In 1930 they had quickly handed over power to civilian politicians. A similar option was not so readily available in April 1964. In fact, the situation was likened to 1889 when it had been considered necessary to hold on to high political office. A paramount concern was the possibility of civil war because pro-Goulart forces were believed to have prepared contingency plans involving a resort to violence should the right wing stage a coup. To counter this perceived threat three high-ranking generals representing the army, navy and air force respectively formed an interim government known as the Revolutionary Supreme Command (*Comando Supremo Revolucionário*). The senior military commander in Rio, General Artur da Costa e Silva, headed the new junta.

While the armed forces were united in agreeing that firmness was essential to maintain order, a division emerged between 'moderates' ('*moderados*') and 'hard-liners' ('*duros*'). The moderates saw the coup as an example of what they preferred to regard as the traditional and legitimate moderating role of the armed forces to avert chaos and act as the guarantor of national unity. They envisaged a limited period of military rule, after which the democratic process would be reinstated. The most prominent moderates were army officers who had attended the Higher War College (*Escola Superior da Guerra* or ESG) and were known as the 'Sorbonne group.' Castelo Branco represented this viewpoint and indicated that 'normalcy' in the form of civilian government

[196]   would be restored within eighteen months. The hard-liners, who included Costa e Silva, believed however that civilian politicians were inherently selfish and corrupt. They regarded the military's acquiescence in allowing Goulart to take power in 1961 as a disastrous mistake and one that should not be repeated. Convinced that the country was locked into a war to defend its 'national security' ('*segurança nacional*') against the internal forces of 'corruption and communism,' the hard-liners advocated a period of lengthy military rule commencing with a 'cleansing' ('*saneamento*') of political life, a policy that would entail a necessary purging of opponents of the new government from Congress, the civil service and the state governments.

Although the anticipated violent resistance to the coup did not materialize, the tough measures advocated by the hard-liners were initially put into effect. Taking advantage of the evident disarray of the pro-Goulart factions caused by the president's sudden departure from the country, the junta acted quickly and used the army and the police to carry out 'Operation Cleanup' ('*Operação Limpeza*') in which a large number of left-wing politicians, trade union officials and militant student leaders were arrested and subjected to summary punishment. At the same time the imposition of military rule was given legal force and 'institutionalized' by the issue of an Institutional Act on April 9. In effect, the military junta simply bypassed the 1946 Constitution and declared itself to be the legitimate governing authority. Their proclaimed aim was no longer just the overthrow of the Goulart regime but became the implementation of a revolutionary program to achieve the 'economic, financial, political, and moral reconstruction of Brazil.'[1] The parallels with the 1937 coup and the establishment of the *Estado Nôvo* were striking. Indeed, the wording of what would become known as Institutional Act No. 1 (AI-1) was directly influenced by Francisco Campos, who had drawn up the 1937 Constitution. Reflecting the conviction that Brazil had suffered unduly from almost two decades of party politics and internecine conflict between the executive and legislature, the act substantially increased the authority of the president while the powers of Congress were correspondingly reduced. Although Congress would continue to meet, an indication of its diminished status was reflected in the peremptory instruction for it to elect an interim president and vice-president within 48 hours. The president would serve until November 1965.

As intended by the military junta, the 48-hour deadline was so brief that it effectively prevented the emergence of civilian candidates and meant that only military figures were seriously considered for the presidency. Despite some support for the former presidential candidates, Juarez Távora and Eduardo Gomes, the strongest candidate was Castelo Branco. The fact that Castelo

Branco was new to national politics and less well-known than his rivals proved [197] a distinct advantage. Avoiding partisan political debate, he was able to stress his impressive record of long service as a military instructor and staff officer. In addition, as a former member of the *Força Expeditionaria Brasileira* (FEB) he possessed close and friendly relations with officials at the American Embassy, especially the influential military attaché, Colonel Vernon Walters. Meanwhile, Congress was purged of most of its critics of the new regime so that the remaining deputies, mostly belonging to the UDN, proved only too willing to ratify the military's choice. Castelo Branco was duly elected as interim president by a large majority on April 11.

Castelo Branco

Influenced by ideas and studies emanating from the ESG and the Institute of Research and Social Studies (*Instituto de Pesquisas e Estudos Sociais* or IPES), the motto adopted by the Castelo Branco administration was 'development and national security.' A 'revolution' was envisaged in which Brazil would be modernized and reshaped by policies ensuring political stability, restoring social order and promoting economic recovery and development. While military officers retained control of the executive and maintained prominent positions in the federal government, civilians were also appointed to office, especially those with 'technocratic' skills in the management of economic policy. The most notable was the celebrated economist, Roberto (de Oliveira) Campos, who became Minister of Planning and Economic Coordination. Stressing the urgent need to 'stabilize' the economy, Campos aimed for a substantial reduction in the headline annual rate of inflation to 10 percent within two years and a target of zero inflation in the following year. Although the resulting economic recovery was slower than planned, inflation was reduced from almost 100 percent in 1964 to 28 percent in 1967.

The authoritarian nature of the new military regime was highlighted not only by the policy of centralized economic control but also by its restrictions on political activities and ruthless repression of opposition. Institutional Act No. 1 enabled the government to deprive 'political undesirables' of their political rights for ten years, a procedure known as 'cassation' (*cassação*). Cassation prevented individuals from voting in elections and holding political office, and was applied to more than 400 persons, including ex-presidents Goulart and Quadros, and notable left-wing politicians such as Luís Carlos Prestes and Leonel Brizola. In effect, a majority of the country's leading

[198]   national political figures was summarily removed from active politics for more than a decade. Moreover, a process was also put into place by which several thousand civil servants and military officers associated with the Quadros and Goulart governments or suspected of left-wing sympathies were identified and dismissed from their posts or required to take early retirement. In addition, a new government agency, the National Intelligence Service (*Serviço Nacional de Informações* or SNI), was created to collect information on internal security, direct investigations, and order arrests of persons suspected of 'subversion' or links with Communists. The SNI became a powerful and greatly-feared tool of the military because it resorted to the systematic use of violence and terror. Moreover, it reported directly to the president and was not accountable to Congress. The indiscriminate and politically partisan nature of the policy of repression was illustrated by the cassation of ex-President Juscelino Kubitschek. Despite the charges brought against Kubitschek of alleged corruption and association with 'subversives,' the real motive of the military government was evidently to demonstrate its rejection of the pre-1964 political system by singling out one of that era's most celebrated figures for public punishment and exclusion from an active role in politics.

Transition to authoritarian military rule

So pervasive was the sense of political, economic and social crisis during the last months of the Goulart administration that the military coup came as a relief not only to the elite but also to the middle class. Criticism surfaced, however, as the regime acted in an increasingly arbitrary and ruthless fashion. Allegations of the systematic mistreatment and torture of political prisoners aroused particular concern. Moreover, the pursuit of economic stabilization resulted in recession, rising unemployment, and a general decline in the pur-chasing power of wages and salaries. Left-wing critics made common cause with nationalists by pointing out the excessive desire of the government to attract foreign capital and investment. They argued that the generals were puppets of American imperialism and that the 1964 coup had actually been planned by the United States.

Criticism only strengthened the conviction of the hard-liners that civilian politicians were unpatriotic and not to be trusted. Although there had been no preconceived plan in 1964 to establish a permanent military dictatorship, the move to a rigidly authoritarian system accelerated as the hard-liners acquired more influence within the military 'high command,' which consisted of the senior commanders of each branch of the armed forces plus all current four-star generals and the army minister. But links with civilian politicians

were still maintained and valued. President Castelo Branco sought and secured [199]
the collaboration of the political leaders of the UDN. Consonant with his
moderate stance, he allowed the holding of direct elections for a number of
state governorships that were scheduled for October 1965. The elections
naturally came to be seen as a test of the military government's national popularity. Considerable attention was focused on the two key states of Guanabara
and Minas Gerais where the anti-government candidates eventually triumphed.
Although pro-government candidates were successful in the other state
contests, the popular perception was that the military had suffered a public
set-back, if not humiliation. Rumors abounded that the hard-liners wanted
not only a repudiation of the election results in Guanabara and Minas Gerais
but also the president's resignation. Castelo Branco remained in office and
the election results were sustained, but only after he accepted the demands of
the hard-liners to rule out the prospect of further elections and an early return
to democratic politics. This was demonstrated by the issue of Institutional
Act No. 2 (AI-2) on October 27, 1965 and No. 3 (AI-3) on February 5, 1966.
The acts removed the element of electoral uncertainty by ending direct
popular elections for president, vice-president, and state governors. In future
the president and vice-president would be elected by Congress while the state
legislatures would choose their own governors.

A remarkable feature of Institutional Act No. 2 was the deliberate attempt
to alter and control the party political system. Reflecting the long-held
distrust of the military for multi-party democratic politics, the act abolished
the existing political parties. These were replaced not with a one-party state
but by an artificial two-party system containing new national political parties
to be known as the National Renovating Alliance (*Aliança Renovadora Nacional*
or ARENA) and the Brazilian Democratic Movement (*Movimento Democrático
Brasileiro* or MDB). ARENA was formed from the UDN and the PSD, and
was intended to support the government. The military sought to ensure
that the new party possessed a large majority in Congress. Another unusual
feature of Institutional Act No. 2 was the creation of the MDB, which was
meant to act as a 'loyal opposition.' Its membership was initially drawn from
the PTB. A beleaguered opposition party within an authoritarian structure,
the MDB appeared at first as a curious political anomaly. Its members, however, were able to discuss and even to criticize the policies of the government,
so that in time the party would serve as a refuge and building-block for opponents of the military regime. Parties of the moderate and extreme left wing
were accorded no role within the new system.

The first two Institutional Acts greatly enhanced both the executive and
legislative powers of the president at both the federal and state level. In fact,

[200]   the position of president became so important that the military was determined that a general should hold the office for the foreseeable future. Castelo
Branco accordingly secured a constitutional amendment to extend his
own presidential term from January 1966 to March 1967. At the same time,
however, he allayed suspicions that he intended to establish a personal
dictatorship by declaring himself ineligible for reelection when his term
expired. In so doing, however, the president became a 'lame duck' and proved
unable to secure a successor who shared his moderate views. Within the
military a consensus emerged in favor of the hard-liner, Costa e Silva, to
succeed Castelo Branco. Costa e Silva announced his candidacy for the presidency in January 1966 and was later formally nominated by ARENA. The
vice-presidential candidate was Pedro Aleixo, a civilian politician and prominent member of the UDN from Minas Gerais. Aleixo, however, lacked influence
within the military and was widely regarded as a token candidate. Although
it made Costa e Silva's victory a certainty, the MDB decided not to nominate
a challenger as a mark of protest against the electoral manipulation practiced
by the military government.

In what was largely a token vote, Costa e Silva was elected president
in October 1966 by a large majority of the members of Congress. In the subsequent congressional elections in November ARENA won 277 seats while
the MDB won 132. The military, however, could take little satisfaction in
ARENA's victory because 21 percent of ballot papers cast were spoiled or left
blank. The unusually high 'blank vote' indicated the widespread unpopularity of the military regime and represented a substantial protest against its overt
attempts to control the political system. The trend towards authoritarianism
continued unabated, however, with the promulgation of a new constitution
on January 24, 1967. This replaced the 1946 Constitution and essentially
legalized the exceptional powers granted to the executive by the various
institutional acts and accompanying complementary legislation. In addition,
shortly before leaving office in March 1967 Castelo Branco decreed the
passage of a National Security Law (*Lei da Segurança Nacional*) that gave the
government virtually unlimited powers to punish any political activity that it
considered to be a danger to 'national security.'

The National Security state

Costa e Silva became president on March 15, 1967. In contrast to the austere
and aloof Castelo Branco, the new president was more personable and congenial. Moreover, despite his reputation as a hard-liner, Costa e Silva had
spoken of 'humanizing' the revolution in his electoral campaign and had

thereby raised the likelihood of a relaxation of the policy of political repression. The important appointments to his cabinet, however, were made to hard-line military officers such as General Afonso (Augusto de) Albuquerque Lima who became Minister of the Interior. Furthermore, the subsequent absence of significant political concessions combined with economic grievances stimulated growing public discontent. Leaders of the Catholic Church, notably Dom Helder Câmara, archbishop of Recife and Olinda, openly criticized the government and singled out its neglect and mistreatment of the poor. Several major demonstrations against the government erupted in 1968, notably a strike of metalworkers at Contagem, a suburb of Belo Horizonte, Minas Gerais, involving 15,000 workers. A series of mass rallies by students took place in Rio de Janeiro and spread to Brasília and other major cities. A more militant attitude was also adopted by extreme left-wing groups who advocated armed resistance and rebellion. Rejecting the traditional policy of the Brazilian Communist Party of achieving socialism by peaceful means, Carlos Marighela resigned from the PCB after a visit to Cuba in 1967 and proceeded to organize the National Liberating Action (*Ação Libertadora Nacional* or ALN) in 1968. Seeking to emulate the success of Fidel Castro in waging revolutionary war and seizing power in Cuba, the ALN developed an urban guerrilla strategy. Though numbering only a few active members, the movement gained considerable publicity by carrying out daring and successful bank robberies that were intended to 'expropriate' money to finance their guerrilla operations.

Asserting that the country's 'national security' was endangered by 'internal enemies,' Costa e Silva responded to dissent by resorting to the ruthless tactics that had been a feature of the early days of the 1964 coup. Talk of 'humanizing' the revolution was forgotten as public demonstrations against the government were met with police violence and mass arrests. In August violent clashes between students and police at the University of Brasília in the federal capital resulted in the police occupying the campus. The policy of coercion eventually provoked a major constitutional clash between the executive and Congress. In December 1968 Congress refused the government's request to lift the parliamentary immunity of Márcio Moreira Alves, an MDB deputy who had made speeches in the Chamber of Deputies that had been critical of the military government. The attempt of the legislature to assert its constitutional powers against the executive, however, was regarded as an act of defiance and precipitated the issue by Costa e Silva of Institutional Act No. 5 (AI-5) on December 13, 1968. The provisions of the act were the most draconian so far. Congress was to be recessed indefinitely, further restrictions were placed on civil rights, and strict censorship was applied to

[202] the press, television and radio. 'How many times,' asked Costa e Silva, 'will we have to reiterate and demonstrate that the Revolution is irreversible?'[2] In effect, the imposition of what was essentially a military dictatorship was a tacit admission that the generals ruled not by consent but by force. This was made evident by the resort to further cassations, including Moreira Alves, and the issue in early 1969 of decrees which suspended all scheduled elections and placed state militia and police forces under the direct control of the federal government. The logical culmination of the policy of repression was reached in March 1969 with a decree prohibiting any criticism in public of the Institutional Acts, government authorities or the armed forces.

The belief of the military that their rule of the country must continue was demonstrated by the 'succession crisis' in 1969. The crisis occurred on August 29 when Costa e Silva was suddenly incapacitated by a massive stroke. According to the 1967 Constitution, which had only been in force for just over two years, Vice-President Pedro Aleixo would immediately succeed to the presidency. Senior generals, however, were resolutely opposed to the succession of a civilian who had expressed criticism of Institutional Act No. 5. The constitution was, therefore, deliberately bypassed as a committee of generals unilaterally declared the office of president vacant and proceeded to decide in private among themselves the question of who was to be Brazil's next president. While Albuquerque Lima was initially the favorite, the nomination was eventually given to a more senior officer, General Emílio Garrastazú Médici. Médici was a four-star general and commander of the Third Army in Rio Grande do Sul. A *gaúcho* like Costa e Silva, he had the advantage of being regarded as the latter's personal choice to succeed to the presidency. Congress, which had been closed since December 1968, was ordered to reconvene and confirm the selection of the generals. This occurred on October 25 when Congress duly carried out its instructions and formally elected Médici to the presidency not just to serve the remainder of Costa e Silva's term but for a full five-year term that would last until March 1974. Prior to the election the military government had also promulgated a new constitution. The 1969 Constitution was little different to its 1967 predecessor and was intended essentially to legitimize the various repressive executive powers passed since 1967.

Authoritarian rule under Garrastazú Médici

In marked contrast to Castelo Branco and Costa e Silva, President Médici gave no hint of any personal inclination or support for a restoration of polit-

ical liberties. He considered that an indefinite period of government by the [203]
military was justified by the need to maintain internal order and ensure the
successful implementation of the policies undertaken since the 1964 coup.
Indeed, an identical rationale had been followed by the new military governments in Argentina in 1966 and Peru in 1968. But the Brazilian military
were uneasy at being closely identified with the despised tradition of
Spanish-American caudillism in which generals sought to establish absolute
dictatorships. Since 1964 the Brazilian military had deliberately reduced
the powers of Congress and carefully controlled the appointment of state
governors and mayors of major cities. Nevertheless, a desire for legitimacy
and popular approval still lingered. This was reflected in the promulgation of
Constitutions in 1967 and 1969 and especially in the creation of the artificial
two-party political system with its provision for a 'loyal' opposition party.
Another indication was the decision to allow the holding of direct elections
for the National Congress and state assemblies in 1970. The choice of candidates, however, was still limited only to members of either ARENA or the
MDB. Moreover, many critics of the military still remained cassated and
were, therefore, excluded from direct participation in the electoral process.
Consequently, the congressional elections in November 1970 resulted, as
expected, in a sizeable majority for ARENA. A large protest vote, however,
was recorded in the form of either blank or spoiled ballot papers amounting
to 30 percent of the total votes that were cast, an even higher proportion
than in 1966.

The hard-line policy of 'cleansing' the political opposition reached its peak
during the Médici administration. An atmosphere of intimidation and terror
was created by the frequency of 'search-and-arrest' operations conducted
by the army and the police, and especially their systematic use of torture to
extract information from those arrested and imprisoned. In addition, there
were unofficial police activities that involved the employment of notorious
'death squads' in Rio de Janeiro and São Paulo to eliminate suspected 'subversives', many of whom turned out to be innocent civilians or petty criminals.
The government justified the policy of repression as a necessary response to
the increased threat posed by left-wing terrorist groups such as the ALN. An
army general recalled that it was 'a war without uniforms, situated in the streets,
where the enemy was mixed within the general population, [where] the police
cannot distinguish by sight the terrorists from good citizens.'[3] In 1969 the
ALN switched from its strategy of mainly emphasizing bank robberies to
include the kidnapping of foreign diplomats. The aim was to expose the weakness of the government and to force the release of imprisoned guerrillas in

return for the kidnapped diplomats. The most celebrated incident occurred during the 'succession crisis' and was the kidnapping of the American ambassador, C. Burke Elbrick, in Rio de Janeiro on September 4, 1969. The ambassador was freed after the government agreed to release fifteen prisoners. The guerrillas hoped that high-profile kidnappings would gain them considerable public support especially in the major cities. But the public generally remained indifferent. In contrast to the well-funded and highly efficient SNI and other government anti-terrorist agencies that were estimated to employ more than 200,000 people, the guerrillas failed to provide a united front and were deeply divided over tactics and ideology. Moreover, they lacked a charismatic leader such as Fidel Castro or Ché Guevara. Their best-known figure, Carlos Marighela, was killed in a police ambush in São Paulo in November 1969. Urban guerrilla activity markedly diminished afterwards and the abduction of the Swiss ambassador in December 1970 proved to be the last kidnapping incident. In fact, the guerrillas never seriously challenged the authority of the government. Nevertheless, they provided the hard-liners with a valuable pretext to justify the continuation of the policy of repression.

The impact of the ruthless and brutal policies of the Médici administration was softened by successful public relations. The Special Advisory Body on Public Relations (*Assessoria Especial de Relações Públicas* or AERP) that had been established in 1968 was particularly effective in promoting a positive image of the regime in the press, on radio and especially on television, a medium of communication that was rapidly expanding its mass audience. The standing of the military government and President Médici also gained from the national pride and good feeling arising from Brazil's victory in the World Cup soccer tournament in Mexico in 1970. In addition, the government claimed credit for the visible improvement in the economy that recorded 10 percent annual growth in 1968 and 1969. Much of the success was directly attributable to (Antonio) Delfim Neto, a *paulista* economist who had been appointed Minister of Finance in the Costa e Silva government. Delfim Neto had adopted a policy of economic expansion by reducing interest rates in 1967 and thereby stimulating a period of rapid economic growth combined with moderate inflation that lasted for six years and coincided with Médici's period of presidential office. Indeed, Médici soon boasted that Brazil was enjoying 'an economic miracle' and was swiftly rising to the status of a world power ('*O Brasil Grande*'). Moreover, the claims of economic achievement could not be easily dismissed by sceptics as government propaganda because they reflected the fact that Brazil actually possessed one of the highest annual rates of economic growth in the world and currently enjoyed a large surplus in its balance of payments.

'Today,' reported a leading British newspaper in 1971, 'Brazilians believe [205] that prosperity can be theirs, that after years of false starts and false promises the country's magnificent resources are being effectively developed.'[4]

Decompression

The outward success of the Médici administration assisted the peaceful and orderly transfer of presidential power in 1974. Some months earlier in June 1973 the military high command had chosen General Ernesto Geisel to succeed Médici. Geisel was currently president of *Petrobrás* and a former head of Castelo Branco's military staff. Although identified as a moderate, Geisel was respected for his administrative ability and had the backing of his influential brother, Orlando, who served as Army Minister in the Médici administration. The selection of Ernesto Geisel was duly endorsed by ARENA. In contrast to their action in 1966, the MDB decided to run an anti-government candidate and chose the civilian politician, Ulysses Guimarães. As expected, Geisel easily won the vote in Congress on January 15, 1974 by 400 to 76 votes and was inaugurated as president in March.

Geisel's election occurred at a time when a growing number of military officers were questioning whether the authoritarian structure of the national security state was still justified. Partly this was a consequence of developments in the wider world where the superpowers were engaging in détente to relax the tensions of the Cold War. In Brazil itself the threat from terrorism was clearly in decline and no longer justified or needed such a large internal security apparatus. The practice of torturing political prisoners was also increasingly condemned. Indeed, there was concern within the military that the exercise of too much direct control over the government and the political system was damaging the professionalism of the armed forces. This was the view of General Golbery (do Couto e Silva), one of Geisel's key advisers, who urged the new president to take the initiative and introduce measures to encourage civilian participation in the political process. The policy of gradual change that emerged was known as 'decompression' ('*descompressão*' or '*distensão*').

Shortly after assuming office Geisel announced that direct elections for Congress would be held in November 1974. In accordance with his proclaimed aim of 'decompression,' he permitted all the candidates to engage in virtually open political debate on television. The electoral results, however, were not what the government expected. The recognition among the public that the elections were not under strict military control clearly benefited the

[206] MDB, which was regarded as the anti-government party and, consequently, recorded impressive gains at the expense of ARENA, whose overall majority in Congress was considerably reduced. Notably fewer blank votes were cast than in the previous elections in 1970.

The 1974 election results were a surprise to Geisel and Golbery and strengthened the influence of the military hard-liners who remained suspicious of any policy that proposed the return of powers from the executive branch to Congress. Seeking to prevent a repetition of anti-government voting in the municipal elections scheduled for November 1976, Geisel instructed the Minister of Justice, Armando Falcão, to issue a decree in August 1976 severely restricting access to radio and television for all political candidates. Although members of ARENA came within the provisions of the '*Lei Falcão*,' the purpose of the measure was clearly to deny the opposition opportunities to publicize and debate their policies. Initially the decree applied purely to municipal elections but was later extended to state and federal elections. In addition, in April 1977 Geisel resorted to the sweeping powers contained in Institutional Act No. 5 to decree measures, known as the 'April package,' which announced that forthcoming elections for state governorships would still be indirect. A new category of appointed senators was also created to ensure a pro-government majority in the Senate.

While Geisel blatantly sought to manipulate the electoral process in order to aid the government party and handicap the opposition, this was balanced with an economic policy that sought to counter the damaging impact of the rise in world oil prices in 1973 with a commitment to promote growth and achieve a redistribution of income that did not disadvantage the poor. In addition, a number of important measures were introduced as part of the policy of 'decompression.' In 1978 *habeas corpus* was restored for political detainees and Institutional Act No. 5 was revoked. Moreover, censorship of the media was relaxed and many political refugees who had sought exile overseas were allowed to return. Military hard-liners led by the Army Minister, General Sylvio Frota, contended that the measures were harmful to national security because they directly aided and encouraged subversives and Communists. Frota sought to win the presidential nomination to succeed Geisel, but was dismissed from his cabinet post by the president in October 1977. Having successfully asserted his authority over the hard-liners, Geisel made known his personal preference for João (Baptista de Oliveira) Figueiredo to be his successor. In 1974 Geisel had appointed Figueiredo as head of the SNI (National Intelligence Service). The process of nomination proceeded smoothly. In March 1978 the military high command confirmed the choice of Figueiredo. ARENA

duly nominated Figueiredo in April along with the governor of Minas Gerais,   [207]
Aureliano Chaves (da Mendonça), for the vice-presidency. The MDB decided
to contest the election and nominated General Euler Bentes Monteiro as
its presidential candidate. In October Figueiredo and Chaves secured a
comfortable victory in the Electoral College.

Abertura

The selection of Figueiredo occurred at a time of economic recession and
increasing public discontent. The 'economic miracle' had begun to falter in
1974 as growth declined and the impact of soaring international oil prices
struck Brazil. Demanding higher wages to compensate for the rise in inflation, a major strike was organized in 1978 by autoworkers in the ABC industrial area of São Paulo, the first major strike since 1968. The strikes spread
to other industries, occupations and professions. In 1979 more than three
million workers went on strike. Encouragement and assistance for the strikers
came from the Catholic Church, which had abandoned its role as a traditional bastion of the establishment to become a foremost leader of protest
against the excesses of the military government. Since the 1960s priests had
been active in assisting the rapid spread of Ecclesiastical Base Communities
(*Communidades Eclesial de Base* or CEBs) that sought to provide a sense of social
awareness and community for peasants and migrants living on the outskirts
of cities. At the senior level the archbishop of São Paulo, Dom Paulo Evaristo
Arns, regularly made speeches critical of the military regime and its frequent
violation of human rights.

The growing movement of social protest evoked a much less violent
response from the military than ten years earlier. In the presidential election
campaign Figueiredo affirmed his support for the process of 'decompression'
that was now renamed as the 'opening' (*abertura*) of the political system.
'I reaffirm my unshakable intention,' he stated in his inauguration speech in
March 1979, 'to make of this country a democracy.'[5] The new president also
intimated that he would allow direct popular elections for Congress at an
unspecified date in the future. In the meantime, he consented to the passage
of an amnesty bill in August 1979 that restored the political rights of nearly
all those individuals who had been cassated, imprisoned or exiled for political
crimes. Shortly afterwards several thousand political exiles including notable
figures such as Leonel Brizola and Luis Carlos Prestes returned to Brazil.
Military hard-liners were appalled at the return of people they regarded as
subversives and Communists, but were mollified by the fact that the terms of

[208]   the bill applied equally to members of the armed forces and internal security forces, including those allegedly involved in torture. This gave them protection from legal prosecution for the violation of human rights.

Figueiredo abolished the two-party political system introduced under Castelo Branco in 1965. The motive was to strengthen ARENA and maintain its congressional majority by encouraging the division and fragmentation of the MDB into several separate opposition parties. ARENA became the Social Democracy Party (*Partido Democrático Social* or PDS), but remained essentially the same party as before. The MDB simply renamed itself as the Party of the Brazilian Democratic Movement (*Partido de Movimento Democrático Brasileiro* or PMDB). As the government intended, however, the strength of the opposition was diluted by other groups which grasped the opportunity to form their own political parties. Some pro-government members of the MDB joined with elements of ARENA to create the Popular Party (*Partido Popular* or PP). Three new parties sprang up to represent the left wing. The Brazilian Labor Party (*Partido Trabalhista Brasileiro* or PTB) was led by Ivete Vargas, a niece of Getúlio Vargas, while the Democratic Labor Party (*Partido Democrático Trabalhista* or PDT) was established by Leonel Brizola. The Workers Party (*Partido dos Trabalhadores* or PT) was created by the new trade unions that had gained members and influence during the industrial development of the past two decades. Its leader was (Luis Inácio) 'Lula' da Silva, the charismatic president of the Metalworkers Union of São Bernardo, an industrial suburb of São Paulo.

Like his predecessor, Figueiredo had to contend with the opposition of the military hard-liners to holding direct elections. The hard-liners, however, suffered a major set-back after an incident at the Rio Centro in Rio de Janeiro in May 1981 in which an army captain and sergeant were killed by a bomb that accidentally exploded in their car. The revelation that the soldiers had intended to plant the bomb at a music concert so that civilians would be killed and injured confirmed public suspicions that the military were directly implicated in a number of recent bomb plots. The resulting public outrage strengthened the pressure on Figueiredo to accelerate *abertura.* Shortly after the Rio Centro incident, he promised to allow direct elections to be held in November 1982 for Congress, state governors and assemblies, mayors and municipalities. In the case of state governors this would be the first direct popular election since 1965.

The 1982 elections occurred at a time of severe economic recession when annual growth was falling while inflation was rising to 100 percent per annum. The country was also suffering from the impact of the international debt crisis and the resulting need to raise foreign exchange urgently to meet the

cost of soaring oil prices and servicing the foreign debt. The dire economic cir-   [209]
cumstances favored the opposition parties, who won most seats at federal, state
and municipal level. The PDS, however, retained overall control of the Senate
but lost its majority in the Chamber of Deputies. Considerable publicity was
attached to the achievement of opposition candidates in winning ten state governorships, especially the triumph of Brizola for the PDT in Rio de Janeiro
State. Notable gubernatorial victories for PMDB candidates were Tancredo
(de Almeida) Neves in Minas Gerais and André Franco Montoro in São Paulo.

President Figueiredo suffered a mild stroke in September 1981 and went
to the United States in July 1983 for bypass heart surgery. The president's
ill-health contributed to a sense of drift and lack of firm leadership at the
head of government. In particular, Figueiredo obstinately refused to indicate
his preferred successor. The president's reticence encouraged the sudden emergence of a national campaign in April 1983 demanding the passage of a constitutional amendment to allow direct popular elections for the presidency in
1985. Adopting the slogan of '*diretas já*' ('direct elections now'), massive public
rallies reminiscent of those organized by Goulart in 1964 were held in the
major cities, culminating in a rally numbering one million in São Paulo on
April 16. The proposed amendment, however, was narrowly beaten in the
Chamber of Deputies on April 25. Although the government and the PDS
had been strong enough to defeat the pressure for direct elections, the military were unable to reassert their authority over the political system as they
had done when similarly challenged in 1965 and 1968. On this occasion,
the combination of a weak president and a mood of demoralization among
the hard-liners resulted in the failure of the high command to nominate a
military candidate to succeed Figueiredo. The 1985 presidential election
would, therefore, be contested between civilians. In August 1984 the PDS
convention nominated Paulo Maluf, a successful businessman and former
governor of São Paulo. The PMDB chose Governor Tancredo Neves of
Minas Gerais as his opponent.

Civilian rule

The selection of Maluf was controversial and prompted some members of the
PDS, including Vice-President Aureliano Chaves and the PDS leader in the
Senate, José Sarney of Maranhão, to leave the party and form the Liberal
Front Party (*Partido da Frente Liberal* or PFL). Reminiscent of the political bar-
gaining of the First Republic, the PFL subsequently allied with the PMDB
to create the Democratic Alliance (*Aliança Democrática*) whose purpose was

[210] to secure the election of Tancredo Neves. In return, Sarney was given the vice-presidential nomination even though he was regarded as a long-standing supporter of the military government. Tancredo's candidacy was also considerably assisted by the fact that, prior to the election, he had privately reassured the military that his administration wished to cooperate with the armed forces and would not seek revenge (*revanchismo*) for the abuse of human rights during the period of military rule. Indeed, while the *mineiro* leader promised the people a 'new republic' ('*nova república*') and to fight against the 'corruption, fraud and thievery that have become routine in Brazilian life,'[6] he also publicly praised the military as an indissoluble pillar of the state and even likened President Figueiredo to the Emperor Pedro II in his dutiful approach to giving up executive power. Figueiredo and the military responded sympathetically by appearing to prefer the PMDB candidate, and showed little visible enthusiasm for Maluf. When the Electoral College met on January 15, 1985, the members were under no great pressure on this occasion to choose the 'official' government candidate. Tancredo Neves defeated Maluf by 480 votes to 180. President Figueiredo accepted the result and welcomed the peaceful return to civilian government.

The 'New Republic'

After more than two decades of authoritarian military rule, the Brazilian public eagerly awaited the beginning of the 'New Republic'. They yearned for a new civilian president of heroic proportions and fastened their hopes upon Tancredo Neves. Moreover, Tancredo's image of integrity and statesmanship was boosted by the widespread public perception of Maluf as an unprincipled politician whose career had been advanced mostly by using his vast wealth to gain votes and favors. But events took an unexpected turn. Suffering from acute ill-health, which he had kept secret prior to the presidential election, Tancredo agreed to undergo an emergency operation on the eve of his inauguration scheduled for March 15. Tancredo failed to recover from the operation and died on April 21, coincidentally the anniversary of the death of Tiradentes. The presidency passed, therefore, to Vice-President-elect José Sarney, who became the first civilian president since 1964.

The elevation of Sarney to the presidency facilitated the acquiescence of the military to the resumption of civilian rule. Indeed, Sarney's political background as a conservative and long-standing government loyalist meant that he was very acceptable to the military. While this alleviated fears of a possible coup to restore military rule, Sarney struggled with the political liability that he was an 'accidental' president who conspicuously lacked both the personal authority and popularity of Tancredo Neves. Moreover, the PMDB were suspicious of a man who had belonged to ARENA and continued to maintain close ties with the military. This ensured that the president's relations with Congress would be awkward and frequently difficult.

President Sarney emphasized the crucial importance of defeating inflation and promoting economic development. The success of his administration was judged therefore by its handling of the economy. In February 1986, to combat a marked surge in inflation, Sarney launched a bold package of economic measures, known as 'the *Cruzado* Plan,' which implemented a freeze on prices, mortgages and rents and introduced a new unit of currency at a rate of one *cruzado* for 1,000 *cruzeiros*. The result was a sharp fall in inflation and a rise in real incomes that stimulated a consumer boom. The Democratic Alliance of the PMDB and PFL was duly rewarded in the 1986 congressional and state elections. In fact, the alliance won all the state governorships, and over three quarters of the Chamber and Senate. The economic boom ended dramatically in 1987, however, leading to criticism that the voters had been cynically manipulated in the elections of the previous year. Despite the issue by the government of further stabilization plans, industrial growth stagnated and inflation renewed its relentless increase, rising to more than 1,000 percent during the final year of Sarney's term of office. The economic downturn and the outbreak of major strikes, some erupting into violent confrontation with the police, conveyed a sense that the country was 'ungovernable.' Sarney, moreover, was also regarded as an ineffective administrator and left office as a highly unpopular president. The first democratic administration of the New Republic did not therefore live up to the high hopes expressed at its birth in 1985 and contributed to the popular perception that the 1980s had been 'a lost decade.'

The standing of the Sarney administration was also adversely affected by the long process of preparing a new constitution to replace the 1969 Constitution. The new Congress that was elected in November 1986 served as a national constituent assembly with the task of preparing a new constitution. After many months of interminable discussion a new constitution was finally approved and promulgated on October 5, 1988. The constitution did not greatly alter the existing form of government, and left this particular issue to be decided by a plebiscite scheduled for 1993. It sought, however, to reverse the tendency towards centralization of the past 50 years and especially during the period of military rule by returning political power and revenue to the states and municipalities. One result was the transfer of funds from the federal government at a time when huge sums were needed for social welfare programs. A run-off electoral system was introduced for presidential elections. The constitution also extended the vote to sixteen-year-olds.

[212]   The transition from military authoritarianism to civilian democracy was symbolically made complete in 1989 by the holding of direct popular elections for the presidency for the first time since 1960. The process was complicated by the fact that restrictions on the formation of political parties had been lifted in 1986, leading to a proliferation of new groupings. Confused by many of the new names, the public saw the election as primarily a battle between particular individual politicians rather than different party platforms and ideologies. The initial favorites were Leonel Brizola of the PDT and Lula da Silva of the PT. Other leading candidates were Ulysses Guimarães of the PMDB and Senator Mário Covas of São Paulo of the Party of Brazilian Social Democracy (*Partido da Social Democracia Brasileira* or PSDB), a new party that had been formed by a breakaway group from the PMDB and included the *paulista* sociologist and politician, Fernando Henrique Cardoso.

All presidential hopefuls were, however, soon eclipsed in the opinion polls by Fernando Collor (de Mello) of the tiny Party of National Reconstruction (*Partido de Reconstrução Nacional* or PRN). Governor of the Northeastern state of Alagoas, Collor emphasized his role as a political outsider. In a manner reminiscent of Jânio Quadros in 1960, he advocated a moral crusade that was especially critical of corruption in government and singled out the 'maharajas' ('*marajás*'), the overpaid officials and civil servants whom he denounced for cynically and systematically defrauding the country. Like Brizola and Lula, Collor claimed to be a critic of the Sarney administration. Despite his radical ideas, however, he was not identified as belonging to the political left wing. Moreover, Collor was just over 40 years old, tall and handsome, and used television to great advantage to inform and appeal directly to an electorate of whom a majority were less than 30 years of age and only 15 percent were over 50 years. Out of 22 official candidates for the presidency, Collor achieved the largest number of votes in the first round of voting. Lula narrowly defeated Brizola for second place, and joined Collor in the runoff. The second round was won by Collor with 53 percent of the total vote. The final tally was 35.1 million votes for Collor against 31.1 for Lula. Itamar (Augusto Cauteiro) Franco, a former senator from Minas Gerais, was elected vice-president.

The inauguration of Collor de Mello took place in March 1990 and was the first of a popularly-elected president since Quadros in 1961. After the lackluster Sarney, the new president was greeted with considerable popular enthusiasm. But Collor faced difficulties in his relations with Congress, where his basis of political support was very narrow. His party, the PRN, possessed only 20 seats in the Chamber and 2 seats in the Senate. As a result, Collor preferred to ignore Congress and resorted to issuing executive decrees to implement his policies. Following on from Sarney, Collor stressed the priority

of achieving economic modernization combined with the 'liquidation' of   [213]
inflation. In what was described as 'a war' against inflation, the new president
delivered an early shock by launching the 'Collor Plan.'

The radical measures proved initially successful as inflation fell to near zero.
Although the economy soon began to falter and inflation resumed its upward
path, the growing criticism of Collor concentrated on his personal integrity
rather than the effectiveness of his economic strategy. The turning point was
the public revelation in May 1992 of massive fraud organized by Collor's
campaign treasurer, P.(Paulo) C.(César) Farias. The discovery that the president's own family was extensively implicated in the corruption aroused public
outrage because it represented a flagrant betrayal of Collor's campaign rhetoric
and promises. Consequently, a national movement began for his impeachment and removal from office. The status of outsider that had once been an
advantage now was a positive disadvantage because it meant that Collor had
few political allies. The free press and media turned against him with a venge-
ance. In September 1992 after a long congressional investigation, the Chamber
of Deputies voted his impeachment. Collor resigned the presidency only hours
before the Senate approved his conviction on December 29. Collor was
declared guilty of the abuse of power. His political rights were suspended for
eight years. The forced removal of a president was not unusual in modern
Brazilian history, but what was remarkable about events in 1992 was the
fact that it had occurred within a democratic political process and that the
military were not actively involved.

Moreover, Collor's downfall did not result in a collapse of the political
system. Vice-President Itamar Franco succeeded to the presidency in a peaceful transition of power. In an attempt to counter the rise in inflation which
soared to a record of 2,670 percent in 1993, Franco transferred Fernando
Henrique Cardoso from the Foreign Ministry to the Finance Ministry. The
new Finance Minister consulted widely with prominent economists and
organized a new anti-inflation plan known as the '*Real* Plan' that was eventually launched in July 1994. Even before the plan was formally introduced
Cardoso had succeeded in reducing inflation to a monthly figure of less than
3 percent. The success of the *Real* Plan made Cardoso the favorite for the
1994 presidential elections. In marked contrast to Collor, Cardoso was a
political insider. Moreover, he was regarded as the only national candidate
who could defeat Lula and, consequently, attracted considerable support from
the middle class and the business interests. Endorsed by President Itamar
Franco and a powerful political coalition consisting of the PDSB, the PFL
and PTB, Cardoso won an overall majority in the first round of voting in
October 1994. He gained more than 34 million votes (54.4 percent) and

[214] defeated Lula da Silva who won just over 17 million. Cardoso attributed his victory to the success of the *Real* Plan: 'At every opportunity, I repeated the principal myth. The *Real* is good, inflation is bad. Whoever is for inflation is bad, whoever is with the *Real* is good. That was all.'[7]

Cardoso assumed office in January 1995 with a number of advantages over his immediate predecessors. Inflation was only 1 percent per annum. The new president had also won an overall majority in the first round of balloting and could claim, therefore, a popular electoral mandate for his policies. Moreover, he possessed considerable political support within Congress. In addition, he was prepared to work closely with Congressional leaders to deregulate the economy and reduce the role of the state in the economy. After the chastening experience of Collor de Mello, the public had lowered their expectations of what a president might achieve. In fact, Cardoso's skill and professionalism in office were so admired that he secured the passage of a constitutional amendment to allow him to run for a second term. Stressing his record as an efficient administrator and experienced statesman, he won the presidency for a second time in October 1998 with an overall majority of 53 percent in the first round of voting. His opponent, Lula da Silva, described Cardoso as 'the executioner of the Brazilian economy' and stated that he 'found it almost incomprehensible that the victims voted for their own execution.'[8] Although Lula won a respectable 31 percent of the vote, the majority of the voters showed more confidence in Cardoso's proven political and administrative skills. In accordance with the procedure laid down in the 1988 Constitution, elections were also held in 1998 for the Chamber of Deputies and one third of the Senate. The successful holding of elections in which millions of citizens had cast their votes was a creditable achievement and meant that Brazil ended the twentieth century as one of the largest functioning democracies in the world.

Economy

Economic stabilization

The economy was in severe crisis when Castelo Branco became president in April 1964. He turned immediately to civilian 'technocrats' and business leaders for advice and quick remedial action. In so doing, he established a collaborative partnership between the military and civilian experts that would be a prominent feature of economic policymaking throughout the period

of military government from 1964 to 1985. The most highly-respected appointments in 1964 were Roberto Campos who became Planning Minister,
and Octávio Gouvéia Bulhões who took the post of Finance Minister. In
August Campos and Bulhões announced a 'Programme of Government
Economic Action' ('*Programa de Ação Econômica do Governo*' or PAEG) whose
purpose was to stimulate a gradual economic recovery and achieve the
publicly-stated goal of slashing the annual rate of inflation from 100 to 10
percent within two years and possibly to zero in the following year. In effect,
the PAEG was a typical package of deflationary measures designed to balance the budget by reducing the spending of the federal government while
seeking to increase revenue by making the collection of taxes more efficient.
The PAEG was unusual, however, in its attempt to improve the balance
of payments by positively stimulating exports rather than concentrate on
restricting and substituting imports of foreign goods. The subsequent
devaluation of the *cruzeiro* made Brazilian exports cheaper but increased the
prices of imported oil and wheat, leading to a rise in the cost of transportation
and staple commodities such as bread. The military government, however,
effectively suppressed any discontent. Indeed, in marked contrast to their
predecessors before the 1964 coup, Campos and Bulhões were able to implement their economic policies with a minimum of political debate and public
scrutiny. For example, by restricting the amount of increase in the minimum
wage, they enforced what amounted to a decline of up to 30 percent in its
real value from 1964 to 1967.

Campos and Bulhões reduced the budget deficit, but did not achieve their
objective of virtually eliminating inflation within two years. Although the
PAEG significantly moderated inflationary pressures arising from previous
excessive government spending and increases in wages and salaries, the
annual rate of inflation still remained high and was more than 25 percent in
1967 at the end of the Castelo Branco administration. Moreover, the government's deflationary policies adversely affected economic growth and put the
economy into recession as GDP fell from 3.4 percent in 1964 to 2.4 percent
in 1965. The figure for 1967 showed only a modest improvement at 4.2
percent. The balance of payments markedly improved, but this reflected not
so much a rise in the volume of exports as a sharp and unplanned reduction in
imports caused by declining domestic demand and a sharp fall in personal
income. After the controversial presidencies of Quadros and Goulart, however,
the combination of political stability and the evident commitment of the
federal government to the pursuit of orthodox economic policies and financial
management was successful in restoring Brazil's international credit rating

[216]   and attracting foreign capital. Indeed, Campos and Bulhões regarded the
inflow of foreign investment as a vital means of providing funds to stimulate
industrial production during a period of reduced government spending. They
were able to renegotiate improved terms for the servicing of the foreign debt
and to secure large loans for economic development from the United States
government, the IMF and the World Bank.

A change of emphasis in economic policy occurred after Costa e Silva
assumed the presidency in 1967. The influence of the economic nationalists
became more pronounced as prominent new cabinet members such as
Minister of the Interior General Albuquerque Lima argued that economic policy
was not primarily just a matter of allowing technocrats to manage the economy
and deal with financial difficulties as they arose. In his opinion, its purpose
should also be the implementation of the fundamental aims of the 1964 Revolution. Most of all, Albuquerque Lima wanted a strong and modern national
economy to help in the fight against internal subversion. It would also fulfill
the long-held views of the nationalists within the military that Brazil should
consciously aim to become economically self-sufficient and reduce its dependence on foreign nations for supplies of industrial goods and especially armaments. This would entail a major role for the state in drawing up ambitious
national development plans and providing investment in economic infrastructure such as transportation, communications and heavy industry. Furthermore,
nationalists believed that as a strong economic power Brazil would possess
prestige and influence in international affairs.

The economic miracle

In March 1967 Costa e Silva assigned the task of promoting economic
expansion to the *paulista* economist, (Antonio) Delfim Neto. On becoming
Finance Minister, Delfim stated that his aim was to achieve rapid economic
growth without at the same time boosting inflation. Where he differed from
Campos and Bulhões was that he favored a substantial expansion in the
money supply to release the country's excess industrial capacity. The policy
was risky and critics predicted that it would stimulate a resurgence of inflation. To combat this danger Delfim stressed the necessity of imposing controls on prices and wages not as temporary expedients but as a systematic
long-term policy. Periodic increases, which were officially described as
'monetary corrections' ('*correção monetária*'), would be allowed and controlled
by 'indexation,' a formula reflecting changes in the cost of living that were

calculated by the government. Indexation was not a new concept and had been introduced earlier during the Castelo Branco administration to encourage the purchase of government bonds and to raise revenue on unpaid taxes. A similar flexibility was applied to the foreign exchange value of the *cruzeiro*. Delfim introduced the 'crawling-peg,' in which the currency was subject to a series of small reductions, and thereby avoided the damaging impact of domestic financial crises caused by sudden devaluations and the activities of foreign exchange speculators.

The economy experienced a marked industrial recovery in 1968 and GDP rose to 11 percent. The boom continued for six years with GDP growing at an annual average rate of almost 11 percent, the highest sustained level since the late 1950s. Despite the forebodings of critics, annual inflation remained at moderate levels and averaged less than 20 percent during the period from 1968 to 1973. Flattering comparisons were drawn with the recent experiences of Western Europe, and Brazil was judged to have achieved an 'economic miracle.' A particular success was the improvement in the balance of payments from deficit to surplus. In fact, exports more than doubled in value from $2.7 billion in 1970 to $6.2 billion in 1973. Agricultural goods were in particular demand and were no longer dominated by coffee, whose share of total exports declined from an average of more than 40 percent during the 1960s to 12 percent in 1974. Indeed, Brazil became a major producer and exporter of lucrative new products such as orange concentrate and soybeans. Industry grew even faster than agriculture. Development was most marked in steel, chemicals, shipbuilding, and armaments. The most spectacular growth, however, was in the automobile industry as Brazil became the eighth largest producer of motor vehicles in the world. Several multinational companies, including General Motors, Ford, Chrysler, Fiat and Volkswagen, made Brazil the center of their manufacturing in South America. Huge factories were located in the 'ABC' region comprising Santo André (A), São Bernardo (B) and São Caetano (C), the industrial suburbs of the city of São Paulo. The most popular model of passenger car was the Volkswagen 'beetle' (*'fusca'*) which was produced and sold in millions throughout Brazil and other countries in Latin America.

A feature of economic policy during the military regime was the growing involvement of the state and military officers in actively stimulating and directing the pattern of economic development. Many of the largest and most successful companies were either owned by the state or dependent upon the government for the supply of much of their investment capital. The military

[218] had traditionally shown a close interest in the strategically-important oil sector and the iron and steel industries. *Petrobrás* and the huge mining company in Minas Gerais, *Companhia Vale do Rio Doce,* were further encouraged to expand their operations both domestically and overseas. Particular attention was directed to developing a national armaments industry, the most prominent example of which was the creation in 1969 of the aircraft company, *Embraer.* Within a decade Brazilian companies were supplying virtually all the needs of the armed forces and also exporting armaments, including tanks and planes, to the value of $800 million in 1980. State control was also maintained over the provision of utilities by such companies as *Electrobrás* for electric power and *Telebrás* for telecommunications. The construction industry, including the building of houses, was aided by funds from the National Housing Bank that had been created in 1965.

The desire of the military to achieve economic growth and promote national security was best exemplified in the decision to proceed with the construction of the 3,000 mile Transamazon Highway in 1970, an ambitious and vast project that was likened to the building of Brasília and was described by President Garrastazú Médici as 'a fundamental commitment of the Revolution.'[9] In their push for economic growth, however, military governments showed indifference to environmental considerations. They assumed that the destruction of the environment was a necessary and inevitable cost of modernization and 'national development.' In response to international criticism that intensive deforestation was destroying animal and plant species and damaging the global climate even to the extent of depleting the ozone layer above Antarctica, Brazilians argued that 'slash and burn' and logging were not only traditional practices but had also been actually carried out on a much smaller scale in Brazil than in other areas of the world.

Delfim Neto was personally credited with having engineered the 'economic miracle.' His belief in the importance of easing credit restrictions and releasing excess industrial capacity appeared to have been vindicated. But a single individual was hardly responsible for major economic change. In effect, the economy was simply recovering from the recession of the early 1960s and resuming the upward path of growth established during the Kubitschek era. Moreover, the rise in GDP and especially the increase in exports were greatly assisted by external as well as internal factors. During the late 1960s world trade boomed as a result of increased American spending on the Cold War and the remarkable growth of the Japanese and West European economies. Furthermore, foreign capital was readily available as bankers in North America, Western Europe and Japan sought investment opportunities and were attracted

by Brazil's political stability under military rule and record of impressive   [219]
economic growth. The military governments were also willing to borrow
heavily to finance imports of capital goods that were considered necessary to
stimulate economic development. This was reflected in the substantial increase
in the foreign debt to over $12 million in 1974, a doubling of the figure for
1971.

Economic crisis

In March 1974 the new president, Ernesto Geisel, chose to replace Delfim
Neto as Finance Minister with Mário Henrique Simonsen. The expectation
of continued high growth was dashed, however, by the tripling of the world
price of oil in 1973 caused by the political action of the Arab-dominated
Organization of Petroleum Exporting Countries (OPEC). Although not a
specific target of OPEC, Brazil was especially vulnerable to the ramifications
of the 'oil shock' because its ambitious plans for economic development
under Kubitschek and subsequently the military governments had been
predicated upon the availability of cheap foreign oil to fuel both its heavy
industries and a communications system that was dominated by highways
and road transportation rather than railroads. Indeed, Brazil had become one
of the largest importers of oil in the developing world and depended on
supplies from the Middle East for 80 percent of its oil consumption.

The dramatic increase in the cost of oil pushed the balance of payments
from a small surplus in 1973 to a deficit of more than $4 billion in 1974. At
the same time the annual increase in the rate of industrial production slumped
to less than 5 percent. The Geisel administration, however, rejected austerity
fiscal measures such as raising taxes and restricting imports. Instead, it determined to continue the policy of promoting industrial growth and maintaining the high levels of investment required to fund the import of capital goods
and the construction of major public works such as highways, bridges and
hydro-electric projects. A desire to avoid political unpopularity and social
discontent partly explained the expansionist attitude. Hopes were also high
that the rise in the price of oil was only temporary and, in the face of opposition from the United States, Japan and Western Europe, could not be sustained
for very long by OPEC. Brazil also attempted to discover and develop alternative sources of energy. As part of the program to increase the exploitation
of the country's hydro-electric resources, approval was given for the construction of the enormous Itaipú hydro-electric complex on the Paraná River

[220] between Brazil and Paraguay. Negotiations were also entered into with foreign companies to provide nuclear power. A contract valued at $10 billion to construct up to ten nuclear reactors in Brazil was agreed in 1975 with a West German consortium. The project which achieved the most worldwide publicity, however, was the National Program for Combustible Alcohol (*Programa Nacional do Álcool* or *Proalcool*) which sought to substitute the gasoline used to power passenger vehicles with 'gasohol,' a fuel produced by the distillation of alcohol from sugar cane. In contrast to oil, Brazil possessed abundant supplies of sugar. All these projects, however, were expensive to initiate. Moreover, in the immediate short term, they could do little to redress the necessity of importing expensive supplies of oil. Over the longer term *Proalcool* proved to be particularly costly and uneconomic.

In the meantime, Brazil contracted large overseas loans to finance a series of budgetary deficits. Ironically, this strategy of 'debt-led growth' was greatly facilitated by the availability of 'petrodollars' from the members of OPEC, the organization that had triggered and prospered from the initial oil shock. While the Brazilian economy grew at an average rate of more than 5 percent per annum, the reluctance of the Geisel administration to restrict the money supply contributed to an upsurge in the annual rate of inflation to more than 30 percent. Growing public discontent was expressed in an outbreak of strikes, notably among the auto workers in São Paulo in 1978. Moreover, the continuation of large trade deficits and rising interest payments on foreign loans meant that the external debt rose from $12.6 billion in 1973 to $43.5 billion in 1978. The annual amount required to service the debt reached $8 billion in 1978 and soared to $10 billion in 1979. This resulted in an annual negative transfer of capital from Brazil to overseas countries that was equivalent to almost 5 percent of GDP.

The resort to overseas borrowing had appeared a sensible strategy after the 1973 oil shock, but turned out to be a miscalculation in 1979 when OPEC again suddenly increased the price of oil. Although he had retained his position as Finance Minister in the new Figueiredo administration, Simonsen resigned in August 1979 and was replaced by Delfim Neto. Now regarded as the 'economic Henry Kissinger,' Delfim promised rapid growth and the working of another 'miracle.' Ever the optimist, the new Finance Minister prepared a 'National Plan,' whose underlying rationale was that 'a developing country with as many potentialities and problems as Brazil cannot give up growth, both because of its citizens' legitimate aspirations for greater prosperity and because of the high social cost of stagnation or decline.'[10] But Brazil could not alter the economic reality that it remained dependent on imports of large quantities of oil and had minimal influence over the international price of this commodity. Consequently, the second oil shock of 1979 not only worsened the deficit in the balance of payments but also contributed to a rapid rise in domestic inflation that was reminiscent of the Goulart era. In 1981 the economy experienced the onset of the worst recession since 1929 as industrial production slumped and the GDP showed an absolute decline for the first time since 1942.

The attempt of Delfim Neto to stimulate economic growth and bring about another 'miracle' was also undermined by a severe contraction in world trade that resulted in a sharp fall in demand for Brazilian exports. Furthermore, the decade of the 1980s began with rising international interest rates which pushed the burden of servicing the growing foreign debt to a crippling level because Brazil's foreign loans had been contracted at floating rates. In some cases rates increased by more than three times the original figure. By the end of 1982 Brazil possessed the largest foreign debt in the world, estimated at $87 billion. Brazil's large population meant, however, that indebtedness in per capita terms was less than most other countries. Nevertheless, foreign exchange reserves became so depleted by debt servicing that Brazil joined Mexico and Argentina in declaring a suspension of payments to foreign creditors. The action was roundly condemned by critics in the developed nations who blamed the profligacy and irresponsible borrowing of countries such as Brazil for causing a 'Latin American debt crisis.' To secure the funding that was necessary to meet short-term obligations, the Brazilian government turned to the IMF in 1983. The action was taken reluctantly because it implied that Brazil was acting as a supplicant and was not fully in control of its own economic affairs. Moreover, ever since Kubitschek had broken off negotiations with the IMF in 1958, that organization was regarded in Brazil as a tool of international capitalism. Nevertheless, the economic position was so desperate that the Figueiredo administration felt compelled to agree to meet national targets drawn up by the IMF that required the implementation of austerity measures to restrict the money supply, reduce the budgetary deficit, impose controls on imports and hold down wages. Nationalist critics described the IMF terms as the externally-imposed 'deindustrialization' of Brazil.

In addition to imposing austerity fiscal measures the Figueiredo administration sought to bring about a favorable balance of payments by boosting exports and restricting imports. A large trade surplus was achieved in 1983 and was followed by a record surplus of $13 billion in 1984. Oil was no longer such a baneful influence as the cost of imports fell owing to a relative

[222] decline in world oil prices and the initial success of the *Proalcool* program in providing supplies of an alternative source of fuel. The domestic economy, however, continued to suffer from 'stagflation,' a combination of industrial stagnation and monetary inflation. In fact, the stress on export-led growth was harmful in the short term. Although the policy of heavily devaluing the foreign exchange value of the *cruzeiro* made exports cheaper, it also raised domestic prices and thereby contributed to inflationary pressures. In addition, the practice of indexation in which wages were adjusted every six months had produced a state of self-perpetuating or 'inertial' inflation so that both business and employees were not only conditioned to rising wages and prices but actually anticipated such increases.

From the *Cruzado* Plan to the *Real* Plan

The transfer of government from the military to a civilian president in April 1985 occurred at a propitious time when the economy was emerging from recession. Inflation continued to rise to record levels, however, as a result of the effects of a prolonged agricultural drought and the new government's decision in 1985 to allow an increase in the minimum wage well above the rate of inflation. Adopting the 'shock' tactics of Argentina's '*Austral* Plan,' Sarney's Finance Minister, Dilson Funaro, launched the *Cruzado* Plan in February 1986. The plan gained its name from the introduction of a new unit of currency at a rate of one *cruzado* for 1,000 *cruzeiros*. The stated aim of the plan was to achieve zero inflation by imposing an indefinite freeze on prices and a one-year freeze on mortgages and rents. 'Inertial' inflation would be undermined by the abolition of indexation. Instead, wages would be automatically adjusted when inflation exceeded an annual rate of 20 percent.

The concept of a freeze on prices and rents was very popular and many citizens volunteered to act as 'Sarney's price inspectors' in order to ensure that companies, stores and even individual street traders would abide by the freeze. The result was a dramatic fall in inflation to single figures and a consequent rise in real incomes that stimulated an unprecedented consumer boom. The GDP rose in line with the increase in domestic economic activity and expenditures, but the release of pent-up demand for imports soon resulted in a deficit in the balance of payments and an increase in the foreign debt to over $100 billion. Administration officials sought to deflect criticism by contending that the excessive interest required to service the debt and the unreasonable attitude of the IMF were to blame for Brazil's economic difficulties.

'Brazil will not pay its foreign debt, with recession nor with unemployment, nor with hunger,' President Sarney had told the United Nations General Assembly in September 1985.[11] More significant, however, was the decision to continue the price freeze for too long a period of time. This became counterproductive because many goods inevitably became scarce and shortages developed. The political popularity of the *Cruzado* Plan, however, tempted the Sarney administration to maintain the freeze until after the congressional and state elections of November 1986. Consequently, the president's reputation suffered irretrievably when a *Cruzado* II Plan was unveiled only five days after the elections and failed to avert economic collapse in 1987. Industrial growth dramatically declined and inflation started to soar until it reached an annual rate of more than 1,000 percent in 1989.

President Fernando Collor de Mello took office in 1990 at a time when the increase in inflation had risen to 100 percent a month and was perceived to be out of control. In what he termed as 'a war to kill inflation,' Collor delivered his own version of 'shock' economic treatment by launching the 'Collor Plan.' In most respects the plan was a typical austerity measure designed to achieve a balanced budget by reducing government spending and increasing taxation. Another common element with previous stabilization measures was the introduction of a new unit of the currency known as the new *cruzeiro* (*cruzeiro novo*) to replace the existing *cruzado*. While the implementation of a freeze on prices was identical to the *Cruzado* Plan, a different and radical aspect of the Collor Plan was an extension of the freeze to include bank deposits, an action that amounted to the temporary confiscation of the assets and savings of companies and individuals. In keeping with his campaign promises to root out inefficiency and corruption in the federal bureaucracy, the new president also declared his intention to seek the compulsory redundancy of thousands of government employees. Moreover, he outlined his plans for the privatization of state companies to gain revenue from their sale and to increase efficiency and productivity by placing them in private ownership. The Collor Plan also sought the liberalization of foreign trade by the removal of protective tariff restrictions and regulations on licensing of foreign trade. Although the amount of the foreign debt continued to rise, Collor renegotiated Brazil's terms of payments so that additional foreign loans would be forthcoming.

The implementation of the Collor Plan was adversely affected by political controversy that ultimately led to the impeachment of the president in 1992. Moreover, as the experience of the *Cruzado* Plan had demonstrated, as soon as the price freeze was relaxed in 1992, high inflation resumed and rose to an

[224]   average of 20 percent per month. Under Collor's successor, President Itamar Franco, the *Real* Plan was introduced by Finance Minister Fernando Henrique Cardoso in July 1994. Once again, the basic aim was economic stabilization by achieving a balanced budget. There was also the introduction of a new unit of currency, the *real*, which would replace the new *cruzeiro*. Cardoso, however, astutely sought to lower public expectations and disclaimed any intention to implement an economic 'shock.' Indeed, the measures were introduced gradually over several months and were often announced in advance. Furthermore, seeking to avoid the perceived mistakes of the *Cruzado* and Collor Plans, the *Real* Plan did not impose a freeze on wages and prices, on the grounds that such controls were only effective for a short period and were ultimately self-defeating in the battle against inflation. A prominent feature of the *Real* Plan was the decision to fix and maintain the *real* at the same value as the US dollar. Devaluation of the currency had become so common, and at times almost a daily occurrence, that a fixed rate against the dollar would have considerable anti-inflationary impact. It would also help to hold down inflation by reducing the cost of foreign imports. As a result, imports rose from $33 billion in 1994 to almost $50 billion in 1995.

Successive military and civilian governments had sought to defeat inflation, but had enjoyed little success. Indeed, Brazilians had come to believe that inflation was inherent and self-perpetuating in their economy, and that, in contrast to Argentina or Chile, it could not be eliminated. The *Real* Plan, however, was successful in reducing inflation by half during 1994 and down to 22 percent in 1996, to 4 percent in 1997 and even close to zero for some months in 1998. Important elements of economic stabilization had also been achieved, such as a reduction in budgetary deficits, a stable foreign exchange value for the *real*, and rising exports especially with Argentina, Uruguay and Paraguay in the newly-created free trade area, *Mercosul*. The chief political beneficiary was Fernando Henrique Cardoso, who won the presidential election in 1994 and re-election in 1998. Under President Cardoso, Brazil weathered the storms arising from financial crises in the Far East and Russia from 1997 to 1999 and ended the 1990s as the tenth largest national economy in the world. Instead of congratulation, however, there was growing concern over the impact on Brazil of the increasing 'globalization' of the world economy. Moreover, persistent worries over inflation, budget deficits and the political difficulty of enacting structural economic reforms meant that the twentieth century closed on a note of pessimism about Brazil's economic future.

Society   [225]

Demography

The national population rose from 71 million in 1960 to 119 million in 1980 and to around 170 million in 2000. Despite the large aggregate increase, the rate of annual growth declined dramatically from the record high point of 3 percent at the beginning of the 1960s to just over 1 percent by the end of the twentieth century. In fact, contrary to previous demographic forecasts population grew more slowly during the 1980s and 1990s than at any period of the twentieth century. The change was not limited to Brazil and occurred throughout Latin America and the developed world. It was attributable to a lower birth rate caused primarily by growing economic prosperity, greater availability of and publicity for the use of birth control and abortion, and also a steady decline in the death rate arising from improving healthcare. Between 1970 and 1991 the proportion of children under 15 years of age fell from 42 to 35 percent of the population. Figures for the group aged 15 to 64 years during the same period showed an increase from 54 to 64 percent, while those aged over 65 years rose from 3 to 5 percent. In effect, Brazilian women were bearing fewer children, who were going on to live healthier and longer lives. In contrast to the early decades of the century, immigration from overseas was negligible and did not compensate for the reduction in the rate of fertility after 1965. Nevertheless, despite the decline in fertility, Brazil's rate of annual population growth remained relatively high in international terms and was considerably above that of the developed countries in the Northern Hemisphere. In 2000 Brazil was the fifth most populated nation in the world and its population was projected to grow to more than 240 million in 2050.

Although the migration of people from the North to the South and from the country to the city continued after 1964, the actual distribution of regional settlement did not alter to the same marked degree as earlier in the .twentieth century. The Center-South remained the most populated section and contained just over half the national population. Inward migration from other regions, however, was offset by a decline in the natural increase of the existing population. But the Northeast continued to lose population. Its proportion of the national population fell from 31 percent in 1960 to 29 percent in 1980. The regions that recorded the largest proportional increases were in the Center-West and the North, especially Mato Grosso and Rondônia where cultivation and settlement were stimulated by gold discoveries and

[226] the construction of federal highways. During the 1970s the population of Rondônia increased by an annual rate of more than 20 percent.

The trend towards increased urbanization intensified after 1964. Indeed, Brazil could be described as a predominantly urban country when the proportion of the population living in cities passed 50 percent for the first time during the early 1960s. The figure rose steadily to 68 percent in 1980 and almost 80 percent by 2000. While urban population more than doubled from 1960 to 2000, the number of people living in the countryside declined in absolute and relative terms. For the decade of the 1970s it was estimated that 17 million or 42 percent of the rural population migrated to the city, pulled by employment opportunities and pushed by the rapid development of agri-business in which machines replaced workers and changed the traditional patterns of land use and cultivation of crops. Although the resulting movement of people from the country to the city was a common feature throughout South America, Brazil retained a relatively high number of people who were still classified as rural dwellers. By the end of the twentieth century only 12 percent of the population in Argentina and Chile lived in the country, whereas in Brazil the figure was 20 percent.

After replacing Rio de Janeiro as the country's most populated city in the mid-1950s, São Paulo subsequently consolidated its leading position. By 1991 the city of São Paulo had a population in excess of 9 million, compared to Rio de Janeiro that had just over 5 million. Salvador was the third most populated city with just over 2 million and Belo Horizonte a close fourth. In 1960 only São Paulo and Rio de Janeiro had more than a million inhabitants, but in 1991 they were joined by nine cities whose populations also passed the million mark. They included, in descending order of population: Salvador, Belo Horizonte, Fortaleza, Brasília, Recife, Porto Alegre, Curitiba, Belém and Manaus. If adjoining suburbs were added, the metropolitan region of São Paulo had more than 15 million inhabitants in 1991 or approximately 10 percent of the national population. The corresponding figure for Rio de Janeiro was almost 10 million, while Belo Horizonte and Porto Alegre possessed over 3 million each. Similar to the relative decline in the increase of the overall national population, the growth of the major metropolitan areas was beginning to slow down towards the end of the twentieth century. In fact, the fastest urban growth occurred in small and medium-sized cities. In this respect, urbanization in Brazil was more widely dispersed and did not show the concentrated hyperurbanization that was a characteristic of most of the other Latin American countries in which from one third to one half of the national population lived in a giant metropolis such as Mexico City or Buenos Aires.

Society [227]

During the period from 1964 to 2000 Brazil experienced considerable economic growth that brought rises in real income and material gains particularly for the upper and middle classes. The visible improvement in the standard of living was most evident in the cities, where households with access to piped running water increased from 16 percent in 1950 to over 70 percent by 1990. The proportion of homes equipped with electricity rose from 25 percent in 1950 to almost 90 percent by 1990. The proportion of individual families possessing television sets increased from 24 percent in 1970 to more than 70 percent in 1990. Only 9 percent of families owned an automobile in 1970. The figure for 1994 was almost 40 percent.

The rise in general material affluence disguised, however, the basic inequality of income distribution that made Brazil one of the most unequal societies in the world. The gap between rich and poor actually widened. The richest 5 percent of the population received 27.7 percent of the national income in 1960 and 35.8 percent in 1990. By contrast, the poorest 20 percent of the population received 3.5 percent in 1960; this proportion declined to 2.3 percent in 1990. Largely reliant on cash as their main means of exchange, the poor were severely disadvantaged by the impact of hyperinflation, and the attitude of the military governments that made economic growth a priority at the expense of policies of progressive taxation and income redistribution. Lack of educational qualifcations also severely restricted employment prospects. For those unskilled and semi-skilled workers who were able to find jobs, pay and conditions of work were relatively poor. Moreover, trade unions were placed under close governmental supervision and protests against low wages and working conditions were unsympathetically and often violently suppressed. Matters did not greatly improve under the civilian governments after 1985. The electoral manifcsto of the Workers Party (PT) in 1994 claimed that 60 million Brazilians were currently living in poverty, of whom 32 million were in absolute poverty and unable to feed themselves adequately, a condition described as 'social apartheid.'

The endemic nature of Brazil's serious social problems was highlighted by statistics on illiteracy and health. Illiteracy among those 10 years and older was reduced from 36 percent in 1970 to 18 percent in 1991. The claims to success, however, rang hollow when Colombia recorded even lower rates of 13 percent and neighboring Argentina only 5 percent. Similarly, the life expectancy figure in Brazil rose from 52 years in 1960 to 62 years in 1980, but compared unfavorably with 72 years in Argentina. Furthermore, infant

[228]   mortality in Brazil persistently remained among the highest in Latin America. In addition, national figures disguised regional imbalances. Life expectancy in the South rose from 60 in 1960 to 68 years in 1980, but similar figures for the Northeast were 42 and 54 years. Infant mortality rates in the Northeast were 50 percent higher than in the South. In 1992 it was estimated that half of those classified as illiterate resided in the Northeast, whereas the illiteracy rate in São Paulo and Rio was less than 10 percent.

Although poverty and deprivation were most deep-rooted in the country-side and especially in the Northeast, the impact of poverty was most visible in the cities. Just as the cities displayed the material gains of economic growth, they also exposed its failings. An absence of town planning and zoning permitted the haphazard construction of factories and the extension and pro-liferation of *favelas*. The perceived plight of the cities prompted the creation of the National Housing Bank in 1965 that was assigned the task of promot-ing urban renewal and improving public access to water and drainage. However, as the cities steadily grew in population, they suffered from traffic congestion and increased pollution. Covered in a dense smog of smoke and toxic chemicals, Cubatão in São Paulo became an internationally infamous example of the consequences of unregulated industrial development. The city's unusually high rate of disease gained it the nickname of 'the valley of death.' Most of all, however, urban life became associated with high rates of violent crime especially in the *favelas*, which often became the centres of organized drug smuggling on a massive scale. Another feature of the major Brazilian cities which aroused international attention and humanitarian concern was the frequent presence of gangs of homeless children whose suspected criminal activities often made them the victims of police harassment and brutality.

Employment and education

Urbanization and industrialization significantly altered the pattern of employment and distribution of occupations. In 1950 14 percent of the total labor force was employed in manufacturing and industry, around 60 percent worked in agriculture and 26 percent had jobs in the service sector. By 1978 the proportion working in industry increased to 20 percent, in agriculture it fell to around 36 percent, while the number employed in services rose to 40 percent. During the 1970s agriculture created virtually no new jobs, while industry, especially in chemicals, automobiles and construction, added more than 500,000 jobs a year. The figure for the service sector was even more impressive with almost one million new jobs a year. The switch from agriculture to industry was highlighted in the statistics for the period from 1950 to 1990, in which the labor force increased from 17 million to 62 million, while employment in agriculture grew by only 40 percent but in manufacturing increased by almost 600 percent and in services by more than 700 percent. Agricultural work, in fact, became increasingly seasonal and temporary with employers relying on workers drawn from the *favelas* and rural towns to work as day laborers on farms. These workers were popularly known as '*boías frías*' (cold meals) because they usually brought along cold rice and beans for their lunch.

A prominent feature of the changing nature of the workforce was the increase in working women. From 2.5 million in 1950, the female labor force increased by more than 5 percent annually, rising to 6 million in 1970 and more than 18 million in 1980. Women made up almost 15 percent of the total labor force in 1950 and 29 percent in 1980. Many of the jobs were in services and were relatively low-paid. Nevertheless, women made a significant contribution to raising the income of their families and lifting those with lower incomes above the poverty level. The increase in working women also contributed to rising material standards and influenced the decline in fertility. Women also became more actively involved and took leadership roles in promoting social and political issues. Often with the support of the Catholic Church, feminist organizations were formed to campaign for equal pay for comparable work, improved access to education and health-care, and the passage of laws against domestic violence.

The concern over the provision of public education was not limited to women's groups. As part of the military's desire for national development and modernization, the government showed a growing awareness in the 1970s that low levels of educational achievement were not only a significant obstacle in promoting personal and career development but also seriously undermined the country's potential for future economic growth. The resulting drive to increase school attendance was successful in lifting the number of pupils from 15.9 million in 1970, to 22.5 million in 1980 and 42 million in 1994. The largest growth was in higher education, whose figure of 456,000 students enrolled in 1970 was tripled to 1.4 million in 1980. The boom reflected the fact that higher education was made a priority during the 1970s and absorbed more than half the annual education budget. The universities were valued by the military governments because they produced 'technocrats.' The emphasis on higher education, however, seriously reduced the funding allocated for primary and secondary education. Moreover, the fact that there was an increase in the numbers of pupils enrolled at primary and secondary level was

[230] misleading because it did not indicate the variable quality of education that was being provided. The drop-out rate was so high that it was reckoned that half the labor force had not completed primary school and that no more than a third had attended secondary school.

Social tensions

Inequality was also evident in the countryside, where the concentration of land tenure was further intensified as a result of economic policies to increase the production of sugarcane to be distilled into alcohol and of new crops such as soya and orange concentrate that were needed to earn foreign exchange. In addition, the military governments stimulated the cultivation and settlement of frontier regions in the North and Center-West. While large landowners and corporations were able to create huge estates, migrant families found it difficult to acquire land. Indeed, the big landowners invariably received the support of the federal and state governments in using violence to protect their estates from invasion by squatters and to expel indigenous peoples from land whose ownership could be legally contested. The murder in 1988 of the political activist, Francisco (Chico) Mendes, attracted considerable international notice and protest. His assassins were eventually arrested and convicted, but soon escaped from prison in suspicious circumstances. In fact, violence has traditionally been a feature of the 'land question' in the frontier regions where from 1964 to 1986 an estimated 1,500 people died as a result of conflicts over land. Indeed, the opening up of unoccupied land by the military government resulted not so much in orderly settlement by peasant farmers (*posseiros*) seeking to establish title to own land by residence but more often in *grilagem* (land-grab) in which ownership was fraudulently claimed by land-grabbers (*grileiros*) usually with the support of influential local landowners and corrupt government officials. Rural conflict also occurred in the Center-South during the 1980s where peasants, with the support of the Catholic Church and the Workers Party (PT), formed the Landless Rural Workers Movement (*Movimento dos Trabalhadores Rurais Sem Terra* or MST) to invade, occupy and cultivate some of the millions of acres of land that was lying fallow and not being put to productive use. 'We fight for agrarian reform in order to work, produce, and guarantee abundant food on the table of every Brazilian,' argued the manifesto of the MST in 1998.[12]

The question of race relations has also revealed divisions within modern Brazilian society. The example of successful national liberation movements in Africa and the well-publicized struggle for civil rights and black power in the United States during the 1960s focused attention on the ambiguity of [231] Brazilian attitudes towards race. The concept of Brazil as a 'racial democracy' remained appealing to whites, but lost further credibility as a series of official reports confirmed that 50 percent of the black population was illiterate and that only 2 percent proceeded to higher education. Moreover, while blacks and mulattos made up more than 40 percent of the national population, they were not similarly represented in top positions in the government, military and judiciary. Provisions against racial discrimination were included in the 1988 Constitution. Nevertheless, only twelve 'non-whites' were elected to the 1990 National Congress. Despite the lack of progress in achieving racial integration and affirmative action in employment, blacks were able to maintain and project their own racial identity and culture by stressing Brazil's links with Africa particularly in art, music, and religious rituals such as *candomblé* and *umbanda*.

The attitude of Brazilian government and society towards the Indian has aroused considerable controversy. Consisting of more than 200 separate tribes with their own languages, the Indians continued to remain in remote regions with little contact with the outside world. This was dramatically changed during the second half of the twentieth century by the government policy of stressing national economic growth. The welfare of the Indian inhabitants was neglected as the frontier regions of the North were opened to business corporations, prospectors (*garimpeiros*) and peasant farmers (*posseiros*). Instead of carrying out its task to protect and promote the welfare of the Indians, the Indian Protection Service (SPI) either seemed helpless or acted in collusion with the invaders. Revelations of corruption and mismanagement resulted in the closure of SPI in 1967 and its replacement by the National Foundation of the Indian (*Fundação Nacional do Índio* or FUNAI).

The creation of FUNAI coincided with a period of intensive economic exploitation of the North, including a gold rush into the Amazon region. By the 1970s the population classified as 'white' in the territory of Roraima had reached 80,000, and rose to 215,000 in 1991. Roraima became a state in 1990. The invasion of prospectors and settlers resulted, however, in conflict with the local Indians. The most damaging consequence was the spread of diseases from which the Indians had no natural immunity. Considerable publicity was given to the suffering of the Yanomami tribe. More than 1,500 or 15 percent of the Yanomami was estimated to have died from disease and malnutrition. Responding to pressure from international opinion to help the Indians and also protect the tropical rainforest from the damage caused by intensive deforestation, the federal government created a Yanomami Reserve

[232] of 36,000 square miles in November 1991. The Indians, however, remained suspicious of the government and regarded FUNAI as an inherently corrupt organization that was not sincerely committed to the protection of Indian rights. With the support of local priests of the Catholic Church, the Indians formed their own separate political movement, the Council of Indigenous Peoples and Organizations of Brazil. Claiming that Indians had been victims of a policy of genocide, the Council pointed out that their population had dwindled from one million in 1900 to 300,000 in 2000.[13] By engaging in political activity, the Indians sought to assert their historical rights and thereby affirm their ethnic identity. In April 2000 hundreds of Indians armed with bows and arrows and wearing traditional war paint symbolically marched in protest against the celebrations in Brasília and Porto Seguro seeking to commemorate and glorify the five-hundredth anniversary of the discovery of Brazil. 'Five hundred years ago began our massacre, suffering and extermination,' an Indian leader told President Fernando Henrique Cardoso.[14]

A feature of modern Brazilian society during the last quarter of the twentieth century was the rapid rise of Protestantism at the expense of Catholicism. With up to 90 percent of the population professing nominal allegiance to the Catholic religion, Brazil still remained the world's largest Catholic nation in 2000. In 1950 Brazil had less than 2 million Protestants or 4 percent of the population. The figure for 2000 was over 20 million and represented 15 percent of the population. In fact, it was argued that more Protestants than Catholics actually attended church services on Sundays. The majority of the new converts to Protestantism were drawn from the urban poor and were attracted to evangelical and Pentecostal groups rather than the well-established denominations such as Anglicans, Presbyterians, Methodists, and Baptists. Although the driving force for the modern movement has come from the proselytizing efforts of North American Pentecostal missionaries, the church known as the Assembly of God was founded by two Swedish missionaries at Belém in 1911. Afflicted by a culture of grinding poverty and despair, millions of Brazilians have found practical relevance in the Pentecostal message of achieving worldly success through personal discipline, hard work and virtuous living. Pentecostal services were also lively and emotional and were regularly broadcast on radio and television. A separate network, TV Record, was purchased for this purpose in 1989.

In his 1995 inaugural address President Fernando Henrique Cardoso promised to govern for 'all' Brazilians. 'But if it becomes necessary,' he remarked, 'to do away with the privileges of the few to do justice to the vast majority of Brazilians, let there be no doubt: I will be on the side of the majority.'[15] However, Brazilian society ended the twentieth century afflicted with uncertainty rather than in a confident mood. At one level, national identity was affirmed by the international success of Brazilian sports stars in soccer, tennis and motor racing and the exotic image of Brazil as the land of the samba and carnival. But the problem of inequality persisted. During the closing decades of the twentieth century, the extremes of wealth and poverty had widened rather than narrowed. The nation's largest cities had become a byword for corrupt government, pollution and crime. In the countryside, poverty and disease remained fixed at Third World levels. Moreover, the comforting concept of Brazil as a 'racial democracy' was belied by irrefutable evidence of widespread discrimination against blacks and mulattos and campaigns of organized violence against the Indians.

Diplomacy

The special relationship

In April 1964 the new military government headed by President Castelo Branco quickly proclaimed a reversal of the independent foreign policy pursued by Quadros and Goulart. Instead, the traditional Brazilian policy of seeking a close and special relationship with the United States was reaffirmed. The move reflected a desire to change the direction of foreign policy away from the left-wing attitudes of the previous government. It also expressed the ideology and geopolitical thinking of the ESG in which the military admiringly regarded the United States as the leader of the free world in the Cold War against International Communism. In addition, access to American trade and investment and cooperation on financial matters was considered vital for the modernization and development of the Brazilian economy. 'What is good for the United States is good for Brazil,' later declared the Brazilian ambassador in Washington, Juracy Magalhães.[16]

The United States government was delighted with the success of the military coup, an event that the American ambassador in Brazil, Lincoln Gordon, effusively described as 'one of the major turning points in world history in the middle of the twentieth century' and similar in significance 'to the Marshall Plan proposal, the Berlin Blockade, the defeat of Communist aggression in Korea, and the resolution of the missile crisis in Cuba.'[17] Indeed, within minutes of the installation of Ranieri Mazzilli as acting-president on April 2, a telegram arrived from President Lyndon Johnson conveying the

[234] support of the American people for the change of government. While the act of diplomatic recognition was very welcome, it was somewhat embarrassing in its speed because ex-president Goulart had not yet actually departed from Brazil. Suspicion existed of American complicity in the coup and was later reinforced by the revelation that a contingency plan involving a naval task force had been prepared by the Johnson administration. 'Our embassy did have far-ranging contacts,' admitted Lincoln Gordon, and he added: 'But we were not participants in the planning of action against Goulart.'[18] Neverthe-less, the Johnson administration was genuine in its good feeling for the milit-ary regime that assumed power. This was demonstrated by its support for internal security measures to suppress subversion and Communism. Priority was also given to the promotion of American financial aid and investment in Brazil. During the period from 1964 to 1970 only South Vietnam and India received more financial assistance from the United States.

The Castelo Branco administration reciprocated by assisting the United States in the battle against International Communism. Especially pleasing to American officials was Brazil's participation in the policy of isolating Cuba in the Western Hemisphere. In contrast to Goulart, who had shown a sympa-thetic attitude towards Fidel Castro and the Cuban Revolution, Castelo Branco broke off diplomatic relations with Cuba only a few weeks after taking office. In June 1965 Brazil sent troops to assist American military intervention to avert an alleged Communist coup in the Dominican Republic. The Brazilian government was also publicly sympathetic to the actions taken by the United States to protect South Vietnam from Communist aggression. In August 1964 Foreign Minister Vasci Leitão da Cunha expressed solidarity with the United States over the Tonkin Gulf incident. A Brazilian medical team was later sent to serve in South Vietnam as a gesture of support for the United States.

While Brazil sought close diplomatic cooperation with the United States, it was neither a formal ally nor a satellite state. In fact, the diplomacy of the military government was similar to the policies pursued by its civilian pre-decessors in seeking both to assert and promote the country's national interest. For example, Castelo Branco stressed that Brazil's intervention in the Do-minican Republic in 1965 was not at American bidding but was an inde-pendent decision and part of a scheme to develop a permanent inter-American 'peace force' under the command of the Organization of American States (OAS). Similarly, while relations were broken off with Cuba, they were main-tained with other Communist countries beyond the Western Hemisphere. Indeed, vigorous efforts were made to expand Brazilian trade with the Soviet Union.

The nationalist foreign policy

When Costa e Silva became president in 1967 he countered domestic criticism that Brazil was too subservient to the United States by implementing what was essentially a return to the 'independent' policy of Quadros and Goulart. To avoid association with the left-wing presidents, however, the military preferred the policy to be described in public as 'nationalist.' Although the new president was a staunch anti-Communist and made a state visit to the United States early in his presidency, he perceived world affairs as no longer so dominated by Cold War ideology and rivalries. Rather than the traditional East–West perspective, more importance was attached to the growing divergence between the affluent nations of the 'North' or 'First World' and the less economically developed countries of the 'South' or 'Third World.' According to this North–South view, the priority of foreign policy was not to cooperate with the United States to contain Communism but to serve as a tool for promoting national economic development so that Brazil could join the First World. 'We want,' stated Foreign Minister José de Magalhães Pinto, 'to put diplomacy at the service of prosperity.'[19] Although Brazil historically identified itself with the nations of the 'North,' the fact that it was a major exporter of primary products and raw materials gave it more in common with the developing countries of the Third World. This was demonstrated when Brazil took a leading role in the formation of the Group of 77 at the Second Meeting of the United Nations Commission on Trade and Development (UNCTAD) in 1968.

Brazil's international prestige and self-esteem was boosted by the achievement of internal political stability and the onset of industrial and financial recovery in 1967 leading to the 'economic miracle.' By projecting the same high annual rate of GDP growth into the future, it was confidently predicted that, by the end of the twentieth century, Brazil would rise to the status of a world power ('*O Brasil Grande*') and become a member of the 'First World.' The idea of 'power' was conceived in terms of economic prosperity and not military strength or territorial conquest. Indeed, the strength of the armed forces was held at a modest level in relation to the country's size and population. More emphasis and expenditure was directed to building economic infrastructure in the form of massive domestic projects such as the Transamazon Highway and the Itaipú Dam. Brazil's remarkable economic progress attracted world attention and admiration. During the visit of President Garrastazú Médici to Washington in December 1971, the American president, Richard Nixon, stated: 'We know that as Brazil goes, so will the rest of the Latin

[236]   American continent.'[20] While the American president's remarks were intended
to be flattering, Brazilians rejected the implication that they were the agents
of American values and business in Latin America.

During the 1970s the relationship with the United States became less
important as the threat of Communist subversion receded in Brazil and
tensions in the Cold War were relaxed by détente between the superpowers.
Moreover, the rise of Western Europe and Japan resulted in America's relative
decline as the world's leading economic power, a development that undermined the value of traditional commercial links. During World War II, the
United States had absorbed more than 50 percent of Brazil's total exports.
The proportion fell to less than 20 percent during the 1970s. Consequently,
Brazil looked further afield for alternative export markets and sources of capital
investment, a drive that was stimulated by the 1973 'oil shock' and the
resulting need to earn more foreign exchange from exports. Particular effort
was directed by Brazilian diplomats to expanding trade with the affluent
nations of Western Europe. New markets were also developed and cultivated
in Africa, the Middle East and Asia. Trade with the Communist Bloc was
markedly increased, especially with the countries of Eastern Europe, where
exports rose from $123 million in 1970 to $421 million in 1973. An opportunity to enter the vast Chinese market was seized in 1974 when full diplomatic relations were established with the People's Republic of China.

The recognition of Communist China predated by four years a similar
action by the American president, Jimmy Carter, and demonstrated Brazil's
determination to exercise autonomy in its foreign policy even if this diverged
from the diplomacy of the United States. Indeed, the pursuit of a 'nationalist'
policy that stressed export-led growth frequently resulted in conflict with
the United States. Despite talk of a special relationship between the two
countries, Brazilian exporters complained of American tariff barriers and discriminatory customs duties that seriously affected their sales of instant coffee,
shoes and steel. Nuclear power was a particularly contentious issue. While
the Costa e Silva administration denied having ambitions to acquire nuclear
weapons, it wanted Brazil to develop atomic energy for peaceful industrial
purposes and adamantly resisted American pressure to sign the Nuclear
Non-Proliferation Treaty. Much to American displeasure, in 1977 President
Geisel signed an agreement with a West German consortium to supply nuclear reactors. Indeed, the suspicion that American officials and businessmen
were seeking to stifle Brazilian commerce and industrial development resulted
in calculated efforts to reduce the country's economic dependence on the

United States. In what was a veiled but unmistakable reference to the United
States, President Geisel stated in 1974 that there would be 'no automatic or
aprioristic alignment' with other countries. In its place, Brazil would adopt
a multilateral policy based upon 'responsible pragmatism.'[21] This was
exemplified by two presidential visits to Western Europe and the negotiation
of large commercial contracts with Britain and France. Brazil refused to join
President Carter's call for a boycott of the Moscow Olympic Games and to
join an embargo on exports of grain to the Soviet Union as a protest against
the Soviet invasion of Afghanistan in 1979. Economic factors also influenced
Brazilian policy towards the Middle East and resulted in disagreement with
the United States over the Arab–Israeli issue. Dependent upon the Middle
East for 80 percent of its oil imports, the Brazilian government adopted
a pro-Arab attitude. Despite American annoyance, Brazil recognized the
Palestine Liberation Organization (PLO) as the representative of the Pales-
tinians in 1979. A similar diplomatic realism was evident in Brazil's cultivation of friendly diplomatic relations during the mid-1970s with the
pro-Marxist governments that won independence from Portugal in Guinea-
Bissau, Angola and Mozambique.

Brazil, however, had no desire to become actively involved in the politics
of the Cold War. The primary purpose of diplomacy remained the global
promotion of commercial relations, a task which became more difficult and
demanding as a result of the damaging effects of the 'oil shocks' of 1973 and
1979 and the debt crisis of the 1980s. Moreover, domestic factors such as
political instability, persistent hyperinflation and the failure to maintain the
high levels of growth of the economic 'miracle' created growing strategic
and economic insecurity. No longer so optimistic about achieving world power
status, successive Brazilian governments were suspicious of what they regarded
as attempts by the great powers to infringe the sovereignty of less powerful
nations and to establish international institutions for their own benefit. Brazil
was, therefore, extremely distrustful of proposals designed to limit the growth
of population, establish international ownership of the seabeds, restrict
arms sales, and regulate world trade. Especially controversial was the issue
of the environment. Indeed, foreign concern over the deforestation of the
Amazon argued that Brazilian actions were affecting the rest of the world
by destroying many rare plant and animal species. Brazil was also charged
with causing catastrophic soil erosion and flooding that was responsible
for destructive climate change including the depletion of the ozone layer
above Antarctica.

A succession of Brazilian governments, both military and civilian, staunchly defended Brazil's sovereignty. In 1970 Brazil unilaterally declared its jurisdiction over territorial waters extending to 200 miles from its coastline. In 1977 President Jimmy Carter's criticism of human rights violations, although ostensibly directed against the Soviet Union, by implication also included Brazil and led the Geisel administration to cancel a military assistance agreement with the United States that had been in operation since 1952. Brazilians were especially sensitive over perceived foreign designs on the Amazonian region. External criticism of deforestation was countered with the argument that 'slash and burn' and logging were not only traditional practices but were on a small scale when compared with the massive programs occurring in Central America, West Africa and Southeast Asia. Furthermore, it was contended that the industrialized nations of the 'North' were actually responsible for much more atmospheric pollution than Brazil.

Nevertheless, Brazil did not want to appear too antagonistic or confrontational. Indeed, Brazilian diplomacy after 1964 was inherently conservative and, in matters of disagreement, sought to challenge and not to overthrow international political and financial institutions. While friendly relations were desired with the nations of the Third World, the opportunity to continue to play a leading role in international meetings and activities of organizations such as UNCTAD was quietly declined. In fact, Brazil gradually felt that it had less in common with these countries as it became a major exporter of manufactured goods and one of the largest industrial economies in the world. During the 1980s economic factors brought about a return to closer cooperation with the United States because Brazil needed American diplomatic assistance in order to negotiate a resolution of the debt crisis. Moreover, the decline in trade between the two countries during the 1970s proved to be only temporary. By the 1990s the United States was once again Brazil's largest single market.

A notable feature of Brazilian diplomacy during the last quarter of the twentieth century was the successful cultivation of closer political and economic relations with the other nations of South America. For much of the 1960s and 1970s Brazil's preoccupation with developing global export markets meant that relations with South America were neglected. This attitude changed, however, as a result of the 'oil shocks' of the 1970s, difficulties with the United States, and the growing awareness of the country's vulnerability to economic decisions made by the developed nations of the 'North.' In 1979 President João Baptista Figueiredo declared that Latin America would be a priority in Brazil's diplomacy. President Geisel had made a similar statement, but Figueiredo differed from his predecessor in actually [239] making a state visit to Buenos Aires in May 1980. The occasion attracted considerable publicity because it marked the first visit of a Brazilian president to Argentina since that of Getúlio Vargas in 1935.

Figueiredo followed up his initiative with further presidential visits to Venezuela, Paraguay and Chile in what a leading American newspaper described as Brazil's attempt 'to woo its neighbors.'[22] Conscious of traditional Spanish-American suspicion of Brazilian motives, Figueiredo was keen to reassure his hosts that Brazil had no expansionist aims. The president sought to project an image of his country as a peaceful and trustworthy partner. In this he was helped by the current poor state of relations between his government and the Carter administration which meant that Brazil did not appear on this occasion as an American agent or surrogate. The diplomatic initiative was also aided by the fact that it took place at a time when regional rivalries were muted by internal political and economic weakness and an awareness of the value of working together to promote shared mutual interests. Ironically, the diplomatic process of improving relations was assisted by the end of Figueiredo's term of office in 1985 and the return of civilian government in Brazil, two years after the election in Argentina of a civilian president, Raúl Alfonsín. In 1985 both governments agreed to the Iguaçu Declaration which created a commission to study the feasibility of economic integration of the two countries. An understanding was signed in the following year that envisaged the creation of a customs union and later a common market within the next ten years. In 1988 the governments of Brazil and Argentina signed the treaty of Integration, Cooperation and Development. A customs union came into being in 1991 and was known as *Mercosul* (*Mercosur* in Spanish). The members were Brazil, Argentina, Paraguay and Uruguay.

During the 1990s Brazilian diplomacy sought to promote the development of *Mercosul* not only for its economic benefits but also to provide a stronger bargaining position in trade negotiations with the economic 'megablocs' of the world such as the European Union and the North American Free Trade Area (NAFTA). Indeed, Brazil became the senior partner in *Mercosul* and took the lead in suggesting a broader South American Free Trade Area (SAFTA) as a logical next step in regional economic integration.

In the wider world, Brazil was sensitive to international charges of its callous mistreatment of the Indians and neglect of the environment. To counter such criticism, Brazil agreed to host the UN Conference on Environment and Development (UNCED) or the 'Earth Summit' in Rio de Janeiro in May 1992. Brazil also revived its ambition to play a more significant role in

[240]   the United Nations and sought a permanent seat in the Security Council. During the 1970s some members of the military government had fondly predicted that Brazil would be a world power by the end of the century. In 2000 Brazil could hardly be described as a world power, but the holding of a meeting of South American presidents at Brasília in August demonstrated that Brazil had successfully risen to a leading position in the region. 'Brazil has earned respect for its international positions, its international goals,' declared Foreign Minister Luiz Felipe Lampreia, and he added: 'We have to be taken seriously.'[23]

CONCLUSION

I n terms of geographical size and population, Brazil is today one of the
giants of the modern world. 'Brazil is the Russia of the South American
continent,' wrote an American visitor in 1899.[1] From its 'discovery' by
Cabral in 1500 to the end of the millennium in 2000 Brazil developed from
a precarious colonial outpost into one of the largest and most populated
nations in the world. At first, the Portuguese perceived the land as a vast and
intimidating wilderness that posed formidable natural obstacles to settlement
and economic exploitation. After a hesitant beginning in the early sixteenth
century, permanent settlements were gradually established close to the coastline. Pioneers and settlers subsequently expanded into the interior and the
remote Amazon region. In the process, land was cleared, settled and cultivated and a nation of more than 3 million square miles in area was formed.
The population also rose from 60,000 in 1585 to 5 million in 1822 at the
beginning of the First Empire. At the start of the Republic in 1889 the population had reached almost 14 million. This leapt to 170 million in 2000,
making Brazil the most populated country in Latin America.

Politics

Despite its size and regional diversity, Brazil formed a viable nation state that
maintained its territorial unity and experienced a more peaceful and stable
political history than its Spanish-American neighbors. For three centuries the
country was a colony ruled from Portugal. The battle for independence in
1822–3 was achieved quickly and with little bloodshed. There was even less
violence in the switch from Empire to Republic in 1889. Relatively peaceful
changes of regime also occurred during the twentieth century in 1930,
1945, 1964 and 1985. But the motto of 'order and progress' that was in-
scribed on the flag of republican Brazil disguised the existence and perpetuation of a political system that was essentially élitist and generally repressive

[242] and corrupt. Political and civil rights of citizens were written into the various constitutions that were promulgated after 1824, but the reluctance of the ruling élite to enact liberal reforms and the failure to develop national political parties stifled political debate and competition. As a result, times of political and economic crisis usually occasioned the imposition of periods of authoritarian rule, as exemplified by the *Estado Nôvo* in 1937 and the intervention of the military in 1964.

Economy

'The country is so well-favored that if it were rightly cultivated, it would yield everything,' reported Pero Vaz de Caminha in 1500.[2] The view of Brazil as a country with enormous economic potential has persisted throughout Brazilian history. The exploitation of natural resources in the past, however, was characterized by recurring economic cycles of 'boom and bust.' This pattern was demonstrated by sugar in the seventeenth century, the mining boom in the eighteenth century, and later by rubber and coffee. Although the concentration on agricultural and mineral exports brought great wealth, it distorted the development and geographical location of the domestic economy. It also made Brazil vulnerable to external shocks in the world economy such as the dramatic contraction of international trade resulting from World War I and the Depression of the 1930s. Brazilian governments responded by seeking to promote the growth of a modern industrial economy. Some success was achieved, but the rise in national income was not evenly distributed among the population. Moreover, the massive increase in the foreign debt and the apparent helplessness of successive governments to halt the relentless rise of inflation during the last half of the twentieth century produced a sense of pervasive domestic economic crisis that raised doubts over the country's future economic prospects.

Society

'There is one thing that will impress itself upon the traveller [to Brazil], and that is the color of its inhabitants,' observed an American journalist in 1910.[3] Salient characteristics of the people of Brazil are that they speak Portuguese and originate from many different ethnic backgrounds. The primacy of the Portuguese language reflects the historical fact that Brazil was discovered and colonized by Portugal. The mixture of races was the consequence of a relative shortage of European women during the early colonial period which resulted in children being born from European fathers and Indian mothers.

In addition, there was the growing importation of large numbers of African slaves to meet the demand for plantation workers. A stratified society emerged in which whites were regarded as superior, while Indians and African slaves were considered to be racially inferior and consigned to the bottom. In the middle were free persons of mixed race. With the exception of an élite led by the wealthy landowning families, the large majority of people have suffered in poverty throughout the history of Brazil. Living in the countryside, their lives revolved around a daily grind of physical labor and subsistence agriculture. In the twentieth century increasing numbers of migrants moved from the country to the cities and industries of the Center-South in search of employment and better wages and working conditions. As a result, society became industrialized and urbanized and no longer predominantly agrarian and rural. The urban middle class increased in numbers, but social divisions based on race still persisted and were intensified by considerations of income, occupation, education and gender.

Diplomacy

During the colonial period Portugal successfully defeated incursions from France and Holland and eventually secured the international recognition of boundaries that confirmed Brazil as the largest country in South America. During the Empire, Brazil often felt a lack of affinity with its Spanish-American neighbors. In particular, there was a history of territorial rivalry with Argentina that developed into competition for regional preeminence. A notable feature of Brazilian diplomacy was the search for allies beyond South America to compensate for its continental insecurity and also to promote overseas trade and investment. Particular effort was directed to maintaining friendly relations with Great Britain during the nineteenth century and the United States during the twentieth century. Although Brazil was generally indifferent to events outside the Western Hemisphere, there were calculated attempts to take an active role in world affairs. This was demonstrated in the decisions in 1917 and 1942 to join the world wars as a belligerent power and the desire to secure a permanent seat on the Council of the League of Nations and later the Security Council of the United Nations. Brazilian diplomats discovered, however, that their country possessed little influence in the wider world beyond South America. The view of the great powers was not dissimilar to that held by diplomats of the sixteenth century in regarding Brazil as an interesting and curiously exotic nation but one that was peripheral to the central issues of international affairs.

NOTES

Notes to Chapter 1

1. Various writers over the centuries have speculated that Europeans discovered Brazil prior to Cabral's expedition and that his change of course was deliberate rather than accidental. The surprise aroused in Europe by Cabral's discovery, however, appeared to be genuine. See J.H. Parry, *The Discovery of South America* (London: Paul Elek, 1979), p. 88.

2. For convenience 'Spain' and 'Spanish' will be used instead of 'Castile' and 'Castilian.'

3. 'The Letter of Pero Vaz de Caminha,' quoted in E. Bradford Burns (ed.), *A Documentary History of Brazil* (New York: Knopf, 1966), p. 28.

4. Exotic birds were also brought to Europe and resulted in some Italians calling the new country the 'Land of the Parrots.' See Boris Fausto, *A Concise History of Brazil* (Cambridge: Cambridge University Press, 1999), p. 9.

5. Luís de Góis (brother of the donatary of São Tome) to João III in 1548, quoted in Leslie Bethell (ed.), *Colonial Brazil* (Cambridge: Cambridge University Press, 1987), p. 19.

6. The 1828 Law of Municipal Organization and the 1834 Additional Act greatly reduced the powers of the municipal councils so that they became virtual administrative agents of the provincial president.

7. For convenience 'Holland' will be used instead of the 'United Provinces' or 'Low Countries.'

8. A comment made in c.1587, quoted in Bethell, *Colonial Brazil*, p. 151.

9. Quoted in E. Bradford Burns, *A History of Brazil* (New York: Columbia University Press, 1980), p. 76.

10. The terms 'England' and 'English' will be used when referring to the period prior to 1800. 'Britain' and 'British' will be used for references after 1800.

11. Treaty of Madrid, 1750, quoted in João Capistrano de Abreu, *Chapters of Brazil's Colonial History, 1500–1800* (New York: Oxford University Press, 1997), p. 170.

12. August 12, 1798, quoted in A.J.R. Russell-Wood (ed.), *From Colony To Nation: Essays on the Independence of Brazil* (Baltimore: Johns Hopkins University Press, 1975), p. 245.

13. Quoted in Kenneth R. Maxwell, *Conflicts and Conspiracies: Brazil and Portugal, 1750–1808* (Cambridge: Cambridge University Press, 1973), p. 222.

14. Despite the efforts of royal officials to supervise the production and transit of gold, illegal production and smuggling took place on a large scale.

15. Religion was another distinction. Jews who had converted to Catholicism were known as 'New Christians.' They were especially prominent in commercial activities and enterprises.

16. People of mixed European and Indian origin were also known as *mestiços*. The term *cafuso* was used for those of Indian and African origin. Though for a long time regarded as a pejorative term, *caboclo* was used to denote people of mixed European, Indian and African origin.

17. Quoted in Stuart B. Schwartz, *Sugar Plantations in the Formation of Brazilian Society: Bahia, 1550–1835* (Cambridge: Cambridge University Press, 1985), p. 273.

18. A list of descriptions for skin colors was drawn up by the Brazilian Institute of Geography and Statistics in 1976 and contained 134 different terms. See Robert M. Levine and John J. Crocitti (eds), *The Brazilian Reader: History, Culture, Politics* (London: Latin American Bureau, 1999), pp. 386–90.

19. Meneses to the Crown, September 1, 1610, quoted in ibid., p. 31.

20. Quoted in Burns, *Documentary History of Brazil*, p. 83.

21. Conditions of work were relatively better for slaves in the mining industry in Minas Gerais. Their working life has been estimated at 12 years and was double that of a field laborer in the sugar plantations of the Northeast.

22. Report of the Overseas Council dated 1768, quoted in José Murilo de Carvalho, 'Political Elites and State Building: The Case of Nineteenth-Century Brazil,' *Comparative Studies in Society and History*, 24 (1982), pp. 383–4.

Notes to Chapter 2

1. Dom João had been appointed Prince Regent in 1792 when his mother, Queen Maria I, had been declared insane. Queen Maria died in 1816.

[246]

2. Letter of Dom Pedro I, June 19, 1822, quoted in Roderick J. Barman, *Brazil: The Forging of a Nation, 1798–1852* (Stanford: Stanford University Press, 1988), p. 72.

3. Quoted in Emilia Viotta da Costa, *The Brazilian Empire: Myths and Histories* (Chicago: University of Chicago Press, 1985), p. 19.

4. The notable exception in Spanish America was Mexico, which tried the experiment of monarchy from 1821 to 1823.

5. 'Statement of the Emperor on the Dissolution of the Constituent Assembly,' November 11, 1823, quoted in E. Bradford Burns (ed.), *A Documentary History of Brazil* (New York: Knopf, 1966), p. 207.

6. 'The Constitution of 1824,' quoted in ibid., p. 214.

7. Henry Chamberlain to Castlereagh, May 15, 1824, quoted in Charles K. Webster (ed.), *Britain and the Independence of Latin America, 1812–1830: Select Documents from the Foreign Office Archives* (London: Oxford University Press, 1938, 2 vols), I, p. 241.

8. Pedro caused public scandal by neglecting his wife, Leopoldina, and openly conducting a love affair with Domitila de Castro, the wife of an army officer.

9. Quoted in Ron Seckinger, *The Brazilian Monarchy and the South American Republics, 1822–1831: Diplomacy and State Building* (Baton Rouge: Louisiana State University Press, 1984), p. 11.

10. Statement dated April 6, 1831, quoted in Barman, *Brazil*, p. 159.

11. Document dated April 7, 1831, quoted in E. Bradford Burns, *A History of Brazil* (New York: Columbia University Press, 1980), pp. 169–70.

12. Letter from Diogo Feijó to José Martiniano de Alencar dated June 1, 1837, quoted in Barman, *Brazil*, p. 187.

13. Quoted in Roderick J. Barman, *Citizen Emperor: Pedro II and the Making of Brazil, 1825–91* (Stanford: Stanford University Press, 1999), p. 173. The words in italics are from the original.

14. A comment made in 1845 by Antonio Carlos (Ribeiro de Andrada Machado e Silva), quoted in Barman, *Brazil*, p. 229.

15. Letter by Paulino José Soares de Sousa (later viscount of Uruguay), December 27, 1852, quoted in Richard Graham, *Patronage and Politics in Nineteenth-Century Brazil* (Stanford: Stanford University Press, 1990), p. 80.

16. The comments of John Mawe, quoted in Robert Conrad, *The Destruction of Brazilian Slavery, 1850–1888* (Berkeley: University of California Press, 1972), p. 11.

17. Memorandum by James Hudson, June 22, 1846, quoted in Leslie Bethell, *The Abolition of the Brazilian Slave Trade: Britain, Brazil and the Slave Trade Question, 1807–1869* (Cambridge: Cambridge University Press, 1970), p. 288.

18. A speech by Rodrigo da Silva in 1887, quoted in Conrad, *Destruction of Brazilian Slavery*, p. 247.

19. 'The Republican Manifesto,' December 1870, quoted in Burns, *Documentary History*, p. 249.

20. Quoted in Viotti da Costa, *Brazilian Empire*, p. 223.

21. Deodoro to Pedro II, February 12, 1887, quoted in June E. Hahner, *Civilian–Military Relations in Brazil, 1889–1898* (Columbia: University of South Carolina Press, 1969), p. 15.

22. Quoted in Barman, *Citizen Emperor*, p. 345.

23. Ouro Preto to Pedro II, June 7, 1889, quoted in Viotti da Costa, *Brazilian Empire*, p. 231.

24. Quoted in Hahner, *Civilian–Military Relations*, p. 29.

25. Statement dated November 15, 1889, quoted in June Hahner, 'Floriano Peixoto: Brazil's "Iron Marshall": A Re-Evaluation,' *The Americas*, 31 (1975), p. 256.

26. Statement dated November 16, 1889, quoted in Burns, *Documentary History of Brazil*, p. 286. Within a month of leaving Brazil the empress died. Pedro died in a hotel in Paris in 1891. The bodies were returned to Brazil for reburial in 1922.

27. Adams to Blaine, no.20, November 19, 1889, Department of State Records, Washington D.C. Record Group (hereafter RG) 59, Brazil, Dispatches, 48. The coup was not entirely bloodless. Protests against the overthrow of the emperor occurred in Florianópolis on November 18 and in Rio de Janeiro, Mato Grosso, and São Luís during December. There was also some opposition to the republic from recently freed blacks who had traditionally regarded Dom Pedro as a champion of their cause. See Gilberto Freyre, *Order and Progress: Brazil from Monarchy to Republic* (New York: Knopf, 1970), p. 8.

28. Teixeira de Macedo to Clarendon, May 16, 1854, quoted in Richard Graham, *Britain and the Onset of Modernization in Brazil, 1850–1914* (Cambridge: Cambridge University Press, 1968), p. 73.

29. Quoted in ibid., p. 202.

30. The foreign exchange value of the *milréis* was traditionally calculated in British pence, in which 240 pence equalled one British pound. The amount of pence could be doubled to give a rough equivalent of the value of the *milréis* in terms of the American dollar, i.e. 25 British pence would be around 50 US cents. During the colonial period the *real* (plural, *réis*) was the basic unit of currency in Brazil. The *milréis* represented 1,000 réis.

31. See Boris Fausto, *A Concise History of Brazil* (Cambridge: Cambridge University Press, 1999), p. 84.

[248]   32. William E. Curtis, *The Capitals of Spanish America* (New York: Praeger, 1969), p. 661.

33. Webb to Seward, May 20, 1862, quoted in Conrad, *Brazilian Slavery*, p. 55.

34. Quoted in Stanley J. Stein, *Vassouras: A Brazilian Coffee County, 1850–1900* (Princeton: Princeton University Press, 1985), p. 135.

35. Professor and Mrs Louis Agassiz, *A Journey in Brazil* (Boston: Ticknor and Fields, 1868), p. 129.

36. Comment on a Report dated September 12, 1882, quoted in T. Lynn Smith, *Brazil: People and Institutions* (Baton Rouge: Louisiana State University Press, 1963), p. 487.

37. Recognition had been given earlier by the African kingdom of Benin and the Yoruba kingdom of Lagos.

38. Chamberlain to Canning, February 9, 1826, quoted in Seckinger, *Brazilian Monarchy*, pp. 42–3.

39. Letter dated July 1823 from Felisberto Caldeira Brant Pontes (later Marquis of Barbacena), quoted in Alan K. Manchester, *British Preeminence in Brazil: Its Rise and Decline* (Chapel Hill: University of North Carolina Press, 1933), p. 193.

40. Canning to Felisberto Caldeira Brant Pontes, May 5, 1825, quoted in Webster, *Britain and the Independence of Latin America*, I, p. 276.

41. Quoted in Bethell, *Brazilian Slave Trade*, p. 266.

42. Diary entry dated 1862, quoted in José Honório Rodrigues, *Interêsse nacional e política externa* (Rio de Janeiro: Civilização Brasileira, 1966), p. 24.

43. Quoted in Seckinger, *Brazilian Monarchy*, pp. 27–8.

44. Henry Chamberlain to Castlereagh, July 18, 1818, quoted in Webster, *Britain and the Independence of Latin America*, I, p. 189.

45. Dudley to Gordon, April 7, 1828, quoted in Seckinger, *Brazilian Monarchy*, p. 149.

Notes to Chapter 3

1. 'The Proclamation Ending the Empire,' November 15, 1889, quoted in E. Bradford Burns (ed.), *A Documentary History of Brazil* (New York: Knopf, 1966), p. 283.

2. Section 2, Article 48 of the 1891 Constitution, quoted in ibid., p. 298.

3. Wyndham to Salisbury, no.137, November 18, 1889. Public Record Office, London. Foreign Office (hereafter FO)13/658, quoted in Joseph Smith, *Illusions of Conflict: Anglo-American Diplomacy Towards Latin America, 1865–1896* (Pittsburgh: University of Pittsburgh Press, 1979), p. 158.

4. Only 14.8 percent of the national population was estimated as literate in 1890. [249]
   See Joseph L. Love, 'Political Participation in Brazil, 1881–1969,' *Luso-Brazilian Review*, 7 (1970), p. 8.

5. The story of Canudos was made famous by Euclides da Cunha, *Os Sertões* and translated by Samuel Putnam as *Rebellion in the Backlands* (Chicago: University of Chicago Press, 1944). Cunha stated that Canudos held out to the last man and that there were only four survivors of the final assault. For evidence that more survived see Robert M. Levine, *Vale of Tears: Revisiting the Canudos Massacre in Northeastern Brazil, 1889–1897* (Berkeley: University of California Press, 1993), pp. 183–4.

6. Manifesto dated October 31, 1897, quoted in Raimundo de Menezes, *Vida e Obra de Campos Sales* (São Paulo: Livraria Martins Editora, 1974), p. 141.

7. Manuel de Ferraz Campos Sales, *Da propaganda à presidência* (São Paulo: 1908), p. 252.

8. But serious riots erupted in Rio de Janeiro in June 1901 protesting against increases in streetcar fares. See June E. Hahner, *Poverty and Politics: The Urban Poor in Brazil, 1870–1920* (Albuquerque: University of New Mexico Press, 1986), pp. 177–8.

9. George Barclay Rives to Knox, no.801, February 10, 1912, Department of State Records, Washington D.C. Record Group (hereafter RG) 59, Decimal File (hereafter DF) 1910–29, 832.00.

10. Quoted in Burns, *Documentary History of Brazil*, p. 333.

11. Letter dated March 1910, quoted in Joseph L. Love, *Rio Grande do Sul and Brazilian Regionalism, 1882–1930* (Stanford: Stanford University Press, 1971), p. 146.

12. Morgan to Secretary of State, no.334, March 10, 1914, RG59, DF 1910–29, 832.00/120.

13. Quoted in Love, *Rio Grande*, p. 194.

14. Quoted in Hélio Silva, *1922 — sangue na areia de Copacabana* (Rio de Janeiro: Civilização Brasileira, 1964), p. 49.

15. Quoted in Thomas E. Skidmore, *Politics in Brazil, 1930–1964: An Experiment in Democracy* (New York: Oxford University Press, 1967), p. 6.

16. Afonso Pena to Rodrigues Alves, July 23, 1907, cited in Steven Topik, *The Political Economy of the Brazilian State, 1889–1930* (Austin: University of Texas Press, 1987), p. 73.

17. Morgan to Bryan, no.497, November 27, 1914, RG59, DF 1910–29, 832.002/18.

18. Robertson to Grey, no.19, April 23, 1915, FO 371/2294.

[250]   19. Message to Congress dated October 17, 1921, quoted in Winston Fritsch, *External Constraints on Economic Policy in Brazil, 1889–1930* (Basingstoke: Macmillan, 1988), p. 63.

20. Quoted in Mauricio A. Font, *Coffee, Contention, and Change in the Making of Modern Brazil* (Oxford: Basil Blackwell, 1990), p. 247.

21. Theodore Roosevelt, *Through the Brazilian Wilderness* (New York: Charles Scribner's Sons, 1914), pp. 346–7, 343.

22. Marie R. Wright, *The New Brazil* (Philadelphia: Barrie and Sons, 1907), p. 102 and *The Times* [London], September 13, 1909.

23. The larger number of 'whites' reflected not just the increase in European immigrants but also a broader definition of the category 'white' on the part of the census-takers to include persons with African or Indian ancestry.

24. Quoted in Robert M. Levine, *Pernambuco in the Brazilian Federation, 1889–1937* (Stanford: Stanford University Press, 1978), p. 11.

25. Quoted in Giberto Freyre, *Order and Progress: Brazil from Monarchy to Republic* (New York: Knopf, 1970), p. 202.

26. See Roosevelt, *Wilderness*, pp. 151–2.

27. United States Congress, *Congressional Record*, 51st Congress, 1st session, December 20, 1889, p. 315.

28. Phipps to Salisbury, no.37, May 21, 1899, FO 13/783.

29. Rio Branco to Gomes Ferreira, no.1, January 31, 1905, AHI 235/2/6.

30. *The Times* [London], August 9, 1906.

31. Domício to Müller, tel., no.74, November 5, 1912, Archivo Histórico, Rio de Janeiro, Archivo Histórico de Itamaraty (hereafter AHI) 234/1/13.

32. Memorandum by British War Trade Intelligence Department, November 30, 1916, FO 371/2900.

33. Peel to Balfour, no.23, March 25, 1918, FO 371/3167.

34. Morgan to Kellogg, no.2398G, July 12, 1925, RG 59, DF 1910–29, 832.00/ 522.

35. *La Prensa* [Buenos Aires], May 19, 1922.

36. Withdrawal required a notice of 2 years, so that Brazil did not technically leave the League until 1928.

37. Hélio Lobo to Ministério das Relações Exteriores, April 8, 1923, quoted in Stanley E. Hilton, 'Brazil and the Post-Versailles World: Elite Images and Foreign Policy Strategy, 1919–1929,' *Journal of Latin American Studies*, 12 (1980), p. 352.

Notes to Chapter 4

1. Vargas did have a military background. As a teenager he had joined the army, attended cadet school and had served as a sergeant in the infantry. He chose, however, to leave the army and to study law.

2. Eduardo, bishop of Ilhéus, quoted in Robert M. Levine, *The Vargas Regime: The Critical Years, 1934–1938* (New York: Columbia University Press, 1970), p. 92.

3. Statement of December 3, 1935, quoted in ibid., p. 124.

4. A democratic gloss was put on the name of the state in 1942 when the fifth anniversary of the *Estado Nôvo* provided an opportunity to change its name to '*Estado Nacional*.'

5. Manifesto dated October 1943, quoted in E. Bradford Burns, *A History of Brazil* (New York: Columbia University Press, 1980), p. 436.

6. Letter from Randolph Harrison dated January 27, 1945, quoted in Frank D. McCann, *The Brazilian–American Alliance, 1837–1945* (Princeton: Princeton University Press, 1973), p. 448.

7. Statement dated October 29, 1945, quoted in Thomas E. Skidmore, *Politics in Brazil, 1930–1964: An Experiment in Democracy* (New York: Oxford University Press, 1967), p. 53.

8. Statement dated November 28,1945, quoted in ibid., p. 63.

9. Campaign speech, quoted in ibid., p. 79.

10. Speech dated May 1, 1954, quoted in ibid., p. 136.

11. Gregório Fortunato was convicted of attempted murder in 1956 and sentenced to 25 years in prison.

12. Quoted in Skidmore, *Politics in Brazil*, p. 139.

13. August 12, 1954, quoted in Alfred Stepan, *The Military in Politics: Changing Patterns in Brazil* (Princeton: Princeton University Press, 1971), p. 90.

14. Letter dated August 25, 1954, quoted in E. Bradford Burns, *A Documentary History of Brazil* (New York: Knopf, 1966), pp. 370–1.

15. See Robert M. Levine, *Father of the Poor? Vargas and His Era* (Cambridge: Cambridge University Press, 1998), p. 138.

16. Café Filho had gone into hospital on November 3, 1955 and was succeeded as acting-president by the president of the Chamber of Deputies, Carlos Luz, who, in turn, was replaced by the speaker of the Senate, Nereu Ramos, on November 11 1955.

17. Remark dated October 8, 1968, quoted in Stepan, *Military in Politics*, p. 92.

18. Speech dated June 27, 1959, quoted in Skidmore, *Politics in Brazil*, p. 181.

[252]   19.   Quoted in John W.F. Dulles, *Unrest in Brazil: Political–Military Crises, 1955–1964* (Austin: University of Texas Press, 1970), p. 108.

20.   Statement dated August 25, 1961, quoted in Skidmore, *Politics in Brazil*, p. 206.

21.   Quoted in Burns, *History of Brazil*, p. 490.

22.   Speech dated March 13, 1964, quoted in Ronald M. Schneider, *'Order and Progress': A Political History of Brazil* (Boulder: Westview Press, 1991), p. 231.

23.   Quoted in Stepan, *Military in Politics*, p. 197.

24.   Quoted in Dulles, *Unrest in Brazil*, p. 301.

25.   Military Order dated March 31, 1964, quoted in Stepan, *Military in Politics*, p. 206.

26.   See Skidmore, *Politics in Brazil*, p. 43.

27.   Brazil was one of eight Latin American countries that made a 'fast recovery' during the 1930s. See Victor Bulmer-Thomas, *The Economic History of Latin America Since Independence* (New York: Cambridge University Press, 1994), p. 212.

28.   Presidential Message to Congress 1951, quoted in Skidmore, *Politics in Brazil*, pp. 93–4.

29.   The national quota for immigrants from Portugal was abolished in 1939.

30.   Edwin Morgan to the State Department, telegram, November 8, 1930, quoted in Joseph Smith, *Unequal Giants: Diplomatic Relations between the United States and Brazil, 1889–1930* (Pittsburgh: University of Pittsburgh Press, 1991), p. 201.

31.   Vargas to Aranha, December 24, 1934, quoted in Stanley E. Hilton, *Brazil and the Great Powers, 1930–1939 : The Politics of Trade Rivalry* (Austin: University of Texas Press, 1975), p. 120.

32.   Aranha to Vargas, November 24, 1939, quoted in Frank D. McCann, 'Brazil, the United States, and World War II: A Commentary,' *Diplomatic History*, 3 (1979), p. 62.

33.   *Newsweek*, November 22, 1937, quoted in Hilton, *Brazil and the Great Powers*, p. 172.

34.   For the policy of 'pragmatic equilibrium' see Gerson Moura, *Autonomia na dependência: a política externa brasileira de 1935 a 1942* (Rio de Janeiro: Nova Fronteira, 1980).

35.   Aranha to MRE, October 5, 1934, quoted in Hilton, *Brazil and the Great Powers*, p. 58.

36.   Brazil did not declare war on Japan until June 5, 1945.

37. Speech dated September 7, 1942, quoted in Robin A. Humphreys, *Latin*   [253]
    America and the Second World War (London: Athlone Press, 2 vols., 1982), II,
    p. 67.

38. Quoted in Frank D. McCann, 'The Brazilian Army and the Problem of Mission,
    1939–1964,' *Journal of Latin American Studies*, 12 (1980), p. 118.

39. Interview with General Edson de Figueiredo dated September 24, 1968,
    quoted in Stepan, *Military in Politics*, p. 242.

40. Brazil was not the first Latin American country to join the war. Mexico did this
    on May 22, 1942.

41. Vargas to Lourival Fontes, July 1951, quoted in Stanley E. Hilton, 'The United
    States, Brazil, and the Cold War, 1945–1960: End of the Special Relation-
    ship,' *Journal of American History*, 68 (1981), p. 611.

42. Johnson to Marshall, December 23, 1948, quoted in Kenneth C. Lanoue, 'An
    Alliance Shaken: Brazil and the United States, 1945–1950' (PhD dissertation,
    Louisiana State University, 1978), p. 84.

43. Fontoura to Vargas, February 1951, quoted in Hilton, 'The United States, Bra-
    zil and the Cold War,' p. 609.

44. Quoted in Ruth Leacock, *Requiem for Revolution: The United States and Brazil,
    1961–1969* (Kent: Kent State University Press, 1990), p. 137.

Notes to Chapter 5

1. See Preamble to Institutional Act No. 1, April 9, 1964, quoted in Thomas E.
   Skidmore, *The Politics of Military Rule in Brazil, 1964–85* (New York: Oxford
   University Press, 1988), p. 20.

2. Quoted in ibid., p. 82.

3. General Carlos Brilhante Ustra, quoted in Martha K. Huggins, *Political Policing:
   The United States and Latin America* (Durham: Duke University Press, 1998),
   p. 158.

4. *The Times* [London], October 25, 1971.

5. Speech dated March 16, 1979, quoted in Skidmore, *Military Rule in Brazil*,
   p. 212.

6. Quoted in *Newsweek*, August 27, 1984.

7. Quoted in Ted G. Goertzel, *Fernando Henrique Cardoso: Reinventing Democracy in
   Brazil* (Boulder: Lynne Rienner, 1999), p. 122.

8. Quoted in ibid., p. 174.

9. Quoted in Skidmore, *Military Rule in Brazil*, p. 147.

10. National Plan, March 1981, quoted in ibid., p. 216.

[254]   11. Speech dated September 1985, quoted in Benjamin Keen and Keith Haynes, *A History of Latin America* (Boston: Houghton Mifflin, 2000), p. 384.

12. Quoted in Robert M. Levine and John J. Crocitti (eds), *The Brazil Reader: History, Culture, Politics* (London: Latin American Bureau, 1999), p. 267.

13. While the Indian population had decreased over the whole of the 20th century, the low point had occurred during the 1950s and there had been an actual increase in numbers since that date.

14. *Washington Post*, April 13, 2000.

15. Inaugural Address dated January 1, 1995, quoted in Levine and Crocitti, *Brazil Reader*, p. 283.

16. Quoted in Robert Wesson, *The United States and Brazil: Limits of Influence* (New York: Praeger, 1981), p. 51.

17. Quoted in Skidmore, *Military Rule in Brazil*, p. 28.

18. *Washington Post*, March 8, 1977.

19. Quoted in H. Jon Rosenbaum, 'Brazil's Foreign Policy: Developmentalism and Beyond,' *Orbis*, 16 (1972), p. 63.

20. Quoted in Jan Knippers Black, *United States Penetration of Brazil* (Philadelphia: University of Pennsylvania Press, 1977), p. 55.

21. Quoted in Moniz Bandeira, *Relações Brasil–EUA no contexto globalização. II, Rivalidade Emergente* (São Paulo: Senac, 1997), p. 126.

22. *Washington Post*, July 16, 1981.

23. Ibid., August 6, 2000.

Notes to Conclusion

1. Frank G. Carpenter, *South America: Social, Industrial, and Political* (Akron: Saalfield Publishing Company, 1903), p. 481.

2. 'The Letter of Pero Vaz de Caminha,' quoted in E. Bradford Burns (ed.), *A Documentary History of Brazil* (New York: Knopf, 1966), p. 28.

3. Nevin O. Winter, *Brazil and Her People of To-day* (Boston: Page Company, 1910), p. 32.

CHRONOLOGY OF MAIN EVENTS

Colonial period

1492	Christopher Columbus sails west and 'discovers' the 'Indies'
1494	Treaty of Tordesillas divides 'New World' between Portugal and Spain
1500	Pedro Álvares Cabral lands in Brazil and claims country for Portugal
1502	King Manoel I grants lease for trade in brazilwood
1530	An expedition under Martim Afonso de Sousa brings settlers to Brazil
1534–6	King João III creates 15 captaincies
1549	Expedition of Tomé da Sousa establishes a central government and capital in Salvador da Bahia
1554	Foundation of São Paulo de Piratininga
1565	Foundation of Rio de Janeiro
1580	Iberian Union established
1630	Dutch invade Northeast Brazil and capture Recife
1640	Portugal breaks away from Spain
1654	Dutch withdraw from Brazil
1695	Gold discovered in Minas Gerais
1727	Coffee introduced into Brazil
1750	Treaty of Madrid establishes boundary between Portuguese and Spanish empires in South America
	Political ascendancy of Pombal begins
1763	Capital transferred from Salvador da Bahia to Rio de Janeiro
1789	*Inconfidência Mineira*
1792	Tiradentes executed
1798	Revolt of the Tailors in Bahia
1808	Portuguese royal family arrives in Brazil
	João VI opens ports to world trade
1810	Commercial treaty signed with Britain
1815	Brazil elevated to status of kingdom
1821	João VI leaves Brazil for Portugal

Imperial period

1822	Brazil becomes an independent empire under Pedro I
1824	First Brazilian Constitution promulgated
1825–8	Cisplatine War between Brazil and Argentina
1831	Abdication of Pedro I. Three-man regency established
1840	Majority of Pedro II declared
1850	Ending of slave trade
1865–70	Paraguayan War
1870	Publication of 'Republican Manifesto'
1871	Passage of Law of the Free Womb
1888	Golden Law abolishes slavery
1889	Military coup overthrows Empire and establishes a republic

Republican period

1894	Prudente de Morais, the first civilian president, takes office
1897	Destruction of Canudos
1906	Valorization of coffee introduced by Convention of Taubaté
	Third Pan-American Conference held in Rio de Janeiro
1917	Brazil joins World War I
1922	Modern Art Week held in São Paulo
	Copacabana Revolt. *Tenente* movement begins
1924	Prestes begins 'Long March' which lasts until 1927
1930	Vargas rises to power
1932	São Paulo revolts
1934	New Constitution promulgated
1937	*Estado Nôvo* declared
1942	Brazil joins World War II
1945	Vargas steps down from presidency
1946	New Constitution promulgated
1950	Vargas elected as president
1954	Suicide of Vargas
1960	Inauguration of the new federal capital in Brasília
1964	President Goulart overthrown by military coup. Castelo Branco elected as president. First Institutional Act implemented
1967	New Constitution promulgated
1978	Revocation of Institutional Acts
1985	Civilian government restored. José Sarney becomes president
1988	New Constitution promulgated
1992	President Collor de Mello resigns
1995	Fernando Henrique Cardoso inaugurated as president

PRESIDENTS OF THE REPUBLIC
SINCE 1889

The First Republic

Deodoro da Fonseca	15 November 1889 to 23 November 1891
Floriano Peixoto	23 November 1891 to 15 November 1894
Prudente José de Morais Barros	15 November 1894 to 15 November 1898
Manuel Ferraz de Campos Sales	15 November 1898 to 15 November 1902
Francisco de Paula Rodrigues Alves	15 November 1902 to 15 November 1906
Afonso Augusto Moreira Pena	15 November 1906 to 14 June 1909
Nilo Peçanha	14 June 1909 to 15 November 1910
Hermes Rodrigues da Fonseca	15 November 1910 to 15 November 1914
Venceslau Brás Pereira Gomes	15 November 1914 to 15 November 1918
Delfim Moreira	15 November 1918 to June 1919
Epitácio Lindolfo da Silva Pessôa	June 1919 to 15 November 1922
Artur da Silva Bernardes	15 November 1922 to 15 November 1926
Washington Luís Pereira de Sousa	15 November 1926 to 24 October 1930

1930–64

Getúlio Dornelles Vargas	3 November 1930 to 29 October 1945
José Linhares (interim)	29 October 1945 to 31 January 1946
Eurico Gaspar Dutra	31 January 1946 to 31 January 1951
Getúlio Dornelles Vargas	31 January 1951 to 24 August 1954
João Café Filho	24 August 1954 to 11 August 1955
Carlos Luz (interim)	11 August 1955 to 11 November 1955
Nereu Ramos (interim)	11 November 1955 to 31 January 1956
Juscelino Kubitschek de Oliveira	31 January 1956 to 31 January 1961
Jânio da Silva Quadros	31 January 1961 to 25 August 1961
João Goulart	7 September 1961 to 31 March 1964

[258]   Since 1964

Ranieri Mazzili (interim)	2 April 1964 to 15 April 1964
Humberto Castelo Branco	15 April 1964 to 15 March 1967
Artur da Costa e Silva	15 March 1967 to 30 July 1969
interim regency	30 July 1969 to 7 October 1969
Emílío Garrastazú Médici	7 October 1969 to 15 March 1974
Ernesto Geisel	15 March 1974 to 15 March 1979
João Baptista Figueiredo	15 March 1979 to 15 March 1985
José Sarney	15 March 1985 to 15 March 1990
Fernando Collor de Mello	15 March 1990 to 29 December 1992
Itamar Franco	1 January 1993 to 1 January 1995
Fernando Henrique Cardoso	1 January 1995–

ACRONYMS OF PRINCIPAL POLITICAL PARTIES

Founded during 1889–1930

AL   *Aliança Liberal/* Liberal Alliance
PD   *Partido Democrático/* Democratic Party
PRC   *Partido Republicano Conservador/* Conservative Republican Party
PRF   *Partido Republicano Federal/* Federal Republican Party

Founded during 1930–1964

AIB   *Ação Integralista Brasileira/* Brazilian Integralist Action
ANL   *Aliança Nacional Libertadora/* National Liberating Alliance
PCB   *Partido Communista Brasileiro/* Brazilian Communist Party
PSD   *Partido Social Democrático/* Social Democratic Party
PSP   *Partido Social Progressista/* Social Progressive Party
PTB   *Partido Trabalhista Brasileiro/* Brazilian Labor Party
UDN   *União Democrática Nacional/* National Democratic Union

Founded since 1964

ALN   *Ação Libertadora Nacional/* National Liberation Action
ARENA   *Aliança Renovadora Nacional/* National Renovating Alliance
MDB   *Movimento Democrático Brasileiro/* Brazilian Democratic Movement
PDS   *Partido Democrático Social/* Social Democracy Party
PDT   *Partido Democrático Trabalhista/* Democratic Workers' or Labor Party
PFL   *Partido da Frente Liberal/* Popular Front Party
PMDB   *Partido Movimento Democrático Brasileiro/* Party of the Brazilian Democratic Movement
PP   *Partido Popular/* Popular Party
PRN   *Partido de Reconstrução Nacional/* National Reconstruction Party

[260] PSDB *Partido da Social Democracia Brasileira*/Party of Brazilian Social Democracy

PT *Partido dos Trabalhadores*/Workers' Party

PTB *Partido Trabalhista Brasileiro*/Brazilian Labor Party

GLOSSARY OF BRAZILIAN TERMS

abertura	process of political opening associated with transition from military to civilian rule from 1978 to 1985
aldeia	Indian village under the control of Jesuits during colonial period
bandeira	flag or banner used to designate a party of explorers or slave-hunters during the colonial period
bandeirante	a member of a *bandeira*
caboclo	person of mixed European, Indian and African origin. Sometimes used as a pejorative term to describe a person from the interior or *sertão*
café com leite	'coffee with milk' — political arrangement between São Paulo (coffee) and Minas Gerais (milk) during the First Republic
capitania	captaincy, i.e. grant of land
coronel (pl. *coronéis*)	rural leader and local political boss
coronelismo	system of boss rule prevalent in the regions during the Empire and First Republic
Côrtes	Portuguese parliament
distensão	period of political 'decompression' from 1974 to 1978
donatario	donor
engenho	sugar-mill, sugar plantation
favela	urban slum or shantytown
fazenda	large farm or ranch
fazendeiro	owner of a *fazenda*
feitoria	fortified trading post
gaúcho	cowboy, horseman, native of Rio Grande do Sul
inconfidência	disloyalty taking the form of a conspiracy to revolt against royal authority during the colonial period
mameluco	offspring of European father and Indian mother
mestiço	person of mixed European and Indian origin
mineiro	inhabitant or native of Minas Gerais

[262]

mulatto	person of European and African origin
pau-brasil	dyewood
paulista	inhabitant or native of the city and state of São Paulo
poder moderador	'moderating power' that allowed emperor to veto legislation and dissolve parliament at his discretion
quilombo	haven for runaway slaves
quinto	royal tax during colonial period amounting to a fifth of the value of goods
Reconquista	War of Reconquest
senhor de engenho	owner of a sugar plantation mill
sertão	backlands of the interior of the Northeast
sesmaria	land grant in colonial period
sindicato	trade union
tenente	junior army officer, usually an army lieutenant
tenentismo	political reform movement of junior army officers that began after 1922 revolt

SELECTIVE GUIDE TO FURTHER READING OF WORKS IN ENGLISH ON BRAZILIAN HISTORY

The rapid emergence of the Internet as a means of gaining access to information is rapidly transforming the study of history. By typing in 'Brazil' or 'Brazilian history', search engines can be used to open up an enormous number of websites that will provide material on all matters relating to the history of Brazil. An excellent website is LANIC at www.lanic.utexas.edu/la/brazil which gives access to official documents and records pertaining to federal and state government departments, journals and newspapers. For links to contemporary views and opinion on Brazilian affairs see also www.info.brazil.com. Titles of books and articles in journals can be accessed by using on-line catalogues available in public and college libraries.

A number of historiographical essays give a convenient guide to the wide range of historical writings on particular periods. For the colonial era see A.J.R. Russell-Wood, 'United States scholarly contributions to the historiography of colonial Brazil', *Hispanic American Historical Review* 65 (1985), pp. 684–723, and 'Brazilian archives and recent historiography on colonial Brazil', *Latin American Research Review* 36 (2001), pp. 75–105. The imperial period is covered in Stanley J. Stein, 'The historiography of Brazil, 1808–1889', *Hispanic American Historical Review* 40 (1960), pp. 234–78. On the republican era after 1889 see Thomas E. Skidmore, 'The historiography of Brazil, 1889–1964', ibid., 55 (1975), pp. 716–48, and ibid., 56 (1976), pp. 81–109. Two other useful historiographical articles are Stuart B. Schwartz, 'Recent trends in the study of slavery in Brazil', *Luso-Brazilian Review* 25 (1988), pp. 1–25, and Mary Lombardi, 'The frontier in Brazilian history: an historiographical essay', *Pacific Historical Review* 44 (1975), pp. 436–57. For works on economic history see Nícia Vilela Luz, 'Brazil', in Stanley J. Stein and Roberto Cortés Conde, eds., *Latin America: A Guide to Economic History, 1830–1930* (Berkeley CA, 1977), pp. 163–272.

General overviews

Several of the most important documents in Brazilian history up to 1964 are collected in E. Bradford Burns, ed., *A Documentary History of Brazil* (New York, 1966).

[264] Robert M. Levine and John J. Crocitti, eds., *The Brazil Reader: History, Culture, Politics* (London, 1999) and Robert E. Conrad, *Children of God's Fire: A Documentary History of Black Slavery in Brazil* (Princeton NJ, 1983) contain interesting selections of documents and readings. Ever since its first publication in 1970 E. Bradford Burns, *A History of Brazil* (New York, 3rd edition, 1993) has been regarded as the standard textbook in English on Brazilian history. A number of excellent surveys, however, have recently appeared. They include Thomas E. Skidmore, *Brazil: Five Centuries of Change* (New York, 1999) and Robert M. Levine, *The History of Brazil* (Westport CT, 1999). Boris Fausto, *A Concise History of Brazil*, trans. Arthur Brakel (Cambridge, 1999) is a translated and abbreviated version of his *História do Brasil* (São Paulo, 1994). An excellent thematic study is Marshall C. Eakin, *Brazil: The Once and Future Country* (New York, 1997). Political history, particularly for the period since 1889, is provided in Ronald M. Schneider, *'Order and Progress': A Political History of Brazil* (Boulder CO, 1991). A parallel but shorter version is contained in the same author's *Brazil: Culture and Politics in a New Industrial Powerhouse* (Boulder CO, 1996). Political developments of the twentieth century up to the early 1970s are also fully covered in Peter Flynn, *Brazil: A Political Analysis* (London, 1978). The political system is lucidly analyzed in Riordan Roett, *Brazil: Politics in a Patrimonial Society* (New York, 5th edition, 1999). Michael L. Conniff and Frank D. McCann, eds., *Modern Brazil: Elites and Masses in Historical Perspective* (Lincoln NB, 1989) is also very informative on politics and society. Wide-ranging interpretive works by Brazilian historians on their country's distinctive past which have been translated into English include José Honório Rodrigues, *The Brazilians: Their Character and Aspirations*, trans. Ralph Edward Dimmick (Austin TX, 1968) and Clodomir Vianna Moog, *Bandeirantes and Pioneers*, trans. L.L. Barnett (New York, 1964). For readers with a reading knowledge of Portuguese, the richness of Brazilian historical scholarship can be found in the collection of essays in Carlos Guilherme Mota, ed., *Brasil em Perspectiva* (São Paulo, 3rd edition, 1971).

Economy

Although it concentrates mainly on developments in the twentieth century, the best one-volume treatment of Brazilian economic history is Werner Baer, *The Brazilian Economy: Growth and Development* (Westport CT, 4th edition, 1995). Celso Furtado, *The Economic Growth of Brazil: A Survey from Colonial to Modern Times*, trans. Ricardo W. de Aguiar and Eric Charles Drysdale (Berkeley CA, 1963) was originally published in 1959 and is a briefer study. See also the relevant sections on Brazil in William P. Glade, *The Latin American Economies: A Study of their Institutional Evolution* (New York, 1969) and Victor Bulmer-Thomas, *The Economic History of Latin America since Independence* (Cambridge, 1994). Thomas W. Merrick and Douglas H. Graham, *Population and Economic Development in Brazil: 1800 to the Present* (Baltimore MD, 1979) contains useful statistical material.

Society

Charles Wagley, *Introduction to Brazil* (New York, 1963) remains a readable and illuminating introductory work. Fernando de Azevedo, *Brazilian Culture: An Introduction*, trans. William Rex Crawford (New York, 1950) is now dated, but is still useful on cultural history. For a comprehensive and detailed study of social institutions see T. Lynn Smith, *Brazil: People and Institutions* (Baton Rouge LA, 1972). The views of Brazil's most prominent sociologist are presented in Gilberto Freyre, *The Masters and the Slaves: A Study in the Development of Brazilian Civilization*, trans. Samuel Putnam (New York, 1946), *The Mansions and the Shanties: The Making of Modern Brazil*, trans. Harriet de Onís (New York, 1963) and *New World in the Tropics: The Culture of Modern Brazil* (New York, 1959). The controversial question of race is explored in Florestan Fernandes, *The Negro in Brazilian Society* (New York, 1969). Roger Bastide, *The African Religions of Brazil: Toward a Sociology of Interpretation of Civilizations*, trans. Helen Sebba (Baltimore MD, 1978) examines the religious background and stresses the importance of slave culture. José Honório Rodrigues, *Brazil and Africa*, trans. Richard A. Mazzara and Sam Hileman (Berkeley CA, 1965) highlights the importance of the relationship between Brazil and Africa. The historical role of the Catholic Church in Brazil is discussed in Thomas C. Bruneau, *The Church in Brazil. The Politics of Religion* (Austin TX, 1982). A major study in Portuguese which contains essays by leading Brazilian historians on social history from the colonial period up to the end of the twentieth century is Fernando A. Novais *et al.*, eds., *História da Vida Privada no Brasil*, 4 vols (São Paulo, 1997–98).

Diplomacy

There is no adequate one-volume history in English of Brazil's foreign relations. A good starting-point is José Honório Rodrigues, 'The foundations of Brazil's foreign policy', *International Affairs* 38 (1962), pp. 324–38. The important relationship with the United States is described in Robert Wesson, *The United States and Brazil: Limits of Influence* (New York, 1981). Recommended works in Portuguese on foreign relations are Amado Luiz Cervo and Clodoaldo Bueno, *História da política exterior do Brasil* (São Paulo, 1982) and Moniz Bandeira, *Presença dos Estados Unidos no Brasil: dois séculos de história* (Rio de Janeiro, 1973).

Colonial period

Politics

The best one-volume guide to the colonial period is Leslie Bethell, ed., *Colonial Brazil* (Cambridge, 1987), a collection of articles from vols. 1 and 2 of Leslie Bethell,

[266]   ed., *Cambridge History of Latin America* (Cambridge, 1984). James Lockhart and Stuart B. Schwartz, *Early Latin America: A History of Colonial Spanish America and Brazil* (Cambridge, 1983) contains excellent chapters on Brazil. N.P. MacDonald, *The Making of Brazil: Portuguese Roots, 1500–1822* (Sussex, England, 1996) is a straightforward narrative history. On the Portuguese background see Bailey W. Diffie and George D. Winius, *Foundations of the Portuguese Empire, 1415–1580* (Minneapolis MN, 1977) and Charles R. Boxer, *The Portuguese Seaborne Empire, 1415–1825* (Oxford, 1963). The captaincy system is explained in Harold B. Johnson, 'The donatary captaincy in perspective: Portuguese backgrounds to settlement in Brazil', *Hispanic American Historical Review* 52 (1972), pp. 203–14. Two readable works by Charles Boxer dealing with the 17th and 18th centuries are *The Dutch in Brazil, 1624–1654* (Oxford, 1957) and *The Golden Age of Brazil: Growing Pains of a Colonial Society, 1695–1750* (Berkeley CA, 1962). Political developments of the late colonial period are considered in Dauril Alden, *Royal Government in Colonial Brazil with Special Reference to the Administration of the Marquis of Lavradio, Viceroy, 1769–1779* (Berkeley CA, 1968) and Kenneth R. Maxwell, *Pombal: Paradox of the Enlightenment* (Cambridge, 1995). The precursors of independence are comprehensively examined in Kenneth R. Maxwell, *Conflicts and Conspiracies: Brazil and Portugal, 1750–1808* (Cambridge, 1973) and in A.J.R. Russell-Wood, ed., *From Colony to Nation: Essays on the Independence of Brazil* (Baltimore MD, 1975). An influential work in Portuguese dealing with the reasons for the decline of Portugal's empire is Fernando A. Novais, *Portugal e Brasil na crise do antigo sistema colonial, 1777–1808* (São Paulo, 1979).

Economy

The development of the sugar industry in Bahia is superbly examined in Stuart B. Schwartz, *Sugar Plantations in the Formation of Brazilian Society: Bahia, 1550–1835* (Cambridge, 1985). Manoel S. Cardozo, 'The Brazilian Gold Rush', *The Americas* 3 (1946), pp. 137–60 remains a classic article on the gold rush into the mining region. Elizabeth Anne Kuznesof, 'The role of the merchants in the economic development of São Paulo, 1765–1850', *Hispanic American Historical Review* 60 (1960), pp. 571–92, examines the activities of the mercantile class. Exploration into the interior and the resulting environmental damage is the subject of Warren Dean, *With Broadax and Firebrand: The Destruction of the Brazilian Atlantic Forest* (Berkeley CA, 1995) and Robin L. Anderson, *Colonization As Exploitation in the Amazon Rain Forest, 1758–1911* (Gainesville FL, 2000). An important work by the economic historian, Caio Prado Júnior, which was originally published in 1963, has been translated as *The Colonial Background of Modern Brazil*, trans. Suzette Macedo (Berkeley CA, 1967).

Society

The story of the *bandeirantes* is recounted in Richard M. Morse, *The Bandeirantes: The Historical Role of the Brazilian Pathfinders* (New York, 1965). Life on the frontier is also

the subject of Alida C. Metcalf, *Family and Frontier in Colonial Brazil: Santana de Parnaíba,*   [267]
1500–1822 (Berkeley CA, 1992). For conditions in the towns see A.J.R. Russell-Wood,
Fidalgos and Philanthropists, the Santa Casa da Misericórdia of Bahia, 1550–1775 (Berkeley
CA, 1968) and Elizabeth Anne Kuznesof, *Household Economy and Urban Development*
(Boulder CO, 1986). The significant role of women is revealed in Muriel Nazarri,
*The Disappearance of the Dowry: Women, Family and Social Change in São Paulo, Brazil
(1600–1900)* (Stanford CA, 1991) and Elizabeth Anne Kuznesof, 'The role of the
female-headed household in Brazilian modernization, 1765–1836', *Journal of Social
History* 13 (1980), pp. 589–613.

The plight of the Indians is recounted in John Hemming, *Red Gold: The Conquest of
the Brazilian Indians, 1500–1760* (London, 1978) and Alexander Marchant, *From Barter to Slavery: The Economic Relations of Portuguese and Indians in the Settlement of Brazil,
1500–1580* (Baltimore MD, 1942). Stuart B. Schwartz, 'Indian labor and New World
plantations: European demands and Indian responses in Northeastern Brazil', *American Historical Review* 83 (1978), pp. 43–79, discusses the attempts of Europeans to
force Indians to work on the sugar plantations. On the daily life of African slaves see
A.J.R. Russell-Wood, *The Black Man in Slavery and Freedom in Colonial Brazil* (London,
1982) and Kátia Maria de Queirós Mattoso, *To Be a Slave in Brazil*, trans. Arthur
Goldhammer (New Brunswick NJ, 1989).

Imperial Period

Politics

Roderick J. Barman, *Brazil: The Forging of a Nation, 1798–1852* (Stanford CA, 1988)
is an excellent analysis which provides considerable information on the transfer of
the royal court and the first decades of the empire. Important articles dealing with
political history are contained in Leslie Bethell, ed., *Brazil, Empire and Republic, 1822–
1930* (Cambridge, 1989). These articles are drawn from vols. 3 and 5 of Leslie Bethell,
ed., *Cambridge History of Latin America* (Cambridge, 1985–6). Clarence H. Haring,
Empire in Brazil — A New World Experiment with Monarchy (Cambridge MA, 1958) is
useful, but is now a dated study. More up-to-date works are James Lang, *Portuguese
Brazil: The King's Plantation* (New York, 1979) and the essays in Dauril Alden, ed.,
The Colonial Roots of Modern Brazil (Berkeley CA, 1973). Roderick Cavaleiro, *The
Independence of Brazil* (London, 1993) provides a descriptive narrative of the events
leading to independence. A full biography of the first emperor is Neill Macaulay,
Dom Pedro: The Struggle for Liberty in Brazil and Portugal, 1798–1834 (Durham NC, 1986).

Emília Viotti da Costa, *The Brazilian Empire: Myths and Histories* (Chicago, 1985) is
a superb analysis of the imperial period. The outstanding interpretative works of José
de Murilo de Carvalho have yet to be translated into English, but this is partly rem-
edied by the publication of two of his articles: 'Brazil 1870–1914 — The force of
tradition', *Journal of Latin American Studies* 24 (1992), pp. 145–62, and 'Political elites

and state building: the case of nineteenth-century Brazil', *Comparative Studies in Society and History* 24 (1982), pp. 378–99. The significance of the bureaucratic élite is also the subject of a pioneering study by Eul-Soo Pang and Ron L. Seckinger, 'The Mandarins of Imperial Brazil', *Comparative Studies in History and Society* 9 (1971), pp. 215–44. See also the perceptive works by Richard Graham: *Patronage and Politics in Nineteenth-Century Brazil* (Stanford CA, 1990) and 'Government expenditures and political change in Brazil, 1880–1899: who got what?', *Journal of Interamerican Studies and World Affairs* 19 (1977), pp. 339–68. Fernando Uricoechea, *The Patrimonial Foundations of the Brazilian Bureaucratic State* (Berkeley CA, 1980) and Thomas Flory, *Judge and Jury in Imperial Brazil, 1808–1871: Social Control and Political Stability in the New State* (Austin TX, 1981) examine the attempts of the imperial government to impose law and order in the regions. Judy Bieber, *Power, Patronage, and Political Violence: State Building on a Brazilian Frontier, 1822–1889* (Lincoln NB, 1999) is a competent case study.

Historical knowledge of the reign of Dom Pedro II has been greatly advanced by the appearance of Roderick J. Barman, *Citizen Emperor: Pedro II and the Making of Brazil, 1825–91* (Stanford CA, 1999). On the 'military question', see Charles W. Simmons, *Marshal Deodoro and the Fall of Dom Pedro II* (Durham NC, 1966) and William S. Dudley, 'Professionalisation and politicisation as motivational factors in the Brazilian Army coup of 15 November 1889', *Journal of Latin American Studies* 8 (1976), pp. 101–25. Richard Graham, 'Landowners and the overthrow of empire', *Luso-Brazilian Review* 7 (1970), pp. 44–56, discusses the attitude of the landed oligarchy. Excellent overviews of the reasons for the 1889 coup are George Boehrer, 'The Brazilian Republican revolution, old and new views', *Luso-Brazilian Review* 3 (1966), pp. 43–57, and the chapter on 'The fall of the Monarchy' in Emília Viotti da Costa, *The Brazilian Empire: Myths and Histories* (Chicago, 1985), pp. 202–33.

Economy

The relative backwardness of the Brazilian economy is discussed in Stephen Haber, ed., *How Latin America Fell Behind: Essays on the Economic History of Brazil and Mexico, 1800–1914* (Stanford CA, 1997) and Nathaniel H. Leff, *Underdevelopment and Development in Brazil*, 2 vols (London, 1982). See also Nathaniel H. Leff, 'Economic retardation in nineteenth century Brazil', *Economic History Review* 25 (1972), pp. 489–507. The growth of the coffee and cotton industries is expertly examined in two studies by Stanley J. Stein: *Vassouras, a Brazilian Coffee County, 1850–1900* (Cambridge MA, 1958) and *The Brazilian Cotton Manufacture: Textile Enterprise in an Underdeveloped Area, 1850–1950* (Cambridge MA, 1957). Developments in the sugar industry are discussed in Peter L. Eisenberg, *The Sugar Industry in Pernambuco: Modernization without Change, 1840–1910* (Berkeley CA, 1974) and B. J. Barickman, *A Bahian Counterpoint: Sugar, Tobacco, Cassava, and Slavery in the Recôncavo, 1780–1860* (Stanford CA, 1998). The significance of slavery on economic development is also examined in Laird W. Bergad, *Slavery and the Demographic and Economic History of Minas Gerais, 1720–1888*

(Cambridge, 1999). Eugene Ridings, *Business Interest Groups in Nineteenth-Century* [269]
Brazil (Cambridge, 1994) studies the attitudes and activities of the business élite,
while the career of the most celebrated Brazilian entrepreneur of the 19th century is
described in Anyda Marchant, *Viscount Mauá and the Empire of Brazil* (Berkeley CA,
1965). The huge influence exercised during the 19th century by Great Britain over
Brazilian politics, economy and culture is revealed in Alan K. Manchester, *British
Preeminence in Brazil: Its Rise and Decline* (Chapel Hill NC, 1933) and Richard Graham,
Britain and the Onset of Modernization in Brazil, 1850–1914 (Cambridge, 1968). Marshall
C. Eakin, *British Enterprise in Brazil: The St. John d'el Rey Company and the Morro Velho
Mine, 1830–1960* (Durham NC, 1989) provides an excellent example of a business
case study. On the development of business in Minas Gerais see also Sérgio de Oliveira
Birchal, *Entrepreneurship in Nineteenth-Century Brazil: The Formation of a Business
Environment* (Basingstoke, 1999).

Society

The controversial issue of slavery was a dominant feature of Brazilian society for
most of the 19th century. Mary C. Karasch, *Slave Life in Rio de Janeiro, 1808–1850*
(Princeton NJ, 1987) and João José Reis, *Slave Rebellion in Brazil: The Muslim Uprising
of 1835 in Bahia*, trans. Arthur Brakel (Baltimore MD, 1993) are illuminating studies
of the life of African slaves during the empire. On the transatlantic slave trade see
Robert E. Conrad, *World of Sorrow: The African Slave Trade to Brazil* (Baton Rouge LA,
1986) and Leslie Bethell, *The Abolition of the Brazilian Slave Trade* (Cambridge, 1970).
Two excellent works on the movement for the abolition of slavery are Robert Brent
Toplin, *The Abolition of Slavery in Brazil* (New York, 1972) and Robert Conrad, *The
Destruction of Brazilian Slavery, 1850–1888* (Berkeley CA, 1972). Richard Graham,
'Causes of the abolition of negro slavery in Brazil: an interpretive essay', *Hispanic
American Historical Review* 46 (1966), pp. 123–37, and Seymour Drescher, 'Brazilian
abolition in comparative perspective', *Hispanic American Historical Review* 68 (1988),
pp. 429–60, are useful articles on the subject of abolition.

During the imperial period the mass of Brazilians lived in poverty. June E. Hahner,
Poverty and Politics: The Urban Poor in Brazil, 1870–1920 (Albuquerque NM, 1986)
looks at this issue in its urban context. The life of the poor in Rio de Janeiro is por-
trayed in Thomas H. Holloway, *Policing Rio de Janeiro: Repression and Resistance in a
Nineteenth Century City* (Stanford CA, 1993), and Sandra Lauderdale Graham, *House
and Street: The Domestic World of Servants and Masters in Nineteenth-Century Rio de Janeiro*
(Cambridge, 1988). Gerald Michael Greenfield, 'The Great Drought and elite dis-
course in imperial Brazil', *Hispanic American Historical Review* 72 (1992), pp. 375–
400, deals with the question of the desperate conditions suffered by the rural poor.
The important role of women is studied in Maria Odila Silva Dias, *Power and Everyday
Life: The Lives of Working Women in Nineteenth-Century Brazil* (New Brunswick NJ, 1995)
and June E. Hahner, 'Women and work in Brazil, 1850–1920: a preliminary investigation,' in Dauril Alden and Warren Dean, eds., *Essays Concerning the Socioeconomic*

History of Brazil and Portuguese India (Gainesville FL, 1977), pp. 86–117. The persistent threat of deadly disease is revealed in Donald B. Cooper, 'The new "Black Death": cholera in Brazil, 1855–56', *Social Science History* 10 (1986), pp. 467–88, and Sidney Chaloub, 'The politics of disease control: yellow fever and race in nineteenth-century Rio de Janeiro', *Journal of Latin American Studies* 25 (1993), pp. 441–6.

Diplomacy

Charles K. Webster, ed., *Britain and the Independence of Latin America, 1812–1830: select documents from the Foreign Office archives*, 2 vols. (London, 1938) provides an informative introduction and important documents on diplomatic relations between Britain, Portugal and Brazil. Ron Seckinger, *The Brazilian Monarchy and the South American Republics, 1822–1831: Diplomacy and State Building* (Baton Rouge LA, 1984) is an excellent overview. On Brazilian diplomacy and the Paraguayan War see Harris Gaylord Warren, 'Brazil's Paraguayan policy, 1869–1876', *The Americas* 25 (1969), pp. 388–406, and Norman T. Straus, 'Brazil after the Paraguayan War: six years of conflict, 1870–6', *Journal of Latin American Studies* 10 (1978), pp. 21–35.

First Republic

Politics

José Maria Bello, *A History of Modern Brazil, 1889–1964*, trans. James L. Taylor (Stanford CA, 1966) is a good example of sound and informative, if old-fashioned, political history. Gilberto Freyre, *Order and Progress: Brazil from Monarchy to Republic*, trans. Rod W. Horton (New York, 1970) offers interesting ideas and themes. The role of the military in establishing the republic and their domination of its early years is examined in June E. Hahner, *Civilian–Military Relations in Brazil, 1889–1898* (Columbia SC, 1969). See also the perceptive assessment of one of the leading military figures in June Hahner, 'Floriano Peixoto, Brazil's "Iron Marshall": a re-evaluation', *The Americas* 31 (1975), pp. 252–71. There is a good deal of information on politics at the national as well as the regional level in Joseph L. Love, *Rio Grande do Sul and Brazilian Regionalism: 1882–1930* (Stanford CA, 1971). Other important regional studies include Joseph L. Love, *São Paulo in the Brazilian Federation, 1889–1937* (Stanford CA, 1980), Robert M. Levine, *Pernambuco in the Brazilian Federation, 1889–1937* (Stanford CA, 1978), John D. Wirth, *Minas Gerais in the Brazilian Federation, 1889–1937* (Stanford CA, 1977), and Eul-Soo Pang, *Bahia in the First Republic: Coronelismo and Oligarchies, 1889–1934* (Gainesville FL, 1979). Linda Lewin, *Politics and Parentela in Paraíba: A Case Study of Family-based Oligarchy in Brazil* (Princeton NJ, 1987) is a well-researched work that emphasizes the significance of family and kinship in regional politics. The subject of *coronelismo* is examined in Victor Nunes Leal, *Coronelismo: The Municipality and Representative Government in Brazil*, trans. June Henfrey (Cambridge, 1977), a classic work that was originally published in Portuguese in 1948.

Os Sertões, the famous account of life and rebellion in the backlands, was first published in 1902 and has been translated as Euclides da Cunha, *Rebellion in the Backlands*, trans. Samuel Putnam (Chicago, 1944). Robert M. Levine, *Vale of Tears: Revisiting the Canudos Massacre in Northeastern Brazil, 1893–1897* (Berkeley CA, 1992) is a very readable study that reflects new research on the subject of events at Canudos. A fictional account is provided by Mario Vargas Llosa, *The War of the End of the World*, trans. Helen R. Lane (New York, 1984). Todd A. Diacon, *Millenarian Vision, Capitalist Reality: Brazil's Contestado Rebellion, 1912–1916* (Durham NC, 1991) lucidly examines another important rebellion that took place during the First Republic. The subject of messianism is assessed in Ralph della Cava, 'Brazilian messianism and national institutions: a reappraisal of Canudos and Joaseiro', *Hispanic American Historical Review* 48 (1968), pp. 402–20. The prevalence of banditry in the countryside is underscored in Billy Jaynes Chandler, *The Bandit King: Lampião of Brazil* (College Station TX, 1978) and Linda Lewin, 'The oligarchical limitations of social banditry in Brazil: the case of the "good" thief, Antonio Silvino', *Past and Present* 82 (1979), pp. 116–46.

The élitist nature of the political system during the First Republic was reflected in the low turn-out at presidential elections, a subject mentioned in Joseph L. Love, 'Political participation in Brazil, 1881–1969', *Luso-Brazilian Review* 7 (1970), pp. 3–24. John W.F. Dulles, *Anarchists and Communists in Brazil, 1900–1935* (Austin TX, 1973) and Neill Macaulay, *The Prestes Column: Revolution in Brazil* (New York, 1974) consider the emergence of radical opposition to the established political élite. For the background to the 1930 Revolution see Jordan M. Young, *The Brazilian Revolution of 1930 and the Aftermath* (New Brunswick NJ, 1967). The influence of economic and military factors is discussed in Maurício A. Font, *Coffee, Contention and Change* (Cambridge MA, 1990) and John D. Wirth, 'Tenentismo in the Brazilian Revolution of 1930', *Hispanic American Historical Review* 44 (1964), pp. 229–42.

Economy

Steven Topik, *The Political Economy of the Brazilian State, 1889–1930* (Austin TX, 1987) is an excellent overview. For the argument emphasizing the important role assumed by central government see also the same author's 'The evolution of the economic role of the Brazilian state, 1889–1930', *Journal of Latin American Studies* 11 (1979), pp. 325–42. The influence of external events is examined in Winston Fritsch, *External Constraints on Economic Policy in Brazil, 1889–1930* (London, 1988), and Bill Albert, *South America and the First World War: The Impact of the War on Brazil, Argentina, Peru and Chile* (Cambridge, 1988). Thomas H. Holloway, *The Brazilian Valorization of 1906: Regional Politics and Economic Independence* (Madison WI, 1975) explains the adoption of the valorization scheme. The dynamic economic development of the city and state of São Paulo is the theme of Warren Dean, *The Industrialization of São Paulo, 1880–1945* (Austin TX, 1969), Robert H. Mattoon, 'Railroads, coffee, and big business in São Paulo, Brazil', *Hispanic American Historical Review* 57 (1977), pp. 273–95, and Richard M. Morse, *From Community to Metropolis: A Biography of São Paulo, Brazil* (Gainesville FL, 1958). Warren Dean, *Brazil and the Struggle for Rubber: A Study in Environmental History* (Cambridge, 1987) and Barbara Weinstein, *The Amazon Rubber Boom, 1850–1920* (Stanford CA, 1983) discuss the rise of the rubber industry. The longstanding difficulties of the Northeast are highlighted in Anthony L. Hall, *Drought and Irrigation in North-East Brazil* (Cambridge, 1978).

Mention must be made of a number of excellent studies by Brazilian economic historians which cover the period since 1889, but have not been translated into English: Annibal Villanova Villela and Wilson Suzigan, *Política do governo e crescimento da economia brasileira, 1889–1945* (Rio de Janeiro, 1973), Nícia Vilela Luz, *A luta pela industrialização do Brasil* (São Paulo, 1975), Carlos Manuel Peláez and Wilson Suzigan, *História monetária do Brasil* (Rio de Janeiro, 1976), Wilson Suzigan, *Indústria brasileira: origem e desenvolvimento* (São Paulo, 1986), and the expert articles in Marcelo da Paiva Abreu, ed., *A ordem do progresso: cem anos de política econômica republicana, 1889–1989* (Rio de Janeiro, 1990).

Society

Two works by Jeffrey D. Needell: *A Tropical Belle Époque: Elite Culture and Society in Turn-of-the-Century Rio de Janeiro* (Cambridge, 1987) and 'The domestic civilizing mission: the cultural role of the state in Brazil, 1808–1930', *Luso-Brazilian Review* 36 (1999), pp. 2–18, perceptively analyze the cultural mindset of the élite. Attempts to 'civilize' and 'modernize' the poor of Rio de Janeiro are the subject of Teresa A. Meade, *'Civilizing' Rio* (University Park PA, 1997) and Jeffrey D. Needell, 'The Revolta Contra Vacina of 1904: the revolt against "modernization" in belle-époque Rio de Janeiro', *Hispanic American Historical Review* 67 (1987), pp. 233–68. Developments in public health are examined in Julyan G. Peard, *Race, Place, and Medicine: The Idea of the Tropics in Nineteenth-Century Brazilian Medicine* (Durham NC, 1999), Nancy Stepan, *Beginnings of Brazilian Science: Oswaldo Cruz, Medical Research, and Policy, 1890–1920* (New York, 1981), and Robin L. Anderson, 'Public health and public healthiness, São Paulo, Brazil, 1876–1893', *Journal of the History of Medicine* 41 (1986), pp. 293–307.

Dain E. Borges, *The Family in Bahia, Brazil, 1870–1945* (Stanford CA, 1992) draws attention to the importance of the family. The increasingly active role assumed by women is considered in June E. Hahner, *Emancipating the Female Sex: The Struggle for Women's Rights in Brazil, 1850–1940* (Durham NC, 1990), Susan K. Besse, *Restructuring Patriarchy: The Modernization of Gender Inequality in Brazil, 1914–1940* (Durham NC, 1990), and Joel Wolfe, *Working Women, Working Men: São Paulo and the Rise of Brazil's Industrial Working Class, 1900–1955* (Chapel Hill NC, 1993). Thomas H.

Holloway, *Immigrants on the Land: Coffee and Society in São Paulo* (Chapel Hill NC, 1980) [273]
and Frederick C. Luebke, *Germans in Brazil* (Baton Rouge LA, 1987) are informative
studies on the arrival of European immigrants in Brazil and their adjustment to
conditions. The less welcoming reception that faced European Jews, and vulnerable
Chinese and Japanese ethnic minorities, is the subject of Jeffrey Lesser, *Welcoming the
Undesirables: Brazil and the Jewish Question* (Berkeley CA, 1995) and *Negotiating National
Identity: Immigrants, Minorities and the Struggle for Ethnicity in Brazil* (Durham NC,
1999). John Hemming, *Amazon Frontier: The Defeat of the Brazilian Indians* (London,
1987) recounts the even darker story of lack of sympathy and violence shown
towards the Indians.

Diplomacy

Joseph Smith, *Unequal Giants: Diplomatic Relations between the United States and the Brazilian
Republic, 1889–1930* (Pittsburgh PA, 1991) concentrates on relations between
Brazil and the United States, but is informative on Brazilian diplomacy during the
period of the First Republic. The crucially important relationship with the United
States is also the subject of E. Bradford Burns, *The Unwritten Alliance: Rio Branco and
Brazilian–American Relations* (New York, 1966), Steven C. Topik, *Trade and Gunboats:
The United States and Brazil in the Age of Empire* (Stanford CA, 1996), and Emily
Rosenberg, 'Anglo–American economic rivalry in Brazil during World War I', *Diplomatic
History* 2 (1978), pp. 131–52. Stanley E. Hilton, 'Brazil and the post-
Versailles world: elite images and foreign policy strategy, 1919–1929', *Journal of
Latin American Studies* 12 (1980), pp. 34–64, provides an expert analysis of Brazilian
foreign policy aims during the 1920s.

Era of Getúlio Vargas to 1964

Politics

Thomas E. Skidmore, *Politics in Brazil, 1930–1964: An Experiment in Democracy* (Oxford,
1967) is an excellent and informative survey. A more theoretical approach is
adopted in Philippe C. Schmitter, *Interest Conflict and Political Change in Brazil* (Stanford
CA, 1971), while Octavio Ianni, *Crisis in Brazil*, trans. Phyllis B. Eveleth (New York,
1970) examines the subject of growing political crisis. Of the many biographical
studies of Getúlio Vargas, John W.F. Dulles, *Vargas of Brazil* (Austin, 1967) is very
detailed and descriptive while Richard Bourne, *Getúlio Vargas of Brazil, 1883–1954:
Sphinx of the Pampas* (London, 1974) is more analytical. A concise and readable study
is Robert M. Levine, *Father of the Poor? Vargas and His Era* (New York, 1998). The
same author's *The Vargas Regime: The Critical Years, 1934–1938* (New York, 1970)
is a thorough and well-researched analysis. The political transition from wartime

[274]   to peacetime is expertly described in Leslie Bethell, 'Brazil', in Bethell and Ian Roxborough, eds., *Latin America between the Second World War and the Cold War, 1944–1948* (Cambridge, 1993), pp. 33–65. John W.F. Dulles, *Unrest in Brazil: Political–Military Crises, 1955–1964* (Austin TX, 1970) characteristically provides detailed information on the period leading up to the 1964 coup.

Michael L. Conniff, 'The Tenentes in power: a new perspective on the Brazilian Revolution of 1930', *Journal of Latin American Studies* 10 (1978), pp. 61–82, considers the political role of the *tenentes*. The growing political significance of Rio Grande do Sul is examined in Carlos E. Cortés, *Gaúcho Politics in Brazil: The Politics of Rio Grande do Sul, 1930–1964* (Albuquerque NM, 1974). Michael L. Conniff, *Urban Politics in Brazil: The Rise of Populism* (Pittsburgh PA, 1981) discusses the impact of Populism during the 1920s and 1930s. Political opposition to Vargas is discussed in John W.F. Dulles, *The São Paulo Law School and the Anti-Vargas Resistance (1938–1945)* (Austin TX, 1986). The essays collected in Alfred Stepan, ed., *Authoritarian Brazil: Origins, Policies, and Future* (New Haven, 1973) consider the background to and the emergence of authoritarian rule. The crucial political role assumed by the military is explained in Alfred Stepan, *The Military in Politics: Changing Patterns in Brazil* (Princeton NJ, 1971) and Frank D. McCann, 'The Brazilian Army and the problem of mission, 1939–1964', *Journal of Latin American Studies* 12 (1980), pp. 107–26. Robert A. Hayes, *The Armed Nation: The Brazilian Corporate Mystique* (Tempe AZ, 1989) is a useful historical survey. Specialist essays on the military's attitude towards politics in the 19th and 20th centuries are contained in Henry H. Keith and Robert A. Hayes, eds., *Perspectives on Armed Politics in Brazil* (Tempe AZ, 1976).

On Communism in Brazil see Ronald H. Chilcote, *The Brazilian Communist Party: Conflict and Integration, 1922–1972* (New York, 1974) and John W.F. Dulles, *Brazilian Communism 1935–1945: Repression during World Upheaval* (Austin TX, 1983). Kenneth Paul Erickson, *The Brazilian Corporative State and Working Class Politics* (Berkeley CA, 1977) and Youssef Cohen, *The Manipulation of Consent: The State and Working-Class Consciousness in Brazil* (Pittsburgh PA, 1989) examine the relationship between the federal government and working-class organizations. John D. French, *The Brazilian Workers' ABC: Class Conflict and Alliances in Modern São Paulo* (Durham NC, 1992) and Cliff Welch, *The Seed Was Planted: The São Paulo Roots of Brazil's Rural Labor Movement* (Philadelphia PA, 1998) deal with the emergence of trade unionism in São Paulo. On the political consequences arising from the deep-rooted economic and social problems of the Northeast see Joseph A. Page, *The Revolution That Never Was: Northeast Brazil, 1955–1964* (New York, 1972) and Riordan Roett, *The Politics of Foreign Aid in the Brazilian Northeast* (Nashville TN, 1972).

Economy

Werner Baer, *Industrialization and Economic Development in Brazil* (Homewood IL, 1965) is a general survey. Luiz Bresser Pereira, *Development and Crisis in Brazil, 1930–1983,*

trans. Marcia Van Dyke (Boulder CO, 1994) presents an expert view of economic   [275]
policy. The development of the steel and petroleum industries is examined in John D.
Wirth, *The Politics of Brazilian Development, 1930–1954* (Stanford CA, 1970), Werner
Baer, *The Development of the Brazilian Steel Industry* (Nashville TN, 1969), and Peter S.
Smith, *Oil and Politics in Modern Brazil* (Toronto, 1976). The influence of economic
factors upon the 1964 coup is discussed in Michael Wallerstein, 'The collapse of
democracy in Brazil: its economic determinants', *Latin American Research Review* 15
(1980), pp. 3–40.

Society

The articles in Edmar L. Bacha and Herbert S. Klein, eds., *Social Change in Brazil,
1945–1985: The Incomplete Transition* (Albuquerque NM, 1989) carefully examine social
and economic change. The enduring controversy over whether a racial democracy
exists in 20th-century Brazil is exemplified in several works, of which the most notable are Carl N. Degler, *Neither Black Nor White: Slavery and Race Relations in Brazil and
the United States* (New York, 1971) and Thomas E. Skidmore, *Black into White: Race
and Nationality in Brazilian Thought* (New York, 1974). An important addition to the
debate is provided by George Reid Andrews, *Blacks and Whites in São Paulo, Brazil,
1888–1988* (Madison WI, 1991) and the same author's 'Brazilian racial democracy,
1900–90: an American counterpoint', *Journal of Contemporary History* 31 (1996),
pp. 483–507. The desperate living conditions of life in the *favelas* during the middle
decades of the 20th century are vividly conveyed in Robert Levine and José Carlos
Sebe Bom Meihy, *The Life and Death of Carolina Maria de Jesus* (Albuquerque NM, 1995).

Diplomacy

Stanley E. Hilton, *Brazil and the Great Powers, 1930–1939: The Politics of Trade Rivalry*
(Austin TX, 1975) is a good introduction to the complex international relations of
the 1930s. Frank D. McCann, *The Brazilian–American Alliance, 1937–1945* (Princeton
NJ, 1973) is an outstanding account of the development of close ties between Brazil
and the United States. Postwar relations are examined in Elizabeth A. Cobbs, *The
Rich Neighbor Policy: Rockefeller and Kaiser in Brazil* (New Haven CT, 1992), Gerald K.
Haines, *The Americanization of Brazil: A Study of U.S. Cold War Diplomacy in the Third
World, 1945–1954* (Wilmington DE, 1989) and Stanley E. Hilton, 'The United States,
Brazil and the Cold War, 1945–1960: end of the Special Relationship', *Journal
of American History* 68 (1981), pp. 599–624. Gabriel Porcile, 'The challenge of
cooperation: Argentina and Brazil, 1939–1955', *Journal of Latin American Studies*
27 (1995), pp. 127–59, and Stanley E. Hilton, 'The Argentine factor in twentieth-
century Brazilian foreign policy strategy', *Political Science Quarterly* 100 (1985), pp. 27–
51, provide a reminder that Argentina has long been influential in the shaping of

Brazilian foreign policy. For the presidential statement on Brazil's 'independent foreign policy', see Jânio Quadros, 'Brazil's new foreign policy', *Foreign Affairs* 40 (1961), pp. 19–27. Wayne A. Selcher, *The Afro–Asian Dimension of Brazilian Foreign Policy, 1956–1972* (Gainesville FL, 1974) examines the desire for closer links with the countries of the Third World. On the role of the United States in the 1964 coup see Phyllis R. Parker, *Brazil and the Quiet Intervention, 1964* (Austin TX, 1979), Ruth Leacock, *Requiem for Revolution: The United States and Brazil, 1961–1969* (Kent OH, 1990), and W. Michael Weis, *Cold Warriors and Coups d'Etat* (Albuquerque NM, 1993).

Since 1964

Politics

Thomas E. Skidmore, *Politics of Military Rule in Brazil, 1964–85* (New York, 1988) characteristically provides an excellent guide to the political history of the period. A much shorter but very readable account is Bernardo Kucinski, *Brazil: State and Struggle* (London, 1982). The strategy of the first two military governments is expertly ana-lyzed in Ronald M. Schneider, *The Political System of Brazil: Emergence of a 'Modernizing' Authoritarian Regime, 1964–1970* (New York, 1971). Wilfred A. Bacchus, *Mission in Mufti: Brazil's Military Regimes, 1968–1985* (Westport CT, 1990) provides a concise overview. On political developments see also Georges-André Fiechter, *Brazil since 1964: Modernization under a Military Regime,* trans. Alan Braley (London, 1975) and Frances Hagopian, *Traditional Politics and Regime Change in Brazil* (Cambridge, 1996).

John W.F. Dulles, *Castello Branco: The Making of a Brazilian President* (College Sta-tion TX, 1978) and *President Castello Branco: Brazilian Reformer* (College Station TX, 1980) offers a sympathetic biographical study. A critical view of the military regime is presented in Maria Helena Moreira Alves, *State and Opposition in Military Brazil* (Austin TX, 1985). Shawn C. Smallman, 'The professionalization of military terror in Brazil, 1945–1964', *Luso-Brazilian Review* 37 (2000), pp. 117–27, analyzes the military's policy of ruthless suppression of perceived opponents. Jan Knippers Black, *United States Penetration of Brazil* (Philadelphia PA, 1977) and Martha K. Huggins, *Political Policing: The United States and Latin America* (Durham NC, 1998) argue that successive American governments supported the policy of coercion. The rise of political opposi-tion to the military is examined in Maria D'Avila G. Kinzo, *Legal Opposition Politics under Authoritarian Rule in Brazil: The Case of the MDB, 1966–79* (New York, 1988) and Scott Mainwaring, *The Catholic Church and Politics in Brazil, 1916–85* (Stanford CA, 1986).

Useful collections of articles dealing with the transition from military to civilian rule during the 1980s are Wayne A. Selcher, ed., *Political Liberalization in Brazil: Dy-namics, Dilemmas, and Future Prospects* (Boulder CO, 1986), Julian Chacel, Pamela Falk, and David V. Fleischer, eds., *Brazil's Economic and Political Future* (Boulder CO, 1988), [277] and Alfred Stepan, ed., *Democratizing Brazil: Problems of Transition and Consolidation* (New York, 1989). Kurt von Mettenheim, *The Brazilian Voter: Mass Politics in Democratic Transition, 1974–1986* (Pittsburgh PA, 1995) considers the impact of the move from authoritarianism to democratic politics. The enduring influence of right-wing political groups is examined in Timothy J. Power, *The Political Right in Postauthoritarian Brazil: Elites, Institutions and Democratization* (University Park PA, 2000).

The dramatic fall of Collor de Mello in 1992 is analyzed in Peter Flynn, 'Collor, corruption and crisis: time for reflection', *Journal of Latin American Studies* 25 (1993), pp. 351–71, and Keith S. Rosenn and Richard Downes, eds., *Corruption and Political Reform in Brazil: The Impact of Collor's Impeachment* (Miami FL, 1999). Emir Sader and Ken Silverstein, *Without Fear of Being Happy: Lula, the Workers Party and Brazil* (London, 1991), Margaret Keck, *The Workers' Party and Democratization in Brazil* (New Haven CT, 1992) and Sue Branford and Bernardo Kucinski, *Brazil, Carnival of the Oppressed: Lula and the Brazilian Workers' Party* (London, 1995) deal with the rise of the Workers' Party and its charismatic leader, Lula, as a new political force. The presidency of Fernando Henrique Cardoso is examined in Ted G. Goertzel, *Fernando Henrique Cardoso: Reinventing Democracy in Brazil* (Boulder CO, 1999) and Susan Kaufman Purcell and Riordan Roett, eds., *Brazil under Cardoso* (New York, 1997).

Economy

Bertha K. Becker and Claudio A.G. Egler, *Brazil: A New Regional Power in the World-Economy: A Regional Geography* (Cambridge, 1992) provides an informative overview. More specialized studies of economic policy and development are Joel Bergsman, *Brazil: Industrialization and Trade Policies* (London, 1970), Donald E. Syvrud, *Foundations of Brazilian Economic Growth* (Stanford CA, 1974) and Vincent Parkin, *Chronic Inflation in an Industrialising Economy: The Brazilian Experience* (Cambridge, 1991). Michael Barzelay, *The Politicized Market Economy: Alcohol in Brazil's Energy Strategy* (Berkeley CA, 1986) analyzes the strategy of using alcohol as a subsititute fuel. Werner Baer and Paul Beckerman, 'The decline and fall of Brazil's cruzado', *Latin American Research Review* 34 (1989): 35–64, is an informative discussion of monetary policy. The views of Brazilian economic experts are collected in Maria J.F. Willumsen and Eduardo Giannetti da Fonseca, eds., *The Brazilian Economy: Structure and Performance in Recent Decades* (Coral Gables FL, 1997).

Society

Robert M. Levine, *Brazilian Legacies* (New York, 1997) is a perceptive and readable introduction to the modern Brazilian way of life. Roberto DaMatta, *Carnivals, Rogues, and Heroes: An Interpretation of the Brazilian Dilemma*, trans. John Drury (South Bend IN,

[278]   1991) is also an insightful study of social customs and behavior. The subject of race relations is explored in Carlos A. Hasenbalg, *Race Relations in Modern Brazil* (Albuquerque NM, 1985). R. Andrew Chestnut, *Born Again in Brazil: The Pentecostal Boom and the Pathogens of Poverty* (New Brunswick NJ, 1997) deals with the rise of Protestantism and its marked attraction for the poor. Joe Foweraker, *The Struggle for Land: A Political Economy of the Pioneer Frontier in Brazil from 1930 to the Present Day* (Cambridge, 1981) and Marta Cehelsky, *Land Reform in Brazil: The Management of Social Change* (Boulder CO, 1979) consider the controversial issue of land reform. The exploitation and development of the Amazon has been the subject of many works including Philip M. Fearnside, *Human Carrying Capacity of the Brazilian Rainforest* (New York, 1986), Stephen G. Bunker, *Underdeveloping the Amazon* (Urbana IL, 1985), and Sue Branford and Oriel Glock, *The Last Frontier: Fighting Over Land in the Amazon* (London, 1985). David Cleary, *Anatomy of the Amazon Gold Rush* (London, 1990) recounts the story of the modern gold rush, while Chico Mendes, *Fight for the Forest: Chico Mendes in His Own Words* (London, 1992) and Jan Rocha, *Murder in the Rainforest: The Yanomami, the Gold Miners and the Amazon* (London, 1999) reflect on the damaging consequences.

Diplomacy

The ambitions of the military governments to turn Brazil into a world power are discussed in Ronald M. Schneider, *Brazil: Foreign Policy of a Future World Power* (Boulder CO, 1977) and William Perry, *Contemporary Brazilian Foreign Policy: The International Strategy of an Emerging Power* (Beverly Hills CA, 1976). Wayne A. Selcher, ed., *Brazil in the International System: The Rise of a Middle Power* (Boulder CO, 1981) reviews Brazil's international status at the beginning of the 1980s. The relationship between Brazil and the United States at the close of the 20th century is assessed in Susan Kaufman Purcell, 'The new U.S.-relationship' in Purcell and Riordan Roett, eds., *Brazil under Cardoso* (New York, 1997) pp. 89–102, and more trenchantly in Moniz Bandeira, *Relações Brasil–EUA no Contexto da Globalização. II. Rivalidade Emergente* (São Paulo, 1997).

INDEX